Praise for *High-Impact Instruct* *A Framework for Great Teaching*

" . . . an extraordinarily powerful, practical, and personal approach to teaching. This book will dramatically transform how teachers work with each other and how they teach students. Every page is filled with detailed descriptions of how to teach difficult content in a very simple, understandable way . . . brilliantly conceptualized and written by one of education's best thinkers and innovators."

—Donald D. Deshler, Williamson Family
Distinguished Professor of Special Education and
Director, Center for Research on Learning, University of Kansas

"Every teacher, instructional coach, and principal who strives for personal excellence in the art and science of teaching will find *High-Impact Instruction* to be a helpful guide on that journey. Written with wit and warmth, Jim Knight's work will guide you to identify both current strengths and actions for improving professional practice. It honors teachers, coaches, and administrators as professionals while clearly communicating that part of professionalism is a desire for growth. *High-Impact Instruction* is a significant step toward articulating how the 'art' of great teaching can be analyzed for the purpose of defining specific and observable actions."

—Randy Sprick, primary author for the *Safe &
Civil Schools* series, Director of Teaching Strategies, Inc.,
and lead consultant for Safe & Civil Schools

"Seasoned author Jim Knight has provided a masterful resource for teachers and other stakeholders to improve student achievement through a host of clearly defined instructional practices. The tools, resources, and examples he provides enable educators to easily implement his framework, which comprises the key ingredients for effective instruction. Furthermore, his writing style makes it an engaging read."

—Kathy Glass, consultant and author of *Curriculum Mapping:
A Step-by-Step Guide to Creating Curriculum Year Overviews* and
Mapping Comprehensive Units to the ELA Common Core Standards, K–5

For my son Geoff Knight

Geoff and his wife, Jenny Peck, have dedicated themselves to saving children's lives in rural Tanzania. A portion of my royalties from the sale of this book will be dedicated to helping Geoff and Jenny do their work in the developing world. You can read more about what they do at http://www.mufindiorphans.org.

Geoff, you make me proud every day.

HIGH-IMPACT INSTRUCTION

A FRAMEWORK FOR GREAT TEACHING

JIM KNIGHT

A JOINT PUBLICATION

CORWIN
A SAGE Company

FOR INFORMATION:

Corwin
A SAGE Company
2455 Teller Road
Thousand Oaks, California 91320
(800) 233-9936
www.corwin.com

SAGE Publications Ltd.
1 Oliver's Yard
55 City Road
London EC1Y 1SP
United Kingdom

SAGE Publications India Pvt. Ltd.
B 1/I 1 Mohan Cooperative Industrial Area
Mathura Road, New Delhi 110 044
India

SAGE Publications Asia-Pacific Pte. Ltd.
3 Church Street
#10-04 Samsung Hub
Singapore 049483

Acquisitions Editor: Dan Alpert
Associate Editor: Kimberly Greenberg
Editorial Assistant: Heidi Arndt
Production Editor: Melanie Birdsall
Typesetter: C&M Digitals (P) Ltd.
Proofreader: Scott Oney
Indexer: Jean Casalegno
Graphic Designer: Janet Kiesel
Permissions Editor: Karen Ehrmann

Cover design by Clinton Carlson.

Printed in the United States of America

A catalog record of this book is available from the Library of Congress.

ISBN 978-1-4129-8177-4

This book is printed on acid-free paper.

15 16 10 9 8 7 6 5 4

CONTENTS

LIST OF COMPANION WEBSITE RESOURCES

Access the following videos and reproducible forms at www.corwin.com/highimpactinstruction

CHAPTER 1

CHAPTER 2

CHAPTER 3

PREFACE

I've been writing this book for more than a decade. In many ways, it began in 1999, when my colleagues and I received a U.S. Department of Education GEAR-UP Grant that helped us set up an instructional coaching program for middle and secondary schools in the Topeka, Kansas School District, USD 501. Our instructional coaches started out sharing Content Enhancement Routines (see http://www.kucrl.org/sim/content.shtml) that teachers could use to teach content more intentionally and inclusively.

The Content Enhancement Routines we used were developed and validated under the guidance of my colleague Keith Lenz, while he worked at the University of Kansas, and teachers who worked with our coaches found them very helpful. However, the instructional coaches realized quickly that some teachers also needed help with classroom management and community building, and I soon began learning from Randy Sprick, a leader in the field of behavior management. Randy and I eventually co-authored *Coaching Classroom Management* (2006) along with Wendy Reinke, Tricia Skyles, and Lynn Barnes-Schuster, and to this day, I continue to learn from Randy.

Not long after this, I met with my former teacher Michael Fullan, and I asked him whose work he thought I should study to broaden my understanding of instruction. Michael quickly recommended Richard Stiggins' work, and before long I was in Richard Stiggins' office at the Assessment Training Institute in Portland, Oregon. After that meeting, my team and I immersed ourselves in Stiggins' and others' research on formative assessment, and we began developing our own version for instructional coaches.

To flesh out our model, I added several instructional strategies that would increase engagement and learning. The result of this exploration and development was a simple framework—the Big Four, addressing Content Planning, Formative Assessment, Instruction, and Community Building. For the past ten years, my research colleagues and I have been working to make the teaching practices, checklists, and observation tools within the Big Four simpler and more powerful. This book summarizes what we created.

To deepen and simplify the materials in this book, instructional coaches on two research projects implemented each of the teaching practices described here. The stories of those instructional coaches and their collaborating teachers are included throughout the book. In addition, to get more feedback, I created beta manuals of most of the teaching practices and made them available on the web at thebigfour.ning.com. That website has been visited by educators from more than 100 countries, and the teachers implementing these practices in North America and around the world have provided feedback on how each strategy can be refined to be simpler and more powerful.

In addition, as we refined these practices, we reviewed hundreds of research articles studying the Big Four teaching practices, and I have reviewed more than 100 books in areas inside and outside education related to the Big Four. For example, I read six business books describing how storytelling can be a cornerstone for a business communication strategy, and I also read most of John Gottman's work on relationships. Although this work is not about education directly, I feel that we would be foolish to ignore studies that speak directly to the work of teachers, addressing topics such as those analyzing teamwork, power, relationships, and happiness.

I also read the excellent work of educational researchers who have created comprehensive instructional models, including Robert Marzano, Charlotte Danielson, Barrie Bennett, Jon Saphier, and John Hattie. After a decade of reading, development, practice, review, and refinement, we have arrived at the high-impact strategies described here.

I want to be clear, however, that this book is not a book for researchers; this is a book for educators working in schools—teachers, coaches, principals, and their students. Thus, it is not a meta-analysis of research articles—excellent meta-analyses already exist authored by Marzano and Hattie, and there is no need to reproduce their work. And although the book was shaped by educational research, I have not limited my study to research conducted in schools. My reading of the literature outside of education, and my work with thousands of teachers in the last decade, has also informed my identification of practices that I conclude have a high impact on learning.

This book is my attempt to create a comprehensive and simple collection of tools that help teachers do the work they love to do: reach students. I encourage you, whether you are a teacher, instructional coach, or administrator, to experiment with these practices, and to let me know how we can make them better. We need to be learning too. You can reach me at jimknight@mac.com.

ACKNOWLEDGMENTS

It takes a village to write a book, just as certainly as it takes a village to raise a child—though in my case it might be more apt to say it took a city to write this one. Without question, this book is the result of the efforts of many, including those whose publications influenced my writing and those who gave their time and support to help turn these ideas into the publication you are looking at right now.

The work of researchers and authors—some whom I know personally, some whom I have met only through their writing—provides the foundation for much of what I have written here. My understanding of content planning, for example, began with what I learned from Keith Lenz, my colleague for many years at the University of Kansas Center for Research on Learning, and was deepened and extended by the work of Grant Wiggins, Jay McTighe, Lynn Erickson, and Kathy Glass.

My understanding of formative assessment began when I interviewed Richard Stiggins at the Assessment Training Institute in Portland and read his book *Student-Involved Assessment for Learning, 4th Edition* (2001). I expanded my understanding by reading the work of his colleague Jan Chappuis, along with other experts in formative assessment, including Dylan Wiliam and James Popham. Mihaly Csikszentmihalyi's research on optimal experience also helped me understand why formative assessment is so important.

I could not have written the community building section in this book without all that I have learned from my friend Randy Sprick whose simple, powerful tools are woven into much of Part III. Others who have influenced my thinking about community building include my colleague Sue Vernon, other leaders in the field such as Fred Jones, Harry Wong, and Robert Marzano, and researchers in related fields outside of education, including relationship expert John Gottman and the many communication experts at the Harvard Negotiation Project.

Finally, my understanding of instruction has been greatly influenced by authors who have dramatically pushed our field forward with their work describing effective instruction. In particular, I am grateful for the work of Robert Marzano, mentioned above, Charlotte Danielson, and Parker Palmer. Marzano and Danielson have helped me understand what great teaching is and how to see it. Palmer has helped me understand what great teaching means.

The authors and researchers just mentioned have been major influences, but many, many others have written books, manuals or research articles that have helped shape this book. I have done my best to always give credit to any author who has created a practice or idea I mention, but if you notice any section here where others deserves to be credited, please write me (jimknight@mac.com) so I can clarify their authorship in future editions.

In writing this book, I have received incredible help from my "city of support" at the Center for Research on Learning. My two primary partners in this process were Marilyn Ruggles and Carol Hatton. Marilyn read hundreds of research articles, transcribed dozens of interviews, and tracked down most of the references I cite in this paper. This book would have taken one or two years more to complete, at least, had it not been for Marilyn's help. Carol created forms and charts, transcribed interviews, reviewed text, looked up references and helped anywhere she could with the development of this book, all while overseeing all the conferences and institutes we hold in Kansas. Indeed, Carol has helped me complete just about every project I've been a part of in the past ten years at the University of Kansas.

My fellow colleagues at the University of Kansas Center for Research on Learning have also provided support, pushed my thinking, and truly inspired me to be better. Don Deshler, our Center Director, is my mentor, my friend, and the one colleague who has most shaped my professional life. And what I have learned about research from Don is nothing compared to what he has taught me about being a good person. Jean Schumaker, our Center's former Associate Director, taught me more about writing than anyone else, and much more important than that, she has been an incredible support and friend to our family. I will always be deeply grateful to Don and Jean, like so many others whom they have mentored.

My fellow researchers at the Center, including Associate Director Mike Hock, Barbara Bradley, Irma Brasseur-Hock, Jan Bulgren, Tom Skrtic, and Susan Harvey, have pushed my thinking, taught me a great deal about professional learning, and helped me better understand research methodology. They also all happen to be wonderful people.

ACKNOWLEDGMENTS

I'm grateful, as well, to my colleagues at the Instructional Coaching Group. Ruth Ryschon has done a phenomenal job organizing every consultation we've conducted in the past four years, and my fellow consultants Michelle Harris, Ann Hoffman, Tricia Skyles, Bill Sommers, Conn Thomas, and Sue Woodruff have done a fantastic job sharing the impact ideas around the world, presenting and consulting.

The ideas in this book are also the result of my work with two great teams of instructional coaches—people who have taught me so much and whom I now consider friends. My colleagues working at the Kansas Coaching Project, instructional coaches Lynn Barnes-Schuster, Stacy Cohen, Jeanne Disney, Devona Dunekack, Marti Elford, Shelly McBeth, and Ric Palma did more than anyone else to help me develop the Big Four teaching practices described in this book, and their work was extended by instructional coaches from the Beaverton School District, Michelle Harris, Susan Leyden, Jenny MacMillan, and Lea Molczan. I also learned an enormous amount from our superstar research team in Beaverton, Sarah Estes, Jeff Levering, and Barb Millikan.

One of the features of this book is the inclusion of Quick Response (QR) codes that link to video clips of teachers implementing or talking about teaching practices. Bill Sommers planted the seed for this idea by telling me about Tony Wagner's book *Creating Innovators* (2012), which beautifully employs this method. I am very grateful to many people at the Teaching Channel (teachingchannel.org) who worked with me to make this feature possible, especially Pat Wasley, the Teaching Channel CEO, Andrew Schulman, Vice President of Strategy and Outreach, and the many awesome teachers, too many to mention, whom I feature here in this book. All of you reinforce my deep belief in teachers and the profession. I am also very grateful to Producer/Director Andrew Benson, who oversaw the development of every video featured here. Andrew, you're way cooler than I am, but I love working with you.

Many people have helped with the production of this book. Clinton Carlson, who has been my design guru and sometime running partner, and who has designed many publications at the Instructional Coaching Group, designed this beautiful cover. Kirsten McBride has edited all of my books and improved almost every page I have written. My colleagues at Corwin have gone out of their way to be true partners with me in book production. I am extremely grateful to my friend and Senior Editor, Dan Alpert, my Production Editor (whom Dan describes as the "best in the business") Melanie Birdsall, and Editorial Assistant Heidi Arndt.

Most important, I am tremendously grateful to my family for supporting, encouraging, and inspiring me to write this. My parents Joan and Doug Knight always told me that I should make a contribution, and this book is one way, I hope, that I can thank them for their unwavering encouragement. My children, Geoff, Cameron, David, Emily, Benjamin, Isaiah, and Luke (30 days old as I write these words), remind me why it is so important to focus my attention on creating the schools our children deserve. Mine do; yours do, too. Finally, my wife Jenny is my soul mate, my partner for life, my thinking partner, and my greatest support. It means the world to me, Jen, that you believe in this work—I hope this book honors your belief in me.

Publisher's Acknowledgments

Corwin gratefully acknowledges the contributions of the following individuals:

Jennifer Abrams, Author and Educational Consultant, Palo Alto, California

Jennifer Bailey, Kilgore ISD, Kilgore, Texas

Don Deshler, Researcher, Author, and Director of the University of Kansas Center for Research on Learning, Lawrence, Kansas

Kathy Glass, Author and Educational Consultant, Woodside, California

Amy Shields, Director of Elementary Learning and Achievement, San Luis Coastal Unified School District, San Luis Obispo, California

Randy Sprick, Author and Director of Safe & Civil Schools, Eugene, Oregon

Karen Taylor, Learning Services Literary Specialist, Arkansas Department of Education, Little Rock, Arkansas

Sharon Thomas, Secondary English Teacher, Cecil County Public Schools, Elkton, Maryland

Sue Woodruff, Educational Consultant, Muskegon, Michigan

ABOUT THE AUTHOR

 **Jim Knight** is a research associate at the University of Kansas Center for Research on Learning and the president of the Instructional Coaching Group. He has spent close to two decades studying professional learning and instructional coaching. He has written or co-authored several books on the topic including *Instructional Coaching: A Partnership Approach to Improving Instruction* published by Corwin and Learning Forward (2007) and *Unmistakable Impact: A Partnership Approach for Dramatically Improving Instruction* (2011). Knight co-authored *Coaching Classroom Management* (2006) and also edited *Coaching: Approaches and Perspectives* (2008).

Knight has authored articles on instructional coaching and professional learning in publications such as *The Journal of Staff Development, Educational Leadership, Principal Leadership, The School Administrator,* and *Kappan.*

Frequently asked to lead professional learning, Knight has presented and consulted in most states and eight countries. Knight also leads the coaching institutes and the Annual Instructional Coaching Conference in Lawrence, Kansas.

He has a PhD in education from the University of Kansas and has won several university teaching, innovation, and service awards. Knight also hosts Talking About Teaching on the Teaching Channel and writes the radicallearners.com blog. Contact Knight at jim knight@mac.com.

Better is possible. It does not take genius. It takes diligence. It takes moral clarity. It takes ingenuity. And above all, it takes a willingness to try.

—Atul Gawande, *Better:*
A Surgeon's Notes on Performance

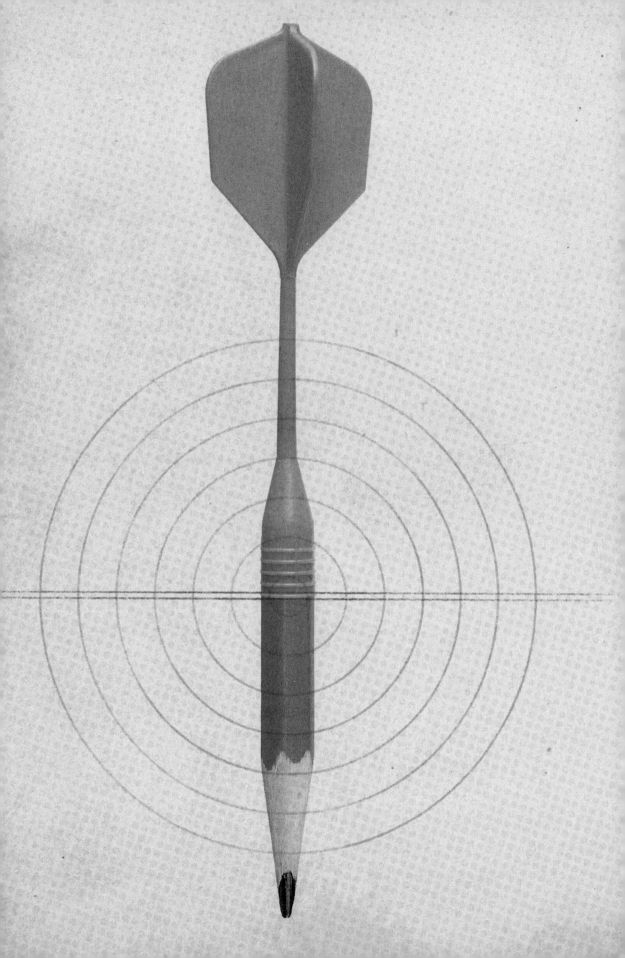

Chapter 1:
Personal
Bests

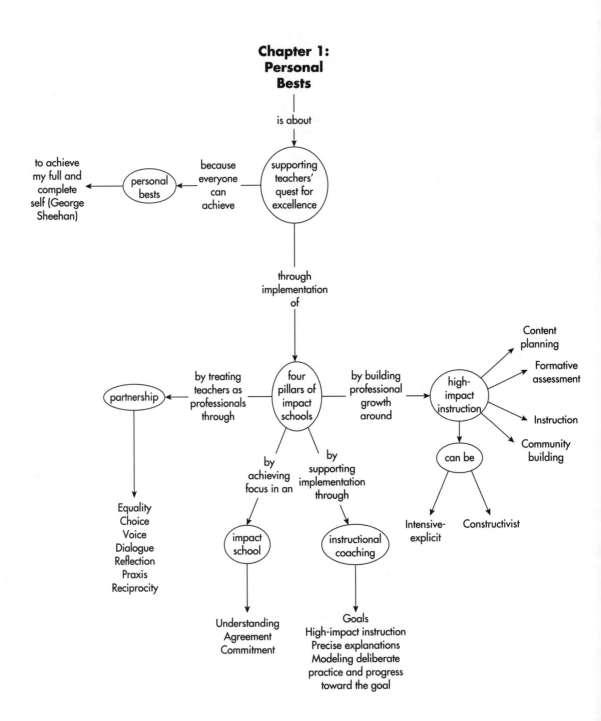

is about

supporting teachers' quest for excellence

because everyone can achieve

personal bests

to achieve my full and complete self (George Sheehan)

through implementation of

four pillars of impact schools

by treating teachers as professionals through

partnership

Equality
Choice
Voice
Dialogue
Reflection
Praxis
Reciprocity

by achieving focus in an

impact school

Understanding
Agreement
Commitment

by supporting implementation through

instructional coaching

Goals
High-impact instruction
Precise explanations
Modeling deliberate
practice and progress
toward the goal

by building professional growth around

high-impact instruction

Content planning

Formative assessment

Instruction

Community building

can be

Intensive-explicit

Constructivist

1

PERSONAL BESTS

The heroic human journey is to function as you are supposed to function, to achieve your personal best.

—George Sheehan, *Personal Best*

On and off for more than five years, I have referred to myself as a runner. I'm not very fast, I don't always stick to a routine, and I certainly don't stick to a healthy diet, but most weeks, I end up running.

My greatest running accomplishment is that even though my times were slow, I have completed three marathons. In fact, my times were so slow that in 2011 an 80-year-old runner, Ed Whitlock, ran the Toronto Marathon 1 hour and 40 minutes faster than my fastest time. That is, I'm almost two hours slower than someone who is 23 years older than me. The good news is that my time did beat Fauja Singh, a 100-year-old who also ran that Toronto marathon.

So, I'm not that fast and I am rounder than your usual runner, but I keep lacing up my shoes and going out on the road. Actually, I do more than that. I've had a personal coach help me develop some basic routines for my running. I've attended a running retreat at Furman University to learn more about my diet and cross training and the difference between speed, tempo, and long runs. I've tried diets, read numerous books, and run on trails, in the mountains, beside three different oceans, and down the country road behind our cabin.

The one question people ask me most about my running is one I struggle to answer. Why? Why do I keep running, trying to set a personal record at 57, to maybe, just maybe, someday qualify for Boston. I've finally come to believe the answer is simple: I just want to get better. Indeed, I believe all of us feel a need to be doing just that—get better. We're wired to do that.

I began thinking about our universal need to get better after reading George Sheehan, the poet laureate for runners around the world. Sheehan, the author of *Personal Best* (1989), writes convincingly and beautifully that running is much more than a simple form of exercise. Running is a way to achieve a happier, more authentic, fully realized life. For Sheehan, running is a way to achieve a "personal best":

> My end is not simple happiness. My need, drive, and desire is to achieve my full and complete self. If I do what I have come to do, if I create the life I was made for, then happiness will follow. (p. 21)

Sheehan's thoughts, of course, are not just about running; they apply to any discipline. Indeed, the research being conducted by Richard Ryan and Edward Deci (2000) into self-development theory confirms Sheehan's beliefs that we are all wired to strive for personal bests. Meaning and happiness, these researchers are finding, arise from the struggle to improve, no matter what we do. Sheehan could be summarizing Deci's research when he writes that the struggle for excellence motivating a dedicated runner is also at the heart of a dedicated writer:

> "I am writing the best I can," said the author of some bestselling popular novels. "If I could write any better I would. This is the peak of my powers." It matters little that she cannot write any better. It matters, more than life, that she is doing it with all her might. (p. 22)

This quest for excellence that Sheehan and Deci describe is also alive in the hearts of great teachers. When teachers strive with all their might, their quest is to do all they can so their students can experience as much growth, joy, power, and learning as possible. This quest is no small thing. "It matters more than life," to borrow Sheehan's phrase, that teachers embrace the challenge to achieve a personal best every day, in every class, for every student.

The rewards of challenging ourselves are enormous. When we pursue excellence, we gain a deeper understanding of our purpose, a fuller knowledge of the contribution we make, and the satisfaction that comes from doing work that makes us proud. When teachers strive to be the best they can be, they have a more positive impact on the lives of children, and their actions encourage their students to start their own journey—to strive for their own personal bests.

This book is a toolkit for teachers who know that "it matters more than life" to strive for personal bests.

Support for Personal Growth

If teachers desire to be excellent, then why, some might ask, does it seem some are no longer interested in that quest? Why aren't more teachers excited about their opportunities to learn?

One reason why many teachers are not striving to be their best is that poorly designed professional learning can actually inhibit growth by de-professionalizing teachers, treating them like workers on an assembly line rather than professionals doing emotionally complicated knowledge work (Knight, 2011). If we are to get the schools our children deserve, we need to start by treating teachers as professionals. Fortunately, there is much we can do to recognize teachers as the professionals that they are.

The Four Pillars of Impact Schools

In my previous writing, I describe a type of school in which all professional development has an unmistakable impact on teaching excellence and student learning—an impact school. In such a school, everything is structured so that teachers can do the important work of striving for personal bests so that students can strive for their own personal bests.

Four factors make it possible for a school to become an impact school. First, professional learning must embody respect for the professionalism of teachers, by involving teachers as true partners in their professional learning. Second, professional learning should provide a clear focus for sustained growth, and teachers should be collaborators in writing their school improvement plan to ensure that everyone (a) understands, (b) agrees with, and (c) is committed to the improvement plan. Third, teachers should have sufficient support to help with implementation of new practices, often provided by instructional coaches. Finally, instructional coaches, principals, educational leaders, and teachers need to have a deep knowledge of high-impact instructional strategies that have a significant, positive impact on students' behavior, attitudes, engagement, and learning.

This book describes those high-impact instructional strategies. However, the other factors, which are described in detail in my two

Michael Covarrubias talks about why he teaches.

Video 1.1
www.corwin.com/
highimpactinstruction

previous books, *Instructional Coaching: A Partnership Approach to Improving Instruction* (2007) and *Unmistakable Impact: A Partnership Approach for Dramatically Improving Instruction* (2011), also need to be taken into account if high-impact instructional strategies are to be implemented. In total, the three books provide a step-by-step guide educational leaders can use to dramatically improve the lives of the children (and adults) in their schools by dramatically improving instruction. The four pillars are as follows.

PILLAR 1: SEEING TEACHERS AS PROFESSIONALS

I've had the pleasure of working with educators in most U.S. states and Canadian provinces, and in other countries around the world. What I've observed wherever I visit is that when teachers truly feel respected, when their ideas and experiences are valued, they engage in meaningful, supportive conversations that lead to substantial improvements in teaching. For example, my colleagues and I at the Kansas Coaching Project at the University of Kansas Center for Research on Learning have watched more than 300 hours of video recordings of coaches and teachers collaborating during our study of instructional coaching in the Beaverton Oregon School District from 2008 to 2011. Again and again, the video shows educators talking about important and difficult topics and interacting with warmth and good humor. Together, in video after video, coaches and teachers engage in what Paulo Freire (1970) refers to as "mutually humanizing" conversations.

One reason why these conversations are productive and positive is that the coaches position themselves as equals with teachers. Michelle Harris, an instructional coach in the Beaverton coaching study, described how important she thought it was to see teachers as equals in the coaching process. For Michelle,

> The partnership approach is EVERYTHING in coaching. It wasn't until I knew those principles, believed in them, and began living them, that I actually felt like I was getting somewhere in my role as a coach. I had to believe that we were equals and that I could always learn something from my person in order to become an effective coach. (personal correspondence, August 17, 2012)

The partnership approach Michelle refers to is the theoretical foundation for the approaches to professional learning described in *Instructional Coaching: A Partnership Approach to Improving Instruction*

(2007) and *Unmistakable Impact: A Partnership Approach for Dramatically Improving Instruction* (2011). In both books, I describe seven principles that educators should use to guide their actions if they want to position their colleagues as equal partners. The principles, described at length in both books, are as follows:

- **Equality.** Each of us is unique, but each of us is equally valuable.
- **Choice.** Although in almost every organization certain initiatives must be implemented, professional educators should be free to make meaningful decisions about their professional practice.
- **Voice.** Teachers should be encouraged to share their honest opinions while learning about, designing, and implementing their own professional learning.
- **Dialogue.** Educational leaders, professional developers, coaches, teachers, and other educators should interact in ways that foster a two-way sharing of ideas.
- **Reflection.** Professional learning should involve "looking back," "looking at," or "looking ahead" at one's practices.
- **Praxis.** Professional learning should involve real-life application of learning.
- **Reciprocity.** Everyone should be learning during professional learning, not just those "receiving" the learning.

The top-down approach of telling professionals what to do and expecting them to do it just as they were told almost always engenders resistance. Therefore, the partnership approach is important. As Edgar Schein explained in *Helping: How to Offer, Give, and Receive Help* (2009), "It is human to want to be granted the status and position that we feel we deserve, no matter how high or low it might be" (p. xi). Schein goes on to explain, "When a conversation has not been equitable we sometimes feel offended. That usually means that the value we have claimed for ourselves has not been acknowledged, that the other person or persons did not realize who we were or how important our communication was (as claimed by us)" (pp. 19–20).

Helping relationships are inhibited, Schein explains, when those being helped feel that they have been put "one down" and that helpers have placed themselves "one up." But this inequality can be ameliorated when instructional coaches see teachers as partners, professionals who can and should make significant choices about the work they do.

A second reason for positioning teachers as partners is because they engage in complex knowledge work that can't be, as Thomas Davenport has written, "reduced to a series of boxes and arrows" (2005, p. 17). Davenport defines knowledge workers in *Thinking for a Living: How to Get Performance and Results From Knowledge Workers* (2005):

> Knowledge workers have high degrees of expertise, education, or experience, and the primary purpose of their job involves the creation, distribution, or application of knowledge. (p. 10)

Teaching perfectly exemplifies the knowledge work Davenport describes. Since teachers use their education and expertise to create, distribute, and apply knowledge, their professional learning must ensure they have sufficient personal autonomy so they can do that thinking. The partnership approach positions teachers as thinkers who can make their own decisions.

Finally, the partnership approach embodies an old idea—that we should treat others the way we want to be treated ourselves. If someone was helping us improve the way we do our work, we would likely want to have some choice in the matter, to have our ideas listened to, and to reflect on and apply the new knowledge to our lives. In sum, we would likely find it easier to accept that help if that person delivering it respected us, had faith in our abilities, and treated us as equals.

Schools can honor teachers as professionals by grounding professional learning in these principles and by positioning teachers as people who can and should shape their own professional learning.[1] Partnership, however, is only one pillar. Schools also need to get a clear picture of current reality and focus their professional learning on practices that, when implemented, will have the greatest impact on student learning and well-being. In *Unmistakable Impact* (2011) I describe how that learning might take place across a school.

PILLAR 2: CREATING A FOCUS FOR PROFESSIONAL LEARNING IN AN IMPACT SCHOOL

Successful and lasting instructional transformation is too complicated to happen in a helter-skelter fashion, and schools will not make sustained improvements if they simply skip from one trend to the next. To lead sustained improvement, school leaders need to do at least two things. First, they need to ensure that there is a clear focus for professional learning. Second, they need to involve every teacher in articulating that focus so that everyone understands, agrees with, and is committed to the plan. In *Unmistakable Impact*, I describe a simple process that educational leaders can employ to achieve these goals. It is briefly summarized below.

Understand. To ensure that everyone fully understands the goals and strategies of a school improvement plan, those writing the plan must strive to write it in its simplest form possible to ensure that everyone understands it. Plans that are long and complex are often too difficult for even their authors to understand, and we can't implement a plan we don't understand. Schools and districts that are creating impact schools, described in *Unmistakable Impact*, create a one-page Target document that summarizes the school's professional development goals for a significant period of time into the future, perhaps as far ahead as three or four years.

Agreement. To ensure that a large majority agrees with the Target, educational leaders should do two things. First, to ensure that every teacher has an opportunity to provide meaningful input into the writing of the Target, a team should be created to gather teachers' ideas about professional learning for their school. In small schools, with 10 or fewer teachers, all teachers and administrators can meet as a team to collaboratively write the Target. However, since most schools have more than 10 teachers, many schools will need to create a Target Design Team.

The Target Design Team is made up of a school's administrators and a small number of teachers, who represent their colleagues (one teacher member for every 10 teachers in a school). Teachers on the team interview their peers and ask them what they think the school improvement focus should be, and then share those perspectives when the first draft of the Target is created.

Second, to ensure that the Target addresses the most important factors for student and teacher learning, leaders should observe every classroom to get a clear picture of teaching and learning in the school. The observation should be a comprehensive assessment of learning and teaching in the entire school, not an evaluation of individual teachers (we discourage sharing the individual data with teachers).

One tool for conducting these observations is the 20-Minute High-Impact Survey (HI-20). The HI-20 assesses teaching and learning in the four areas described in this book: (a) Instruction, (b) Content Planning, (c) Formative Assessment, and (d) Community Building. Download a beta version of the HI-20 at www.corwin.com/highimpactinstruction.

Download the 20-Minute High-Impact survey at www.corwin.com/highimpactinstruction

After all observations have been conducted and every teacher has been interviewed, the Target Design Team meets to create a Target that addresses the issues pointed to by the observation data and that genuinely embodies the concerns raised by teachers during interviews.

Commitment. Once a draft of the Target has been created, principals meet with groups within the school to review the proposed Target and to ask teachers to vote on whether they agree with and are committed to implementing the draft Target. The vote must be anonymous, and teachers must be strongly encouraged to give their honest opinion. If the results suggest that a large majority of staff agree with and are committed to the Target, the plan can proceed.

If there is a lack of commitment or agreement, leaders should ask teachers to write down the modifications to the plan they feel are necessary before they are willing to agree and commit, and revisions should be made until the plan is one that everyone can support. Teachers who are especially opposed to the plan may be invited to join the Target Design Team to help create a plan that the large majority of educators in the school are excited about implementing.

Professional learning will only succeed when teachers understand, agree with, and are committed to the plan. If teachers are not committed, their involvement will be half-hearted. In addition, few teachers will commit to a plan if they don't agree with it, and educators can only agree with a plan if they understand it. The process described in detail in *Unmistakable Impact* is designed to ensure that everyone has a voice in creating a plan that everyone wants to see become a reality.

Once the Target has been identified, efforts turn to translating the Target into action. Such work, however, requires sufficient, meaningful support. Instructional coaches, described in *Instructional Coaching: A Partnership Approach to Improving Instruction* (2007), provide that support.

PILLAR 3: INSTRUCTIONAL COACHES

For many of us, the journey toward a personal best, although highly attractive, can feel overwhelming, especially if we feel we are embarking on the journey all by ourselves. For example, teachers need a clear picture of the current reality in their classroom, but they may not know what data to gather to get an objective, accurate picture. They need a goal, but they may need help in defining an appropriate goal and measuring movement toward it. They need high-impact teaching strategies that can help them achieve their goal, but they probably don't know those strategies, or else they would already be using them. And they need someone who can help them learn and use those strategies until the strategies become habits of practice.

One person who can help with all of these important aspects of professional growth is an instructional coach (IC). An IC is a second set of hands, a second set of eyes, a learning partner who collaborates with teachers to identify goals, suggests teaching practices to learn, explains and models the new practices, and observes and supports teachers as they master and integrate those new practices into their teaching and meet their goals. An instructional coach provides the vital follow-up and support a teacher needs to implement new practices. "Coaching done well," Atul Gawande (2009) wrote, "may be the most effective intervention designed for human performance" (p. 53).

For more than a decade, my colleagues and I at the Kansas Coaching Project at the University of Kansas Center for Research on Learning have conducted research to design, develop, and validate instructional coaching. In *Instructional Coaching: A Partnership Approach to Improving Instruction* (2007), I first described the theory and practice of instructional coaching. Below is a short description of what coaches do.

Goals. To pursue a personal best in the classroom, teachers need a clear understanding of how well their students are learning. This isn't always easy. To see the classroom exactly as it is, teachers must have the courage to venture outside their comfort zone. Sheehan (1989) writes, "It's more comfortable not to try. But life is, or should be, a struggle: Comfort should make us uncomfortable; contentment should make us discontented" (p. 30). Real learning requires an honest assessment of current reality. The best teachers understand this and, consequently, they are never completely satisfied. They have a clear understanding of how their students are doing, and they restlessly strive to create better experiences and more learning for their students.

More than two decades ago, Robert Fritz (1989) wrote about the creative tension that lies at the heart of the quest for a personal best. Growth, he wrote, requires two factors: (a) a clear picture of current reality and (b) a clear goal that motivates an individual to move beyond that current reality. Knowing where we are and knowing where we want to go, Fritz argued, creates a tension that can only be resolved successfully through growth. Peter Senge summarized Fritz's ideas in *The Fifth Discipline* (1990):

> The juxtaposition of vision (what we want) and a clear picture of current reality (where we are relative to what we want) generates what we call "creative tension": a force to bring them together, caused by the natural tendency of tension to seek resolution. The essence of personal mastery is learning how to generate and sustain creative tension in our lives. (p. 132)

Ginger Grant talks about the power of one-to-one conversations during coaching.

Video 1.2
www.corwin.com/
highimpactinstruction

Instructional coaches begin the coaching process by partnering with teachers to set up the creative tension between a vision for the future and a clear picture of current reality that Robert Fritz described. First, to create a clear picture of current reality, ICs gather data on what is happening in a teacher's classroom. The data may be student achievement measures, student opinions gathered through surveys such as those developed by Harvard researcher Ron Ferguson at the Tripod Project,[2] or more frequently, video data gathered in a teacher's classroom using a Flip camera or some other camera, such as a Go Pro, iPhone, or iPad (Knight et al., 2012).

Instructional coaches share the data with teachers and ask them to review them. Using video has proven to be especially powerful since we have found that teachers (like most professionals) are often unaware of what their professional practice looks like until they see video of their lessons.

After teacher and coach have reviewed the data, together they identify a goal. An appropriate goal could be a student goal related to behavior (fewer than four disruptions per 10 minutes), achievement (95% mastery of questions on exit tickets), or attitudes (90% of students will say they enjoy reading on our quarterly survey). Effective goals are (a) specific, (b) measurable, and (c) compelling to the people who set them. Most important, however, as Chip and Dan Heath wrote, the best goal "kicks you in the gut" (2010, p. 76); that is, the best goal truly matters to the individual setting the goal.

High-Impact Instruction. After the teacher and coach have identified a goal, they discuss strategies the teacher might implement in an effort to meet the goal. For this reason, instructional coaches need to have a deep understanding of teaching practices. This book describes those teaching strategies, organized around four areas: (a) content planning, (b) formative assessment, (c) instructional practices, and (d) community building.

Precise Explanations. Once a teaching strategy has been identified, the instructional coach explains the practice in a way that makes it easiest for the teacher to implement it. This is a two-part process.

On the one hand, when coaches describe new teaching practices, their explanations must be clear and easy to act on; teachers will struggle to implement practices they don't understand. For that reason, instructional coaches must have a deep, complete understanding of the practices they describe *and* be able to explain those practices so that everyone can learn, internalize, and use them. Support for the importance of precise explanations is found in Gawande's studies of doctors and medical teams (2009) for the World Health Organization, which demonstrated that precise explanations embodied in checklists could save thousands of lives and billions of dollars.

Simply telling teachers how to implement practices is usually unsuccessful because it positions the collaborating teacher as someone who must passively consume practices; besides, few practices fit every classroom exactly the same way. Therefore, instructional coaches not only explain practices precisely; they also explain them provisionally. In other words, as coaches explain the aspects of a teaching practice, they point out that it may need to be adapted to best meet the needs of individual students and teachers. As they explain each aspect of a practice, instructional coaches stop and ask teachers whether or not the practice needs to be adapted in any way to meet the unique strengths or needs of students or their own strengths or needs. In short, they adopt Eric Liu's (2004) dictum that "Teaching is not one-size-fits-all; it's one-size-fits-one" (p. 47).

Modeling. While explanations can introduce practices to teachers, teachers usually need to see those practices in action to be ready to implement them fluently (Patterson, Grenny, Maxfield, McMillan, & Switzler, 2008). For this reason, modeling is an important part of the learning that is at the heart of instructional coaching. Most frequently, modeling occurs when a coach demonstrates a practice in a teacher's classroom. However, modeling can occur in several other ways. For example, the coach can demonstrate a practice in the teacher's classroom with only the coach and the teacher present, or the coach and teacher can co-teach. On some occasions, the coach and teacher visit another teacher's classroom, or the teacher visits another teacher's classroom while the coach covers the teacher's classroom. In yet other instances, modeling occurs when the teacher watches a video of the new practice.

Deliberate Practice and Progress Toward the Goal. Turning ideas into habits takes practice, feedback, and reflection (Syed, 2010). Thus, during the process of instructional coaching, teachers try out a new way of teaching, such as frequent checks for understanding, and instructional coaches gather data on how the new practice is being implemented and whether or not it is improving student behavior, achievement, or attitude. Instructional coaches might gather data from video recordings of the teacher or student, student survey data (such as that gathered from the Tripod survey), or achievement data from standardized or formative assessment, like that gathered from formative assessments such as exit tickets.

Instructional coaches gather data to monitor progress toward the goal and to provide an objective standard teachers can use to assess the effectiveness of the practice they are implementing. Thus, if coach and teacher have identified 90% engagement or 95% correct answers on a summative assessment as a goal, they monitor student performance until the goal is met. In addition, the teacher might review a checklist to determine, from her own perspective, how effectively she implemented a given practice.

Once the goal has been met, time on task is higher than 90%, for example, and the teacher is using the practice habitually and fluently, the coach and teacher can repeat the process by identifying another goal to be pursued.

PILLAR 4: HIGH-IMPACT INSTRUCTION

As I explained in *Unmistakable Impact*, a critical task for educational leaders is to identify those practices that have the greatest impact with the smallest effort. Peter Senge (1990) explains this in *The Fifth Discipline*:

> Small, well-focused actions can sometimes produce significant, enduring improvements, if they're in the right place. Systems thinkers refer to this as "leverage." . . . Tackling a difficult problem is often a matter of seeing where the high leverage lies, a change which—with a minimum of effort—would lead to lasting change. (p. 64)

In their exploration of successful change agents, *Influencer: The Power to Change Anything* (2008), Patterson, Grenny, Maxfield, McMillan, and Switzler made a similar observation: "Enormous influence comes from focusing on just a few *vital behaviors*. Even the most pervasive problems will often yield to changes in a handful of high-leverage behaviors. Find these, and you've found the beginning of influence" (p. 23). The findings from our study of instructional coaching reinforce the findings of Senge (1990), Patterson and his colleagues, Sims (2011), and others. That is, when it comes to teaching, little changes can make a big difference. This book describes those practices.

Is This Constructivist or Intensive-Explicit Pedagogy?

The high-impact instructional strategies described here are "agnostic," so to speak, because they can be employed by teachers adopting either a constructivist or intensive-explicit ideology. How practices are used should vary significantly depending on each teacher's approach. For that reason, I'll provide a brief review of the constructivist and intensive-explicit practices and a quick explanation of their implications for teachers using high-impact instructional strategies. I have written a longer treatment of these issues previously (Knight, 2005), and some of the ideas in that paper appear here.

INTENSIVE-EXPLICIT INSTRUCTION

I coined the term "intensive-explicit instruction" (IE) (Knight, 2005) to refer to a number of approaches to instruction variously referred to as direct instruction (Hattie, 2011; Roehler & Duffy, 1984), explicit instruction (Archer & Hughes, 2011), explicit, direct instruction (Hollingsworth & Ybarra, 2008), and strategic instruction (Ellis, Deshler, Lenz, Schumaker, & Clark, 1991). Teachers use intensive-explicit instruction to efficiently and effectively teach content and significantly increase the likelihood that students will master that content. Intensive-explicit instruction is *intensive* because it involves teaching practices that ensure students are engaged in learning and actively mastering content (Archer & Hughes, 2011; Ellis et al.). It is *explicit* because it involves teachers clearly modeling covert thinking (Roehler & Duffy) and providing detailed feedback as students move toward mastery of content (Hollingsworth & Ybarra, 2009; Kline, Schumaker, & Deshler, 1991).

The principal goal for teachers using IE is for students to understand, remember, and generalize content they teach. During IE, as John Hattie (2008) has written about direct instruction, "the teacher decides learning intentions and success criteria, makes them transparent to the students, demonstrates them by modeling, evaluates if they understand what they have been told by checking for understanding, and re-telling them what they have told by tying it together with closure" (p. 206). Similarly, in *Explicit Instruction: Effective and Efficient Teaching* (2011), Anita Archer and Charles A. Hughes define explicit instruction as follows:

> Explicit instruction [is] a structured, systematic, and effective methodology for teaching academic skills. It is called explicit because it is an unambiguous and direct approach to teaching that includes both instructional design and delivery procedures. Explicit instruction is characterized by a series of supports or scaffolds, whereby students are guided through the learning process with clear statements about the purpose and rationale for learning the new skill, clear explanations and demonstrations of the instructional target, and supported practice with feedback until independent mastery has been achieved. (p. 1)

CONSTRUCTIVIST INSTRUCTION

Constructivist instruction is grounded in the belief that, as Brooks and Brooks (1993) stated, "each of us makes sense of the world by synthesizing new experiences into what we have previously come to understand" (p. 4). Piaget (1954) first named this process of individually fitting new information into our prior knowledge by overcoming incongruities between old and new knowledge "assimilation." For Piaget,

> No behavior, even it if is new to the individual, constitutes an absolute beginning. It is always grafted onto previous schemes and therefore amounts to assimilating new elements to already constructed structures. (Glaserfield, 1995, p. 62)

Lev Vygotsky built on Piaget's concept of assimilation by proposing a second important concept within constructivist instruction, the "zone of proximal development." According to Vygotsky (1978), the zone defines "those functions that have not yet matured but are in the process of maturing . . . functions that will mature tomorrow but are currently in an embryonic state" (p. 86). The zone is "the distance between the actual developmental level as determined by independent problem solving and the level of potential development as determined through problem solving under adult guidance or in collaboration with more capable peers" (p. 86). Simply put, the zone is the gap between a person's current intellectual level and his or her potential level.

Constructivist teachers provide scaffolding (Wood, Bruner, & Ross, 1976) to enable students to develop their full potential within their zone of proximal development. In addition, constructivist teachers facilitate discourse and dialogue to provide students opportunities to assimilate new learning into their prior knowledge (Mariage, 2000). Within constructivist instruction, then, a teacher is more of a facilitator than an expert.

Brooks and Brooks (1993) helped clarify constructivist instruction by creating a list of constructivist traits. Specifically, they suggest that constructivist teachers

a. "encourage and accept student autonomy and initiative" (p. 103);

b. "use cognitive terminology . . . when framing tasks" (p. 104);

c. "allow student responses to drive lessons, shift instructional strategies and alter content" (p. 105);

d. "inquire about students' understandings of concepts before sharing their own understanding of those concepts" (p. 107);

  e. "encourage students to engage in dialogue" (p. 108);

  f. "provide time for students to construct relationships and create metaphors" (p. 115); and

  g. "nurture students' natural curiosity through frequent use of the learning cycle model" (p. 116).

COMPARING APPROACHES

During IE, the teacher guides students to a predetermined right or wrong outcome. The teacher's goal is that students will create a picture of knowledge in their heads that is similar to the picture the teacher holds in his or her head. By comparison, during constructivist instruction, the teacher presents many opportunities for students to assimilate learning into their prior knowledge. The teacher's goal is that students will create their own pictures of what they are learning.

The teaching strategies in this book can be employed from either perspective, but they should be employed in significantly different ways by IE versus constructivist teachers. Intensive-explicit teachers, for example, ask a lot of questions and use questions to gauge whether or not students have mastered the predetermined content. Constructivist teachers, on the other hand, ask only a few questions, usually to seek students' opinions, not right or wrong answers.

In addition, cooperative learning, for example, serves very different purposes within the two approaches. During IE, cooperative learning is employed to increase and confirm mastery of content; thus students might work together to ensure that they have a complete, accurate understanding of some information. During constructivist instruction, on the other hand, cooperative learning is used so that students can tackle complex problems, engage in dialogue, and progress at their own pace. During constructivist instruction, cooperative learning often arrives at unpredictable points as students mediate their own learning.

Some teachers are entirely committed to constructivist practices, while others entirely subscribe to an intensive-explicit ideology. My belief is that both approaches have their place. When my goal is to ensure that students master content as I teach it, such as learning grammatical terms, phonetic sounds, or math facts, I adopt an intensive-explicit approach. When my goal is to provide an opportunity for students to make their own sense of what they are learning, such as interpreting a poem, solving a problem, or writing a personal vision, then I adopt a constructivist approach.

What matters is that teachers determine what approach works best for their students and then use the appropriate high-impact strategies. In the pages of this book, I will explain where and how each high-impact strategy can be used for each approach.

What You Will Find in This Book

PART I: PLANNING

Part I describes high-impact planning, simple strategies teachers can use to

a. create guiding questions that point to the essential knowledge, skills, and big ideas to be learned;

b. identify what is to be assessed and how it will be assessed;

c. create a learning map depicting what is to be learned; and

d. integrate the questions, assessments, and maps into lessons so that every student understands what they are learning and how well they are progressing.

Chapter 2, Guiding Questions, describes a method teachers can use to develop their own understanding of the objectives and content that they will be teaching in their classes. In addition, guiding questions enhance student learning by providing clear explanations of what will be learned in a unit. Effective guiding questions address state or core standards, identify how students should learn and understand content, explain how content is meaningful or important, and identify critical concepts, ideas, or content structures to be learned.

Chapter 3, Formative Assessment, introduces an easy and powerful method for designing and implementing assessment for learning in the classroom. Used effectively, formative assessment increases student engagement, enables students to see how well their learning is progressing, and surfaces essential data that enable teachers to see how well their students are learning. The chapter also describes 18 easy-to-use informal assessments that teachers can use every day to determine whether or not students have learned their content. Finally, the chapter describes how teachers can use the data gathered from ongoing assessment for learning to rethink their lessons and their assessments and in-class assessment practices.

Chapter 4, Learning Maps, describes a variety of approaches to mapping (cluster maps, mind maps, concept maps, thinking maps, and content structures), explains how teachers can use graphic organizers to map out what students will learn in a unit, and describes how teachers should share learning maps and guiding questions with students on the first day of a unit, during a unit, and at the end of a unit. Also, the chapter describes how all students can use learning maps to note essential information and for ongoing review of learning.

PART II: INSTRUCTION

Part II introduces five high-impact instructional practices that teachers can use to engage students, to increase student mastery of content, and to empower students to make connections and apply their learning to their lives.

Chapter 5, Thinking Prompts, describes how teachers can use video clips, photographs, newspaper articles, popular songs, and other devices as catalysts for discussion, dialogue, and higher order thinking in the classroom. Thinking prompts capture student attention through the use of media and topics that are especially relevant to students. Thus, they enable students to see connections between new content to be covered and their own way of seeing the world, and they can promote positive cultural norms and a positive learning environment in the classroom.

Chapter 6, Effective Questions, describes different kinds of questions that can be used as catalysts for student thinking, classroom conversation, and dialogue. During direct instruction, closed-ended, right-or-wrong questions are often most effective. During constructivist instruction, open-ended, opinion questions are often most effective. The chapter also distinguishes between three levels of questions, knowledge, skill, and big ideas, and discusses effective questioning techniques.

Chapter 7, Stories, describes how teachers can use stories to link abstract learning to concrete, personally relevant narratives to connect new learning to prior knowledge, to create positive learning communities, and to increase students' interest in whatever lesson is being learned. Teachers can use stories to illustrate important ideas being delivered, especially since stories are often the part of a lesson that students recall most vividly. Teachers should use stories to illustrate content that is especially noteworthy, so that students can carry away strong recollections of important material.

Chapter 8, Cooperative Learning, describes learning that is mediated by students rather than the instructor. Thus, in cooperative learning, students work in groups or pairs to teach themselves what is being learned. Teachers can use cooperative learning as a way for groups to cover material, problem solve, brainstorm, and explore or invent new ideas. Cooperative learning can also be used to inject variety into lessons, to increase engagement, and to provide a setting for students to learn important social skills. Finally, cooperative learning can involve groups of any size, from two students to very large groups.

Chapter 9, Authentic Learning, describes how teachers can design assignments that are optimally challenging for students. Effective, challenging assignments are (a) matched to the learning goal, (b) designed to produce authentic learning, (c) personally relevant and optimally challenging (not too easy; not too hard), (d) differentiated according to student strengths, (e) designed to promote appropriate levels of thinking, and (f) produce a meaningful product.

Authentic learning also describes experiential learning that provides students with opportunities to see how well they can use the new concepts they are learning, reminds them of the concrete attributes of a particular phenomenon being studied, or allows students to gain new insights into their thoughts, assumptions, and behaviors.

PART III: COMMUNITY BUILDING

Part III describes six powerful teaching strategies that teachers can use to build a safe, productive, joyous learning community in their classrooms.

Chapter 10, Learner-Friendly Culture, describes strategies for shaping a classroom culture that promotes safety, joy, well-being, and learning. Strategies include co-constructing classroom norms, attending to student behavior, and creating a positive physical learning environment in the classroom.

Chapter 11, Power With, Not Power Over, distinguishes between "power over," during which teachers try to force students to comply with demands, and "power with," during which teachers interact respectfully and provide students with choices in order to foster meaningful learning.

Chapter 12, Freedom Within Form, describes steps teachers can take to encourage students to creatively and freely experience learning while also providing structures that allow that creativity to progress productively. Too much freedom can lead to anarchy, but too much structure destroys learning.

Chapter 13, Expectations, describes why effective community building begins with establishing clear expectations for activities and transitions. In addition, the chapter describes the three critical elements of expectations: action, talking, and movement.

Chapter 14, Witness to the Good, describes how teachers should reinforce student behavior by noticing and commenting when students act consistently with expectations. The chapter also includes information on building connections with students and fostering positive emotions in classrooms.

Chapter 15, Fluent Corrections, describes how teachers can attend to students and correct them consistently when they act in ways that disrupt their own or others' learning.

Each chapter begins with a learning map, similar to the learning maps described in Chapter 4, that visually depicts the key concepts in the chapter. Each chapter also contains these features:

- **Turning Ideas Into Action,** suggestions for how students, teachers, coaches, and principals can use chapter ideas to improve instruction
- **What It Looks Like,** with suggestions on how to observe for the teaching practices described
- A summary of the chapter under the heading **To Sum Up**
- A **Going Deeper** section that introduces resources readers can explore to extend their knowledge of the ideas and strategies discussed

Each chapter also contains QR codes with links to videos from the Teaching Channel, which I have chosen to illustrate the practices I describe here. Some video links are taken from my program, Talking About Teaching, and others are Short Cuts, where I highlight other teachers doing amazing practices. Finally, throughout the book, I include numerous checklists to clarify precisely how the high-impact teaching practices should be implemented.

Turning Ideas Into Action

Students

1. Consider involving students in writing a school improvement target by interviewing students or by including students on the Target Design Team.

2. Consider using student survey data, from a survey such as the Tripod Survey, when gathering data on current reality in schools.

Teachers

1. Consider committing to striving for personal bests.

2. Write a personal vision that states exactly what you want to accomplish in your life and work.

3. Hold your school accountable once it has identified a Target.

Instructional Coaches

1. Strive to be your best in at least three critical areas:

   a. Master the teaching practices, such as those described in this book, that are the focus of your instructional coaching.

   b. Master the components of instructional coaching described in *Instructional Coaching* (2007).

   c. Communicate and lead effectively by deeply understanding the partnership principles, communication strategies, and leadership tactics described in *Instructional Coaching* (2007) and *Unmistakable Impact* (2011).

Principals

1. Communicate with central office district leaders to ensure that they support your pursuit of the Target.

2. Resist the pressure to implement new practices before the Target has been achieved.

3. As with your instructional coaches, communicate and lead effectively by deeply understanding the partnership principles, communication strategies, and leadership tactics described in *Instructional Coaching* (2007) and *Unmistakable Impact* (2011).

What It Looks Like

In an impact school, all professional learning leads directly to improvements on teacher effectiveness, and student development, growth, and happiness. A comprehensive tool for looking at all of the high-impact teaching strategies, the High Impact Instruction 20-Minute Survey (HI-20) is available online at www.corwin.com/highimpactinstruction.

To Sum Up

- Professionals in all fields find meaning in the challenge of striving to achieve a personal best.

- When teachers strive to achieve a personal best, their students benefit because instruction improves and because they may be inspired by their teachers' love of learning.

- If teachers are to experience professional learning that helps them strive for a personal best, the school must be organized in a way that supports their learning.

- In impact schools, the entire staff comes together around achieving a Target for improvement that each teacher understands, agrees with, and is committed to implementing.

- In impact schools, teachers receive the support they need to translate the Target into action from instructional coaches who collaborate with them to assist them in setting goals and identifying practices to achieve those goals by explaining and modeling those practices and by observing teachers and exploring implementation data until teachers achieve their goals and are fluent and habitual in their use of new practices.

- The high-impact instructional strategies described in this book, organized around the themes of Instruction, Content Planning, Formative Assessment, and Community Building, are the practices that I believe have the most positive impact on teacher effectiveness and student development, growth, and well-being.

Going Deeper

Teachers as Professionals. My two books *Instructional Coaching* (2007) and *Unmistakable Impact* (2011) describe the partnership principles and an approach to professional learning that begins with respect for the professionalism of teachers. Thomas Davenport's *Thinking for a Living* (2005) provides a description of the characteristics of knowledge workers. Daniel Pink's *Drive* (2009) is an engaging summary of Edward Deci's self-determination theory and other theories of motivation.

Schoolwide Change. Michael Fullan's work on educational change, nicely summarized in *Motion Leadership: The Skinny on Becoming Change Savvy* (2009), was the major influence on my book *Unmistakable Impact*. Readers interested in leading instructional improvement would benefit greatly from reading his work. Randy Sprick's work on comprehensive school reform focused on behavior has also greatly influenced my thinking. Other books worth reviewing are Michael Schmokers' *Focus* (2011) and Wayne Sailor, Glen Dunlap, George Sugai, and Rob Horner's *Handbook of Positive Behavior Supports* (2010).

Instructional Coaching. My book *Instructional Coaching* (2007) provides an overview of the theory and practice of instructional coaching. Cheryl Jones and Mary Vreeman have published *Instructional Coaches & Classroom Teachers: Sharing the Road to Success* (2008). Robert Hargrove's *Masterful Coaching* (2008) makes the distinction between pull and push coaching. Stephen Barkley's *Instructional Coaching With the End in Mind* (2011) is another valuable resource for instructional coaches.

Other useful books on coaching in general include Joellen Killion and Cindy Harrison's *Taking the Lead: New Roles for Teachers and School-Based Coaches* (2006), Nancy Love's *Data Coaching: Using Data to Improve Learning for All: A Collaborative Inquiry Approach* (2009), Lucy West and Fritz Staub's *Content-Focused Coaching* (2003), and Art Costa and Robert Garmston's *Cognitive Coaching* (2002).

Other Comprehensive Models of Instruction. Several other comprehensive models of instruction have been published recently, and many have influenced the writing of this book. Charlotte Danielson's *Framework for Teaching* (2007) provides a rich description of aspects of instruction and is used internationally as a method for observing teaching. Doug Lemov's *Teach Like a Champion: 49 Techniques That Put Students on the Path to College* (2010) describes easy-to-learn teaching techniques designed to increase student engagement and learning. John Hattie's *Visual Learning* (2009) and Robert Marzano, Jane E. Pollock, and Debra J. Pickering's *Classroom Instruction That Works: Research-Based Strategies for Increasing Student Achievement* (2001) both offer meta-analyses of effective instructional practices. Finally, Jon Saphier, Mary Ann Haley-Speca, and Robert Gower's *The Skillful Teacher: Building Your Teaching Skill* (2008) is a comprehensive and practical overview of instructional practices.

Notes

1. You can read about research conducted on the partnership approach at http://instructionalcoach.org/research.
2. See www.metproject.com for more information on the Tripod survey.

PART I

PLANNING

What you leave behind is not what is engraved in stone monuments, but what is woven into the lives of others.

—Pericles

If your actions create a legacy that inspires others to dream more, learn more, do more and become more, then, you are an excellent leader.

—Dolly Parton

I grew up on a farm in Southern Ontario in Canada. My parents and I lived with my grandparents and my aunt in a big farmhouse about 60 miles west of Toronto. In the first years of my life, my grandfather made a lot of time for me. He let me pretend to help when he built things around the farm, brought me along when he did chores, and taught me to love books and how to read.

When I was four years old, my grandfather started a tree-planting project with me. Grampa would walk with me a half-mile down the gravel road to a large willow tree at the end of the farm, and we would we cut small shoots of branches off the tree. Then we put the shoots in mason jars filled with water and waited for roots to sprout. Eventually, little roots grew out of our twigs, and our willow shoots were ready to be planted as little trees. We planted them in many places on the farm and around the little village of Sheffield where my grandparents eventually moved.

At the time I didn't realize it, but with hindsight I believe that my grandfather was planting those trees with me so that I would remember him. The trees were something I could go and see to be reminded of him after he died. And he was gone much too soon. My grandfather died of a heart attack when I was seven years old.

Unfortunately, one by one, the trees had to be removed. One was too close to a fence; one was too close to the house, and eventually none was left. For a while I felt sad about that, but then I realized that the actual trees were not what was important. What mattered was the act. What I remember was my grandfather and me doing the planting together. The trees were gone, but the legacy my grandfather left me lived on. Now writing this when I am 57 years old, I still remember my grandfather like I was 4.

To leave a legacy is as important in teaching as it is in life. Like my grandfather with his grandson, teachers have the chance every day to plant something that takes root and shapes the minds, hearts, and lives of their students. I learned this firsthand when I started doing research on learning at the University of Kansas Center for Research on Learning.

For my first research project, I studied what happens when teachers write personal visions. One of the teachers I was working with was Maryfrances Wagner, a wonderful language arts teacher in the Raytown School District, outside of Kansas City. One day I met Maryfrances to discuss the vision study, and I asked her how her day was going. "Today," she said, "is a good day." She had received a letter from one of her former students, a girl she had taught in twelfth-grade English. Mary shared the letter, written on the letterhead of a legal firm. In part, as I recall, it read as follows:

> Dear Mrs. Wagner,
>
> You may not remember me, but 12 years ago I was in your AP English class. During the class you asked me what my plans were after I graduated. I told you I was planning to be a legal secretary, and you told me, don't be a secretary, be a lawyer. Well, today I was just named partner in my law firm. I want you to know that it wouldn't have happened if it hadn't been for you . . .

This letter was a beautiful testament to Ms. Wagner's successful teaching and a gracious gesture by a student, demonstrating the impact teachers can have on their students. But I don't believe the impact that Maryfrances had on her former student was exceptional.

This is what teachers do. Through their love of learning and their love of children and young adults, teachers profoundly affect the future.

Teachers have the chance, each day, to open their students up to possibilities that children often don't have any inkling they hold within them. With what they teach, what they believe, and how they act, teachers help shape the lives of their students. There is no doubt that teachers leave a legacy with every student they teach. To teach is to leave a legacy.

This then is the critical question: What is the legacy I want to leave with my students?

Teachers answer that question every day they meet with children, and their legacy is passed on through modeling, instruction, encouragement, feedback, smiles, and suggestions. But the importance of considering the legacy is nowhere more important than when teachers sit down to plan their courses, units, and lessons. When teachers think about what to emphasize, what to ensure students master, what to skip, and where to go deep, their driving question should be this: Ten years from now, what do I want my students to remember about our class? High-impact planning is where teachers begin to answer that question.

What Is High-Impact Planning?

High-impact planning involves (a) creating guiding questions that point toward the big ideas, skills, and knowledge students need to learn; (b) developing formative assessments that enable teachers and students to monitor progress and that serve to guide teachers as they adapt and differentiate instruction to increase learning; and (c) crafting learning maps that graphically depict the learning students will experience. Guiding questions, formative assessments, and learning maps provide a structure for student learning, and they make the outcomes and sequence of learning transparent so that students understand the key ideas and when they will be learned.

There seems to be no preferred or correct order for high-impact planning. Wiggins and McTighe (2005) suggest that some teachers benefit from starting with assessments and working backward in a kind of creative and artful task analysis. They write, "Backward design calls for us to make our goals or standards specific and concrete, in terms of assessment evidence, as we begin to plan a unit or course" (p. 19). For many teachers, backward design means starting with the assessment, and they aren't comfortable writing their questions or drafting learning maps until they're sure what they will be assessing.

Other teachers, in my experience, prefer to write their guiding questions at the start of planning. They say that they need to create the guiding questions first because they have to think deeply about the learning objectives before they write the assessments.

A third group of teachers would rather start with the map. "I have to get all the content out there so I can see it before I can write my questions and assessments," they say.

Having worked with hundreds of teachers on curriculum development, I've found that most teachers prefer to start in one of these three places, guiding questions, learning maps, or formative assessment, and most know what they prefer. Teachers, I've concluded, should start where it feels most appropriate for them, in part, because that is where they will start anyway. What matters is that all three aspects of the planning process help refine the other parts of development.

Teachers who have written guiding questions may find the questions focus their development of their learning maps; similarly, developing a learning map may enrich a teacher's guiding questions. In addition, when a teacher creates formative assessments—which is largely about breaking down and clearly articulating the knowledge, skills, and big ideas into what I call specific proficiencies and then determining how to assess students' acquisition of those specific proficiencies—that act often leads them to refine their questions and learning maps. On many occasions, I've observed that after teachers write the specific proficiencies for their guiding questions, they realize they have to change the questions to better point to the answers they want students to discover. "If I can't answer this question," they say, "how can I expect my students to?"

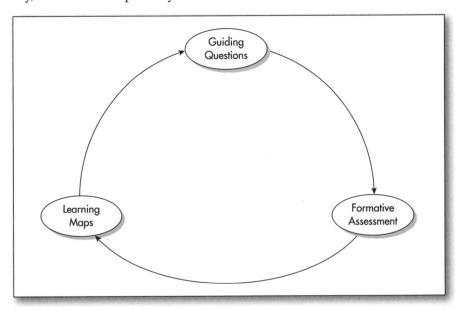

High-impact planning is largely about using all three components of planning to be intentional about what students will be learning and how learning will proceed. When we live unintentionally in learning, we make a big mistake. As Wayne Dyer has famously stated, "Our intention creates our reality." An unintentional life squanders opportunity because days, months, and sometimes years fly by before we realize that we are missing what is most important. The same can be said about teaching. An unintentional classroom is one in which opportunities are lost because too little thought is given to what is most important. Hours, days, and months fly by and opportunities for learning evaporate.

High-impact planning helps teachers create an intentional classroom by guiding teachers to think deeply about each learning opportunity. When teachers create guiding questions, they identify what is most important for their students to learn. When they create formative assessments, teachers ensure they know and their students know how well they are learning, and teachers are able to use that knowledge to appropriately adjust learning in school. And when they create learning maps, teachers consider the sequence of their instruction and the connections between the knowledge, skills, and big ideas their students will be learning.

In Chapter 2, I'll describe how to develop guiding questions. In Chapter 3, I'll describe how teachers can (a) identify the knowledge, skills, and big ideas that students need to learn; (b) assess whether students have learned what they are supposed to learn; and (c) adjust instruction to ensure that students do learn the content. In Chapter 4, I'll describe how to develop learning maps and how teachers should integrate guiding questions and learning maps into the daily rituals and routines in the classroom to enhance teaching and, especially, learning.

Chapter 2:
Guiding
Questions

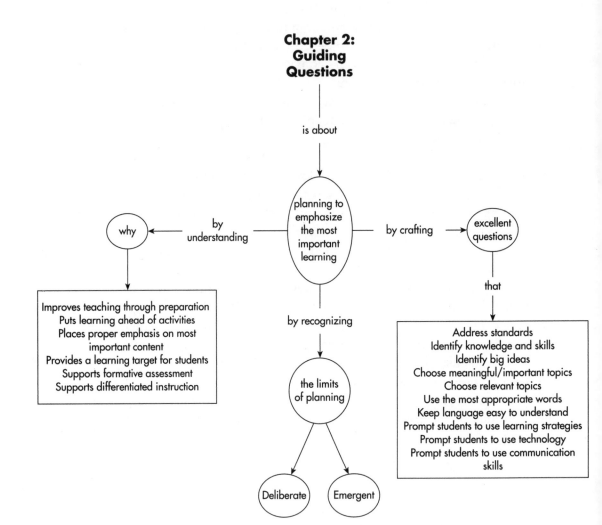

is about

planning to emphasize the most important learning

by understanding

why

Improves teaching through preparation
Puts learning ahead of activities
Places proper emphasis on most important content
Provides a learning target for students
Supports formative assessment
Supports differentiated instruction

by recognizing

the limits of planning

Deliberate

Emergent

by crafting

excellent questions

that

Address standards
Identify knowledge and skills
Identify big ideas
Choose meaningful/important topics
Choose relevant topics
Use the most appropriate words
Keep language easy to understand
Prompt students to use learning strategies
Prompt students to use technology
Prompt students to use communication skills

2

GUIDING QUESTIONS

Success depends upon previous preparation, and without prepa-
ration there is sure to be failure.

—Confucius

Pay attention to where you are going because without meaning
you might get nowhere.

—A. A. Milne

E thel Edwards, a former curriculum director for mathematics in
Topeka, Kansas, worked with me on many projects when the
Kansas Coaching Project partnered with USD 501. A mathematics
expert, a former state employee, and a district administrator, Ethel is a
woman of many surprises. A passionate educator deeply committed
to students, she also happens to be a former triathelete who completed
Ironman competitions and a person who still likes to take her Harley
Davidson out for long rides on her vacations with her husband.

Ethel and I created a process, intensive learning teams (ILTs),
which I described in *Unmistakable Impact: A Partnership Approach for*
Dramatically Improving Instruction (2011). Intensive learning teams
bring together all the teachers who teach the same course—we started
with seventh-grade math—so that they can collectively do planning.
Together, the teachers create the guiding questions, learning maps,
and formative assessments for a course.

During the first hours of our first ILT, Ethel and I realized that
some special kind of magic was taking place in the group. When

teachers had time to think deeply about what to teach, how to organize that instruction, and how to assess the subsequent learning, their
content knowledge shot up like a rocket. Their deeper knowledge, we
realized, would help their teaching be more efficient, precise, and
effective. When teachers have a precise understanding of exactly
what students will learn, and they clearly communicate those learning goals, students learn more.[1]

What Ethel and I saw as we observed the seventh-grade teachers
creating guiding questions and learning maps for their students also
was observed by instructional coaches when they worked with individual teachers planning their units. For example, when Jenny
MacMillan, one of the coaches in our intensive study of instructional
coaching in Beaverton, Oregon, spent a lot of time working with
Robin Turner on guiding questions, Jenny saw that Robin's experiences mirrored those of Ethel and me.

Robin and Jenny worked together on developing guiding questions because Robin wanted to become clearer about her instructional
targets. Jenny scheduled a substitute teacher to cover Robin's class
one afternoon and met with Robin to, as Jenny said, "crank out" the
questions for a unit. The simple task of clarifying exactly what will be
taught proved to be extremely helpful.

After writing guiding questions, Robin, Jenny reported, "sees the
beauty of knowing where she is going." Robin realized this change
herself and told Jenny, "This has helped me so much because I feel
like I am clearer. I know where I am going with my students. I know
what I want. I am able to ask them better questions as we go along. I
am able to check in with them." "It's clearer for her," Jenny said. "It
gives her more focus in her teaching."

When teachers think deeply about what they will be teaching, in
communities or on their own, their teaching, and consequently student learning, improves. In *Where Great Teaching Begins: Planning for
Student Thinking and Learning* (2001), Ann Reeves writes about the
importance of teacher planning:

> This is the "deep work" of teaching: designing instruction that
> takes teachers deep into content and deep into consideration
> of their students' learning . . . it goes far beyond selecting
> activities and writing tests; it extends past the teachers' per-
> formance to address the bedrock of the whole educational
> enterprise—demonstrated student learning. (p. 8)

Effective guiding questions provide a clear target for student
learning, pointing to both the final destination and the knowledge,

skills, and big ideas to be learned along the way. In total, guiding questions lead students toward a complete understanding of what they are to learn in a unit. If students can construct complete answers to each guiding question, they should receive an A or B grade on the unit because they will have demonstrated mastery of the knowledge, skills, and big ideas in the unit.

The act of writing guiding questions compels teachers to create precise, focused plans for learning, and that focus and precision helps students better understand the learning expectations for each unit and lesson. Good questions evoke a rigorous education, but they should be written in easy-to-understand language and involve the smallest number of questions for each unit. Great questions are accessible, easy-to-understand, but complete illustrations of what will be learned.

Why Teachers Should Create Guiding Questions

Guiding Questions Improve Teaching Through Preparation. When asked why he was so successful as a football coach, the two-time national champion Urban Meyer replied, "Well-prepared players make plays. I have yet to be in a game where the most prepared team didn't win." What is true on the football field is also true in the classroom. Preparation reaps significant benefits. When teachers think through what will be learned and how learning will happen, their lessons are more focused, efficient, and accessible to all learners.

When I interview teachers about the value of content planning, their first response is usually, "I know these are supposed to help students be organized, but what they really do is help me be organized." When teachers are clear on their plan, everyone benefits.

Guiding Questions Put Learning Ahead of Activities. When teachers craft effective guiding questions, they look at learning through their students' eyes, considering what the students will learn, rather than through their own eyes, considering what activities or lessons they will assign the students. In fact, Wiggins and McTighe (2005) consider a focus on activities rather than learning to be one of the main sins of instructors:

> The error of activity-oriented design might be called "hands-on without being minds-on"—engaging experiences that lead only accidentally, if at all, to insight or achievement. The activities though fun and interesting do not lead anywhere intellectually. (p. 16)

Wendy Hopf talks about the importance of content planning.

Video 2.1
www.corwin.com/
highimpactinstruction

High-impact planning starts with the most fundamental question: What do I want my students to remember 5, 10, or 20 years after this class is over? As such, it compels teachers to be precise about exactly what students will learn and how their mastery of the knowledge, skills, and big ideas will be measured.

Guiding Questions Place Proper Emphasis on Most Important Content. The knowledge, skills, and big ideas learned in a class are not all equally important. For students reading Langston Hughes' poem "Dreams," for example, remembering the exact day Hughes was born, February 1, 1902, might not be very important, but making a personal connection with the closing lines of the poem could be very important:

> *Hold fast to dreams*
>
> *For when dreams go*
>
> *Life is a barren field*
>
> *Frozen with snow.*

Source: "Dreams" from *The Collected Poems of Langston Hughes* by Langston Hughes, edited by Arnold Rampersad with David Roessel, Associate Editor, copyright © 1994 by the Estate of Langston Hughes. Used by permission of Alfred A. Knopf, a division of Random House, Inc. Any third party use of this material, outside of this publication, is prohibited. Interested parties must apply directly to Random House, Inc. for permission.

When teachers are poorly prepared, the distinction between important and unimportant becomes blurred, and everything can seem to be equally important. Content planning guides teachers to think deeply about what is most important and then to teach in a way that ensures that the most important learning is given the emphasis it requires.

Guiding Questions Provide a Learning Target for Students. Guiding questions help students by giving them a clear target for each day's learning. As Richard Stiggins noted, "Students can hit any target they can see and that holds still for them" (cited by Sparks, 1999, p. 3). When teachers write good questions and create maps, they are forced to become very clear about what they are teaching. That clarity gives focus to their teaching, but also makes it much easier for students to learn. When students understand what they are supposed to learn, the chances are much higher that they will actually learn it.

Guiding Questions Support Formative Assessment. Guiding questions represent a starting point for formative assessment. Indeed, the in-depth thinking that is a necessary part of formative assessment will enhance the quality of teachers' guiding questions and learning maps. Formative assessment is easier when a teacher has developed guiding questions, but the development of detailed answers and specific proficiencies, as described in Chapter 3, will inform the development of guiding questions and learning maps.

Guiding Questions Support Differentiated Instruction. When teachers teach classes with diverse learners, and most teachers do these days, they frequently need to differentiate learning so that it meets the needs of all students (Tomlinson, 1999). When teachers differentiate, they tailor the content, processes, products, or learning environment to the unique needs of students. Differentiation happens best when teachers carefully plan their instruction so that they can reflect on where and how learning needs to be transformed.

Guiding questions provide an excellent starting point for differentiation. After teachers have created their guiding questions, they have a much clearer understanding of where they need to make modifications to ensure that learning is accessible for every student. Guiding questions provide a firm foundation for thinking about how and where to differentiate learning.

The Limitations of Planning

But planning instruction, like most things in life, isn't as simple as it seems. On the surface, the task seems easy enough. Identify what your students need to learn, make a plan to teach what you have identified, measure whether or not your students have learned it, and modify your teaching if students aren't learning. Easy to say; not so easy to do. Or as the Yiddish proverb states, "Man makes plans. God laughs."

Plans are great in theory, but once real human beings start to interact with those plans, teaching becomes more complicated. The reality is that student progress rarely follows a linear path. Some years students learn material much quicker than others; other years, for whatever reason, learning takes more time. Most years, different students progress at different paces, and teachers struggle to decide what to do when some students are bored because they have mastered the material and others are frustrated because they still don't understand.

Life itself presents wonderful opportunities for learning that also can sidetrack a well-thought-out plan. During the 2000 presidential election between George Bush and Al Gore, for example, social studies teachers tell me that their students showed unprecedented interest in the workings of the electoral college, the Supreme Court, and other components of the U.S. government. A teacher who slavishly followed a plan but missed the chance to take advantage of student interest in life around them would not be serving students well.

Other events can lead to rich and powerful detours in an instructional plan. A natural disaster can lead to rich learning in science. The release of a new movie can deepen student interest in a related novel, and an event such as the financial crisis can pull students into learning about economics and mathematics. Even smaller events in a school, a change in prices in the cafeteria, for example, can lead to meaningful conversations.

For all these reasons, although planning is essential, teachers must remember that no plan is ever more important than authentic learning and that sometimes the map for learning must be set aside to make sure that the best learning occurs. Planning, then, involves a paradox of sorts. On the one hand, planning is essential, but on the other hand, when planning a unit or lesson, teachers must enter into the process aware that they may have to shift directions at some point if they are going to meet the needs of all their students and if they are going to exploit all the opportunities for learning that arise, like gifts, in the environment.

Henry Mintztberg, an internationally renowned academic studying business, points to the same paradox in strategic planning (1985). On the one hand, businesses have to make plans based on anticipated outcomes—what Mintzberg refers to as deliberate strategy. But at the same time, businesses need to be ready to pivot when circumstances reveal that a change in strategy is necessary—what he refers to as emergent strategy. Businesses need deliberate plans to focus and organize effort, but they also need to be ready for emergent plans when they are needed.

In his book on understanding critical life decisions, *How Will You Measure Your Life?* (2012), Harvard Business School professor Clayton Christensen suggests that Mintzberg's ideas about strategic planning also apply to life planning.

> Each approach [deliberate and emergent] is vying for our minds and our hearts, making its best case to become our actual strategy. . . . In our lives and in our careers, whether we are aware of it or not, we are constantly navigating a path by deciding between our deliberate strategies and the unanticipated alternatives that emerge. (p. 48)

As in business and life, so too in the classroom. Planning is absolutely essential, and the better prepared teachers are, in general, the more students will learn. However, plans must be flexible enough to accommodate the unique needs of individual students and the unique opportunities for connected learning that arise every day. Great plans provide a detailed map for the journey, but teachers should be prepared to fold the map and set it aside whenever a more important opportunity or need comes along.

A Focus on Units and Questions

Planning can occur at the course, unit, or lesson level. I have worked with hundreds of teachers who have benefited from using Keith Lenz's *Course Organizer Routine* (Lenz, Schumaker, Deshler, & Bulgren, 1998) to write course questions, identify concepts, develop course maps, and create other plans for a course. Some teachers report that they feel they have to see the whole course laid out before they can plan units and lessons.

For others, the unit of focus is the lesson. Moss and Brookhart (2011), for example, write that "improving student learning happens in the immediacy of an individual lesson . . . or it doesn't happen at all" (p. 2). In my experience with teachers, again, I find that some educators do find it most helpful to carry out their planning at the lesson level, and certainly all teaching requires some lesson planning.

In the majority of cases, however, I find that teachers find it most helpful to plan at the unit level. Course planning requires a breadth of thinking that occurs best over time, indeed a year, as teachers implement and adapt unit plans. Lesson planning is too particular to account for the themes and other big ideas to be learned in a unit. If teachers want to think about big ideas, and if they want to create plans that show how knowledge, skills, and big ideas connect, they may find it most useful to plan at the unit level. For that reason, in this book I describe unit planning; however, the strategies described in this section might be used at the course or lesson level as well.

Indeed, my experience is similar to that of Wiggins and McTighe (2005), who wrote:

> In working with thousands of teachers over the years, we have found that the unit provides a comfortable and practical entry point for this design process. Although it may seem natural to apply the UbD [Understanding by Design] approach to a system of daily lesson planning, we discourage it. Individual lessons are simply too short to allow for in-depth development of big ideas, exploration of essential questions, and authentic applications. (p. 8)

I have chosen, as do Lenz (Lenz et al., 1998) and Wiggins and McTighe (2005), to describe creating questions rather than objectives, outcomes, or learning targets. Others may prefer a different approach. Ann Reeves, for example, describes how to write instructional objectives, which she defines as "statements of what students will know and be able to do at the end of the lesson or unit of instruction. They describe the learning outcomes for students that the lesson is designed to produce" (2011, p. 15). Robert Marzano, in *The Art and Science of Teaching* (2007), recommends teachers write learning goals, "even though . . . there appears to be some confusion as to its [the term learning goals] exact nature" (p. 17). A learning goal, Marzano writes, "is a statement of what students will know or be able to do" (p. 17).

Marzano recommends that learning goals be stated in one of two formats:

Students will be able to _____.

or

Students will understand _____.

Moss and Brookhart (2012) suggest that teachers plan by creating learning targets. They define learning targets and distinguish them from instructional objectives as follows:

> Learning targets differ from instructional objectives in both design and purpose. As the name implies, instructional objectives guide instruction, and we write them from the teacher's point of view. . . . They describe, in language that students understand, the lesson-sized chunks of information, skills, and reasoning processes that students will come to know deeply. (p. 3)

No doubt, much can be learned by developing questions, objectives, outcomes, and targets. For my purposes, however, I find it best to consider what questions students should be answering as they encounter and learn the knowledge, skills, and big ideas in a unit. My own experience creating guiding questions was influenced by Keith Lenz, who writes:

> An effective way to achieve learning goals is to translate the critical outcomes into a small set of "big idea" questions that

reflect what is critical in and about the content to be learned. You can shape these critical questions by asking yourself what is really critical for all students to know and understand in whatever course, unit, or lesson you are planning to teach. How can learning outcomes be cast as critical questions that capture the essence of what students need to learn? And just as importantly, what are the central or big ideas that tie all of the information together? (Lenz, Deshler, & Kissam, 2004, p. 62)

Creating Excellent Guiding Questions

Developing the questions, assessments, and learning maps for a unit is as creative an act as writing a song, painting a watercolor, or writing a short story, and up front, it presents opportunities and challenges as significant as those confronted by any artist. In her book about creativity, *The Creative Habit* (2005), choreographer Twyla Tharp describes how she feels just before she starts to develop a new ballet. On the day of the first rehearsal, she goes to her studio early so she can sit and experience the empty workspace before the dancers and other artists arrive. Tharp writes:

> To some people this empty room symbolizes something profound, mysterious, and terrifying: the task of starting with nothing and working your way toward creating something whole and beautiful and satisfying. It's no different for a writer rolling a fresh sheet of paper into his typewriter (or more likely firing up the blank screen on his computer), or a painter confronting a virginal canvas, a sculptor starting a raw chunk of stone, a composer at the piano with his fingers hovering just above the keys. Some people find this moment—the moment before creativity begins—so painful that they simply cannot deal with it. They get up and walk away from the computer, the canvas, the keyboard; they take a nap or go shopping or fix lunch or do chores around the house. They procrastinate. In its most extreme form, this terror totally paralyzes people.
>
> The blank space can be humbling. But I've faced it my whole professional life. It's my job. It's also my calling. Bottom line: Filling this empty space constitutes my identity. (pp. 5–6)

When they begin writing units, like other creative artists, teachers may feel the paralysis and even fear that can inhibit creation. This fear, which author and creativity expert Stephen Pressfield (2002) has named "The Resistance," can stop teachers before they start. Shayne Coyne summarizes Pressfield's ideas about this resistance as follows:

> Call it writer's block, artistic *agita*, or general malaise, that malignant internal entity that keeps us from our calling can be a killer. Painting, writing, starting a new business venture, doing charity work, or even just putting everything into the work we're already doing is waylaid again and again by that chattering critic inside our heads. (2012, p. ii)

Step one for teachers, then, is to set aside their fears and dive in and begin to identify the knowledge, skills, and big ideas their students will learn. Writing a unit, like writing anything, is more about editing than it is about creating a stellar first draft. Ultimately, the construction of formative assessments described in Chapter 3 and the development of learning maps described in Chapter 4 will refine any guiding questions. But to create a great unit, we have to start somewhere, and for many the starting point is the guiding questions. After all, not writing out a unit because we're afraid it won't be perfect doesn't make it perfect. It just hides our own misunderstandings. Better to write out a first draft of our guiding questions so at least we have a place to start. I've included the following suggestions (see Figure 2.1) to guide teachers as they go about the challenging and important creative work of writing guiding questions.

Address the Standards. Starting with standards, in most cases the Common Core State Standards, may seem like the last thing a creative person would want to do. And certainly, a slavish focus on the test, with little attention to the importance, relevance, or joy of learning, is a recipe for disaster. But ignoring the standards is equally ill advised. To do so risks failing to prepare students for the learning they will experience in future grades or wasting students' time by teaching them content or skills they have learned before or will encounter later. Like it or not, each class is not an island, and understanding the standards ensures that students learn in ways that best prepare them for the learning they will experience in other classes and that course content addresses foundational learning that everyone should master.

Larry Ainsworth (2004), Grant Wiggins and Jay McTighe (2005), and others have described strategies teachers can use to unpack standards. The principal strategy is deceptively simple: When teachers dig into standards, they will discover that most nouns describe

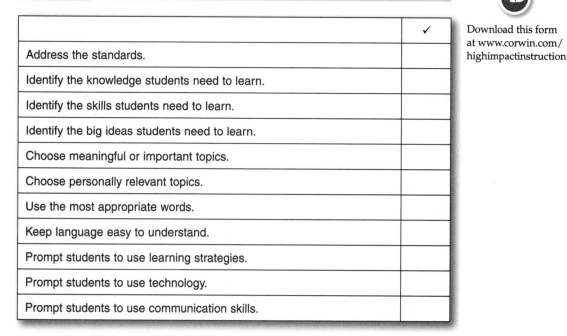

Figure 2.1 How to Create Great Guiding Questions

	✓
Address the standards.	
Identify the knowledge students need to learn.	
Identify the skills students need to learn.	
Identify the big ideas students need to learn.	
Choose meaningful or important topics.	
Choose personally relevant topics.	
Use the most appropriate words.	
Keep language easy to understand.	
Prompt students to use learning strategies.	
Prompt students to use technology.	
Prompt students to use communication skills.	

Download this form at www.corwin.com/highimpactinstruction

knowledge and most verbs describe skills. According to Ainsworth, teachers can benefit from going through each standard and indicator and circling the nouns and verbs to become more aware of what students need to know and do.

Teachers using a commercial textbook to teach algebra, for example, can look at each standard and indicator and then identify which pages in the text are necessary to learn the indicator. However, teachers need to be careful about an overdependence on a text. I suggest teachers work collaboratively or individually to ensure that their questions are guided by standards and not the pages and chapters of a text. What matters most at this point is that teachers have a deep understanding of the standards and indicators for their course.

Developing questions is most productive and effective when teachers work with colleagues who teach the same class to review each standard and indicator and list each indicator that is to be taught and what reference materials students will need to review to learn the material (usually articles, websites, or textbooks). In *Unmistakable Impact* (2011), I describe a process, involving Intensive Learning Teams, districts can put in place so that teachers can collaboratively unpack standards and create guiding questions, formative assessments, and learning maps.

Identify the Knowledge and Skills Students Need to Learn. For most lessons, there is certain content that students need to master. For example, students may need to learn vocabulary, facts, formulas, or definitions. Thus, students in a literature class might need to learn that a simile is a comparison that uses "like" or "as," or students in a science class may need to learn the parts of animal and plant cells. Knowledge refers to factual knowledge that students need to learn to gain access to anything being learned.

In addition to the knowledge students need to learn, there are certain skills they may need to learn during lessons. For example, students might need to know how to identify main ideas, or how to paraphrase, use *Evernote*, or use the scientific method. Skills can include other practices such as strategies, procedures, or performances. Standards (Common Core and otherwise) usually identify the knowledge and skills students need to learn.

Identify the Big Ideas Students Need to Learn. While much of learning involves knowledge and skills, some of the most important learning involves the bigger themes, concepts, content structures, and principles. As Lynn Erickson (2007) has written, these bigger ideas are an essential part of learning:

> In addition to specific content knowledge and skills, a district curriculum needs to articulate the concepts, generalizations, and principles for each grade level and discipline. These statements are the essential enduring ideas that students must *understand* at a deeper level. The factual knowledge is what students must know in order to describe, discuss, explain, or analyze the deeper concepts. One cannot understand the conceptual level without the supporting factual knowledge. But there must be a synergy between the two levels if we are going to systematically develop intelligence. (pp. 2–3)

Big ideas are the principles, themes, and concepts that recur throughout a course. When students recognize big ideas, they often have an "aha" moment that puts their learning into perspective. One type of big idea is a concept. One of my colleagues at the Center for Research on Learning, Jan Bulgren, who has studied concept acquisition for more than two decades, defines a concept as "a category or class into which events, ideas, or subjects can be grouped" (1994, p. 7). Thus, a word like "tragedy" is a concept because we can organize our understanding of different dramas by deciding whether or not a play demonstrates all the characteristics of a tragedy, or a word like "congruent" is a concept because it helps you describe different shapes that have the same size and same size angles. Concepts, like most big ideas, transcend individual lessons, so a concept like revolution might be applicable in many different lessons during a course.

Another big idea is a content structure. Content structures are the patterns that reveal how various parts of the content relate to other parts of the content. When teachers teach students to see content structures, students can better organize, remember, and apply content. In the same way that understanding text structures can help students comprehend texts, understanding content structures helps students better comprehend content.

David Scanlon, the author of *The Order Routine* (Scanlon, Deshler, & Schumaker, 2004), identifies four content structures as most important for comprehending content: descriptive, sequential, compare and contrast, and problem-solution. Students who see descriptive structures learn how to sort complicated information into patterns that are orderly and comprehensible. Recognizing sequential structures helps students sort such content as events and processes. Compare and contrast structures help students deepen their understanding by finding similarities and differences between concepts and ideas. Finally, problem-solution structures help students generate options and sort out possible solutions. (I include more information on content structures in Chapter 4.)

A separate but important category of big ideas includes attitudes, sensibilities, and ways of being that are much bigger than the specific content of a unit. For example, Carol Dweck's (2006) assertion that a "growth mindset" leads to more success than a fixed mindset and John Gottman's (2002) assertion that every relationship is shaped by each single interaction are both big ideas. Teachers need to think broadly and deeply about big ideas when they write guiding questions.

We can get a deeper understanding of the distinctions among knowledge, skills, and big ideas by analyzing how those dimensions of learning apply to a much anthologized poem, Ezra Pound's "The River-Merchant's Wife: A Letter."

The River-Merchant's Wife: A Letter

by Ezra Pound

While my hair was still cut straight across my forehead
I played about the front gate, pulling flowers.
You came by on bamboo stilts, playing horse,

You walked about my seat, playing with blue plums.

And we went on living in the village of Chokan:

Two small people, without dislike or suspicion.

At fourteen I married My Lord you.

I never laughed, being bashful.

Lowering my head, I looked at the wall.

Called to, a thousand times, I never looked back.

At fifteen I stopped scowling,

I desired my dust to be mingled with yours

Forever and forever and forever.

Why should I climb the look out?

At sixteen you departed,

You went into far Ku-to-yen, by the river of swirling eddies,

And you have been gone five months.

The monkeys make sorrowful noise overhead.

You dragged your feet when you went out.

By the gate now, the moss is grown, the different mosses,

Too deep to clear them away!

The leaves fall early this autumn, in wind.

The paired butterflies are already yellow with August

Over the grass in the West garden;

They hurt me. I grow older.

If you are coming down through the narrows of the river Kiang,

Please let me know beforehand,

And I will come out to meet you

As far as Cho-fu-Sa.

Source: Monroe & Henderson (1917).

Knowledge

To appreciate the poem, readers need certain knowledge. At the most basic level, they need to know how to read the words in the poem. Assuming readers have that basic knowledge, other knowledge would help them comprehend the poem. For example, they might benefit from knowing literary terms such as pathetic fallacy—which M. H. Abrams describes as "a common phenomenon in descriptive poetry, in which the ascription of human traits to inanimate nature is less formally managed than in the figure called personification" (1971, p. 268)—to better understand how Pound uses images to convey emotion. In addition, readers who know Pound's ideas about the imagist movement, which promoted poetry that exploits clear images to convey meaning, would be better prepared to appreciate what Pound is trying to accomplish with various images in the poem.

Skills

Particular skills can enable a deeper appreciation of the poem. First off, readers would need to be able to translate the language of verse into an understandable narrative and be able to see and describe the events that take place in the poem. Next, readers would need to identify where Pound used poetic devices such as imagery and pathetic fallacy, mentioned above, to communicate his poetic message. Good readers would recognize, for example, that the sorrowful monkeys and deeply grown moss are external pictures of the wife's internal state of mind.

Big Ideas

If the analysis of the poem ends with knowledge and skills, then much of the true joy of reading the poem will be missed. As Erickson (2007) has written, "artful teachers engage students emotionally, creatively, and intellectually to instill deep and passionate curiosity in learning" (p. 6). To do that, teachers need to guide students to explore big ideas. Teachers might lead students to explore the deeper meaning of the poem and ask them to explore what the poem says to them about relationships of all sorts, and, in particular, whether the fear of losing someone can keep us from embracing others with all of our hearts. Such a conversation could lead students to a deeper understanding of their own fears and hopes in all relationships. Alternatively, classroom discussion could explore how art employs indirect communication (in this case, images) to produce a work that can touch readers much more deeply than direct statements.

When teachers leave out big ideas, reading a poem can be reduced to one more mundane task to be completed as quickly as possible. Leaving out big ideas may leave out joy, passion, humanity, and depth of knowledge. However, meaningful learning isn't possible if readers can't read the words and if they can't apply their knowledge through skills that help them decode the narrative. Knowledge, skills, and big ideas are all important aspects of learning. All three must be considered when teachers develop their guiding questions.

Meaningful, Important, and Relevant. Guiding questions that address the knowledge, skills, and big ideas articulated in standards, but bore children to tears, won't create the kind of learning most parents want for their children. If we want students to be engaged by their learning, they need to understand why they are learning what they are learning. While it may be true that the personal relevance of every lesson cannot be clearly stated, it is also true that the relevance of learning can be stated much more often than it is. Students, just like adults, want to know why they have to learn something, and explaining why something is important and how it is relevant goes a long way toward motivating learners.

Considering why learning is meaningful, relevant, or important is also an important filter for deciding what to include and what to leave out of a unit. If a teacher cannot explain why something is taught, maybe it shouldn't be taught. Also, when teachers think about the connections students make between their lives and what they are learning, they deepen their understanding of the content they are teaching and make it easier for them to explain complicated ideas in ways that lead to understanding.

There is ample evidence, particularly in the field of research known as social development theory (Ryan & Deci, 2000), that learners are most motivated to learn when they can see personal connections between what they are learning and their own lives. Teachers should strive to design learning experiences and activities so that students can see how the learning is relevant to them.

Easy to Understand. Another way to increase student motivation is to write questions that are easy to comprehend. In some settings, guiding questions are written in abstract language or at reading levels that are way above those of the targeted students. In addition, some guiding questions are too vague. Questions that students don't understand don't help them learn. To create questions that their students understand, teachers must first be very clear of their own understanding and then write in language that honors the complexity and richness of learning while also communicating clearly and simply.

Most Appropriate Words. Words matter, and as teachers write guiding questions, they need to be careful to use the words that most precisely describe the knowledge, skills, and big ideas students need to learn. In part, finding the right words is about considering how students will hear them. Political media guru Frank Luntz (2007) puts it this way:

> It's not enough to be correct, or reasonable, or even brilliant. The key to successful communication is to take the imaginative leap of stuffing yourself right into your listener's shoes to know what they are thinking and feeling in the deepest recesses of their mind and heart. How that person perceives what you say is even more *real*, at least in a practical sense, than how you perceive yourself. (p. xiii)

Ann Reeves' (2011) suggestions for writing objectives also serve as excellent suggestions for writing excellent questions. Objectives, Reeves writes, should be (a) student centered, by focusing on what students must do and using the active voice; (b) thinking centered by describing what students will learn to do; and (c) professional rather than colloquial, by precisely describing learning outcomes, and in particular by choosing the most correct verbs. One way to increase precision is to think carefully about the level of thinking you propose for students.

Identify Learning Strategies. Teaching students how to learn is likely at least as important as teaching students what to learn. Many teachers explicitly teach learning strategies to help students acquire, remember, or express knowledge, skills, and understandings. For more than three decades, researchers at the University of Kansas Center for Research on Learning have been developing and validating strategies that improve student learning in socially significant ways. When teachers teach these strategies, students might learn *The Paraphrasing Strategy* (Schumaker, Denton, & Deshler, 1984) to improve their reading comprehension, *The FIRST Letter Mnemonic Strategy* (Nagel, Schumaker, & Deshler, 1986) to improve their ability to remember lists of facts, or the *Sentence Writing Strategy* (Schumaker & Sheldon, 1985) to improve the clarity of their writing.

If students are going to internalize their use of strategies, they benefit from many cues reminding them when and how to use them. The guiding questions are a great place to embed those cues.

Identify Technology. Another important goal of most classrooms is to teach students how to use various technological tools. For example, students writing essays might learn to use *Evernote* to organize information gathered during research or *Inspiration* to create a mind map during the prewriting phase of writing. Students also might be prompted to create a Facebook page to organize their collaborative work with a team or use PowerPoint to create a slide deck for a presentation.

Identify Communication Skills. Another important skill is learning how to interact effectively with peers. Many students are taught how to listen, find common ground, use objective standards to resolve conflicts, build relationships, and share positive and corrective feedback with their peers. Guiding questions can remind students of when and how to use those skills during learning.

Putting Guiding Questions Together With Formative Assessments and Learning Maps

The suggestions listed here for developing guiding questions are only a start for high-impact planning. Indeed, if teachers only develop questions, without thinking about formative assessments or learning maps, their plans may not go deep enough into the knowledge, skills, and big ideas that students need to learn.

High-impact planning involves all three components, with each component acting as a check or balance for the other two. Formative assessment ensures that questions have fully addressed the standards, and learning maps ensure that learning is coherent and complete. In addition, each of the high-impact planning components involves strategies that may be used to surface better questions. For example, in Chapter 4 I introduce a five-step process that could be employed, in part, to develop excellent guiding questions.

What matters is that the questions, assessments, and learning maps in combination provide a complete picture of the knowledge, skills, and big ideas that make up an effective unit. When teachers think deeply about what students need to learn, why that learning is important, and what students can do to become learners, they bring focus and clarity to their teaching. That focus and clarity makes it easier for teachers to do their most important work—leave a legacy with their students.

Turning Ideas Into Action

Students

1. Consider involving students in the writing of critical questions at the start of a unit by asking them what they find interesting about a topic. While most of the content to be covered will be determined by standards, students can provide their perspective on how learning could be more interesting or what strategies they could use to learn the material.

2. Test out questions with students to make sure the questions are clear and easy to understand.

Teachers

1. Consider posting the questions in the classroom so that they are always visible to students.

2. Refer to the guiding questions frequently so that students have many opportunities to construct their answers.

3. Whenever possible, collaborate with colleagues to refine and deepen your guiding questions.

Instructional Coaches

1. Use the checklist for guiding questions included above to work through the development of guiding questions with teachers.

2. Offer to review the guiding questions from the students' perspective and comment on the questions as you think students would.

3. Offer to share the guiding questions with students to see if they think they are clear and interesting.

Principals

1. Consider advocating with central office leaders for districtwide meetings of teachers who teach the same course, during which they can create guiding questions for the units they teach.

2. Advocate for time for teachers to work with their peers to develop guiding questions.

What It Looks Like

1. When administrators observe teachers' classrooms, they should consider watching for evidence related to the following two questions:

   Is there evidence the teacher has a plan for the unit?

   Does the teacher explain how the lesson fits into the larger plan?

(Continued)

(Continued)

2. Grant Wiggins and Jay McTighe (2005) have suggested the following questions to ask students to see how well planning is affecting their learning. Principals, coaches, or teachers can ask students these questions in the middle of learning. Teachers might ask students to complete an exit ticket with these questions to see how students perceive their learning:

What are you doing?

Why are you doing it?

Why are you being asked to do it?

What will it help you do?

How does it fit with what you have previously done?

How will you show what you have learned? (p. 17)

To Sum Up

• When teachers create guiding questions, they frequently increase student learning because they are better prepared, place correct emphasis on the most important content, focus on learning more than on activities, provide a target for students, keep themselves and their students on task, and are better able to differentiate learning.

• Planning instruction involves a paradox. On the one hand, teachers need to make deliberate plans that lay out exactly what will be learned. On the other hand, teachers need to be ready to adjust their plan when opportunity or slow progress suggests they need to change.

• Effective guiding questions (a) address the standards; (b) identify the knowledge, skills, and big ideas students need to learn; (c) are meaningful and important; (d) are personally relevant; (e) use the most appropriate words; (f) are easy to understand; (g) identify learning strategies; (h) identify technology; and (i) identify communication skills.

Going Deeper

This content planning section would not have been possible without the work of my colleague Keith Lenz, who spent many years developing and researching Content Enhancement Routines at the University of Kansas Center for Research on Learning. Lenz's work is pioneering, and anyone who wants to gain a deeper understanding of how to plan to make content more accessible to more students would gain a great deal by reading Lenz's *Course Organizer Routine* (Lenz, Schumaker, Deshler, & Bulgren, 2004), *Unit Organizer Routine* (Lenz, Bulgren, Schumaker, Deshler, & Boudah, 1994), and *Lesson Organizer Routine* (Lenz, Marrs, Schumaker, & Deshler, 1993), all part of the Content Enhancement Routine series published by Edge Enterprises in Lawrence, Kansas (www.edgeenterprisesinc.com).

Those interested in deeper planning and inclusive instruction would also benefit greatly from reviewing the work of my colleagues Jan Bulgren, Jean Schumaker, Don Deshler, Ed Ellis, and others, who have created a collection of teaching routines all designed to increase accessibility and rigor of instruction. You can learn more about Content Enhancement at http://www.kucrl.org/research/topic/category/content-enhancement.

Keith Lenz is also principal author of *Teaching Content to All: Evidence-Based Inclusive Practices in Middle and Secondary Schools* (Lenz, Deshler, & Kissam, 2003), a comprehensive and detailed overview of how to plan and teach in a way that includes all students. This is another valuable resource for those interested in creating rigorous, accessible instruction.

Likely more than any other work, Grant Wiggins and Jay McTighe's *Understanding by Design* (2005) has taught educators how to conduct backward design, content planning that starts by asking what students need to learn. Wiggins and McTighe provide a methodology teachers can use to think deeply about the instructional goals, understandings, performance tasks, and activities of their units.

Lynn Erickson's *Concept-Based Curriculum and Instruction for the Thinking Classroom* (2007) gives teachers a vocabulary they can use to talk about what is most important in a lesson. Erickson argues persuasively that good instruction must include knowledge, skills, and understandings (which I refer to as big ideas), and her work has taught me about the importance of the conceptual level of learning.

Ann Reeves' *Where Great Teaching Begins: Planning for Student Thinking and Learning* (2011) contains excellent suggestions on how to create learning objectives, while also addressing such issues as the language and validity of objectives. This book is an excellent resource for anyone who prefers writing objectives rather than guiding questions; however, her suggestions would be helpful to anyone writing learning targets, learning goals, guiding questions, or any other form of curriculum planning.

Like Reeves' book, Moss and Brookhart's *Learning Targets: Helping Students Aim for Understanding in Today's Lesson* (2012) provides excellent suggestions on how to write targets for lessons, and the authors' suggestions apply to most other forms of curriculum development.

Note

1. For information on preliminary research I've conducted on the impact of ILTs on the content knowledge of teachers, see *Unmistakable Impact: A Partnership Approach for Dramatically Improving Instruction* (Knight, 2011).

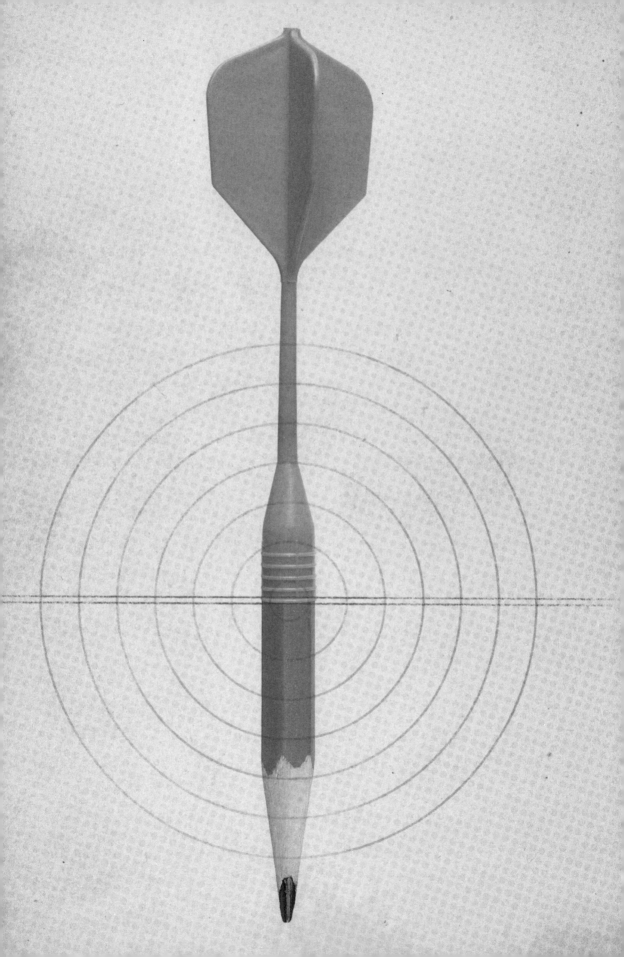

Chapter 3:
Formative
Assessment

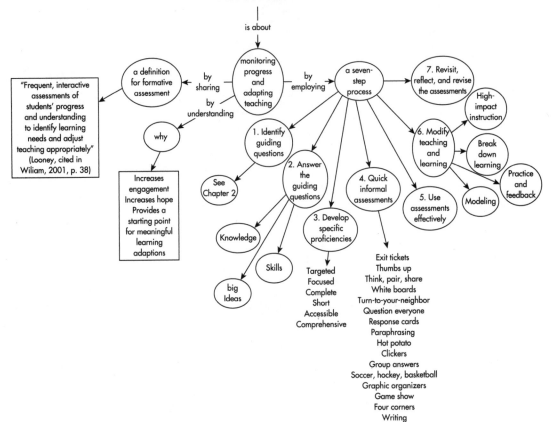

is about

monitoring progress and adapting teaching

by sharing

by understanding

a definition for formative assessment

"Frequent, interactive assessments of students' progress and understanding to identify learning needs and adjust teaching appropriately" (Looney, cited in Wiliam, 2001, p. 38)

why

Increases engagement
Increases hope
Provides a starting point for meaningful learning adaptions

by employing

a seven-step process

7. Revisit, reflect, and revise the assessments

High-impact instruction

6. Modify teaching and learning

Break down learning

Practice and feedback

Modeling

1. Identify guiding questions

2. Answer the guiding questions

4. Quick informal assessments

5. Use assessments effectively

See Chapter 2

Knowledge

3. Develop specific proficiencies

Skills

big Ideas

Targeted
Focused
Complete
Short
Accessible
Comprehensive

Exit tickets
Thumbs up
Think, pair, share
White boards
Turn-to-your-neighbor
Question everyone
Response cards
Paraphrasing
Hot potato
Clickers
Group answers
Soccer, hockey, basketball
Graphic organizers
Game show
Four corners
Writing
...

3

FORMATIVE ASSESSMENT

You can't tell me that kids don't want to learn. Sometimes they don't want to learn the things that adults say they should, . . . but once they begin to experience success, that target becomes a whole lot more attractive. . . . We've got to find a way to turn them on to the possibilities.

—Richard Stiggins (personal communication)

During our research discussions with coaches from the Beaverton Coaching Study, instructional coach Michelle Harris loved to talk about Sarah Langton, a collaborating teacher who taught sixth-grade science and math. Michelle described the positive climate in Sarah's classroom and how Sarah carried herself in a calm, peaceful way that was reflected in her students' behavior. Sarah, Michelle said, is the kind of teacher that orchestrates every move in the classroom. Before giving students a cooperative learning activity, for example, Sarah taught students how to have a nonjudgmental face, modeled it, and then had the students practice it so that they would be better listeners and collaborators during the activity. Sarah's "questioning skills," Michelle said, "are better than those of any teacher I have ever seen. I've learned a ton," Michelle said, "from working with Sarah."

"Sarah," Michelle explained, "really, really cares about students . . . especially those kids who struggle. She genuinely wants to help them." Perhaps because of how much she cares, Sarah was "hungry for [new] ways to teach," and she embraced the opportunity to work with an instructional coach to try and be even better. For someone who is already such a phenomenal teacher, coaching provided a way for her to see how much more she could be doing.

Michelle video recorded Sarah's class and asked her to watch the video to identify what she wanted to work on through coaching. Sarah was teaching a new science curriculum, and it was causing her a lot of "angst" because she hadn't worked out how to teach every lesson and didn't know how students might respond to lessons. The makeup of the class also presented challenges, Michelle said. "She has 26 kids in the class and she has a wide range. . . . She has ELL; she has kids on IEPs; and she has kids who are reading at the twelfth-grade level."

Sarah and Michelle watched the video separately, and then they met to identify a goal for instructional coaching. "It was pretty clear," Michelle said, "that what she wanted to work on was formative assessment—she needed to know where the kids were."

Sarah's new science curriculum provided big learning targets, but the targets were not written in student-friendly language, and they were so broad that they gave little guidance as to what students needed to learn in each lesson or unit. Sarah and Michelle decided to deconstruct each learning goal, identify exactly what students needed to learn, and create simple checks for understanding to see if students had learned the knowledge, skills, and big ideas identified for that day. They decided to use exit tickets, described below, as their informal assessments. Sarah planned to organize student responses into three categories: (a) highly proficient, (b) proficient, and (c) working toward proficient.

The first day she gathered the informal assessments, Sarah realized that five children had not learned the content. "Sarah," Michelle said "was stuck right there." She asked, "How do I do this? What am I going to do with these five kids?"

During their coaching conversation, Sarah and Michelle decided that Sarah could show the students what understanding looked like by discussing some of the highly proficient answers. Sarah displayed some answers on her document camera (after covering the students' names) and then asked the students to identify the characteristics of a highly proficient answer. "What do you see about this answer? Why would this be highly proficient?"

The conversations about quality work were beneficial for all students, Michelle said. "The kids who were proficient, the next time, a lot of them became highly proficient . . . and 100% of students became proficient. There was so much happening in those conversations."

Sarah used formative assessment to show her students that they could learn the content, and she used what she had learned from their responses to plan instruction that would make it easier for her students to succeed. Assessment for learning helped Sarah understand that there were better ways to ensure her students mastered what was being taught, and it led her, as Michelle said, to "think really deeply about the content."

"When teachers don't know how well their students are learning," Michelle says, "they are just teaching. They don't know what the students are learning. They are just covering content." By using assessment for learning as part of her daily teaching routine, Sarah obtains a clear understanding of how well her students are learning, and her students understand how much they are learning. Now before every lesson "she sits down and figures out, what exactly am I targeting on this lesson, and how exactly am I going to know that the students know it." "Sarah," Michelle says, "gives the kids a chance to let her know what they know every single day."

Defining Assessment for Learning

The simple ideas that Sarah was implementing are the basic components of formative assessment: (a) knowing how well her students were learning, (b) ensuring her students knew how well they were learning, and (c) using the data she gathered from the assessments to modify her teaching to ensure students mastered their learning. Several definitions have been offered for formative assessment (see Wiliam, 2011, p. 37, for a summary of the definitions). For our purposes, we will adopt the definition proposed by the Organisation for Economic Co-operation and Development (OECD) that formative assessment is "frequent, interactive assessments of students' progress and understanding to identify learning needs and adjust teaching appropriately" (Looney, 2005, cited in Wiliam, 2001, p. 38).

Formative assessment, then, is a collection of strategies teachers employ to get clarity on what they will be teaching and to assess how well students have learned what they are teaching. The understanding teachers gain from formative assessment then serves as the foundation for teachers to make adjustments to the way they teach so students will learn what is being taught. Formative assessment is also a way for teachers and students to monitor students' progress toward mastery.

Why Use Formative Assessment?

We can learn a lot about formative assessment just by watching children play a video game. As most parents can tell you, children would play games far beyond their bedtime given the chance. And while they play, children (and many adults) are usually 100% engaged in what they are doing—and more than anything else, what they are doing is learning.

I gained some insight into why people are so engaged by video games when Mihaly Csikszentmihalyi, the author of *Flow: The Psychology of Optimal Experience* (1990), came to the Center for Research on Learning at the University of Kansas to meet with us to discuss his research on happiness.

During his visit, Dr. Csikszentmihalyi explained that an important key to happiness is engagement. When we are fully engaged in an activity, we are happier and more likely to be at our best—to have optimal experience. Furthermore, he explained, engaging activities, which he refers to as "flow experiences," usually have the same structural elements. Among other things, "flow experiences" provide the right kind of challenge for our level of skill. Engaging experiences are not so difficult that they frustrate us or so easy that they bore us. The sweet spot for engagement, and learning, is just a little bit more challenging than our skill level.

"Flow experiences," Csikszentmihalyi explained, are also goal-directed activities during which people receive extensive feedback on how close they are to their goal. If we enjoy playing golf or a video game, for example, we likely enjoy it because we experience the right kind of challenge for our skill level and because the game provides immediate feedback on how well we are progressing toward a goal.

A major reason why people love video games, then, according to Csikszentmihalyi's research, is that they have a clear goal and receive clear feedback on progress toward their goal. Every second of the game, a gamer knows exactly what he is hoping to do, and his score tells him exactly how close he is to his goal. An equally important reason why gamers love their games is the way games are structured. Most video games are organized into several levels, with level one being easiest, and each new level progressively more challenging. This multilevel structure ensures that people are always playing at the most engaging level of challenge—just a bit more challenging than their current skill level.

How engaging would a video game be if it didn't provide a clear goal, if there was no score, and if it was always at the same level so that when players mastered a level, they had nowhere to go for greater challenge? Without these characteristics, pretty quickly the game would be set aside either because it wasn't motivating or because it was boring. And yet, for many students, school is just like this boring game, with no clear goals, too little feedback on progress, and always the same level of challenge.

One major reason for using formative assessment is that it provides a way for teachers to dramatically increase engagement. That is, formative assessment is a way by which teachers can clarify learning goals, provide students with frequent, clear feedback on their progress toward the goal, and adjust learning so it is more frequently at the optimal level of challenge for students. Formative assessment may not turn a classroom into a video game experience, but it does allow teachers to employ the same strategies that game designers employ to maintain gamer engagement.

What Csikszentmihalyi says about happiness echoes what Richard Stiggins has said about the role of assessment in student motivation. Dr. Stiggins is one of the nation's leading experts on formative assessment and the author of numerous books and articles on the topic, including the classic text *An Introduction to Student-Involved Assessment for Learning, 6th Edition* (2011). In an interview I conducted in Portland, Oregon, at the Assessment Training Institute, Stiggins echoed Csikszentmihalyi: "Unless we can keep students believing that the goal is within reach, they'll stop trying . . . [and] when the feedback suggests to me that I'm not making it, leading me to an inference that I'm incapable of making it, then I give up in hopelessness and I stop trying. . . . I've got to get them [students] to somehow believe that effort is of value, that there is some relationship between effort and their level of success. If I can't get them to believe that, then I can't help them."

Stiggins' comments point to perhaps an even more important reason for using formative assessment: It increases students' belief that they can succeed. When students receive daily feedback on their progress, when they see clear evidence that they are progressing, they are more much confident that they can tackle the learning tasks they experience in school. Progress is encouraging, and it gives people hope.

Harvard researchers Teresa Amabile and Steven Kramer have found that progress at work is the single most important factor contributing to attitude, which they refer to as "inner work life," and long-term performance. After conducting an extensive qualitative study of "238 people in 26 project teams in 7 companies and 3 industries" (Amabile & Kramer, 2011, p. 5), they concluded the following:

Real progress triggers positive emotions like satisfaction, gladness, even joy. It leads to a sense of accomplishment and self-worth as well as positive views of the work and, sometimes, the organization. Such thoughts and perceptions (along with those positive emotions) feed the motivation, the deep engagement, that is crucial for ongoing blockbuster performance. (p. 68)

Amabile and Kramer referred to the experience of ongoing success, even in small wins, as "the progress principle," and their findings apply to children in school. When students experience small wins on a daily basis and see clear evidence of their progress, they are much more motivated to take on greater learning challenges. Stiggins makes precisely the same point in *Student-Involved Assessment for Learning* (2001):

> If these students are to come to believe in themselves, then they must first experience some believable (credible) form of academic success as reflected in real and rigorous classroom assessment. A small success can rekindle a small spark of confidence, which can in turn encourage more trying. If that new trying brings more success, their academic self-concept will begin to shift in a positive direction. Our goal then is to perpetuate that cycle. . . . This begins to build their self-confidence, which ultimately pays off in their ability to risk failure to find immense success. (p. 45)

The potential rewards of formative assessment are great. First, by tapping into the technology of engagement, goals and feedback, challenge, and skills, formative assessment can dramatically increase student engagement. Second, by exploiting the progress principle, the motivation that occurs when people experience many small successes, formative assessment can motivate students to achieve. Finally, by helping teachers see their students' progress, formative assessment can be profoundly motivating for teachers.

When Sarah Langton saw her students get results, she was very happy to see students succeed who had experienced very few successes in the past. But she was also motivated personally. Her coach, Michelle Harris, said that although Sarah had always been an accomplished teacher, formative assessment pushed her forward. "Being confident and knowing that the kids are actually learning something are not the same thing. Going through this, Sarah came out on the other side so much more confident of her abilities because she knew her students got it. Sarah wants to accelerate everybody. She's a learner, and so are her students."

To implement assessment for learning, Michelle guided Sarah through the high-impact approach. It involves seven steps, each described in the sections below.

Assessment for Learning

1. Identify Guiding Questions

2. Answer the Questions: What Do Students Need to Know, Understand, and Be Able to Do?

3. Identify Specific Proficiencies

4. Identify Assessments

5. Use Assessments Effectively

6. Modify Teaching and Learning

7. Revisit, Reflect, Revise

1. IDENTIFY GUIDING QUESTIONS

The most common point of departure for formative assessment within high-impact planning, identifying guiding questions, was described in Chapter 2. In my experience, many teachers need to clarify what they are going to teach before they decide what to assess. To accomplish this, teachers should develop guiding questions for a unit, employing the strategies described in Chapter 2.

Starting with the questions before the assessments goes against the advice of many who would advocate for identifying assessments first. The thinking here is that we shouldn't articulate questions until we know what we want to assess, and I think this is good advice if it works for you. I suggest teachers start at the place that seems most natural, but do all three components of high-impact planning whenever possible. Each component (guiding questions, formative assessment, learning maps) refines the other two components and should ensure that the unit plans adequately address the knowledge, skills, and big ideas students need to learn.

2. ANSWER THE QUESTIONS: WHAT DO STUDENTS NEED TO KNOW, UNDERSTAND, AND BE ABLE TO DO?

Once the guiding questions have been identified, teachers need to uncover the answers to those questions. This can be done in several ways. Many educators create comprehensive answers to their guiding questions by writing answers that address the levels of thinking described in Bloom's taxonomy (1956)—(a) Knowledge, (b) Comprehension, (c) Application, (d) Analysis, (e) Synthesis, and (f) Evaluation—or Anderson and colleagues' revision (2001) of Bloom's taxonomy—(a) Remember, (b) Understand, (c) Apply, (d) Analyze, (e) Evaluate, and (f) Create. Still others use Marzano et al.'s taxonomy (2001)—(a) Knowing, (b) Organizing, (c) Applying, (d) Integrating, (e) Analyzing, and (f) Generating—or yet other taxonomies.

The many ways of thinking about thinking can be overwhelming, even before a teacher writes a single word. One useful simplification is provided by Lenz:

> We have found in talking to teachers over the years that, in practice, they find the six levels of Bloom's taxonomy cumbersome, and that the levels overlap a great deal. We have reconfigured the taxonomy of cognitive objectives to three levels: acquisition, manipulation, and generalization. Acquisitions correspond to

Bloom's levels of knowledge and comprehension; manipulation corresponds to application, analysis, and synthesis; and generalization corresponds to evaluation. (2004, p. 57)

Instructional coaches, teachers, and other educators working with the Kansas Coaching Project have adopted an alternative three levels, Knowledge, Skills, and Big Ideas, first introduced in Chapter 2. As Lynn Erickson has written in *Concept-Based Curriculum and Instruction for the Thinking Classroom* (2007), instruction must address all three levels of thinking. Learning has to involve the knowledge students need to learn, the skills they need to do any learning task, and the big ideas they need to grasp the themes, concepts, patterns, and "aha" aspects of learning.

Whether an educator uses the ideas of Bloom, Marzano, Anderson, or Lenz is a matter for each person or team to decide. Regardless, educators must use some framework for levels of thinking to create a comprehensive and complete answer for each guiding question. If they have not clearly articulated the answers to their questions, their teaching may lack focus, and time may be wasted on learning that isn't that important. In addition, by answering the questions, teachers can ensure that their questions are indeed answerable. In guiding teachers through the practice of writing answers to their questions, frequently I have seen that during this process they discover that their questions, because they lack clarity or do not point to the most important learning, simply cannot be answered.

To avoid this trap, I suggest teachers write down in outline form every answer to each question. These notes will provide a focus for the units and lessons to be taught. They also provide a starting point for step three, identifying specific proficiencies. An example of how a teacher might answer a guiding question is presented in Figure 3.1.

Figure 3.1   Sample Answer to a Guiding Question

Guiding Question: How do I identify subjects and verbs in a sentence?

Answer:

Know: Students need to know the definitions for subjects and verbs.

Do: Students need to be able to find verbs and subjects.

Understand: Students need to understand that (a) clear writing will enable them to get many things they will want in life and (b) identifying subjects and verbs is important for editing, discussing correct writing, and ensuring one's writing is clear and correct.

Figure 3.2	Specific Proficiency Checklist

The specific proficiency is . . .	✓
Targeted: . . . a partial answer to a guiding question.	
Focused: . . . contains one idea.	
Complete: . . . written as a complete sentence.	
Short: . . . as concise as possible.	
Accessible: . . . easily understood by students.	
Comprehensive: . . . in combination with all other specific proficiencies, represents a complete answer to the question.	

Download this form at www.corwin.com/ highimpactinstruction

3. IDENTIFY SPECIFIC PROFICIENCIES

After identifying answers to all guiding questions, the next step is to determine all the components of the answers that you think need to be assessed. I refer to these components as "specific proficiencies." Specific proficiencies are sentences that state, in exact terms, the knowledge, skills, and big ideas students need to learn. A specific proficiency describes a discrete item that has to be assessed.[1]

To create specific proficiencies, after broadly describing the knowledge, skills, and ideas students need to learn, teachers should write short, concise, and precise sentences that describe each component of the answer to the guiding question (see Figure 3.2). The complete list of specific proficiencies forms a complete answer to the guiding question.

We can get a deeper understanding of specific proficiencies by revisiting the answers that were created for the question: How do I identify subjects and verbs in a sentence?

Each answer contains within it specific proficiencies. When teachers identify the specific proficiencies, they know exactly what to teach and what to assess.

The first answer about knowledge indicates that students need to know the definitions for nouns and verbs. It might contain the following specific proficiencies.

1. A subject is a noun that says what the sentence is all about.

2. A noun is a word that describes a person, place, thing, idea, or quality.

3. A verb describes a mental or physical action or a state of being.

4. State-of-being verbs are often called linking verbs. They describe any form of the verb *to be*, including, *am, is, are, was, were, been, being*, and *become*.

5. State-of-being verbs do not express action.

The second answer about skills indicates that students need to master the skills involved in finding subjects and verbs. These skills might be written in the following specific proficiencies:
To find subjects and verbs, students need to . . .

1. Find the verb in the sentence and

2. Ask who or what plus the verb to find the subject.

The third answer about big ideas indicates that (a) clear writing will enable students to get many things they will want in life and (b) identifying subjects and verbs is essential for editing, discussing correct writing, and ensuring your writing is clear and correct. This might be articulated in the following propositions:

1. When we can say what we want, we have a better chance of getting what we want.

2. Subjects and verbs are important concepts for understanding sentence structure, complete sentences, punctuation, and subject-verb agreement.

3. Active voice puts the subjects ahead of the verbs in a sentence so it is clear who is doing what.

4. Passive voice puts the verbs ahead of subjects in a sentence, often making it unclear who does what.

The act of creating specific proficiencies deepens teachers' understanding of what must be taught and often prompts teachers to rewrite their guiding questions and learning maps. Once created, the propositions provide clarity for teachers' instructional plans and clear goals for student learning. In addition, each specific proficiency provides the focus for assessment, the next step of this process.

4. IDENTIFY ASSESSMENTS

The following joke is often told in various forms by people who believe in formative assessment: A mother comes home and finds her son and husband in the front yard. Her son is sitting on the ground beside his shiny new bicycle. Mom asks, "What have you two been up to today?" The father looks up, grins, and says, "I taught Isaiah how to ride his bike." "Well, Isaiah," the mother asks, "why aren't you riding?" "Well, I taught him," Dad replies, "but he didn't learn it."

When teachers are unclear on the specific proficiencies involved and don't know how well their students are learning, they run the risk of being a little like the father in the story, saying, "I taught it, but they just didn't get it." A better alternative is to clearly identify knowledge, skills, and big ideas in specific proficiencies, assess whether or not students have learned the proficiencies, and make adjustments, when necessary, to ensure mastery.

To accomplish this, we suggest teachers identify assessments for every identified specific proficiency. The form in Figure 3.3 is one way of organizing thinking around assessment.

To use the form, teachers write the guiding question in section 1. In section 2, they list all of the specific proficiencies. Finally, in section 3, they list the assessments they will use to assess whether or not students have learned each specific proficiency. There are numerous ways that what students are learning can be assessed. Some of the more popular ways of checking for understanding include the following.

Exit Tickets. Exit tickets are short tasks students can do before they leave class. Usually students complete the tasks by writing on small pieces of paper or index cards, and students hand their paper to their teacher as they exit class, in the same way they might hand over a ticket at a movie theater as they enter. The task could be a writing assignment, a short quiz, or a question students are to answer. Some teachers use exit tickets at the end of every class as a closing routine. Teachers can give students tasks that are untimed, such as "write as much as you know about this topic up until you hear the bell," to ensure that students stay engaged until the end of class.

Quick Informal Assessments

Exit tickets	Hot potato
White boards	Soccer, hockey, basketball
Response cards	
Clickers	Graphic organizers
Thumbs up, thumbs down, thumbs wiggly	Writing
	Game show
Turn-to-your-neighbor	Jigsaw or gallery walk
Paraphrasing	Four corners
Group answers	Bell work
Think, pair, share	Quizzes or tests
Question everyone	

Figure 3.3 Proficiency Assessment Form

1. Guiding Question	
2. Specific Proficiency	3. Assessment

White Boards. When prompting students to use white boards, teachers give students questions or tasks and ask them to write their answer on a white board. Then, they ask all students to hold up the white board at the same time. If students give conflicting answers, teachers can open a discussion by saying something like, "It looks like we've got a disagreement here. Let's discuss this to come to an agreement." Then they can lead a clarifying discussion.

Response Cards. Teachers use response cards in a way that is similar to how they might use white boards. Response cards can include index cards with a *yes* on one side and a *no* on the other side, or drawings of traffic lights with red meaning no or I don't understand, yellow meaning not sure, and green meaning yes or I understand. You can also hand out red, yellow, and green index cards to show the same meaning or create cards with other messages. Students use response cards to communicate their level of understanding by holding them up in response to teacher questions during a lesson.

Clickers. Various companies sell electronic devices that enable students to respond to questions and send their responses directly to a teacher's computer or tablet. Using such tools, teachers can see immediately which students answered correctly and incorrectly, and tallies of answers can be displayed via a projector or Smart Board.

Thumbs Up, Thumbs Down, Thumbs Wiggly. When teachers don't have Smart Boards or clickers, they can do things the old-fashioned way, asking student to use their thumbs. Teachers should explain to students that thumbs up means "I understand/agree," thumbs down means "I don't understand/agree," and holding thumbs horizontally and wiggling your hand means "I'm not sure if I understand or agree."

Turn-to-Your-Neighbor. After students complete a learning task, teachers can ask them to compare their answer or idea with their neighbor's (another student) to see if they have the same answer. If yes, students give the teacher a "thumbs up." If no, students give the teacher a "thumbs down." This simple process helps teachers get a clear picture of how well students are learning, or not learning.

Paraphrasing. Teachers can assess student understanding by asking students to retell in their own words what they have learned, using words other than those they heard or read when they learned whatever is being learned.

Group Answers. Teachers use this strategy to check student understanding by putting students in groups, keeping in mind the ideas about cooperative learning discussed in Chapter 8. Teachers should give students a task to complete, a question to answer, a term to memorize, or some other assignment. They should explain that in

Carrie Hochgrebe explains how she uses clickers for formative assessment.

Video 3.1
www.corwin.com/
highimpactinstruction

groups everyone is responsible for everyone's learning and that they'll check with one group member, to be determined, to check that everyone has learned what needs to be learned. Thus, all students need to ensure that everyone knows whatever is being learned.

Think, Pair, Share. Teachers give students a task to do on their own and then have them share their work with one other person to identify similarities and differences. Sometimes teachers prompt students to consider revising their answers based on what they've learned from their partner. After this, teachers ask the partners to share their answers with the class. You can find more information on this learning structure in Chapter 8.

Question Everyone. Tell students to be prepared to answer questions (either open or closed questions). Then call on students randomly or make a point of targeting groups of students (such as HALO questioning, High, Average, Low, Other). Some teachers say, "I'll be picking the student who looks least interested." Others draw names from a brown bag or write student names on Popsicle sticks and pull names out randomly. Teachers can apply the questioning practices described in Chapter 8 when they use this method of checking for understanding.

Hot Potato. Ask a student a question to test his or her understanding of content. If the student gets the answer right, he gets to ask another question that tests another student's understanding. The student asking the question must know the answer so he or she can confirm whether or not the new student gets the correct answer. Sometimes teachers let students pick who will answer the question; at other times, teachers pick who will answer the question.

Soccer, Hockey, Basketball. Teachers organize the class into two teams. For example, let students choose their team based on their allegiance to a particular team or assign students to the green and blue teams. Before questioning begins, the teacher draws a playing field on the white board and explains that soccer, hockey, or basketball is about to begin. Then the teacher draws a ball or puck on the white board at the center of the newly drawn field or rink.

The rules of the game are simple. If a team gets a correct answer, the teacher moves the ball or puck closer to the other team's goal by erasing the drawing and redrawing the puck closer to the goal. If a member of a team gets an answer wrong, the ball or puck moves toward their own goal. If the ball or puck gets in their zone, and they get a wrong answer, or the other team gets a right answer, a goal or basket is scored. You can play this game using the hot potato routine described above as well.

Graphic Organizers. In Chapter 4, I describe a variety of graphic organizers students can draw to organize and demonstrate the knowledge, skills, and big ideas they have learned. Asking students to create graphic organizers, such as the descriptive, sequential, problem-solution, and compare and contrast organizers described by David Scanlon (2004), is a good check of student understanding because in most cases students won't be able to create correct graphic organizers unless they understand the content.

Writing. Students' understanding can be assessed using numerous writing assessments. For example, students can be prompted to write a response to a passage they've read, answer a question with a few sentences, write a letter to an author, write a letter of complaint, write a short story to illustrate a concept that has been learned, and so forth. In Maryland, students statewide are prompted to write Brief Constructed Responses (BCRs) to demonstrate their knowledge and thinking.

Game Show. With a little effort, teachers can develop their own version of popular game shows such as *Jeopardy, Who Wants to Be a Millionaire, Wheel of Fortune*, or *Family Feud*. Teachers should divide the class into teams and give each team review time prior to the game.

Jigsaw or Gallery Walk. As described in Chapter 8, during this form of cooperative learning students are organized into groups. Students create a poster on chart paper that they can display in the room. The poster should demonstrate the students' knowledge of content covered; for example, a poster might consist of a few bullet points, a picture, a metaphor, or a graphic organizer. After this part of the activity, put students into other groups so that each new group includes a member from the group that created a poster. Have the groups rotate around the room, stopping at each poster. Whoever created the poster explains it to the rest of their new group.

Four Corners. This is a quick way to get students moving around a room to demonstrate what they do or do not know about a topic. For this activity, teachers give students a question and then ask them to move to a corner of the room based on their answer. For example, a teacher might pose a multiple-choice question and designate each different corner as a, b, c, or d.

Bell Work. When prompting students to do bell work, teachers create a short task for students to do as they walk into class. The task could be a writing assignment, a short quiz, a question that students can respond to in their journals, or some other task. Teachers need to ensure that students know that they are to start the task when the bell goes at the start of class. After providing sufficient time for students to complete the task, gather student work and discuss it with the class. Some teachers use bell work as a starting routine for every class.

Quizzes or Tests. Multiple-choice, true-or-false, fill-in-the-blanks, and short-answer quizzes and tests are used frequently to gauge student performance. Quizzes or tests can be used with many of the above assessment techniques.

Numerous other assessments may be used. What matters is that the chosen method for checking for understanding accurately assesses the specific proficiency. In addition, to be effective, assessments must clearly communicate to students and teachers how well students are performing. Finally, the best assessments are easy to use and take little time to implement (see Figure 3.4).

We can get a deeper understanding of how the specific proficiency form can be used to assess understanding of specific

Download this form
at www.corwin.com/
highimpactinstruction

Figure 3.4 Quality Assessment Checklist

The informal assessment . . .	✓
Clearly tells students how well they are performing.	
Clearly tells teachers how well all students are performing.	
Is easy to use.	
Takes little time to implement.	

proficiencies by returning to our question about subjects and verbs. Figure 3.5 shows what a completed form for that question might look like.

5. USE ASSESSMENTS EFFECTIVELY

Formative assessments have many benefits, but those benefits won't be realized unless the assessments are used effectively (see Figure 3.6). There are very specific practices teachers should employ to increase the likelihood that the assessments will be effective.

Ensure That All Students Respond. Since a major goal of formative assessment is to obtain a clear picture of how well students are progressing, teachers need to ensure that they gather data from all students. This is easily done when students use pen-and-paper forms of assessments, such as quizzes or exit tickets, but more difficult when students are responding in the moment during class using response cards or white boards. In those kinds of situations, the following strategy is very important.

Develop a Group Response Ritual. A group response ritual is a routine teachers implement in the same way every time students respond

Figure 3.5 Sample Proficiency Form

1. Guiding Question	How do I identify subjects and verbs?
2. Specific Proficiency	3. Assessment
A subject is a noun that says what the sentence is all about.	Bell work and response cards
A verb describes a mental or physical action or state of being.	Bell work and response cards
State-of-being verbs include any form of the verb "to be," such as "am, is, are, was, were, been, being, and become."	Exit tickets
To find subjects and verbs, students need to find the verb in the sentence and ask who or what plus the verb to find the subject.	Turn-to-your-neighbor, quizzes

Figure 3.6	Checklist for Using Assessments Effectively

Use assessments effectively to . . .	✓
Ensure that all students respond.	
Develop a group response ritual.	
Ask students to explain their responses.	
Use effective questioning techniques.	
Reinforce students as they respond.	
Read nonverbal cues.	
Create a mistake-friendly culture.	
Consider giving students progress charts.	

in class using an in-class assessment such as response cards, thumbs up, or white boards. Anita Archer and Charles Hughes (2011) recommend that teachers let students know they are going to be asked to respond by counting down 3, 2, 1 and then giving students a signal, perhaps a hand signal such as moving the hand down to the side of the body, to let them know exactly when to respond. Everybody needs to respond together at the precise moment they see the hand signal.

Such a structured form of teaching does not fit with every teacher's style, but for those comfortable with such rituals, this practice has certain advantages. First, by counting down the teacher gives students who process information slowly a little more time to think through their answer. Second, by having everyone respond at exactly the same time, the teacher makes it much more difficult for students to sneak a peek at their neighbor before responding. When everyone responds at the same time without checking their neighbor's response, teachers get a clearer picture of what students know and don't know. Finally, by having everyone respond at exactly the same time, the teacher increases engagement and energy in the classroom. Doing something together with others is energizing. Group responses to checks for understanding generate the kind of energy people experience in many other group actions such as singing together in a choir or moving together in a dance routine, and most students enjoy the idea of responding together at exactly the same time.

Ask Students to Explain Their Responses. Usually when students respond to checks for understanding, they provide different answers. This sets up an excellent learning opportunity. When students give different responses, teachers can ask them to explain why they answered the way they did. For example, a teacher might say, "It looks like we have a difference of opinion here. Who can explain why they answered the way they did?" Often during the discussion, students correct each other's misconceptions without any guidance from the teacher. At other times, the teacher has to guide students to deeper, correct understandings.

Use Effective Questioning Techniques. All of the questioning strategies mentioned in Chapter 6 should be applied to ensure effective formative assessment. Thus, teachers should be careful not to give away the answer when asking questions or checking for understanding, and use the connect and redirect strategy when students give the wrong response (affirm and encourage each student response but ask clarifying questions of students—or call on other students) to expand and correct answers.

Reinforce Students as They Respond. Teachers who wish to encourage behavior need to make sure they give it significant attention. Checking for understanding provides many opportunities for teachers to give positive feedback and reinforce learner-friendly behavior. Effective feedback emphasizes effort rather than student intelligence, and studies in psychology and organizational behavior suggest that interactions should be at least five times more positive than negative. Much more on this topic is included in Chapter 14.

Read Nonverbal Cues. One of the easiest ways to check for understanding is to pay attention to students' nonverbal messages. When students pinch their forehead together in the middle of their brow, shake their head back and forth, avoid eye contact, scratch their head, frown, and so forth, those cues are powerful messages that the students don't understand what they have been studying. Similarly, when students nod their heads yes, smile, gesture emphatically (such as making a small fist pump in the air), or make direct eye contact, those cues are powerful messages that students do understand the content.

Nonverbal cues are important because they provide extra information that confirms or contradicts students' verbal or written responses. When teachers see a student's eyes light up when he or she answers a question, they can be more confident that the student understands what is being taught. On the other hand, when nonverbal cues suggest that students are confused, that may be a sign that teachers need to review content or provide more practice time for students. Teachers should keep in mind, however, that over time many students learn teacher-pleasing behaviors, and one of those behaviors is to look like you understand when you don't. Nonverbal cues, therefore, by themselves, are not sufficient for assessing understanding, and many of the other methods for checking for understanding described here should be used as well.

Create a Mistake-Friendly Culture. Alfred Adler wrote about the importance of mistakes in life, saying, "Do not be afraid of making mistakes, for there is no other way of learning how to live!" Certainly Adler's advice is true in the classroom. A great deal of powerful learning arises only from taking risks and making mistakes. Using the methods described in Chapter 10, teachers need to create a culture where students embrace the chance to make mistakes because they know that mistakes are an important part of learning.

To create a mistake-friendly culture, more than anything else, teachers must repeatedly reinforce students for effort and speak explicitly about the importance of risk-taking as a part of learning. Also, teachers must avoid teasing or ridiculing students who give wrong responses. Wrong responses are the window through which real insight enters, for, as one famous learner, Albert Einstein, has written, "Anyone who has never made a mistake has never tried anything new."

Consider Giving Students Progress Charts. One way to make it easier for students to monitor their progress is for them to plot their scores on a progress chart such as the one included in Figure 3.7. Progress charts give students clear evidence of their success, and like the score on a video game, they motivate and encourage students to keep moving forward.

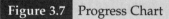

Figure 3.7 Progress Chart

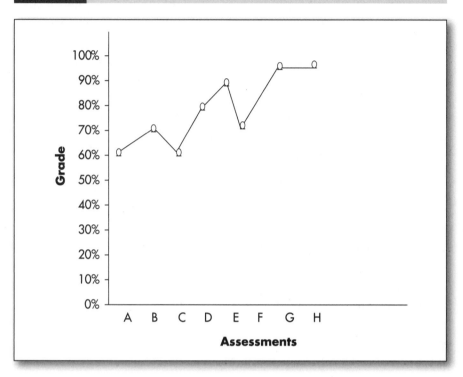

6. MODIFY TEACHING AND LEARNING

When Sarah Langton first saw her students' formative assessments, her coach, Michelle Harris, tells us, she was "stuck" because she didn't know what to do to help the students who hadn't learned what she had taught. This is perhaps the biggest challenge teachers face when using formative assessment: What do I do if the students haven't learned it? Fortunately, there are many, many things teachers can do to adapt their teaching to increase student learning.

High-Impact Instructional Strategies. Chapters 5 to 9 describe five high-impact strategies that teachers can use to increase engagement, mastery, and generalization of learning. Each strategy should be considered as an alternative way to enhance learning. Stories, for example, can be used to help students grasp a complex concept or to provide a real-world example of material that is being learned. Thinking prompts can be used to present students with problems that could lead to insight as they are solved by students or to expand or deepen students' appreciation of a topic. Cooperative learning could be used to provide opportunities for students to practice new learning with fellow students or to explore learning from multiple perspectives.

Other high-impact strategies can be used to find different ways to enhance student learning. For example, authentic learning could be used to provide concrete experiences of ideas being learned. Also, effective questioning could be used to guide students to deeper understanding of what they are learning. The five high-impact teaching strategies (thinking prompts, effective questions, stories, cooperative learning, and authentic learning) should be the first areas to consider when teachers think about how to enhance student learning, but many other practices can be reconsidered.

High-Impact Community-Building Strategies. If checks for understanding show that students are not learning, teachers should also consider whether they have created the most learner-friendly learning community by reflecting on the community-building strategies that are described in Chapters 10 to 15. Thus, teachers might work with coaches to get a measure of time on task or ask students to self-report their level of engagement. If students aren't engaged, the first step in rethinking their learning is to ensure that teaching practices are being used to increase engagement. More on time on task is found throughout this book.

Teachers might also want to get a measure of how often they praise and how often they criticize students. Ironically, as explained in Chapter 14, if teachers spend a lot of time correcting students, the attention they give students while correcting them actually encourages students to act up. Many students will do what it takes to get their teachers' attention, and if the only way they can get that attention is by acting up, many will act up.

At the most fundamental level, teachers could rethink how they encourage and connect with students or how they use power in the classroom (see Chapter 11). Finally, teachers could consider whether they have clearly taught and consistently reinforced the expectations (see Chapters 13, 14, and 15) and whether they have created a classroom community that truly is learner friendly (see Chapter 10). Formative assessment is a powerful point of departure for the entire instructional coaching process, and modifying teaching to meet students can involve high-impact strategies along with the additional teaching strategies described below.

Modeling. For some students, learning is enhanced when teachers model learning practices. Most often this involves a process referred to as "I do it," as in the teacher models how to do something, "we do it," where the teacher and student do something together, and "you do it," whereby the student practices on his or her own. Ed Ellis, a researcher from the University of Alabama, adds a step that comes right before "you do it," which he refers to as "ya'll do it." This is a stage where students practice with a partner before doing independent practice. See Figure 3.8.

Figure 3.8	I Do It, We Do It, You Do It

Download this form at www.corwin.com/highimpactinstruction

I Do It	✓
Review prior learning.	
Explain why today's learning is important.	
Tell students what they need to do.	
Think out loud.	
Problem solve.	
Attack the challenge in different ways.	
Address categories of error that arose in the previous day's work.	

We Do It	✓
Ask the students how to do what they are learning.	
Call on several students to explain how to do the task being learned.	
Ask students to explain their thinking.	
Shape students' responses (connect and redirect).	
Encourage students with praise for effort.	
Assess student understanding (perhaps with a quick assessment like response cards).	
Reteach if necessary.	

(Continued)

(Continued)

You Do It	✓
Let students perform independently.	
Give brief constructive feedback.	
Give feedback on the fly.	
Identify categories of error if students haven't mastered the learning.	
Plan how to address the categories of error in the next lesson.	

Aisha Santos discusses "I do it, We do it, You do it."

Video 3.2
www.corwin.com/
highimpactinstruction

Teachers frequently use the "I do it, We do it, You do it" teaching routine to ensure that students master skills. What matters with this routine is that teachers take the time to clearly model for students exactly what they are learning to do. Then, teachers need to involve students in collectively performing the skill to ensure that everyone knows how to do what is being learned. Finally, teachers need to give students a chance to perform the task independently and provide feedback that ensures students master the skill.

Breaking Down Learning. Another modification teachers can make when checks for understanding suggest that students have not learned what was taught is to consider whether the knowledge, skills, and big ideas being learned can be broken down into smaller components to ensure students master each component. Language arts teachers, for example, teaching students how to write paragraphs may decide they need to focus on topic sentences rather than all of the components of paragraph writing, and then they may decide they need to identify different types of topic sentences and teach each one individually.

Discussing Student Work. Sarah Langton helped her students better understand what they were to learn by showing them various answers to student questions. She used her document camera to show different responses to questions, and then together the students discussed the characteristics of a highly proficient response. This approach can be used in all subject areas. In language arts, for example, teachers who are teaching students about voice in writing can share different writing samples and then have the students identify criteria for writing in which authors have used voice effectively.

Feedback. More than two decades ago, Frank Kline conducted pioneering research (1991) at the Center for Research on Learning that showed that students learn more when teachers identify categories of error in student work and provide elaborated feedback and modeling to ensure students learn how to move forward. Since that time, researchers have expanded and refined our understanding of feedback by conducting numerous studies on the topic.

A recent issue of the journal *Educational Leadership* ("Feedback," 2012) provides a useful summary of what many of the leading researchers studying feedback now have to say about the characteristics of effective feedback. First, many agree that effective feedback should be guided by student goals. As Brookhart writes, "feedback can't work if students aren't trying to reach a learning target—or don't know what the target is or don't care" (p. 28). Similarly, Wiggins writes, "effective feedback requires that a person has a goal, takes action to achieve the goal, and receives goal-related information about his or her actions" (p. 13). Second, effective feedback, the authors generally agree, is focused on objective data and not a judgment of the student receiving the feedback. Dylan Wiliam writes, "effective feedback . . . focuses on the task at hand, not the recipient's ego" (p. 34).

Third, effective feedback should also be given as soon as possible after students complete a task. Timeliness was considered by many to be very important. In addition, as T. Phillip Nichols has written, "There is a great deal of value in setting aside time to speak with students one-on-one about the course, their work, their strengths and weaknesses, and the things that confuse and interest them" (p. 73). Fourth, effective feedback, as Grant Wiggins writes, is actionable. "Effective feedback is concrete, specific, and useful; it provides actionable information" (p. 14).

In addition, effective feedback should be easy to understand (Wiggins), have clear criteria (Brookhart), focus on the most information (Chappuis), focus on patterns in student errors (Fisher & Frye), prompt students to do their own thinking (Chappuis), and clearly guide students to see the next steps they need to take to improve (Brookhart).

7. REVISIT, REFLECT, REVISE

From time to time while moving through a unit, teachers should stop and consider whether their questions, specific proficiencies, and assessments are doing what they are supposed to do. The following six questions are intended to help teachers get an accurate understanding of what worked and what didn't work in their current approach to formative assessment.

Did My Question(s) Effectively Address the Key Learning and Standards?

Lessons that fail to address the knowledge, skills, and big ideas outlined in the Common Core State Standards or other state standards may leave students unprepared for the next level of learning. In addition, when lessons do not address standards, the learning that students experience may not be reflected in external measures of success such as standardized test scores. For these reasons, teachers should consider whether unit questions can be refined to better address what is intended for the unit. Simply put, the first question teachers should ask is whether they taught the right stuff or if they need to adjust the guiding questions to ensure they are more focused on the learning that is most important.

Should I Change My Questions in Any Way to Make Them More Effective?

The checklist in Chapter 2 for creating effective guiding questions offers several suggestions for writing effective questions. Teachers should consult these guidelines when first writing guiding questions, but they should also review them at the end of the unit to see if their questions can be improved. Teachers should consider whether the questions address all the important knowledge, skills, and big ideas in a unit and whether they can be written in more student-friendly language. In addition, teachers should consider whether the questions could help more students to think about how they learn and how technology might enhance their learning. Finally, teachers should consider whether their questions help students see how meaningful and relevant learning in a unit will be.

Did the Assessments Assess the Right Things?

Teachers must ensure that their assessments actually measure what they are designed to measure. For example, asking students to hold up a red, yellow, or green response card to indicate whether or not they know how to multiply fractions is not the same as asking students to actually demonstrate how to multiply fractions. Similarly, asking students to write down a memorized definition for subjects and verbs does not mean that students can actually identify subjects and verbs.

A common issue to be considered is whether or not assessments are assessing (a) attitude, (b) awareness, (c) deep knowledge, or (d) application of learning. When teachers assess attitude, they are trying to determine what students think about content—not whether or not students know the content. Asking, "How confident are you that you know the content?" yields valuable information about students' attitudes, but it doesn't tell the teacher whether or not the student knows what has been taught.

Clarifying how deeply students need to know content also helps improve assessments. In particular, teachers should consider whether students need to internalize content at a deep level or whether they merely need to know how to access the knowledge. With so much information available on the Internet and elsewhere these days, perhaps it is more important that students are able to find information than remember information. And as a result, assessments need to reflect this distinction.

Finally, as any teacher can tell you, just because a student has memorized something doesn't mean that he or she will apply that knowledge. If teachers really want to know whether or not students can apply their learning in real-life contexts, they should create and use assessments that measure whether or not students are able to apply their learning.

Was I Able to Monitor All Students' Progress?

If effectively implemented, formative assessment should benefit all students, and teachers need to consider whether or not their assessments yield data on all students. This is especially important when using questioning to check for understanding since a few correct answers by a small number of students can give the false impression that all students know what is being learned. Effective assessments paint a clear picture of how well all students are progressing, not just a few.

Did Students Have a Clear Understanding of Their Progress?

Formative assessment is an essential tool for teachers as data serve as the foundation for adjusting instruction to ensure students learn what is being taught. However, it is equally important that formative assessment shows students exactly how well they are progressing. The progress principle described by Teresa Amabile and Steven Kramer (2011) is as at least as important for students in school as it is for adults at work.

If it appears students do not clearly understand their progress, teachers should consider whether they should give more frequent assessments so students receive feedback more frequently. In addition, teachers could prompt students to plot their progress on charts such as the one included earlier in this chapter.

Were the Assessments Fun?

Lynn Erickson (2007) warns us that not all learning has to be "fun." Erickson writes, "I'm not opposed to students experiencing pleasure in their work; pleasure is a kid magnet after all. It's just that I've come to understand that some things that are devilishly hard and most distinctly not fun can also be very engaging and deeply satisfying when we conquer them" (p. ix).

Nevertheless, fun remains a worthwhile outcome to strive for because it increases engagement, pleasure, intrinsic motivation, and joy—outcomes that are inherently valuable. When formative assessments are used effectively, they can be a lot of fun. When students answer questions in a game show, create graphic organizers, or play a version of soccer to demonstrate their learning, they should enjoy themselves. In fact, most of the time just getting an answer right is a pleasant experience for anyone.

If students don't appear to enjoy using assessments, if asking students to get out their white boards elicits groans, teachers need to rethink the way assessments are being used. Most often, the easiest way to increase students' enjoyment of assessments is to use a number of different checks for understanding and to vary when they are used. When teachers rotate through several different forms of assessments and keep learning experiences fresh, students will enjoy classes more, and because of their enjoyment, they will learn more.

Turning Ideas Into Action

Students

1. Involve students in identifying quality work. Give students examples, as Sarah Langton did, of highly proficient work and ask them to identify the characteristics that produce highly proficient products. When students are actively involved in identifying the attributes of high-quality work, they are more likely to demonstrate that quality in their own work.

2. Involve students in identifying methods of assessment. Explain that the goal is to ensure that everyone knows how well they are learning, and ask students for suggestions on how they would assess themselves.

3. Ask students to assess the assessments. Prompt students to provide anonymous feedback on how well they understand their own progress and ask for suggestions for how assessments could be modified to produce more helpful information for them.

Teachers

1. Consider adopting a no-learning-gaps policy; that is, you will not teach something unless you have identified a specific proficiency and method of assessment for what is to be taught.

2. Find time to collaborate with your peers, especially colleagues who teach the same course as you. Share your assessments and borrow assessments from your colleagues.

3. Commit to working with a coach to master how you share your checks for understanding with students.

4. Continually ask yourself, "Do I know how well all my students are doing? Do all my students know how well they are doing?"

Instructional Coaches

1. Offer to serve in the role of "child's advocate" when you work with teachers on formative assessment. When you are a child's advocate, you scrutinize all aspects of the assessment process for anything that might be unclear or confusing, and then you ask the teacher to clarify what might be confusing to some students. If you are uncertain about anything, be sure to communicate that to the teacher.

(Continued)

(Continued)

2. Use your smartphone or digital camera to create a library of video clips of teachers using assessments in class (such as response cards, thumbs up, thumbs down, and so on). Of course, be certain to get the teacher's approval before recording a class or sharing a video.

3. Keep copies of teachers' proficiency forms to share with other teachers so that they can see how others have addressed assessment issues.

4. Offer to interview students to get their perspective on formative assessment and learning. Ask students what helps them learn and what gets in the way of their learning. Ask students about the effectiveness of the assessments they are completing.

5. Keep a learning journal in which you record how you have helped other teachers change their teaching when students are not learning.

6. Develop a deep understanding of all of the teaching practices described in this book (and other practices) so that you can provide meaningful support to teachers when they need to make changes to increase student learning. Some of the most powerful coaching occurs when coaches collaborate with teachers to help them change their teaching to ensure all students are learning.

7. Find a professional learning community, either online or face-to-face, to find out how others are helping teachers adapt their instruction to meet the different needs of their students. The Twitter group #educoach is one place to start.

Principals

1. Encourage central office decision makers to establish Intensive Learning Teams, described in Chapter 6 of *Unmistakable Impact: A Partnership Approach for Dramatically Improving Instruction* (2011), during which teachers who teach the same course collaborate to create high-impact plans for their course.

2. Lead schoolwide and team discussions about formative assessment to ensure that staff have a deep understanding and common vocabulary around terms like "guiding questions," "specific proficiencies," "I do it, We do it, You do it," and so forth.

3. Fight to get extra planning time so that teachers will have an opportunity to develop guiding questions, learning maps, and specific proficiencies. Given how busy and emotionally complicated the knowledge work of teaching is, extra time is likely needed for teachers to do the deep reflective work of high-impact planning.

4. Hold assessment exhibitions on professional development days during which teachers can share poster-size versions of the specific proficiencies forms that they have created.

5. Make assessment a part of everyday conversation and build it into meetings, professional learning communities, and other group gatherings in school.

6. During conversations with teachers, ask them about their guiding questions and specific proficiencies.

7. Consider making assessment for learning a part of the school improvement target, as described in Chapter 3 of *Unmistakable Impact: A Partnership Approach for Dramatically Improving Instruction* (2011).

What It Looks Like

1. Look to see if have teachers have posted guiding questions or specific proficiencies in the classroom.

2. Look to see if teachers are checking for understanding in various ways throughout a lesson.

3. Observe whether all students respond at the same time when teachers use assessments.

4. Check with students to see if they can accurately describe how well they are progressing in the class.

To Sum Up

- Janet Looney defines formative assessment as "frequent, interactive assessments of students' progress and understanding to identify learning needs and adjust teaching appropriately" (cited in Wiliam, 2001, p. 38).

- Formative assessment increases student engagement, and providing feedback on progress increases student hope.

- Formative assessment data are a starting point for adapting instruction.

- Formative assessment as described in this chapter involves seven steps:

1. Identifying guiding questions

2. Answering guiding questions

3. Developing specific proficiencies

4. Choosing quick, informal assessments

5. Using assessments effectively

6. Modifying teaching and learning

7. Revising assessments, reflecting on what worked and what didn't work, and revising questions, assessments, and lesson plans

Going Deeper

My understanding of assessment for learning began with Richard Stiggins. Dr. Stiggins met with me on two occasions when I was preparing to write *Instructional Coaching: A Partnership Approach to Improving Instruction* (2007), and during those discussions, he laid the groundwork for my knowledge of formative assessment. My copy of his book *Student-Involved Classroom Assessment, 3rd Edition* (2001), now titled *Student-Involved Assessment for Learning, 6th Edition* (2011), is dog-eared, marked up, and covered with sticky notes. If there are good ideas in this chapter, many, if not most of them, came from Stiggins' work.

Richard Stiggins' colleague Jan Chappuis has written an accessible and highly useful book, *Seven Strategies of Assessment for Learning* (2009), which would be an excellent source for readers wishing to deepen their knowledge of formative assessment. Here are Chappuis' seven strategies:

1. Provide students with a clear and understandable vision of the learning target.

2. Use examples and models of strong and weak work.

3. Offer regular descriptive feedback.

4. Teach students to self-assess and set goals.

5. Design lessons to focus on one learning target or aspect of quality at a time.

6. Teach students focused revision.

7. Engage students in self-reflection, and help them keep track of their learning.

Two others works, James Popham's *Transformative Assessment* (2008) and Dylan Wiliam's *Embedded Formative Assessment* (2011), have both helped me clarify my own understanding of what formative assessment is and is not, and I am certain those books would help others with their own similar learning.

Finally, Douglas Fisher and Nancy Frey have written many very useful resources. Anyone interested in deepening their knowledge about techniques for checking for understanding would benefit greatly from reading their book *Checking for Understanding: Formative Assessment Techniques for Your Classroom* (2007). In addition, anyone interested in learning more about the "I do it, We do it, You do it" routine, which they describe as gradual release, would find their book *Better Learning Through Structured Teaching: A Framework for the Gradual Release of Responsibility* (2008) to be very useful.

Note

1. Specific proficiencies are similar to test items known as propositions. Stiggins explains that to create propositions you should "capture the elements you wish to test in the form of clearly stated sentences that reflect important elements of content and stipulate the kind of cognitive operations respondents must carry out" (p. 132).

Chapter 4:
Learning Maps

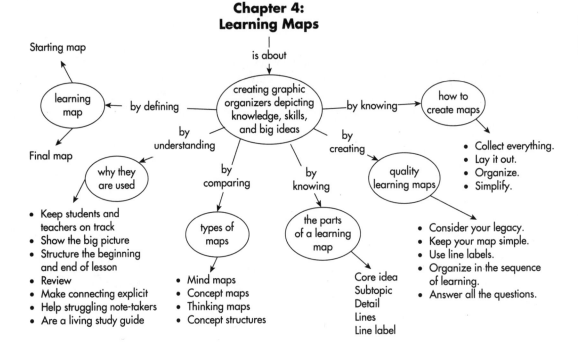

Starting map

learning map

by defining

is about

creating graphic organizers depicting knowledge, skills, and big ideas

by knowing

how to create maps

Final map

by understanding

by comparing

by creating

by knowing

quality learning maps

- Collect everything.
- Lay it out.
- Organize.
- Simplify.

why they are used

types of maps

the parts of a learning map

- Keep students and teachers on track
- Show the big picture
- Structure the beginning and end of lesson
- Review
- Make connecting explicit
- Help struggling note-takers
- Are a living study guide

- Mind maps
- Concept maps
- Thinking maps
- Concept structures

Core idea
Subtopic
Detail
Lines
Line label

- Consider your legacy.
- Keep your map simple.
- Use line labels.
- Organize in the sequence of learning.
- Answer all the questions.

4

LEARNING MAPS

A good map is both a useful tool and a magic carpet to faraway places.

—Author unknown

During the first half of my twenties, I lived in the heart of the Canadian Rockies, in Jasper, Alberta, my favorite part of the world. Surrounded by beautiful mountains, I was consumed by a desire to stand on some of the major peaks. I usually went into the backwoods to mountaineer every weekend, and I rock climbed after work on the cliffs just outside of town.

One climb was up Mount Andromeda, a wall of ice and snow that towers above the Columbia ice fields. My climbing partner and I had to hike some distance across the ice fields to get to the start of the climb. Roped together, we walked across the glacier with our ice axes in hand, ready in case one of us should fall into a crevasse.

Poking his ice ax ahead of himself as he walked, like a soldier walking through a minefield, my climbing partner discovered a crevasse that blocked our progress. Certain he could jump across it, he asked me to feed him about 15 feet. He leapt into the air, but the gap was wider than he thought, and in less than a second the rope between us tightened, and he went hurtling into the crevasse. I jumped on my ax to try and stop him before he hit the icy bottom.

I stuck the wide end of my ax into the ground and did my best to drag us to a stop. The extra 15 feet had sent him into the crevasse quickly, and I was pulled across the ice at a frightening pace. A park warden who was watching us through binoculars as we went across the glacier told me later that I looked like I was water skiing as I skipped across the ice. Quickly, though, I pulled us to a stop and my partner used his ice climbing gear to get back up to the surface.

People who look for ominous signs about the future might have seen my fellow climber's dive into the bowels of the glacier as a pretty clear indication that that day was not our day, but we decided to keep going. We started the actual climb about two hours late. Near the top, we realized that there was a cloud at the summit, and on top we couldn't see more than a few feet ahead of us. Most troubling, we couldn't see our route back down the mountain. After stumbling around in the cloud on the backside of the mountain, we decided that going on was too risky, so we tied ourselves to some rocks on a little ledge and settled in for the night.

After a restless night, we awoke to clear skies and a beautiful but unrecognizable landscape. We were tired, cold, running out of food, and, clearly, lost. We decided to hike down the edge of the mountain since we had to try to get somewhere, and eventually we landed in a valley. About midmorning we watched a rescue helicopter fly overhead, missing us completely. Being lost started to feel a little more frightening.

We edged our way across the valley, not sure what direction we were going, hoping to find a landmark that could help us get out. After a few hours, we came to a cliff at the end of the valley, and more than 1,000 feet down I could see a huge sheet of ice with the distinctive markings of the Saskatchewan Glacier. As soon as I saw the glacier, I knew we would be able to follow it back to the highway. We weren't lost anymore. Now we could get home.

Chances are you've been lost a few times in your life and know what it feels like. When lost, we feel helpless. We don't know which way to turn. We walk around in circles. Sometimes when people are lost, they just give up and hope that someone will find them. And people don't have to climb a mountain to get lost. Too many students get lost in schools all the time. Like my friend and me on the back of Mount Andromeda, they look up from what they are learning and don't know where they are. And, as a result, they may give up.

One way to avoid getting lost is, of course, consulting a map. If my friend and I had remembered to bring a topographical map, we could have used it to find the valley, identified our exit, and made our way home. A map would have been an incredibly helpful tool. Learning maps, in exactly the same way, can be incredibly helpful in the classroom. Learning maps help students stay on course and make it easier for them to learn.

Learning Maps

A learning map is a graphic organizer that highlights the knowledge, skills, and big ideas that students should get from a lesson, unit, or course. The map depicts the most important information to be learned and how the different pieces of learning are connected. A learning map is a visual cue for the advance organizer (the introduction of learning at the start of a lesson) and post organizer (the summary discussion at the end of a of a lesson), and a living study guide that students and teachers complete after each new learning.

In this chapter I will focus on using learning maps to depict what will be learned in a unit, but learning maps can also be used to organize and visually depict the information to be learned in a course or lesson. Learning maps are two-dimensional depictions of information that usually include (a) a core idea, often the name of the unit; (b) subtopics (usually surrounded by shapes such as ovals, rectangles, squares, or stars); (c) details; (d) lines that show the relationship between the different parts of the map; and (e) line labels that explain the relationship between the core idea and the subtopics. My colleague Keith Lenz, whose *Unit Organizer Routine* (Lenz, Bulgren, Schumaker, Deshler, & Boudah, 2005) introduced me to learning maps, suggests that maps also include a paraphrase of the core idea of the unit.

I suggest creating two types of learning maps: starting maps, which usually only include the core idea, paraphrase, and supporting details (see Figure 4.1), and ending maps, which are constructed throughout the unit as details are added and finished when the unit is completed (see Figure 4.2).

Like the climber's topographical map, a learning map points out the most important features of the landscape. On learning maps, the landscape is the knowledge, skills, and big ideas to be learned in a class. The learning map highlights the most important information students need to learn and provides students with guideposts for following the sequence of instruction.

Why Learning Maps Are Useful

Seeing Supports Learning. In his book *The Back of the Napkin: Solving Problems and Selling Ideas With Pictures* (2008), Dan Roam illustrates how helpful visual learning can be with a legendary story about the founding of Southwest Airlines:

> Herb Kelleher was a lawyer from New Jersey who decided
> that the big open spaces of his wife's native Texas looked like

Carrie Hochgrebe learns about learning maps.

Video 4.1
www.corwin.com/
highimpactinstruction

Figure 4.1   Sample Learning Map for a Sentence Writing Unit—Starting Map

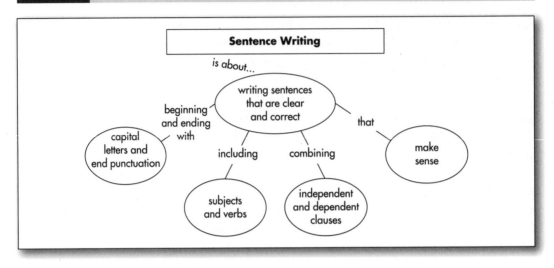

Figure 4.2   Sample Learning Map for a Sentence Writing Unit—Ending Map

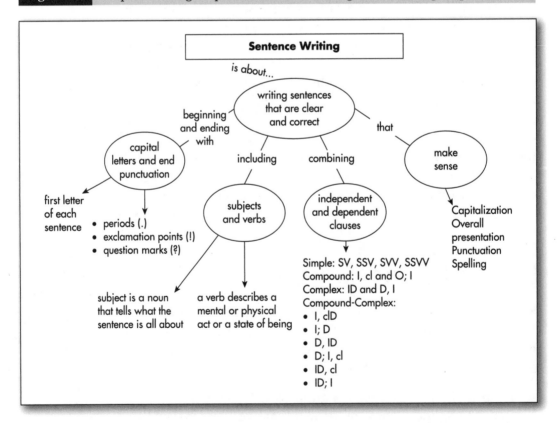

a good place to set up business, so he packed up the family and headed to San Antonio.

One afternoon in 1967, Kelleher was sitting at the prestigious St. Anthony Club, helping his client Rollin King finish up the paperwork that would close Rollin's failed airline. But Rollin wasn't through with the airline business. He picked up a napkin and sketched a triangle on it. As he wrote San Antonio, Houston, and Dallas on each of the three points, Rollin explained another crazy idea to Herb—an idea that four years later became Southwest Airlines.

Rather than running a small airline that serviced small towns, why not run a small airline that serviced big cities—the three biggest boomtowns in Texas, in fact? Because it flew to only three cities, the airline would not come under regulation of the Texas Civil Aeronautics Board, thus freeing it up to financially operate pretty much as it pleased. And by flying to Dallas' otherwise deserted Love Field, it would offer a far easier commute for Dallas-based business travelers.

Southwest legend has it that Herb agreed with Rollin on two things: first, that the idea was crazy, and second that the idea was brilliant. On its own, the simple map illustrated the fundamental operating principles of the company that Herb and Rollin agreed to start that evening: fly short routes between busy cities, avoid hubs, and where possible fly into smaller, secondary airfields. One napkin; one good idea; one profitable airline. (pp. 120–121)

Southwest Airlines might have been launched without the sketch on the back of the napkin, but there is plenty of evidence that visual depictions of information such Rollin King's drawing significantly enhance understanding. In *Brain Rules: 12 Principles for Surviving and Thriving at Work, Home, and School* (2008), John Medina, the director of the Brain Center for Applied Learning Research at Seattle Pacific University, generalizes from the existing research: "Vision is probably the best single tool for learning anything. . . . Put simply, the more visual the input becomes, the more likely it is to be recognized—and recalled" (p. 233). Learning maps enhance student learning by providing a picture of what students will learn.

They Show the Big Picture. Teachers who have used learning maps report that seeing the entire unit laid out on one page helps them make decisions about how to differentiate learning. They can look over the unit from start to finish and pinpoint where they may need to modify instruction to increase the likelihood that all children will learn. As one teacher explained in a workshop, "the map gives me the whole gestalt. It helps me get a much clearer idea of what and how I need to teach."

What helps teachers also helps students. When students see the unit displayed on one page at any point in the unit, they can see what has been learned and what remains to be learned, all in one shot. And as a result, they can estimate what they need to do and how long it will take them to master the unit's knowledge, skills, and big ideas. The map also becomes a visual reference point for much of the learning that happens in the class, especially the advance and post organizers for each day's lessons.

They Keep Students and Teachers on Track. I have interviewed dozens of teachers after they have used learning maps, and they almost always report that they like them because they keep them on track. Learning maps are daily reminders of what should be taught and what should be emphasized, and many teachers have told me those daily reminders are very helpful.

Again, the benefits teachers experience are also experienced by students. Like road maps, learning maps give students a turn-by-turn, or at least idea-by-idea, picture of what will be learned in each lesson. When teachers use learning maps fluently, every day, students get a chance to picture what they have learned and what they are about to learn, and for many students that kind of scaffolding is very important.

They Structure the Beginning and Ending of Lessons. Many studies have been conducted to show that the first and last information we experience is the easiest to remember. Psychologists studying these phenomena refer to the primacy and recency effect (Atkinson & Shifrin, 1968; Ebbinghaus, 1913; Glanzer & Cunitz, 1966; Murdock, 1962: Terry, 2005). I include more on this topic later in this chapter.

In the classroom, this means that the first few minutes and the last few minutes of a class are extremely important for introducing and reinforcing student learning. There is also ample evidence to suggest that advance organizers and post organizers, in part because of the primacy and recency effect, enhance student learning (Lenz, 1987; Marzano, Pickering, & Pollock, 2001). Learning maps provide a picture of the unit that teachers can use to begin and end lessons in a way that best supports student learning.

They Serve as a Mechanism for Repeated Review. When teachers begin and end each day's lesson by discussing the learning map, students are able to take stock of how well they understand what is being learned in a unit. In Chapter 5, I describe many ways in which teachers can prompt students to review the learning depicted on the map. Whether the map is used individually or with other students, learners benefit by reviewing the learning depicted on the map.

They Make Connections Explicit. When my colleague at the University of Kansas Center for Research on Learning, Keith Lenz, studied the characteristics of students who are at risk for failure, he found that many of these students did not see the connections between the knowledge, skills, and big ideas they were learning. For students who struggle in school, each day can bring just another piece of unrelated stuff to be experienced or perhaps endured. Therefore, teachers need to do what they can to organize what they teach so that students see the connections between the knowledge, skills, and big ideas being learned.

Learning maps are designed to show how everything being learned is connected. In the learning maps throughout this book and described below, the maps explicitly show the connections between various words on the map. The line label "is communicated by" in the map in Figure 4.3, for example, makes it clear how body language, respect, and the details are related.

Figure 4.3 Learning Map

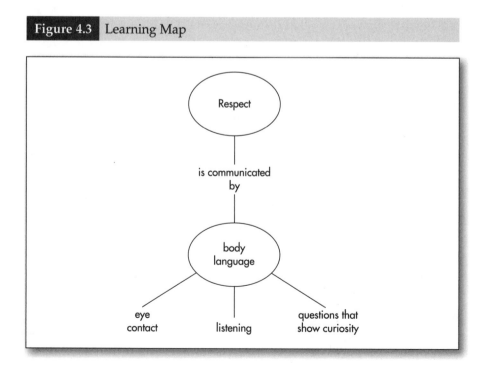

Teachers can help students see how various aspects of learning are connected by creating maps that explicitly show connections and by pointing out those connections during learning experiences.

They Help Struggling Note-Takers. Students who are at risk for failure often have not mastered the complex task of taking notes. For some students who have been diagnosed as having learning disabilities, for example, distinguishing between important and unimportant information is a daunting task, and students often either try to write down every bit of information that is taught or give up, overwhelmed by the challenge. In addition, in heterogeneous classrooms with diverse learners, slow note-takers present a significant challenge for teachers. If the teachers move the learning at a pace that most students can handle, some students will be left behind, but if the teachers allow enough time for all students to keep up with notes, intensity will be lost, and some students will become bored or off task.

Learning maps accommodate learner needs by providing a scaffold for note taking. Although a learning map does not replace notes, it does provide a format for all students to record information about what they are learning, and with teacher guidance, students can be sure they are recording the most important information. In extremely diverse classrooms, teachers can create a fill-in-the-blanks form of the learning map so that every student can complete the map quickly.

They Serve as a Living Study Guide. In some learning settings, teachers give students study guides a few days before the end of a unit so that the students can prepare for the final test. Learning maps can provide a similar support for students, but they are created with students throughout the unit, not simply handed out at the end. In addition, since students interact with the map by taking notes, using it in discussions and activities, reviewing it during advance and post organizers, using it to monitor and check learning, referring to it to stay organized and focused during class, and frequently using it as the starting point to create their own maps, the map becomes a central part of learning. For all these reasons, a map that is built throughout the unit has a greater impact on retention of ideas than a teacher-constructed study guide handed out at the end of a unit.

Types of Maps

Many authors have written about the power of mapping as a part of learning. Mapping models include clustering (Rico, 2000), mind maps (Buzan, 1993; Margulies, 2001), concept maps (Novack, 1998), thinking

Figure 4.4 Map of Mapping Ideas

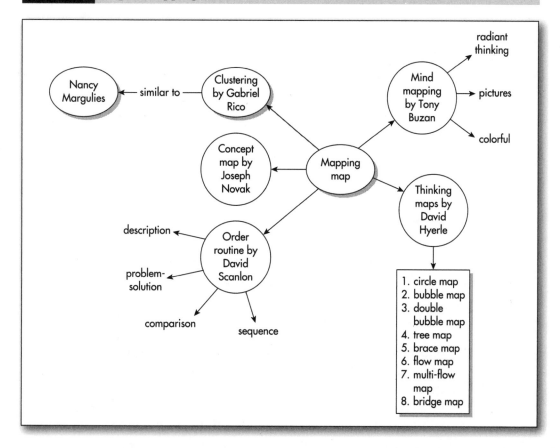

maps (Hyerle, 2009), and content structures (Scanlon, 2004). Each author has constructed useful and interesting theoretical and practical approaches to mapping. Before I describe how to create learning maps, I will offer a brief overview of each of these approaches (see Figure 4.4).

Mind Maps. Mind mapping was originally introduced through the writing of Gabriel Rico, who describes clustering as a part of the writing process in *Writing the Natural Way* (2000), and Nancy Margulies in *Mapping Inner Space* (1991) and Tony Buzan in *The Mind Map Book* (1993). In their simplest form, mind maps are webs of words or shapes filled with words that flow out from the center of a page in a way that naturally extends whatever is being explored.

In my experience, clustering or mind mapping is a bit like brainstorming with bubbles. Since first reading *Writing the Natural Way*, more than two decades ago, I have used Rico's cluster maps to organize almost all my writing projects (see Figure 4.5). Buzan's mind maps are more elaborate forms of mapping, involving pictures and colors, and are often used for note taking.

Figure 4.5	A Prewriting Cluster Map

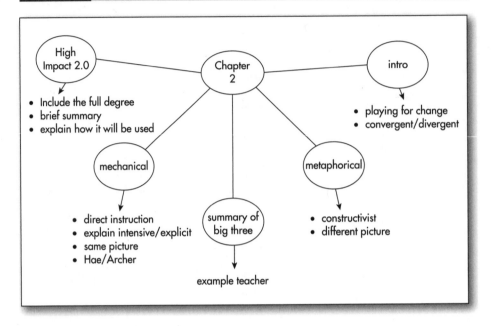

Concept Maps. Developed by Joseph Novak (1998), concept maps are hierarchically organized maps of concepts where the relationship between concepts is communicated through line labels (see Figure 4.6). According to Novak, "concept maps are a knowledge representation tool . . . [that] . . . should be read from the top to the bottom, proceeding from the higher order—more general—concepts at the top to the lower order—more specific—concepts at the bottom. Concept maps also have crosslinks that show relationships between ideas in different segments of the map" (pp. 4–5).

Thinking Maps. Developed by David Hyerle (2009), thinking maps are depictions of cognitive processes designed to enhance people's ability to think in ways that Hyerle convincingly asserts are universal. Hyerle writes:

around the world, like universal human emotional patterns such as love, joy, and pain, there are basic cognitive processes: Every child born into this world, for example, comes to learn how to sequence the day, categorize ideas and objects around them, break down objects whole to parts and assemble them parts to whole, survive by casual reason, and reason by analogy. (p. 119)

| Figure 4.6 | The Five Elements That Compose an Educational Event: Teacher, Learner, Knowledge, Evaluation, and Context. All elements are present in an educative event and combine to construct or reconstruct the meaning of experience. |

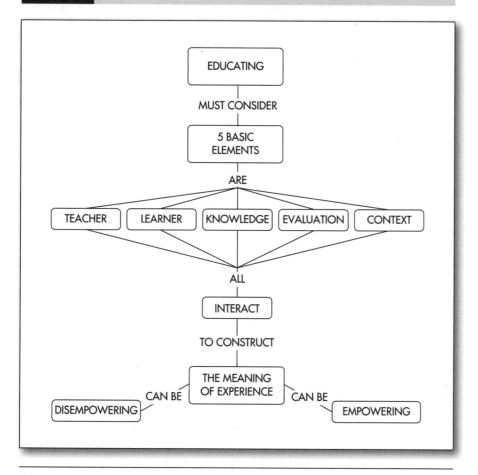

Source: Novak (1998).

Hyerle describes eight maps designed to enhance learners' ability to think (see Figure 4.7):

1. **Circle Map.** How are you defining this (concept) and in what context?

2. **Bubble Map.** What are the attributes?

3. **Double-Bubble Map.** How are these alike and different?

Figure 4.7   The Cognitive Bridge to Literacy

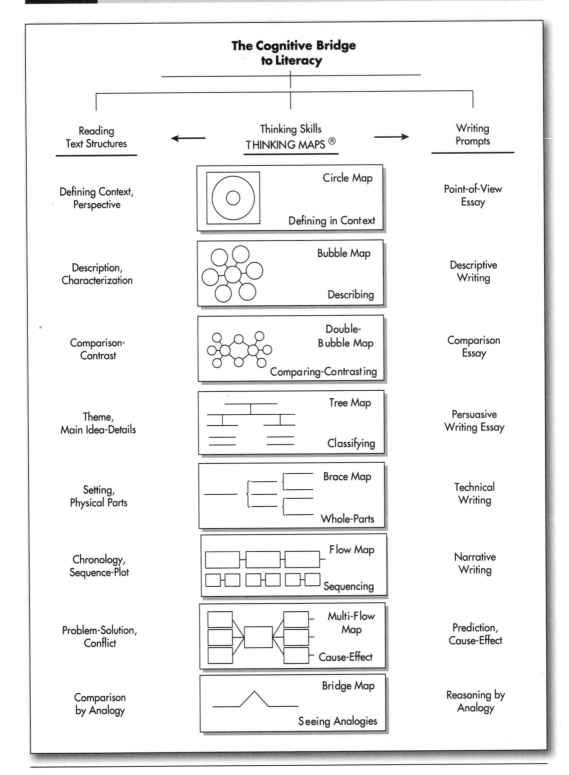

Source: Hyerle (2009).

4. **Tree Map.** How are these grouped together?

5. **Brace Map.** What are the parts of a physical whole object?

6. **Flow Map.** What was the sequence of events?

7. **Multi-Flow Map.** What were the causes and effects?

8. **Bridge Map.** Is there an analogy between these ideas?

Order Routine. Building on the pioneering work of many of the authors described above, David Scanlon created and scientifically validated *The Order Routine* (Scanlon, Schumaker, & Deshler, 2004), which teachers can use to help students identify important information and organize it into one of four graphic organizers: sequential, compare and contrast, problem-solution, and descriptive.

Sequential structures organize events, the steps of a process, or other information into a step-by-step pattern. For example, a sequential pattern could be depicted using a number line to show the events occurring during a historical time such as the civil rights movement, as depicted in the number line in Figure 4.8.

Figure 4.8	Sequential Structure: Civil Rights Movement

Civil Rights Movement	
1954 —	*Brown v. Board of Education*
1955–56 —	Rosa Parks and the Montgomery Bus Boycott
1957 —	Desegregation of Little Rock
1960 —	Sit-ins
1961 —	Freedom Rides
1961–62 —	Albany Movement
1963 —	March on Washington
1963–64 —	Birmingham Campaign
1963–64 —	St. Augustine, Florida
1964 —	Mississippi Freedom Summer
1964 —	Civil Rights Act
1964 —	Mississippi Freedom Democratic Party
	Dr. King awarded Nobel Peace Prize
1965 —	Selma and the Voting Rights Act
1968 —	Dr. King assassinated

Compare and contrast patterns organize information so that similarities and differences are easy to see. A common type of compare and contrast diagram is a compare/contrast grid, which is used to highlight similarities and differences between concepts, characters, geographic locations, objects, and so forth. For example, a comparison diagram showing how a rock band is similar to a cooperative learning group could be used to ground new ideas about cooperative learning groups in information that everyone knows (see Figure 4.9).

Another common form of content structure is a *problem-solution* graphic organizer. This type of organizer illustrates a problem, options for solving the problem, pros and cons of each option, and a proposed solution. In Figure 4.10, students explore options they can use if they are falling behind on their homework.

Figure 4.9 Sample Compare and Contrast Organizer

Cooperative Group		Rock Band
host, timekeeper, scribe	*roles*	guitarist, singer, drummer
everyone contributes	*cooperation*	everyone plays
learning product	*outcome*	music
joy of learning	*reason*	joy of music

Figure 4.10 Problem-Solution Organizer

Problem	Options	Pros/Cons	Solution
Falling behind on homework	1. ignore it	pro – easy con – I might fail I'll worry I'll be unhappy	
	2. ask my parents	pro – they are easy to find con – they might be busy I'd have to work after supper	After-school tutor
	3. After-school tutor	pro – free they know the content I don't have to do it at home con – I have to do it after school	

| Figure 4.11 | Sample Descriptive Organizer |

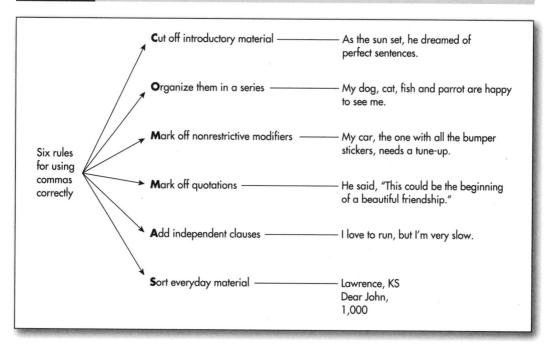

Probably the most common type of content structure is the *descriptive organizer*. This type of organizer is organized around key ideas, with supportive details or examples listed underneath the organizing idea. Figure 4.11 is a descriptive organizer illustrating six rules about punctuation.

The Parts of a Learning Map

Learning maps combine various elements of cluster maps, mind maps, thinking maps, concept maps, and content structures to depict what students will learn in a unit. As the map in Figure 4.12 illustrates, learning maps usually involve (a) a core idea (usually the name of the unit); (b) a core idea paraphrase (usually a paraphrase of the unit); (c) subtopics usually surrounded by ovals, rectangles, or stars; (d) details beneath the subtopics; and (e) line labels to show the relationship between different parts of the map.

The Characteristics of a Quality Learning Map

As mentioned, the learning map is really two maps: the *starting map*, which is introduced on the first day of the unit, and the *ending map*,

Figure 4.12 Parts of a Learning Map

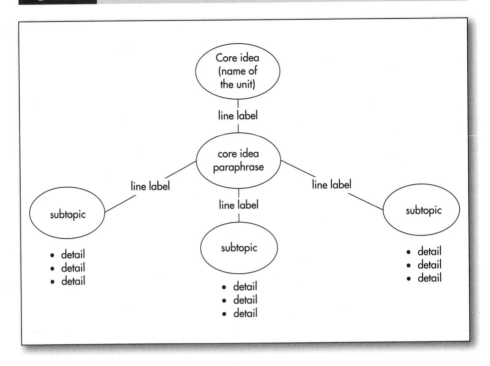

which is built throughout the unit until the end. Although teachers usually only share the starting map on the first day, they should create a complete ending map before they begin teaching. When teachers create the entire learning map, they are able to estimate how much time to spend on each component of the unit, and as pointed out above, they are able to use the map to help them differentiate instruction. In addition, when teachers also create guiding questions and formative assessments, they are better able to get a complete picture of the knowledge, skills, and big ideas students need to learn in a unit.

To share the learning map, teachers usually guide students to write their guiding questions on one side of a piece of paper and put the map on the other side. Students can either draw the starting map themselves on a blank page (and write the guiding questions on the back) or fill in the blanks on a partially completed starting map handed out by their teacher. The map then becomes a point of departure for learning that takes place throughout the unit.

For the highest impact, teachers must make the highest quality map possible, but this can be a creative challenge. For example, teachers who love their content often struggle when creating their learning maps. Since each part of their subject is fascinating, they want to include every detail and can easily convince themselves that students need to hear everything. However, presenting them with too much information often means that students remember less. Grant Wiggins and Jay McTighe (2005) refer to this as the "coverage orientation," an approach that they suggest might be labeled as "Teach, test, and hope for the best" (p. 5). They write:

> [A coverage orientation is] . . . an approach in which students march through a textbook, page by page (or teachers through lecture notes) in a valiant attempt to traverse all the factual material within a prescribed time. . . . Coverage is thus like a whirlwind tour of Europe, perfectly summarized by that old movie title, *If It's Tuesday, This Must Be Belgium*, which properly suggests that no overarching goals inform the tour. (p. 16)

But the opposite extreme also fails students. Creating a content-light, rigor-free course or unit that doesn't challenge students does not inspire authentic learning. If teachers dummy-down the content and give students a mile-wide and inch-deep learning experience, they make it impossible for students to have authentic, meaningful learning experiences, and worse, they take away the opportunity for students to see what they are capable of achieving.

A third way is for teachers to find the simplest way to map learning without sacrificing rigor and depth. The goal is simplicity, which, in the words of simplicity expert Bill Jensen, is "the art of making the complex clear" (2000, p. 2). "Simplicity," Jensen writes, "is power" (p. 1). Teachers can move closer to making simple learning maps, that is, maps that support rigorous *and* accessible instruction, by following a few simple guidelines, as presented below.

Answer All the Guiding Questions. A learning map that doesn't prepare students for success on assessments will likely be ignored. Teachers need to create maps that provide excellent answers to the guiding questions. There are many strategies for constructing great answers to guiding questions. First, teachers should think about the knowledge, skills, and big ideas their students need to learn. If teachers have created specific proficiencies for guiding questions as a part of formative assessment as described in Chapter 3, they will already be very clear on what has to be included on the map.

Other strategies can also be helpful. Some teachers create their own maps to answer all the questions so that they deepen and broaden their appreciation of what students will learn. Some teachers use sticky notes to answer their questions and then move the notes around when they develop their maps. Discussing questions and answers with fellow teachers also helps clarify what should go on the map.

The benefit of all this work is that when teachers have a deep understanding of the unit's knowledge, skills, and ideas, their lessons are much more focused and effective. More on how to create maps is included later in this chapter.

Keep Your Map Simple. A few guidelines help to keep the map as "simple as possible but no simpler." First, the starting map should include only the core idea or name of the unit, the unit paraphrase, and the subtopics. It is a good idea to keep the starting map to no more than seven bubbles.

Second, the ending map should never be more than one page. Putting everything on one page compels the teacher to resist the temptation to create too broad a map. A good map is comprehensive but not overwhelming. If teachers cannot convey the whole unit on one page, there is a good chance they may have slipped into focusing more on covering content than on learning. Creating a one-page map forces deep thinking. Bill Jensen (2000) includes CIO Kent Green's comments on one-page documents in *Simplicity,* and Green's comments nicely explain why one-page documents can help teachers and students alike:

> We get people focused through one-page tools. . . . If you can actually get everything on one page—and not just editing stuff out—that means the tool and the process caused you to reflect on what it is you want to do. If you limit the number of pages people have to explain themselves, it forces them to reflect first and think about what they're trying to do. That's very important. (pp. 52–53)

Use Line Labels. Joseph D. Novak, the inventor of concept maps, suggests that line labels be used to link concepts with one or two words: "The linking word should define the relationship between the two concepts so that it reads like a valid statement or proposition" (1998, p. 228). Jenny MacMillan, an instructional coach in our Beaverton, Oregon, study, found it easiest to create learning maps by writing the sentences that linked the unit paraphrase with the subtopics (see Figure 4.13).

Creating the map also can provoke deep thinking on the part of teachers. When teachers cannot identify what to write on the line labels, chances are they need to think more about the connections between the ideas and details on the map. During one of our focus group sessions, Jenny explained that she and her teacher "ended up writing the sentence that she wanted to be the gist of her unit first, and then we made the map match the sentence. We built the content bubbles off of that . . . and that's what we highlighted. She really loved it."

Organize the Map in the Sequence of the Learning Occurring in the Class. Although it may not be possible with every learning map, there are many advantages to organizing the map in the sequence of the learning that will take place in a unit (see Figure 4.14). This usually involves positioning the subtopics so that they reflect the sequence of instruction. In the Sentence Writing Starting Map above, the first few lessons will be on capital letters and end punctuation. Lessons will then focus on subjects and verbs. Those lessons will be followed by instruction on sentence structure, and the unit will conclude with lessons on using the COPS (Capitalization, Overall Presentation, Punctuation, Spelling) editing strategy.

Figure 4.13	Sample Linking Words	
through	including	by analyzing
defined by	grounded in	caused by
by being	by creating	organized by
leading to	involving	by always
based on	embodied in	developed by

Download this list at www.corwin.com/ highimpactinstruction

Figure 4.14	Quality Map Checklist	
A quality map . . .		✓
Answers all the guiding questions		
Has a starting map with only the core idea, paraphrase, and subtopics		
Has a complete ending map on no more than one page		
Shows connections through line labels		
Is organized in the sequence of the learning in the unit		

Download this form at www.corwin.com/ highimpactinstruction

Organizing the map to reflect the sequence of instruction makes it much easier for teachers to review content throughout the unit. In some cases, such as when a key theme or concept is returned to throughout a unit, other organizational patterns make more sense. As always, teachers need to use their professional decision to make the best map to support student learning. For that reason, it serves teachers well if they understand the different types of maps that they might create.

How to Create Learning Maps

As with any planning process, each person finds his or her own best way to go about creating learning maps. As I've mentioned in other parts of this book, the entire planning process involves three components, developing guiding questions, learning maps, and formative assessments, and each aspect of planning informs other aspects.

I have collaborated with hundreds of teachers developing units, some working with teams and some working independently, and I've found the five steps described in Figure 4.15 very helpful for creating learning maps.

1. IDENTIFY THE KNOWLEDGE, SKILLS, AND BIG IDEAS

Learning maps depict the most important information students need to remember as they progress through a unit, so the point of departure for creating a learning map is to bring together all the information that might end up being learned in a unit. In most cases, this involves identifying answers to the guiding questions. In Chapter 3, Formative Assessment, I proposed answering guiding questions by

---

Figure 4.15 Creating Learning Maps

1. **Identify** the knowledge, skills, and big ideas and other information that need to be in the map.

2. **Display** everything by transferring information to sticky notes and putting it out where it can be seen.

3. **Organize** information into a map.

4. **Connect** information using line labels.

5. **Refine** the map by asking, subtracting, and contracting.

creating specific proficiencies, short sentences that describe the knowledge, skills, and big ideas students need to learn in a unit. Many teachers find that creating and revising specific proficiencies helps ensure that their maps depict all the important information.

Whether they work from the specific proficiencies for formative assessments or some other list of knowledge, skills, and big ideas, teachers need to consider all of the resources that they will reference as they teach their unit. This means that they might look at the standards for a unit, textbooks, or other reading material students will read for the unit, websites, national, state, common core, or district curricula, and any other information that might be of use in planning the learning taking place during a unit. The goal here is to look at everything that might inform instruction before pinning down the details of the learning map.

2. DISPLAY EVERYTHING

Once all the resources have been located and reviewed, the next step is to transfer all ideas to sticky notes. Every fact, skill, concept, and theme should be individually noted on a separate sticky note. Then, each sticky note should be placed on a surface where the whole range of ideas can be viewed. For teachers, the best place might be their classroom's white board. Dan Roam (2008) described a similar model for generating visual displays of information. He writes that it is incredibly helpful to lay all the possible parts of a map out where everything can be seen:

> Having collected everything, we now have to lay it out where we can really look at it. This is such an obvious rule that it often gets ignored, and yet it is the single best way to effectively look at a broad range of inputs—take everything we've collected and lay it out side by side, where our eyes can scan it all in a few passes. . . . When it is packed away in individual files and records it's impossible to look at the big picture—but getting everything out in the open makes invisible connections visible. (pp. 61–62)

Many teachers choose to use software designed for creating maps, such as *Inspiration*, and if digital thinking seems natural and effective, that is a good idea. In my experience, however, there is value in getting away from your computer during this stage of unit development. Garr Reynolds, who has revolutionized the way people create and deliver presentations through his book *Presentation Zen* (2008), explains it this way:

> A fundamental mistake people make is spending almost the entire time thinking about their talk and preparing their content while sitting in front of a computer screen. Before you design your presentation, you must see the big picture and identify your core messages—or the single core message. This can be difficult unless you create a stillness of mind for yourself, something that is hard to do while puttering around in slideware.
>
> Right from the start, most people plan their presentations using software tools. In fact, the software makers encourage this, but I don't recommend it. There's just something about paper and pen and sketching out rough ideas in the "analog world" in the early stages that seems to lead to more clarity and better, more creative results when we finally get down to representing our ideas digitally. . . . I call preparing the presentation away from the computer "going analog," as opposed to "going digital" at the computer. (p. 45)

3. ORGANIZE

Once everything has been written on a sticky note and posted where it can be clearly seen, the teacher can start to sort the ideas into groups that will eventually become the learning map. When reviewing the sticky notes, the teacher can group information around big ideas and consider the sequence of instruction. Teachers report that it helps with instruction if the first part of the map is the first part to be taught in a unit, with the rest of the map laid out in the sequence in which content will be learned.

Teachers should also consider the hierarchy of content. Which sticky notes describe big ideas and which ones describe skills and knowledge. Which sticky notes identify words, concepts, or ideas that might end up as a subtopics on the learning map and which ones identify details that will be listed underneath the subtopics.

Teachers should also think about what kind of map to use. Although the most common learning map is the descriptive map, other maps, such as a number line or comparison-contrast grid, may be used. Often a learning map is a hybrid map using a concept map structure, but also including a number line or other map to depict the information related to a subtopic. In the learning map in Figure 4.16, a teacher used a sequential flow chart map for a unit on paragraph writing.

Figure 4.16 Sequential Flow Chart Map: Paragraph Writing

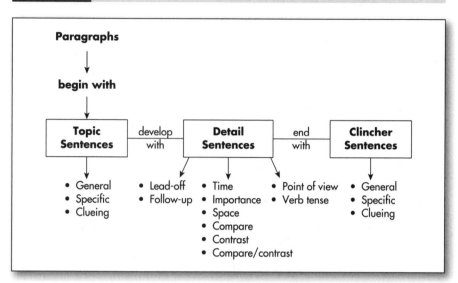

4. CONNECT

Once the map is created, the next step is to identify the line labels that show how the parts of the map relate to each other. In *Learning, Creating, and Using Knowledge: Concept Maps as Facilitative Tools in Schools and Corporations* (1998), Joseph Novak describes the characteristics of effective line labels:

> Label the lines with one or a few linking words. The linking words should define the relationship between the two concepts so that it reads as a valid statement or proposition. The connection creates meaning. When you hierarchically link together a number of related ideas, you can see the structure of meaning for a given subject domain. (p. 221)

Keith Lenz also gives excellent advice on how to create and use line labels. In the *Unit Organizer Routine* (Lenz, Bulgren, Schumaker, Deshler, & Boudah, 1994), he and his co-authors write:

> To identify how information in your Unit Map is related, begin by thinking about the words that you would use to describe the link or relationship depicted by the lines you have drawn between the geometric shapes. To identify these concept connections, ask yourself, "What is the connection represented by each line that I have drawn and that I want to

emphasize so students will understand how to think about this information?" (p. 23)

5. REFINE

After the entire map has been created, the final step is to add, subtract, or contract information. Teachers who are refining their maps should first ask whether they need to add information to ensure that the map points toward a complete answer for each guiding question.

Second, teachers should consider whether there is any information that can be removed. As Dan Roam (2008) has written, "there is always far more visual information out there than we can process, so our vision system needs to be picky about what it lets past the front door" (p. 70). As a general rule, if information can be removed without diminishing the answer to a question, it should be removed.

Finally, teachers should consider whether information can be combined or contracted. If several ideas or details can be expressed in a larger concept without losing any important information, they probably should be.

I like to imagine the core idea, subtopics, and details on a map as the tips of icebergs, with all the related knowledge, skills, and big ideas extending beneath the page. The words and ideas on the learning maps in total should point to a complete answer to the guiding questions, but too much information can be overwhelming.

The five-step process for creating learning maps, like other ideas in this book, does not have to be followed to the letter. Each person or team will need to experiment to find the creative process that works best for them. However, if teachers and teams employ these strategies, they will create high-quality maps that enhance their teaching and student learning.

Marlo Warburton uses a graphic organizer to explain equations.

Video 4.2
www.corwin.com/
highimpactinstruction

Sharing Learning Maps With Students

Learning maps can enhance student learning in many ways, but they won't have much impact if they stay in students' backpacks. For that reason, teachers should develop rituals, which Loehr and Schwartz (2003) refer to as "highly specific routines" (p. 11), that integrate learning maps into learning. In particular, the teachers should employ specific rituals (a) at the start of a unit, (b) during the daily lessons, and (c) at the end of the unit. Each is described below.

RITUALS FOR INTRODUCING LEARNING MAPS

On the first day of a unit, the teacher usually introduces the guiding questions and learning map to give students a clear outline of what they will be learning in the unit (see Figure 4.17). During this introduction, the teacher only reveals the first level of the learning map. Students will be guided to add new information to the map as they learn it, building their maps as learning progresses. An example of an introductory learning map for a unit on narrative writing is included in Figures 4.18 and 4.19.

Students Construct Their Personal Map. Many teachers are tempted to hand out a beautifully crafted, desktop-published, complete map to students on the first day of a unit. I strongly advise against this. If students don't create their own map, or at least a part of the map, there is a good chance that their map will end up on the floor of the bus. Students need to interact with and "own" the map, and that means they need to create their own personal version.

If students can write quickly and legibly, the teacher should simply ask them to copy the map as she reveals it to them, usually on a white board, Smart Board, overhead, or document camera (my preferred method is the document camera).

Figure 4.17	Introducing the Learning Map and Guiding Questions

Download this form at www.corwin.com/highimpactinstruction

Teaching Behavior	Yes or No
The teacher takes 25 to 45 minutes to thoroughly introduce the unit.	
Students complete their personal map in their own handwriting (at least partially).	
The teacher co-constructs the map with students.	
The teacher provides many opportunities for students to respond to learning so that learning is highly interactive.	
Students store their map in a place where it will be easy for them to retrieve it.	

Figure 4.18 Sample Introductory Learning Map

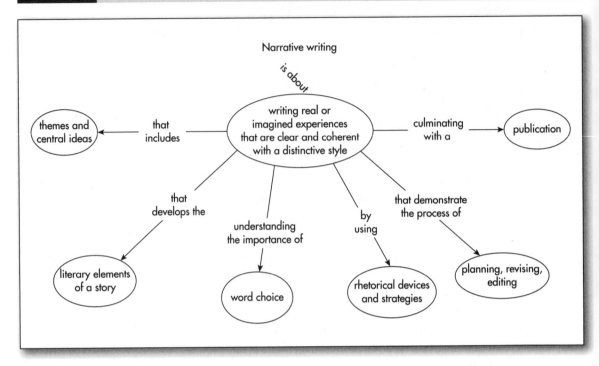

Figure 4.19 Sample Partially Completed Learning Map

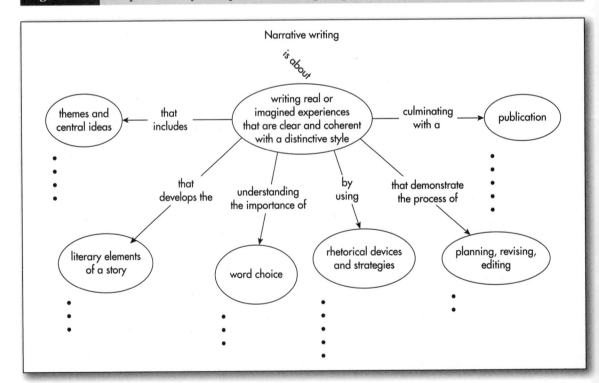

If some students struggle to write quickly and legibly, the teacher may prefer to hand out a partially completed learning map and prompt students to fill in the blanks. When this is the case, spaces need to be included on the map for all the key information that will be noted. An example of a partially completed map is presented in Figure 4.19.

The Teacher Co-Constructs the Learning Map With Students. Teachers need to create their own complete map before teaching the unit, but they should reveal the map to students in a way that feels as if the plans are being constructed in the moment, right before their eyes. The introductory class is an opportunity to light students' desire to learn all about something new, to engage their curiosity, and to lay out the exciting possibilities for the upcoming unit.

Unfolding the learning map and guiding questions in a way that excites students is an artful dance that hinges on the kinds of questions the teacher asks. Teachers need to ask questions that get to the heart of what students will learn and why it will be exciting. Indeed, perhaps the first thing teachers need to do before teaching a unit is to remind themselves of why they are passionate about the unit they are about to teach. A passionate teacher inspires passionate students. Chapter 6 contains many strategies teachers can use for effective questioning.

Students Store Their Map in an Easy-to-Retrieve Location. Teachers must ensure that students have a special place to keep their map so that they can find it quickly at the start of every day. Some teachers provide plastic sleeves that have been three-hole punched (the kind often used to protect overheads) where students place their maps and questions, and direct students to put them in the very front of their binders so that the students can easily find their maps and have them ready for the start of their class. Other teachers color code learning maps and any other handouts so that an entire unit's handouts are the same color or copy the learning maps onto a firmer stock of paper so that the form is easy to find.

Students need to be able to locate their learning map quickly before the start of class. If students forget or lose their map, they simply need to copy out another version at the beginning of class. Rewriting the map may not be highly enjoyable, but it might reinforce learning, and encourage a student not to lose the map again.

RITUALS FOR DAILY USE

Learning maps have their greatest impact on student learning when they are routinely used by teachers and students in the classroom. Maps aid understanding of advance and post organizers, and are used to record new information as it is learned and focus post organizers.

Advance Organizers. In Psychology 101, we learned that our first and last experiences are often the most memorable. Psychologists have labeled this the primacy effect and recency effect. In the classroom, this means that the first few minutes and last few minutes are prime learning times, so teachers must be especially aware of how they start and finish their class or day.

Many teachers begin their classes by focusing on the learning map. Using the map as a visual aid and asking many questions, teachers guide students to see what they will learn, why it is important, what they need to do to learn, and how the day's lesson fits with what they have already learned (see Figure 4.20).

Post Organizers. The last few minutes of class can reinforce student learning by prompting students to add newly learned content to their learning map. Teachers can also simply ensure that every class ends with a post organizer in which the teacher guides students, through questions, to discuss such topics as (a) what was learned today, (b) how it fits with the bigger ideas being learned in a unit, and (c) what will be learned the next day (see Figure 4.21).

USING MAPS ROUTINELY

Learning maps should be used routinely by both students and teachers. Students need to be guided by their teachers to develop a habit of having their map and questions out on their desk before the lesson begins. Students waste valuable learning time if they are fishing in their backpack looking for their paper when they should be engaging in classroom learning.

Teachers also have to develop habits of use if learning maps are to have full benefit for students. The truth is that teachers can create

---

Figure 4.20 Components of an Advance Organizer

Through questioning, activities, or direct instruction, guide students to an understanding of

- What will be learned
- What they need to do to learn
- How today's lesson fits with previous learning
- Why it is important

| Figure 4.21 | Daily Use of the Learning Map and Guiding Questions |

Teaching Behavior	Yes or No
Students have their map open on their desk when the bell rings to start the class.	
Class begins with a review of the content covered up until the current point in the unit.	
The learning map is used to introduce the day's lesson.	
Students record new content learned on the learning map.	
Each day ends with a review of the material depicted on the learning map.	

excellent guiding questions and then drop the ball and fail to keep using them. Needless to say, if teachers don't use the maps, they aren't of much help.

Sarah Weller, from Beaverton, Oregon, employed a simple method to develop the habit of starting and ending all her classes with learning maps. When she first introduced the idea of learning maps, Sarah told her students that she thought the maps would help them learn and that every class would begin with a review of the learning map, during which she would discuss (a) what students have learned, (b) what they will be learning today, (c) why it is important, (d) what they have to do in class, and (e) how today's learning fits with other learning they have done in the unit.

Then Sarah explained that because she really wanted them to help her remember to do all five things at the start of the class, students were to watch carefully to make sure she did each part of a complete advance organizer. "If I don't do one part," Sarah said, "I'm going to put a dollar in an envelope. Then at the end of the year, we'll decide to what charity we'll donate the money."

This little strategy ended up costing Sarah about $35.00, but it worked like a charm. The students watched Sarah with rapt attention at the start of each lesson to see if she did all the components of the advance organizer. Sarah had to face a slightly painful consequence on the days when she forgot to use an advance organizer. In the end, a charity got a small donation, Sarah developed an important instructional practice, and her students started every class with a review of what they had learned, knowing what they were learning, why it was important, what they had to do, and how their new learning fit with what they already knew.

VARY THE WAY THE MAPS ARE SHARED

Learning maps and guiding questions are high-impact instructional strategies, but they aren't effective if they put students to sleep. And if teachers share learning maps the same way every day, pretty soon students will let their teacher know they're getting tired of the same old routine.

Teachers need to vary the way they use maps with students. If each day is a new way for students to experience the map, student learning will remain fresh and alive. Teachers can keep things fresh by showing connections between learning and students' personal experiences, telling stories about what they will be learning, using the element of surprise, and using a variety of formative assessment practices to assess how well students are learning. Most of these practices are described in different sections of this book, so I will only talk about them briefly here.

Making Connections. One way teachers can make connections between students' experiences and what they are learning is through the use of a high-impact instructional strategy, thinking prompts (described in Chapter 5). For example, a highly persuasive television commercial may be shown to students to introduce the idea of persuasive writing.

Using a Variety of Checks for Understanding. In Chapter 3, I introduced a variety of checks for understanding. Teachers can mix things up by trying a different strategy every day. For example, one day students can work with a partner, and another day they can use response cards. On other occasions they can take part in a game show review or use white boards.

What matters is that the start of class does not become a boring routine. These strategies and others can help keep the learning fresh. More important, however, is that the teacher shares her passion for the unit to be learned. If students are excited about what they are going to learn, they are much less likely to complain of being bored.

END-OF-UNIT REVIEW

By the end of the unit, teachers and students will have created a highly useful study guide for the learning that has occurred as everyone has progressed through the unit. Unlike the study guides sometimes handed out at the end of a unit, this study guide is one that students have helped create and interacted with throughout the unit. By the end of a unit, a complete learning map, such as the one in Figure 4.22, will have been reviewed so many times that it should be as familiar as an old friend when students open it to study for the end-of-unit assessment.

Most teachers have their own way of conducting end-of-unit reviews prior to the final unit assessment. Learning maps simply make it easier to conduct that review. Teachers can integrate learning maps and guiding questions into their end-of-unit review by dividing students into cooperative learning groups and giving each group one guiding question to answer. Then students should be prompted to create a learning map that summarizes their answer. Students who have learned about the structure of learning maps can be asked to first identify what kind of map is most appropriate for their answer, (a) sequence, (b) description, (c) problem-solution, (d) compare-contrast, or (e) cause and effect, and then start the process of creating an appropriate map that summarizes their answer.

Figure 4.22 Complete Learning Map

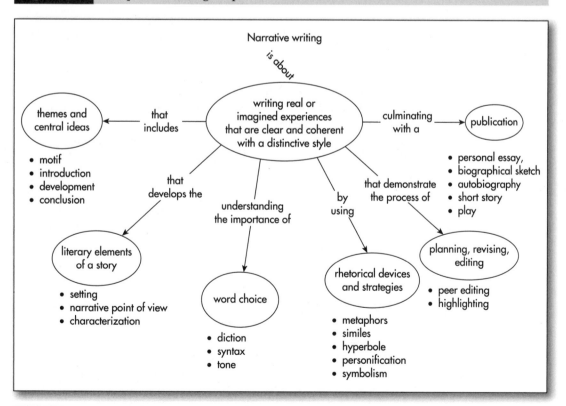

Source: This learning map was first created by Jeff Baxter, Leavenworth High School, Leavenworth, KS.

All of the components of effective cooperative learning, described in Chapter 8, should be taken into account. In some cases, students could create their map by writing all the key information on slips of paper or sticky notes, arranging the sticky notes into the organizer, and then drawing the map on chart paper, an overhead projector sheet, or a piece of paper to be shown via the document camera.

In classes with learner-friendly cultures (Chapter 10), students can choose which question they wish to answer. After the learning maps have been created, students can share their ideas via a gallery walk (see Chapter 8) or simply teach their map to the rest of the class, one group answering one question at a time.

While this process is going on, the teacher rotates from group to group to check that students' answers are correct. In some cases, the teacher will need to provide a mini-review in the middle of the students' group practice to ensure that misunderstandings are quickly corrected. In this way, the teacher also makes sure that students don't share their misunderstandings when they share their learning maps with the rest of the class.

Turning Ideas Into Action

Students

1. Most books and articles on maps (including learning maps, concept maps, clustering, mind maps, graphic organizers, thinking maps, or nonlinguistic representations) describe how maps can be used by learners to enhance their learning. Hyerle, for example, writes that "ultimately, this is about power sharing or construction of knowledge" (2009, p.13). Robert Marzano and his colleagues, in his meta-analysis of research on instruction (2001), concludes that "the more we use both systems of representation—linguistic and nonlinguistic—the better we are able to think about and recall knowledge" (p. 72). Many students benefit when they have the opportunity to construct their maps to deepen their understanding of what they are learning.

2. Teachers should discuss with their students why they are using learning maps and ask students for their feedback on what works and what doesn't work for them. Students can also give feedback on how they like to interact with the map and suggest ways in which exploration of the map can be made more meaningful, useful, or fun.

Teachers

1. The best way to learn about maps is to use them. Teachers can experiment with maps for all kinds of tasks and see what works and doesn't work for them. For example, cluster maps can be used as a prewriting strategy for reports or other writing practices or as a way to organize a day's tasks. Concept maps can be used to clarify understanding of new curricula. And mind maps can be used to take notes during professional learning workshops.

2. Many teachers use learning maps to plan their own lessons and units even though they may not at first feel comfortable sharing the maps with students. This approach may be a good starting point for some teachers, but ultimately the power of a learning map is revealed in sharing it with students.

3. An easy way to start using learning maps is to experiment with them by designing maps for lessons. After a few days of planning and sharing maps, teachers will have a better idea whether learning maps can increase student learning.

4. Teachers can gather data on how effective learning maps are by conducting action research. Such research would involve sharing maps with students in half of their classes and then comparing and contrasting the growth in achievement of students who did versus those who did not see learning maps. If learning maps are used in a lesson, comparing the results of students on formative assessments, described in Chapter 3, would help teachers make decisions about whether or not they are worth the work. Chances are that the results of such research will be enlightening.

Instructional Coaches

1. Coaches can collaborate with teachers to create learning maps by using the checklists included in this chapter.

2. Instructional coaches should develop a deep understanding of learning maps by reading this chapter carefully, studying some of the additional works referenced in the Going Deeper section, and using maps for taking notes, creating, and even taking notes on books and articles about mapping.

3. Coaches can also deepen their understanding of maps and model their use by using them in any workshops they may do on the topic.

4. Since learning maps depict knowledge, skills, and big ideas, the amount of content knowledge a coach has will affect how the coach approaches teachers. If a coach is an expert in the content being

(Continued)

(Continued)

discussed (a veteran science teacher discussing a course she loved to teach, for example), then the coach will often take on the role of being a full collaborator in developing the map. On the other hand, if an instructional coach does not have content expertise, he or she plays the role of seeing the map through the eyes of students, asking clarifying questions to increase the chances that more students will learn the content. Both roles are important. When coaches know the content, they can really push a teacher's thinking. But our research at the Kansas Coaching Project has shown that when coaches are not content experts, they are more quickly able to establish a partnership relationship, with the IC being the expert on learning maps and the coach being the expert on content.

Principals

1. The most important activity a principal can do in support of learning maps is to fight for time for teachers to reflect and create learning maps. In my experience, it takes four to five days of sustained, reflective practice for teams of teachers to write guiding questions, learning maps, and formative assessments for an entire course if the group is organized, well-functioning, and motivated. Teachers working alone will need more time to create maps.

2. A second challenge principals and other administrators face is to resist the temptation to create the questions, maps, and formative assessments and hand them out to teachers, ready to be used. What we know about knowledge work and motivation (Knight, 2011, Chapter 2) suggests that such a strategy does not change teaching practice because professionals need to be a part of the thinking if they are going to embrace something as comprehensive as new plans for guiding questions, learning maps, and assessments for a unit. A better strategy is for entire teams of teachers teaching the same course to collaboratively develop guiding questions, learning maps, and formative assessments.

What It Looks Like

Learning maps will only make a difference if students see them and use them. The checklists included here, on introducing the learning map and daily use of the map, can prompt teachers to share the maps with students and can be effectively used as tools for observing effective implementation. The checklists can be used by teachers as they watch videos of their instruction and by coaches and principals observing lessons. I've found observations work best when the observer and teacher review and modify them to fit the teachers' approach before the observation. Similarly, the quality map checklist can be used during the writing of learning maps and to review how learning maps have been constructed.

To Sum Up

Learning maps . . .

- Are visual depictions of knowledge, skills, and big ideas students will learn in a unit
- Can be included as an element of most parts of learning in a unit
- Enhance student learning by being visual, keeping students and teachers on track, making connections explicit, and being a living study guide
- Combine aspects of mind maps, concept maps, thinking maps, content structures, and nonlinguistic representations
- Include (a) a core idea (usually the main idea of the unit); (b) subtopics (usually surrounded by a geographical shape such as an oval, rectangle, or star); (c) details; (d) lines; and (e) line labels
- Are most effective if they are simple, answer all the guiding questions, and make connections explicit

Going Deeper

Writing this chapter would not have been possible were it not for all I have learned working with Keith Lenz, the editor of the Content Enhancement Routine Series and the author of the *Course Organizer Routine* (Lenz, Schumaker, Deshler, & Bulgren), *Unit Organizer Routine* (Lenz, Bulgren, Schumaker, Deshler, & Boudah, 2005), and *Lesson Organizer Routine* (Lenz, Marrs, Schumaker, & Deshler, 1993), which all have been successfully field-tested in general education classrooms characterized by significant academic diversity.

Keith Lenz's unit organizer is a comprehensive graphic organizer that includes (in addition to guiding questions and learning maps) sections for noting current, previous, and upcoming units, a schedule, and means for identifying the relationships between bits of information being learned. Anyone interested in a routine that communicates more information and that can be used for a more comprehensive advance organizer should consider experimenting with *The Unit Organizer Routine.*

The Course Organizer Routine is, as its name would indicate, an organizer for an entire course. This organizer contains sections for a course map (usually made up of all the units), course questions, critical concepts, course standards, community principles, learning rituals, and performance options. In my experience, the *Course Organizer*

Routine guides teachers to think deeply about many important aspects of their unit and provides a student tool that can be used to communicate those aspects of the course.

The *Lesson Organizer Routine* provides a tool for planning and teaching a lesson. It contains sections for background information, relationships, task-related strategies, self-test questions, a learning map, and a list of tasks. More information on Content Enhancement Routines and the research validating them may be found at www.crl.org.

David Scanlon's *Order Routine* (Scanlon, Schumaker, & Deshler, 2004) describes four different content structures, description, compare/contrast, problem-solution, and sequence, and includes a strategy students can use to create their own organizers: Step 1, open your mind and take notes; Step 2, recommend the structures; Step 3, draw an organizer; Step 4, explain it; and Step 5, recycle it. The *Order Routine* also includes guidelines for instructional routines that Scanlon's research has shown will increase learning for all students, especially students with learning disabilities.

Barrie Bennett and Robert Marzano have also created two excellent concise overviews of mapping. In *Beyond Monet: The Artful Science of Instructional Integration* (2008), Bennett provides an excellent overview of concept maps and mind maps along with descriptions of several other types of maps, including Venn diagrams, word webs, and fishbone maps. I especially appreciated Bennett's many color examples and the fact that he integrates mind mapping and concept mapping into a bigger, richer framework for teaching.

In *Classroom Instruction That Works: Research-Based Strategies for Increasing Student Achievement* (2001), Robert Marzano and his colleagues describe the research in support of nonlinguinistic representations, and they provide many useful examples of graphic organizers. A teacher can get an excellent overview of mapping by reading Bennett and Marzano's chapters.

Teachers who are interested in a more comprehensive overview of mapping can find it in David Hyerle's *Visual Tools for Transforming Information Into Knowledge* (2009), which gives the history and theoretical foundations of mappinig and organizes maps into three categories: brainstorming, graphic organizers, and conceptual maps. The book also provides a detailed overview of thinking maps. However, teachers who are primarily interested in how to use thinking maps may wish to use Hyerle's *Student Successes With Thinking Maps: School-Based Research, Results, and Models for Achievement Using Visual Tools* (2011).

Joseph Novak's *Learning, Creating, and Using Knowledge: Concept Maps as Facilitative Tools in Schools and Corporations* (1998) explains how concept maps were discovered and how their use is supported through research and theory on how humans create knowledge. Novak's book also explains what concept maps are and how they should be created. I found Novak's explanation of how concept maps integrate with Ausubuel's research (1998) on advance organizers and assimilation learning theory to be especially helpful.

My own use of cluster maps, and my interest in maps in general, was greatly influenced by Gabriel Rico's *Writing the Natural Way* (2000). I begin almost everything I write with the clustering process Rico describes, and I've used clustering to plan my day, problem solve, decide on Christmas presents, and a host of other creative activities.

Tony Buzan's *The Mind Map Book,* with the ambitious subtitle *How to Use Radiant Thinking to Maximize Your Brain's Untapped Potential* (1993), is a beautifully designed, accessible, step-by-step guide on how to create mind maps. The book makes the case that mind maps are a more natural way to create, express, and remember knowledge than more traditional methods because mind maps embody the radiant patterns of thought. Finally, the book includes exercises teachers and students can use to deepen their knowledge of and experience with mind maps.

PART II

INSTRUCTION

It is by being fully involved with every detail of our lives, whether good or bad, that we find happiness.

—Mihaly Csikszentmihalyi

During my workshops on high-impact instruction, I show a film clip from the Playing for Change project. Playing for Change involves videographers around the world video and audio recording singers and musicians all playing the same song. Then the filmmakers mash the various recordings together into one video that makes it look like everyone is playing the song at the same time. Even though the recordings were made days and thousands of miles apart, in the short films everyone plays the same song harmoniously.

The particular clip I use shows musicians around the world singing Bob Marley's "One Love." The video begins with Robert Luti playing a dobro in Livorno, Italy, and then shifts to Menyatso Nathole playing a Les Paul electric guitar in Mamelodi, South Africa, and then Menu Choo playing an acoustic guitar in Paris, France. In the less than two minutes, we see and hear singers and musicians in Kathmandu, Tel Aviv, The Congo, Johannesburg, and Umalizi.

After I show the video, I ask teachers in the workshop for their ideas on how they might use the clip as a thinking prompt with a class. Their ideas are amazing. Some suggest using the clip to prompt discussion about principles for a learning community. Others suggest using it as a catalyst for conversation about respecting diversity. I've heard ideas for using the video in every subject area, for learning outside of the classroom, for parent-welcoming sessions, and for kick-off staff meetings. One teacher even mentioned using it to teach the concept of common denominators.

After the teachers have shared a number of ideas, I propose the following scenario.

> Let's say an English teacher finds that clip and decides to use it to reinforce the concept of theme with her students. After she shows the clip, she asks her students, "Who can tell me what the theme is in that video?"
>
> One girl raises her hand and says, "I think the theme is that technology can bring us together."
>
> "Nope. That's not right. Who else wants to try?" responds the teacher, shaking her head.
>
> A boy in the class then raises his hand and says, "I think the theme is love can bring us together."
>
> The teacher shakes her head again. "No. That's not it either."
>
> The teacher keeps shaking her head and asking questions until she gets the answer she wants, her personal interpretation of the video.

When they hear this line of questioning, teachers react strongly and negatively, claiming, "Such an approach would do damage to the learning, and if the students can defend their theme, who says the teacher's version is the only right one." Some teachers go on to share their personal stories about how their love of literature was damaged by a teacher who insisted a poem meant only what she said it meant, not what they felt and thought on their own. In most discussions, most teachers disapprove of the fictional teacher's attempt to find the one right answer—her answer.

But using questions to find the right answer is not always the wrong goal for questioning. In fact, seeking the right answer is an effective strategy in some learning situations. For example, I hope the people who inspect my plane's engine before the plane takes off were asked a lot of right or wrong questions as they learned how to ensure that a plane is safe for take off. What matters is that teachers understand when to ask the questions that are appropriate for the kind of learning students are experiencing. Good questions, asked at the right time, are a catalyst for powerful, exciting, memorable learning. However, the same questions do not have the same impact for all forms of learning, and a good question for one learning situation may be an impediment to engagement, enthusiasm, and learning in another situation.

The Importance of Engagement

Choosing the right type, kind, and level of question, and using that question in the most effective way is one of five high-impact instructional strategies described in this section. Each of these strategies has been chosen because it can increase engagement and learning.

Engagement is essential for learning because students won't learn what the teacher intends for them to learn if they are off task. However, engagement is important for reasons far beyond learning what the teacher wants students to learn. Engagement is a vital part of a happy, productive, fulfilling life, and if students are allowed to spend their days, weeks, and years off task, they may not learn an incredibly important lesson—that engagement is central to a satisfying and meaningful life.

Engagement at work, for example, seems absolutely essential for success and satisfaction. Jim Loehr and Tony Schwartz, who lead the Human Performance Institute, assert that lack of engagement is the primary reason why many people find their work unrewarding. In the *Power of Full Engagement* (2003), the authors write:

> Less than 30 percent of American workers are fully engaged at work according to data collected by the Gallup Organization in early 2001. Some 55 percent are "not engaged." Another 19 percent are "actively disengaged," meaning not just are they unhappy at work, but that they regularly share those feelings with colleagues. The costs of a disengaged workforce run into the trillions of dollars. (p. 7)

At the Human Performance Institute, Loehr and Schwartz help their clients, who include a wide range of people—from professional athletes to corporate CEOs—"ignite their potential" by learning how to increase their engagement in what they do. Full engagement, the authors state, is essential for high performance. And to be "fully engaged," the authors write, "we must be physically energized, emotionally connected, mentally focused, and spiritually aligned with a purpose beyond our immediate self-interest" (p. 5). They explain,

> Full engagement begins with feeling eager to get to work in the morning, equally happy to return home in the evening and capable of setting boundaries between the two. It means being able to immerse yourself in the mission you are on, whether that is grappling with a creative challenge at work, managing a group of people on a project, spending time with

loved ones or simply having fun. Full engagement implies a fundamental shift in the way we live our lives. (p. 5)

Mihaly Csikszentmihalyi's findings from his research on happiness, which he refers to as "optimal experience," also reveal the importance of engagement. In his landmark book *Flow: The Psychology of Optimal Experience* (1990), Csikszentmihalyi explains that to study happiness, he and other researchers interviewed thousands of people from around the world. In doing so, they employed the experience sampling method, which involves asking people to wear an electronic paging device for a week and to write down how they feel and what they are thinking whenever the pager signals, which is at random times about eight times a day. The researchers gathered more than 100,000 samples of experience from different parts of the world. What they found suggests just how important engagement is to a happy life.

Csikszentmihalyi shared his research with us at the University of Kansas Center for Research on Learning. During the visit, he clarified his finding that people who are happy are almost always people who are engaged. When people achieve optimal experience, he said, they are 100% engaged in what they do. As he wrote in *Flow* (1990), "The mark of a person who is in control of consciousness is the ability to focus attention at will, to be oblivious to distractions, to concentrate for as long as it takes to achieve a goal, and not longer. And the person who can do this usually enjoys the normal course of everyday life" (p. 31). Being engaged in what we do, then, is an essential aspect of happiness.

John Gottman's research at the Gottman Relationship Institute (2002) further illustrates the vital importance of engagement. Gottman, perhaps the world's leading expert on relationships, concludes that engagement is the essential characteristic of a healthy relationship. Engagement, which he refers to as "emotional connection," leads to loving, enduring partnerships. Lack of engagement, or connection, on the contrary, most highly predicts a future divorce. Gottman writes:

Husbands headed for divorce disregard their wives' bids for connection 82 percent of the time, while husbands in stable relationships disregard their wives' bids just 19 percent of the time. Wives headed for divorce act preoccupied with other activities when their husbands bid for their attention 50 percent of the time, while happily married wives act preoccupied in response to their husbands' bids just 14 percent of the time. (p. 4)

Gottman's findings led him to conclude that the ability to connect is essential for relationships between intimate partners, parents and their children, and colleagues at work. According to Gottman (2002), "failure to connect can hinder your career. It can interfere with friendships. It can weaken your relationships with relatives, including your kids. It can even ruin your marriage" (p. 25). Furthermore, if you are not engaged, you are not able to connect. "If you don't pay attention, you don't connect. . . . Achieving . . . connection is possible with friends, relatives, and coworkers . . . [only if] . . . you are willing to give your full attention to another person and his or her feelings" (p. 66).

Engagement is essential for a successful career, a healthy marriage, and a happy life. And yet, I fear our schools may be unintentionally teaching students that a disengaged life is acceptable, even the norm. That is, when we allow students to move from class to class, day to day, and year to year, bored and not engaged by school, we allow them to develop habits of practice in which not being engaged is the norm. If we want students to grow up and embrace living, we need to teach them the rewards and pleasures of engagement. For the truly committed teacher, nothing less than 100% authentic engagement is acceptable.

What Is Student Engagement?

In *Engaging Students* (2011), Phil Schlechty identifies five levels of student involvement in learning tasks, which he divides into three categories. Category One, Engagement, Schlechty says, occurs when students (a) attend to the tasks they are engaged in, (b) are committed to the tasks—whether or not there are extrinsic rewards, (c) persist in completing the task even when the work gets difficult, and (d) find meaning and value in the tasks that are involved in the work. For example, students enthusiastically turning the pages of a new Harry Potter novel or staying up as late as they can to play a new video game are authentically engaged. Similarly, students passionately discussing an important topic or working on authentic schoolwork that they see as important or relevant are also engaged.

Category Two, Compliance, occurs when students do what they are supposed to do, even though their heart isn't in the work. According to Schlechty (2011), students can be either strategically compliant or ritually compliant. Students are strategically compliant when they do what they are supposed to do because they believe they will receive a reward if they do the work. Strategically compliant

Watch Sandi Silbernagel describe how she assesses whether students are engaged, strategically compliant, or noncompliant.

Video P2.1
www.corwin.com/
highimpactinstruction

students, Schlechty writes, "almost always have a conditional commitment to the work; they are willing to do the work only so long as the extrinsic reward is present. Remove the reward, they withdraw the effort" (p. 17).

On the other hand, students are ritually compliant when they do the minimum amount of work possible. Ritually compliant students seek any opportunity to avoid doing the work and do the smallest amount possible. These students would rather talk, move around the room, or text friends than tackle the task at hand, and if the work is difficult, they give up quickly. While not openly rebellious, the ritually compliant student tries to avoid work as much as possible.

Category Three, Noncompliance, Schlechty writes, is manifested at two levels. "Retreatism" refers to students who simply don't do the work. These students find ways to avoid the tasks at hand without calling attention to their lack of engagement. "They do nothing and bother no one." Schlechty quotes the comedian Bill Cosby in describing noncompliant students: they are skilled at "going to sleep with their eyes open" (cited in *Engaging Students*, 2011, p. 21).

"Rebellion," another form of retreatism, refers to students who openly resist engagement in learning activities. Students who are rebelling might listen to their iPod or play a video game rather than work on the assigned task. As Schlechty writes, "students who rebel are not only refusing to comply; they are choosing to fasten their attention on other matters. And sometimes what they attend to is disruptive to the work of others" (2011, p. 21).

All the high-impact teaching strategies in this book are designed to increase engagement and learning. For example, the planning and assessment strategies described in Part I have a significant, positive impact on student engagement. When teachers have a clear plan for learning, and students use learning maps to follow the plan, they are more likely to be successful, and success will lead to engagement. When students have clear targets for their learning and are clear on how well they are progressing toward those targets, they can be drawn into learning in the same way that a person can be drawn into a video game.

High-Impact Instructional Strategies

1. Thinking prompts
2. Effective questions
3. Stories
4. Cooperative learning
5. Authentic learning

Similarly, the community-building strategies presented in Part III also positively affect student engagement. When teachers create positive learning communities, teach expectations, and reinforce and correct behavior to create learner-friendly cultures, those strategies increase engagement.

In this section of the book, I describe five high-impact instructional strategies that each, in its own way, has a dramatic impact on learning and engagement:

1. **Thinking prompts**; that is, provocative devices such as video clips, works of art, or newspaper clippings that are rich in dialogue

2. **Effective questions** that reinforce and intensify different kinds of learning

3. **Stories** teachers can tell to clarify and reinforce student learning

4. **Cooperative learning** where students mediate their learning rather than being directed by the teacher

5. **Authentic learning**—activities that are relevant and meaningful for students

**Chapter 5:
Thinking
Prompts**

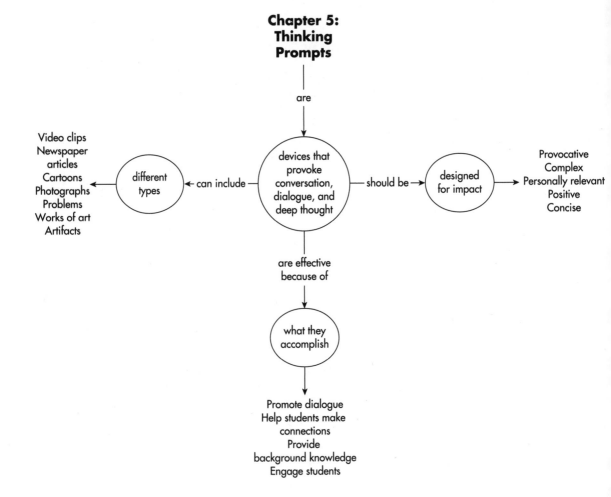

are

devices that provoke conversation, dialogue, and deep thought

can include

different types

Video clips
Newspaper articles
Cartoons
Photographs
Problems
Works of art
Artifacts

should be

designed for impact

Provocative
Complex
Personally relevant
Positive
Concise

are effective because of

what they accomplish

Promote dialogue
Help students make connections
Provide background knowledge
Engage students

5

THINKING PROMPTS

How can one learn the truth by thinking? As one learns to see a face better if one draws it.

—Ludwig Wittgenstein

Thinking is where intelligent actions begin. We pause long enough to look more carefully at a situation, to see more of its character, to think about why it's happening, to notice how it's affecting us and others.

—Margaret Wheatley

Instructional coach Shelly McBeth and language arts teacher Juli Watson worked together at Highland Park Secondary School in Topeka, Kansas. Shelly lit up when she talked about her experiences coaching Juli. "She is fabulous. Very creative . . . very constructivist. She is hyperkinetic almost. She is always doing something, always on the move, always wanting to go further. Teachers, students, everyone, she wants everyone to go deeper."

Juli and Shelly shared a deep commitment to the students at Highland Park. Many of the students faced significant challenges, with more than 88% receiving free or reduced-price lunch. "They are the students who need the most," Shelly said, "because they have the least."

Juli chose to work with Shelly because she wanted her students to have a deeper understanding of the novel they were reading, and through that novel, she wanted them to have a deeper appreciation of and love for reading in general. "Juli," Shelly told me, "wanted her students to know that there are elements woven throughout a story that make it richer and that if you understand what those elements are, you learn how to read a book and see the deeper meanings in the symbolism, themes, and relationships." In short, Juli wanted her students to love reading.

Juli chose *November's Blues* for her students to read. The novel's author, Sharon M. Draper, explains on her website that she wrote the book because she believes young adults need to read material that "recognizes that teenagers live in a stressful and confusing world and face difficult decisions every day. Instead of avoiding issues they must deal with," the author said, "I choose to address the problems they might encounter though fictional characters and situations" (Sharon Draper's comments were taken from the website sharondraper.com).

Juli believed her students would better understand how to read if they personally connected with the story. She bought extra copies of the novel so that all students could read their own book instead of having to share copies, and she even persuaded the author to fly from Ohio and spend a day at Highland Park to meet the students and discuss her work.

After talking about the novel with her instructional coach, Juli wanted Shelly to help her use thinking prompts as a way to provide important background knowledge—an understanding of the blues— and to help students connect with the novel. Juli was afraid that her students would not understand the many references to the blues throughout the novel, so she used some blues songs as thinking prompts, playing the songs and asking students to describe how the music made them feel and how the music related to what the main character in the book, November, experienced. Shelly explained:

> Music was an important factor, and Juli wanted her students to really understand the duality of the blues throughout the book. But it wasn't just about the music. It wasn't just music for the sake of being music. It was . . . there is that kind of weighty, mourning, kind of bluesy emotion that was very indicative of what the main character was feeling at the time. You know, the blues is usually about somebody who has been done wrong and whose life sucks, and Juli wanted her students to understand what the music was saying about what November was feeling. That is, there was a dual purpose to the music.

Blues music was one form of thinking prompt, but Juli also wanted to help students connect with November and her decisions. To do that, she and Shelly decided to use clips from the movie *Juno* as thinking prompts for classroom discussion about critical points in the novel. For example, Juli showed a scene where Juno, the movie's main character, told her parents she was pregnant, and the students discussed how difficult that experience might be.

Thanks to the thinking prompts, Shelly said, "there were wonderful classroom discussions around the clips about such things as social stigma and how it would feel if you were in November's position." By the end of the unit, informal assessments showed that the students had made significant gains in their learning. While the pretest results demonstrated that students didn't understand the blues or realize how understanding literary features could enhance reading, students' posttest scores were dramatically better. In fact, perhaps because they connected with the book, Shelly said, "many of the kids went on to read Sharon Draper's entire series of books."

Another teacher who uses thinking prompts masterfully is Mark Bulgutch, a professor at Ryerson University in Toronto, Canada. Mark was the chief editor for *The National*, Canada's top nighttime news program on the Canadian Broadcasting Corporation, and he occasionally taught courses within the journalism program at Ryerson. Since *The National* was the most-watched news show in Canada, and since Mark's job was to decide what would and would not be shown on the program, he played an important role in shaping what was news in Canada.

I watched Mark teach at Ryerson University, where I was also teaching at the time. His classes ignited fiery discussion and dialogue among future journalists, media liaisons, or public relations experts as they considered what news should (and should not) be shown on television. His classes led students to significant breakthroughs in their understandings, and yet he provided no direct instruction or lecturing.

What he did, instead, in his courses was simple in conception but sophisticated in reality. Mark showed provocative film clips of newsworthy items and then asked the students to talk about whether or not each clip should be shown on the news. I watched these lessons on numerous occasions, and each time, the conversation was so animated that it almost took my breath away. The discussions were so intense and powerful that course leaders sometimes scheduled two-hour breaks after Mark's class so students could cool down.

Mark was careful to pick video clips that were powerful, provocative, emotional—and sometimes profound, sometimes trivial. One clip that I will never forget showed a mother in JFK airport at the very instant she found out that her daughter had died in a plane crash. The mother's reaction was, as you can imagine, agonizing, intimate, and incredibly personal, the camera capturing every one of her movements at one of the most vulnerable points in her life. The talk in the classroom following the clip was dizzying. Some students were adamant that such a personal moment should never be shown on TV because showing the clip would be a violation of the grieving mother's right to some semblance of privacy. Others were just as convinced that the clip should be shown since it showed the intense personal consequences of real news, the weight of grief felt by those who have lost a loved one. "If you don't show the clip," they would say, "you are editing and sanitizing the news before anyone sees it."

Mark didn't tell the students what to think. He used video clips that prompted them to think and then created an opportunity for students to explore the boundaries of their own journalistic principles. Because of Mark's thinking prompts, and the dialogue they provoked, most students left the class with a much deeper understanding of their own beliefs about what constitutes news.

When I wrote Mark about his experiences teaching the class, he sent the following email: "There are usually a few students who come up to me when it's over to tell me it was the most meaningful day they've spent in college. THAT is rewarding."

What Are Thinking Prompts?

Both Juli Watson and Mark Bulgutch used video clips as thinking prompts, and for reasons discussed below, video clips, used effectively, are very effective catalysts for thought and dialogue. However, a thinking prompt, as I define it, can be any device a teacher puts in front of students to prompt thinking, discussion, and dialogue. Thinking prompts can include video clips, newspaper articles or columns, cartoons, photographs, problems, works of art, and artifacts. Even individual words can be used as thinking prompts. What matters is that the prompt, whatever form it takes, provokes discussion, dialogue, and thought. Below, we will take a look at some of the most powerful thinking prompts, including film clips, cases, short stories, poems, works of art, newspaper articles and columns, and advertisements.

Film Clips. As Juli Watson and Mark Bulgutch's classes showed, film clips can be powerful thinking prompts because they tend to engage students fully. Teachers can use short films to augment student learning in every subject area. For example, video can be used to help elementary students understand place value and to introduce high school students to statistics, to provide a context for a kindergarten story about sharing, or to prompt discussion among seniors about women's rights.

Cases. Cases, perhaps most famously developed by Harvard Business School, can also serve as effective thinking prompts. Business cases, often used in higher education, are short narratives that describe an individual or an organization at an important point in professional or personal life. As Golich, Boyer, Franko, and Lamy have written (2000), "cases recount, as objectively and meticulously as possible, real events or problems so that the reader relives the complexities, ambiguities, and uncertainties confronted by the original participants in the case" (p. 1). A case, Swanson, Elliott, and Harmon (2011) suggest,

> represents a type of dilemma or problem that arises with some frequency. The dilemmas themselves and the factors that contribute to their complexity provide the grist for focusing discussions, debates, and collaborative learning. (pp. 8–9)

But students don't have to go to Harvard to learn from cases. Teachers can prompt thought by using cases that put students at the heart of important decisions in any subject area. Students could read and discuss cases that depict people confronting environmental or ethical issues or that present mathematical problems students need to resolve.

The case format can also be used to prompt discussion of historical events or literary works. Students reading about westward migration in the United States, for example, could discuss real-life decisions that pioneers would have had to make during their journey west, and students reading novels such as *To Kill a Mockingbird* could discuss the complicated decisions the characters face at critical points in the works.

Short Stories. Teachers have always used short stories as thinking prompts, though they probably didn't refer to them in that way. For example, many teachers have used Richard Connell's *The Most Dangerous Game* as a catalyst for discussion of ethical principles related to the sanctity of life. Others have used Raymond Carver's *A Small, Good Thing* (Rubenstein, 2005) to prompt discussion of issues related to compassion, forgiveness, or community. Like cases, stories take readers inside others' thinking, and as such, they can help students reconsider their own thinking about any issue described in a case.

Poems. Poems can also serve as thinking prompts for discussing whatever topic is addressed by a poem, which can be pretty much anything. Thus, the issues raised by poets can range from ethics, as prompted by

Earl Birney's "David," to love, as prompted by E. E. Cummings' "Somewhere I Have Travelled, Gladly Beyond," to the impact technology may have on our lives, as in Wendell Berry's "How to Be a Poet," or to eating someone else's grapes in the refrigerator, as in William Carlos Williams' "This Is Just to Say." Indeed, Billy Collins' poem "Introduction to Poetry" is a great thinking prompt for discussing what poetry is and how we should experience it.

Photographs. Simple photographs can prompt spirited and meaningful discussion and dialogue. Photographs of environmental disasters or the impact of climate change shown in science or social studies classrooms, for example, can lead to lively discussion about ethical actions of businesses or policy decisions of governments. Historical photographs, such as those from the civil rights marches, can be used to provoke students to think more deeply about the significance of events or to provide a context for deeper student understanding. When used effectively as a thinking prompt, a photograph can be worth much more than a thousand words.

Words and Metaphors. Even single words can function as thinking prompts. If a teacher writes the word "respect" on the white board, for example, and asks students for their opinion on what the word means, she is using the word as a thinking prompt.

Metaphors, too, can be powerful thinking prompts. In his book *Imaginization* (1993), organizational theorist Gareth Morgan suggests that we use metaphors to broaden our thinking about topics or think more creatively by

> pursuing the implications of a resonant image or metaphor to develop new insights that can help us organize in new ways. . . . [Using metaphors as thinking prompts] . . . allows us to break free of the constraints of traditional thinking and to create the opportunity for new behaviors rooted in a new image of what one is doing. (p. 87)

As should be clear, there are many different kinds of thinking prompts, and there are also many reasons why teachers should consider using them.

Why Use Thinking Prompts?

They Promote Dialogue. Dialogue occurs when people use conversation to dig deeply into a topic and explore ideas with others. As David

Bohm (1996) has written, dialogue is "thinking together." Since dialogue is a way of communicating, where there is equality between speakers, where ideas are shared, and where every person's ideas are respected, dialogue changes the way teachers approach facilitating learning in the classroom.

Bohm's short book *On Dialogue* (1996) is a concise introduction to this way of interacting. Bohm uncovers the etymology of the word "dialogue," explaining that the original Greek meaning of "logos" is "meaning" and that the original Greek meaning of "dia" is "through." Thus, dialogue is a form of communication in which meaning moves back and forth between and through people. Bohm explains:

> The picture or image that this derivation suggests is of a *stream of meaning* flowing among and through us and between us . . . out of which will emerge some new understanding. It's something new, which may not have been in the starting point at all. It's something creative. And this *shared meaning* is the "glue" or "cement" that holds people and societies together. (p. 1)

In the *Pedagogy of the Oppressed*, Paulo Freire (1970) describes the dialogical approach to learning that he developed while working mostly with illiterate and impoverished workers in Brazil. Freire rejects traditional forms of teaching where the teacher tells the students what to do and learn, what he calls "banking education," and instead proposes problem-posing learning, where teacher and learner work together as partners. Problem-posing learning is dialogical, designed to free students through reflection, not fill them with facts.

Freire sees thinking prompts, which he refers to as "cognizable objects," as powerful tools for creating a setting where dialogue is possible. Freire writes:

> The cognizable object . . . intermediates the cognitive actors—teacher on the one hand and students on the other. . . . Through dialogue, the teacher-of-the-students and the students-of-the-teacher cease to exist and a new term emerges: teacher-student with students-teachers. The teacher is no longer merely the one-who-teaches, but one who is himself taught in dialogue with the students, who in turn while being taught also teach. (p. 67)

Thinking prompts decentralize the classroom; that is, they turn students' attention away from the teacher to something else, such as a film clip, a poem, or a newspaper column, that everyone can comment on equally, whether teacher or student. While the teacher mediates discussion, maintains some focus, mediates conflict, and calls attention to connections, in a real sense, the teacher is a learner, a participant in the dialogue just like the students. When true dialogue occurs, teachers can be as swept up in the conversation as the students are.

Parker Palmer (2009) writes about the power of thinking prompts, which he refers to as "third things," to promote dialogue and meaningful conversation. According to Palmer, teachers can use thinking prompts to explore topics metaphorically

> via a poem, a story, a piece of music, or a work of art that embodies it [the topic for discussion]. I call these embodiments "third things" because they represent neither the voice of the facilitator nor the voice of the participant. . . . Mediated by a third thing, truth can emerge from, and return to, our awareness at whatever pace and depth we are able to handle— sometimes inwardly in silence, sometimes aloud in community— giving the shy soul the protective cover it needs.
>
> Rightly used, a third thing functions a bit like the old Rorschach inkblot test, evoking from us whatever the soul wants us to attend to. (pp. 92–93)

They Help Students Make Connections. Teachers today recognize that they can increase student learning by increasing students' ability to see connections with and between the various knowledge, skills, and big ideas they are learning. Juli Watson, mentioned earlier in the chapter, for example, used thinking prompts in her class to make it easier for students to connect with the experiences of November, the central character in the novel they were reading.

Researchers on reading have long emphasized the importance of students making connections. Keene and Zimmeran (1997), for example, discussed the importance of text-to-self, text-to-text, and text-to-world connections. As Cris Tovani has written (2000), readers get a lot more out of reading when they make connections because connections, which are often increased by thinking prompts, help students empathize with characters and understand their motivation, visualize what they are reading, stay focused, set a purpose, be actively involved in reading, and remember what they have read.

They Provide Background Knowledge. Sandi Silbernagel—a teacher I met and interviewed for my program Talking About Teaching on the Teaching Channel, and whom I write about in more detail in other parts of this book—guided her second-grade students to use text-to-self, text-to-text, and text-to-world connections while they read the short story "Feliciana Feydra LeRoux: A Cajun Tale." Specifically, she used video clips and photographs to help her students better understand what it would be like for Feliciana, the central character, to venture into a swamp filled with slimy reptiles. The video she used, displayed on her Smart Board, showing alligators, snakes, and spiders, elicited gasps from the students and helped them better understand the story.

As Robert Marzano has written in *Building Background Knowledge for Academic Achievement* (2004), ensuring that students have appropriate background knowledge is one of the most important variables contributing to student learning. Marzano writes:

> What students *already know* about the content is one of the strongest indicators of how well they will learn new information relative to the content. Commonly, researchers and theorists refer to what a person already knows about a topic as "background knowledge." (p. 1)

Numerous studies have confirmed the relationship between background knowledge and achievement (Dochy, Segers, & Buehl, 1999). Thus, students who have a great deal of background knowledge in a given subject area are likely to learn new information readily and quite well.

Thinking prompts are frequently used successfully to increase student background knowledge. For example, students who see pictures of the dustbowl and discuss what life would have been like during that time will better understand John Steinbeck's *The Grapes of Wrath*. Because thinking prompts are often visual or auditory, and because they prompt students to discuss whatever they depict, they can be a window into content in any subject area, helping students see experience through others' eyes instead of their own.

They Engage Students. I have shown hundreds of thinking prompts to thousands of people, children and adults, and have seen one thing firsthand: They capture people's attention. Thinking prompts that are visual—video clips, photographs, even words or short cases visually displayed—engage learners because increasingly people are drawn to visual stimuli.

Ian Jukes, Ted McCain, and Lee Crockett, in their book *Understanding the Digital Generation* (2010), make a strong case that today's students are very visual. Citing the research of Eric Jensen and others, the authors conclude that

> at least 60 percent of students in any given classroom are not auditory or text-based learners. Increasingly, because of digital bombardment, because they think graphically, and because they've grown up in the new digital landscape, they're either visual or visual kinesthetic learners, or a combination of the two. (p. 29)

Thinking prompts also engage students in other ways. As Robert Marzano explained in *The Art and Science of Teaching* (2007), a number of studies have shown that students are engaged when they take part in a dialogue that involves mild controversy or when they have opportunities to talk about themselves. Both of these situations are frequently the outcome of the use of thinking prompts.

Finally, research on the brain suggests, what educators have always known, that variety increases engagement. Thinking prompts, like other teaching practices discussed in this section of the book, shift what occurs in the class, and consequently increase engagement. In my observations of teachers, I frequently see that every student appears to be authentically engaged when teachers use thinking prompts effectively.

What Are the Attributes of Effective Thinking Prompts?

Download a checklist for the attributes of effective thinking prompts at www .corwin.com/high impactinstruction

One of my favorite thinking prompts is a video clip of NBA basketball coach Maurice Cheeks interacting with a 13-year-old eighth-grade student, Natalie Gilbert. In the clip, Natalie, who won a Portland Trailblazer "Get the Feeling of a Star" promotion, stands before basketball fans at the Portland Trailblazers' first home game of the NBA playoffs, ready to sing the national anthem. After singing a few words, Natalie stumbles, and in front of 17,000 fans and millions of television viewers loses all composure, forgets the words, and desperately looks around for anyone who can help her. She looks absolutely terrified, and a day or two after the event, when interviewed on *The Today Show*, Natalie admitted, "I thought it was going to be the worst day of my life."

However, the day did not turn out to be the worst experience of her life. A few seconds after she stumbles, Coach Cheeks ran to her side, sang the words with her, gestured to the crowd to sing along, and compassionately communicated to Natalie that she was going to be okay. And she was! With the coach's help, the eighth grader finds her voice, and singing along with 17,000 others in the audience, the players on the court, and even Don Nelson, the opposing team's coach, Natalie finishes strong, showing she is a very accomplished and powerful singer. She told Katie Couric, "It turned out to be one of the best days of my life."

My colleague Amy Petti was at the game, and she told me about her experience: "This tiny girl, all dressed up in a prom dress, came out to sing. She looked at all the people in the stands, became overwhelmed, and just couldn't do it. All of us took in our breath and felt for this kid. Then, when Maurice Cheeks came out and fed her the words, we all just lost it, grown men—everyone—was crying and singing the national anthem."

The video of Coach Cheeks and Natalie Gilbert never fails to elicit lively conversation because it embodies several attributes of effective thinking prompts. That is, it is provocative, complex, concise, and positive, and it builds community. Each of these attributes is described below.

Provocative. The best thinking prompts are so stimulating that after experiencing them people cannot wait to talk about what they've seen or heard. The Maurice Cheeks clip certainly meets this criterion. Natalie's helplessness, the coach giving her exactly the kind of positive support she needs, and the patriotic context of the national anthem combine to create a powerful story. The clip is so provocative that on dozens of occasions when I have used it as a thinking prompt, I have watched audiences break into spontaneous applause after watching it. And it takes no prodding at all to get them to turn to each other and talk about what they have just experienced. People can't wait to talk about the video, and they do.

Complex. The Cheeks/Gilbert film clip is also effective because there are so many different ways people can see and vicariously experience what is going on. The story couldn't be much simpler: an eighth-grade student stumbles, and a gracious man provides support. But when I ask my workshop participants the simple question, "How do the actions of this athletic coach mirror the actions you like to see in an instructional coach or an instructional leader?" they offer a wide range of opinions representing many different perspectives.

Some comment that Coach Cheeks is supportive throughout, he communicates that the young girl can do it, that failure is not an option. Others point out that although the coach may not rival Pavarotti when it comes to singing, he has exactly what Natalie needs: the words and encouragement to go on. Some note that the coach had to show courage and step far beyond his comfort zone and sing in front of thousands in the stands and millions on TV. Some comment that after Natalie finished successfully, Maurice Cheeks stepped out of the way so that Natalie could be in the limelight and hear the applause. Yet others suggest that the coach's only motive appears to be to do the right thing—he wasn't going to let this little girl go down.

I have experimented with thinking prompts that have very clear, single messages, but my own and the experiences of others show that thinking prompts that provoke only one response probably don't provoke a lot of thought. The best prompts can be seen from many different perspectives; indeed, it is their complexity that makes them effective.

Personally Relevant. People are almost always moved when they see Maurice Cheeks support Natalie. For some, the clip reminds them of their own experiences, perhaps when they faltered in public or their own fear of public performance. Others think of their own children or students they have taught who have found themselves in similar circumstances. Some see Maurice Cheeks' compassion as a call to action. In a leadership workshop that I led for principals in Richardson, Texas, after I showed the thinking prompt and before I could even ask for responses, one principal shouted out, "That's what I want to do right there. I want to do that for children." Her colleagues applauded and agreed.

Such is the impact of a great thinking prompt. It speaks to us personally, and because it feels like the prompt speaks directly to our individual selves, we are drawn in and compelled to think, respond, and share ideas. Students take good thinking prompts personally, and for that reason, they are more likely to learn important information.

Positive. When I show different groups Maurice Cheeks' compassionate, supportive actions, I often witness a shift in the group's culture. After seeing a moving depiction of a person who cares, who is respectful, and who treats another with such humanity, groups are often inclined to adjust their interactions to be more respectful and humane. As Daniel Goleman explained in his book *Social Intelligence* (2006), emotions are infectious, and thinking prompts that communicate positive emotions can have a salutary impact on the mood of a community of learners. For this reason, teachers should recognize that everything they do shapes the culture of their learning community.

It is true that after I show the Maurice Cheeks film clip, I always feel a palpable difference in the way people talk and listen with each other, but not every thinking prompt can exclusively promote positive emotions. In Mark Bulgutch's classes, which explore the boundaries of what can be shown on TV, Mark had to show some clips that communicated very negative emotions. Teachers need to simply recognize that each thinking prompt will impact the culture in their classroom. For more on this, see Chapter 10, Learner-Friendly Culture.

Concise. The Cheeks/Gilbert clip is also effective simply because it isn't too long (it is only a second or two longer than it takes most people to sing the U.S. national anthem). The fact that the clip packs so much into a short amount of time intensifies the viewers' experience and increases the thinking prompt's effectiveness.

When video clips that are too long are used as thinking prompts, they can lose their power to evoke emotion, conversation, and thought in an audience. In fact, I use many clips that are less than a minute long. When a thinking prompt is provocative, personally relevant, complex, positive, and concise, you have the makings of an effective thinking prompt. Shorter clips also leave more time for thinking and learning.

How to Use Thinking Prompts

How a teacher uses thinking prompts in a classroom depends on whether the teacher takes a constructivist or intensive-explicit approach to teaching. A simple television commercial for a well-known airline, for example, would be used in completely different ways for intensive-explicit and constructivist learning.

The commercial is a cartoon that tells the story of a young man who flies to a distant city to interview for a job. Along the way, he realizes, to his horror, that he is wearing one brown and one black shoe. He goes through an intense interview, leaving the interview dejected, sure he didn't get the job because of his shoes. Eventually, however, he receives a call telling him that he landed the job. On the flight home, a kind-looking flight attendant covers him with a blanket as he sleeps, and the ad concludes with a voice-over: "Where you go in life is up to you. There's one airline in life that can take you there . . ."

Intensive-Explicit. When teachers use thinking prompts for intensive-explicit instruction, they use the prompt to ensure that students have a clear and correct understanding of the knowledge, skills, or big ideas they are learning. That is, the teacher wants the students to see what they are learning just as she sees it. A teacher who uses the airline commercial as a thinking prompt for intensive-explicit teaching, for example, could use the clip to illustrate the elements of a story and lead students to identify the settings, plot elements, conflict, character, point of view, and theme elements in the 60-second cartoon. Indeed, a teacher might even use a simple graphic organizer such as the one in Figure 5.1 to solidify every student's learning.

When teachers use thinking prompts for intensive-explicit learning, they accomplish something important: They provide helpful anchors for student learning. Many studies have shown that students remember information when they can anchor learning in something else. Malcolm Gladwell, in his book *The Tipping Point: How Little Things Can Make a Big Difference* (2000), gives us a name for such anchoring: stickiness. Gladwell writes, "the hard part of communication is often figuring out how to make sure a message doesn't go in one ear and out the other. Stickiness means that a message makes an impact. You can't get it out of your head. It sticks in your memory" (p. 25).

Gladwell's comments are especially applicable to teachers. When a teacher uses a TV commercial to anchor student learning about the elements of a story, perhaps more than anything else, she is making that learning "sticky."

| Figure 5.1 | Graphic Organizer |

Story Elements	Examples
Settings	Apartment, airplane, boardroom, city street
Character	Our hero is a flat character
Plot	**Exposition:** Our hero is tying his tie for his job interview **Rising Action:** He's got mismatched shoes; he goes to the job interview **Climax:** He gets the job **Falling Action:** Flight attendant covers our hero with a blanket **Resolution:** Final comment by announcer
Conflict	His shoes don't match
Point of view	Third person
Theme	This airline will help you get where you decide to go

Constructivist Learning. When teachers use thinking prompts for constructivist reasons, on the other hand, their goal is to push student thinking, to broaden students' perspectives, to provide an opportunity for students to consider an idea from multiple perspectives. There is no right answer when a teacher uses thinking prompts for constructivist learning. The critical thing is to create a dialogue that prompts everyone, including the teacher, to test her or his assumptions. There is no single right answer because each person's personal response is what is desired.

If a teacher was to use the airline commercial thinking prompt for constructivist learning, perhaps as an introduction to a persuasive writing unit, she might show the commercial and ask a few simple questions: Were you persuaded by this video? Does the video make you want to fly on that airline? Why were you persuaded? Why not? Teachers might even show a few other commercials, or share photos of billboards, magazine advertisements, and other print advertisements and have students compare and contrast perspectives on the learning.

Once students have explored persuasion from multiple perspectives, the teacher could then point out connections to content to be learned, such as Aristotle's rhetorical appeals to emotion, credibility, and logic. In this way, the dialogue around persuasion would provide a context or anchor for learning, and eventually student writing.

Wendy Hopf discusses thinking prompts and effective questions.

Video 5.1
www.corwin.com/
highimpactinstruction

Six Suggestions for Sharing Thinking Prompts

Whether teachers use thinking prompts for intensive-explicit or constructivist reasons, several other issues should be considered. In my experience, the following suggestions are important:

1. Establish respectful norms for all classroom dialogue (respect each response, listen to others before you start talking, wait until the speaker is finished before raising your hand to talk, don't blurt out responses, and so forth). There are no "right" norms. Each class and teacher is unique, but it is important that classroom norms be consistent. (Chapter 10 in Part III provides extensive information on how to create a learner-friendly environment.)

2. Use the right kind, type, and level of question. Each of these distinctions is explained in detail in Chapter 6, Effective Questions.

3. Listen empathetically to all student responses.

4. Encourage students by frequently offering authentic praise. When students' comments are convoluted or confusing, listen intently to decipher the main idea. Then paraphrase it using simple language and, finally, ask the student if you've heard her or him correctly.

5. Suggest connections between various ideas offered by students.

6. Keep the dialogue session short enough so that all students remain engaged but long enough to prompt meaningful reflection.

Turning Ideas Into Action

Students

1. Many teachers ask students to bring their own thinking prompts to class to promote discussion and dialogue.

2. Students can learn to lead classroom discussion around thinking prompts, perhaps learning to ask the appropriate type, kind, and level of questions as described in Chapter 6.

3. Asking students to identify thinking prompts that depict examples and non-examples of concepts can help students with concept acquisition (Bennett & Rolheiser, 2008) and can broaden or deepen their knowledge, skills, or big ideas.

Teachers

1. The challenge with thinking prompts at first is to find them. Teachers need to become detectives, always on the lookout for the photograph, advertisement, or video clip that can create meaningful dialogue. Frequently, great thinking prompts can be found by doing a Google search or searching YouTube for a theme. When I typed in "statistics" recently on YouTube, for example, I found many excellent clips I could use for thinking prompts.

2. Teachers can also make finding thinking prompts a part of many everyday experiences. When I read a magazine, go to a movie, or surf through YouTube, I try to keep in mind that the next scene in the movie could be a perfect thinking prompt. This is not to say that teachers need to spend every minute on the hunt for the next big thinking prompt, but if they are sitting through a movie, for example, that wasn't their choice and they are not particularly enjoying it, looking for thinking prompts might make the experience a little more enjoyable.

Instructional Coaches

1. Like teachers, coaches need to be on the lookout for thinking prompts.

2. Coaches can create a digital bank of prompts that they can share with others. If possible, an instructional coach can make the bank available digitally to all teachers in a district.

3. Instructional coaches should also be skilled at observing time on task (described in Part III) and helping teachers design and use formative assessments (described in Chapter 3). Time-on-task data can help teachers see whether or not student engagement is increased through the use of thinking prompts, and results from formative assessments can indicate whether or not thinking prompts are helping students learn the knowledge, skills, and big ideas in the class.

Principals

1. Principals should encourage conversation about thinking prompts so that the term is recognized and used frequently by educators.

2. Principals can encourage the use of thinking prompts by using them in their own presentations. For example, they can show short clips of teachers on the Teaching Channel during workshops they lead and encourage teachers to share their perspectives on what they see. In addition, principals might share cases, short articles, or other thinking prompts and then ask effective questions (as described in Chapter 6) to initiate dialogue during meetings and presentations.

What It Looks Like

When people observe the use of thinking prompts (teachers watching themselves on video, instructional coaches, or principals), several data points are important. First, they can observe for time on task as described in Chapter 12 to see if the prompt is truly increasing engagement. Second, they can observe students' test results or check for understanding to see if learning that is explored through a thinking prompt is different than learning without thinking prompts. Third, they can observe to gather data on how much time teachers talk versus how much time students talk. Finally, they can look at the type, kind, and level of questions being asked during discussion of thinking prompts. Effective questioning is described in the next chapter.

To Sum Up

- Thinking prompts are devices that provoke conversation, dialogue, and deep thought.

- They can be video clips, newspaper articles and columns, cartoons, photographs, problems, works of art, and artifacts.

- Thinking prompts promote dialogue, help students make connections, provide background knowledge, and engage students.

- Effective thinking prompts are provocative, complex, personally relevant, positive, and concise.

Going Deeper

Parker Palmer's *A Hidden Wholeness* (2004) addresses topics far beyond the scope of most books on teaching. As he explains, this book is about life, community, teaching and learning for transformation, and nonviolent social change. The primary readership are facilitators who lead groups of adults and various forms of professional learning communities. However, the book beautifully describes how thinking prompts, which Palmer refers to as "third things," can be used to facilitate meaningful dialogue. The book has also taught me a great deal about how to live and integrate my private and professional life.

Paulo Freire's *Pedagogy of the Oppressed* (1970) is for me a "desert-island book" (if I could take only 10 books with me to a desert island, this would be one of them). The book is not an easy read; for me, it reads like a complex poem that requires multiple readings. Like a great poem, however, repeated reading of the book is highly rewarding. Freire's defense of humanity in instruction, his argument for dialogue, reflection, and praxis, are foundational ideas within my work, and I believe any teacher will find that deeply reflecting on what he has to say will be rewarding. Freire's discussion of "cognizable objects" as vehicles for creating dialogue provides another perspective on thinking prompts.

Many authors have written excellent works on the concept of dialogue; I have found two books to be especially helpful. William Isaac's *Dialogue* is a comprehensive and very practical major work (399 pages on dialogue) that, to my mind, is the most extensive treatment of the topic. David Bohm's *On Dialogue* (1996) is a concise (less than 60 pages) but extremely wise introduction to dialogue. Most people who write on the topic of dialogue, including Isaacs, are deeply indebted to the simple and powerful ideas in Bohm's work. A teacher who wishes to increase dialogue in the classroom can learn a great deal from both authors.

Chip and Dan Heath's *Made to Stick: Why Some Ideas Survive and Others Die* (2007) is an extended riff on the concept of stickiness in Malcolm Gladwell's *Tipping Point* (2000). The authors "poured over hundreds of sticky ideas" (p. 16) and concluded that six ideas over and over are at work: simplicity, unexpectedness, concreteness, credibility, emotions, and stories.

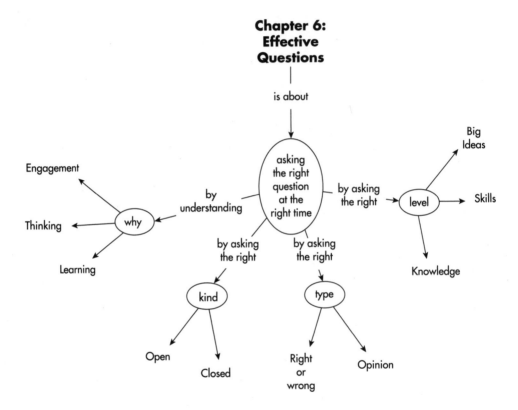

**Chapter 6:
Effective
Questions**

is about

asking
the right
question
at the
right time

by
understanding

why

Engagement

Thinking

Learning

by asking
the right

kind

Open

Closed

by asking
the right

type

Right
or
wrong

Opinion

by asking
the right

level

Big
Ideas

Skills

Knowledge

6

EFFECTIVE QUESTIONS

Always the beautiful answer who asks a more beautiful question.

—E. E. Cummings

When I interviewed instructional coach Marti Elford about her experiences working for the Kansas Coaching Project, she was quick to tell me that she wanted to talk about questioning. "It's powerful," Marti said. "I've seen how effective it can be." Effective questioning, she told me, "raises engagement in the student population and forces teachers to think about what their instruction is really doing and how they can facilitate the learning of students."

Marti told me about collaborating with Lana Thompson (not her real name), an English teacher who came to Marti for assistance. "To her credit," Marti said, she wanted "to learn to ask better questions." Despite her 25 years of experience, Lana knew she had to change the way she taught. A few days after their initial conversation, Marti was observing her teaching *Macbeth*.

When Marti observed the class, she told me "it was staggering." Mrs. Thompson "had a number of questions, but she was asking the same thing. They were all clarifying questions . . . She was asking, 'Who did Macbeth encounter?' 'What were the witches around?'" Low-level, clarifying questions had become "a behavioral habit . . . that was her way of engaging students."

The students, Marti said, "weren't learning anything. A couple of kids in the front row had their heads on their desks, and many of the students were doing something else, drawing, reading a book, or doing homework from another class. A few were looking at Mrs. Thompson, and every once in a while she'd point to one and the child would answer, but students didn't even have to read the section to be able to answer the questions . . . So their minds were not engaged even if their bodies were."

Marti noted on a form, similar to one included later in this chapter, every question that Lana asked. After the class, coach and teacher met to review the data. Lana was very surprised to see how many questions she had asked, and when she and Marti coded the questions, it became clear that almost all of them were low-level, closed questions. Marti said, "I think that in that particular lesson she had asked two open questions and probably 50 that were closed."

After reviewing the data, Marti and Lana met again to plan for a different approach to questioning. Marti asked Lana to identify the instructional goal ahead of the meeting. Then together they constructed questions that "would be like a roadmap to get to that instructional goal." After a lot of collaboration, they had come up with "five or six really big questions for that 90-minutes class." Lana was all set to try a different approach in the next lesson.

When Mrs. Thompson tried out the new questions, Marti said, "it was laborious . . . it looked unnatural; she felt unnatural; extremely uncomfortable. Her body language just said, 'I don't like this.'" But Lana persevered. "I mean, she could look out at the class and see that the students weren't engaged; her test scores were low; and she was dissatisfied with her own performance. So even though it was uncomfortable, she was willing to do whatever it took."

At first, Marti said, "the kids just looked at her as if to say, who are you and what have you done with our teacher?" But bit by bit the students "started actually paying attention to what was being said." As the class progressed, the students stopped sleeping and started, Marti said, "feeding off of each other." By the end of the class, there was "this flurry of engagement . . . and every kid in the class except two or three wanted to offer their opinion."

The students "had gone from having their heads on the desk to having a conversation . . . a dramatic change." According to Marti, the percentage of students authentically engaged went from maybe 2% in the first class to better than 90% in the second class. "That one thing made such a big difference, and I might not have figured that out on my own," Marti admitted. "I stumbled onto something really great because this teacher was interested in making a change."

What Marti learned firsthand when she collaborated with Lana was that, as she told me, "planning questions ahead of time, being strategic about how to ask those questions, and learning when to use certain types of questions can have a profound impact on how students are learning."

Why Should Teachers Reflect on the Effectiveness of Their Questions?

My own experiences mirror Marti's—choosing and using the right kind, type, and level of question is one of the most important aspects of high-impact instruction. In my observations, when classroom conversation is dull and lacks energy, it is often because the teacher is trying to move conversation forward with questions that generally provoke simple, short responses that don't require much thought. Mrs. Thompson's questions about *Macbeth* ("Who was around the cauldron?" "What did the witches prophesize?") did little to stimulate thought, and consequently, the students were not engaged during the lesson. In a classroom where low-level questions are being asked, there can be a palpable lack of engagement, thinking, and learning. Students look like they are barely awake, and observers who watch the class might think that the students don't care about their learning at all.

If those same observers were to see the students in the cafeteria, however, they might see that the students can have extremely animated conversations about the latest video game, who should be the number one ranked college basketball team, politics, the upcoming play they are in, or the events that are happening in the lives of friends and family. If students are interested in a topic, chances are they will be very engaged in it.

The challenge for teachers is to ask questions that prompt the same level of engagement, thought, and (ultimately) learning that take place during high-energy cafeteria conversations. Good questions engage students intellectually; they hook students and get them thinking. Once students are engaged and thinking, learning happens.

In this chapter, I describe different (a) types (open and closed); (b) kinds (right or wrong); and (c) levels (knowledge, skill, big idea) of questions. I also discuss where and how each type, kind, and level of question should be used.

Type of Question: Open or Closed

Open Questions. The terms *open* (or *open-ended*) and *closed* (or *closed-ended*) are used almost every time people talk about questions in schools, and yet there are no universally agreed-upon definitions for these terms. A quick web search for open and closed questions shows that there are lots of definitions. Usually, authors refer to the length of the answer produced by a question. An open question prompts a long response; a closed question provokes a short response. In my work with instructional coaches, however, I've found it helpful to adopt a more precise working definition to ensure clarity during conversations about types of questions.

I define open questions as those that have an unlimited (or open) number of responses (see Figure 6.1). For example, if you ask, "What do you like about The Beatles?" there are many different ways to answer the question. People could talk about the way The Beatles continuously revised "Sergeant Pepper" until it was exactly how they wanted it to be. They could talk about how much they enjoyed the Fab Four's acting in the film *A Hard Day's Night*. Or people might relate their memories of the first time they heard "Hey Jude" or tell you why they like The Beatles' politics. The number of possible answers can't be counted, and that is what makes the question, for our purposes, an open question.

Closed Questions. Closed questions, as I define them, are the opposite of open questions in that they have a finite number of possible answers (see Figure 6.2). If you keep answering a closed question correctly, eventually you will get to a point where no more correct answers are left. For example, if you ask, "What are all the capital cities of the Canadian provinces?" the person answering the question will either run out of cities he can name or reach the point where he has named all 10 cities (with extra points for naming the capital cities of the three territories). Since the possible number of answers for a closed question is limited, at some point the question can be

Figure 6.1 Sample Open Questions

What would you do if you were the president when Pearl Harbor was bombed?

How does Pablo Neruda use images to move his reader?

What is an example of a system at work in nature?

How would you solve this problem?

How do people act when they treat each other with respect?

How do we decide what is good or bad behavior?

| Figure 6.2 | Sample Closed Questions |

How old are you?

What is the setting of the story?

Which word in the sentence is an adverb?

How is the periodic table organized?

What is the Pythagorean theorem?

What would be the five albums you'd take to a desert island?

completely answered. That is, every closed question has a complete response even though the person answering the question may not give the complete response.

Most frequently, closed questions elicit short answers, but again, what defines a closed question is not the length of the answer but the finite number of possible answers. The question "What are the names of all the communities in Kansas?" would require a very long response if it was complete, but it would still be a closed question as we define it.

You can visualize the difference between the two types of questions by imagining a closed and an open field. A closed field would be surrounded by a fence, and someone running in the field would only be able to go as far as the fence allowed. An open field, on the other hand, would have no fences, so a runner could run as far as she wished with no barriers to limit how far she could go. A closed question, like a fenced-in field, is finite, with a limited number of responses. An open question, like an open and unfenced horizon, theoretically, has an infinite number of responses.

Neither type of question is necessarily good or bad, and open questions are not superior to closed questions in all circumstances. However, when classroom conversation is dull and lacks energy, it is often because the teacher is trying to move conversation forward with closed questions when open questions would be more likely to provoke real thinking.

When closed questions are effective, it is usually when they are used to confirm and check student understanding. I have seen many stimulating classes, with 100% engagement and with students sitting literally on the edge of their chairs ready to reply to the next question, when teachers use questions to confirm student understanding through verbal practice.

Jean Schumaker and Jan Sheldon, in *The Sentence Writing Strategy* (1985), explain how closed questions can be used to confirm understanding and maintain engagement while students learn a strategy for correctly writing different types of sentences:

> Before students are asked to use the strategy, they must learn to define certain concepts and name the strategy steps at an automatic level. During this instructional stage, therefore, you will ask students to verbally rehearse the definitions of important terms and strategy steps.... The Verbal Practice stage can be very effectively and quickly carried out with a group of students through "rapid-fire" practice. Using this method, you will point to each student in succession, and require the contribution of the next definition or the next step of the strategy. (p. 5)

Closed questions embedded within a verbal practice stage of instruction can be a very effective way to determine whether or not students have memorized key vocabulary. However, knowing the steps of a strategy and using them in writing are two different proficiencies. That is why the verbal practice that Schumaker and Sheldon describe is part of an eight-stage, intensive-explicit instructional process that involves (a) generating student commitments, (b) describing, (c) modeling, (d) verbally practicing, as described above, (e) controlled practice, (f) advanced practice, (g) generating student commitments to generalization, and (h) generalization (Ellis, Deshler, Lenz, Schumaker, & Clark, 1991).

Just asking closed questions would do little to move students toward mastery and integration of learning, but embedding the questions within such an intense and explicit sequence of instruction can be very effective.

Some teachers don't employ intensive-explicit instructional practices and, therefore, rarely ask closed questions. Other teachers dedicate a great deal of time to intensive-explicit instruction and, therefore, ask a large number of closed along with open questions. What matters here is that the right question is asked for the right instructional goal, and the same distinction is true for the kind of question asked.

Kind of Question: Right or Wrong or Opinion

Right or Wrong Questions. Right or wrong questions, as the term suggests, have correct or incorrect answers (see Figure 6.3). The

| Figure 6.3 | Sample Right or Wrong Questions |

Who is the prime minister of Canada?

What is the subject of the sentence?

What are the steps of the scientific method?

What are the definitions for mean, median, and mode?

When did you start going to spin class?

purpose of a right or a wrong question is to determine whether or not students understand something that has been taught or learned. In most cases, right or wrong questions are closed questions.

According to Jackie Acree Walsh and Beth Dankert Sattes (2004), who cite the research of Gall (1984), about 80% of questions are low-level, fact, recall, or knowledge questions, all forms of right or wrong questions. As with closed and open questions, there is nothing inferior or superior about right or wrong questions, but teachers must be careful to use them when they are appropriate.

Opinion Questions. In contrast to right or wrong questions, opinion questions don't have right or wrong answers; in fact, it is very difficult to give an incorrect answer to a skillfully crafted opinion question (see Figure 6.4). For example, if you ask someone, "What did you think of the movie tonight?" you are prompting the person to give his opinion, not checking to see what he knows or doesn't know. Opinions are personal and individual, so he can only answer the question correctly, giving his opinion.

Opinion questions are effective catalysts for conversation because they remove the main reason why many students (children and adults alike) don't speak up in class—they are afraid of giving an incorrect answer in front of their peers. Since they can't be wrong when they are asked to share their opinion, students are much more willing to participate in classroom discussion when teachers use this approach to questioning. Indeed, the single most common barrier to lively discussion I see when observing teachers is that they use closed, right or wrong questions to start a discussion when open, opinion questions would be much better prompts for discussion.

Nevertheless, while most opinion questions are open questions, this is not always the case. If you asked, "On a scale of 1 to 10, how much did you like the show?" that would be a closed question, but it

Figure 6.4 Sample Opinion Questions

What is your opinion of the president?

What would you do if you were the character at this point in the story?

What is a puzzle in nature that you would like to understand?

Do statistics make sports more or less interesting for you?

Chris Korinek talks about questions.

Video 6.1
www.corwin.com/
highimpactinstruction

is also an opinion question. As with all answers to opinion questions, whatever you say is precisely and correctly your opinion.

Levels of Questions: Knowledge, Skills, and Big Ideas

As explained in Part I of this book, several taxonomies have been created to identify levels of questions. Teachers can use any of them to identify the appropriate level for their questions, and any of the taxonomies prompts us to think more deeply about questions. I have found it helpful, as have many others, including Keith Lenz (2004), Lynn Erickson (2007), and Art Costa (2009), to consider three levels of questions. As I've written in Chapter 2, the three levels of questions for high-impact instruction are knowledge, skills, and big ideas.

Knowledge Questions. Knowledge questions prompt students to demonstrate that they can remember information they have learned (see Figure 6.5). Knowledge questions are frequently closed questions.

Skill Questions. Skill questions prompt students to apply their knowledge to new situations or settings (see Figure 6.6). Simply put, skill questions prompt people to explain how to do something, and they are often open or closed.

Figure 6.5 Sample Knowledge Questions

What is 4×4?

What is a noun?

What are the five steps of the strategy?

What are some countries that border Tanzania?

| Figure 6.6 | Sample Skill Questions |

Given what we've learned about how to read poetry, what do you think this poem is meant to convey?

How can you use what we have learned about problem solving in math to solve a personal problem?

What are the implications of what we have learned about the Vietnam War for future U.S. foreign policy?

Big Ideas. Big idea questions communicate the themes, concepts, overarching ideas, and content structures that recur throughout a course (see Figure 6.7). Big idea questions prompt students to demonstrate that they comprehend the implications of the information they have learned. They are the questions that often lead students to "aha," deeper insights. Such questions are usually open.

The high-impact questions described here are by no means the only way to rethink questioning. Additional ways of thinking about questions are suggested below. However, my experience has shown that considering the type, kind, and level of question is a great place to start improving questioning skills.

Improving Questioning Skills

Improving questioning, like many forms of learning, involves seeing the world around us (in this case, our methods of questioning) clearly and in new ways. Without a strategy for clearly looking at their questions, teachers may not improve in the ways that they would like and that would most help their students. In *Quality Questioning: Research-Based Practice to Engage Every Learner* (2005), Walsh and Sattes summarize a

| Figure 6.7 | Sample Big Idea Questions |

How did the geographical differences between the North and the South lead to the start of the Civil War?

What does the structure of a tragedy suggest about human nature?

What would happen if you injected pure water into an animal cell and how do you know this?

If you dropped a 10-pound rock and a 1-pound rock from the top of the Empire State Building, which would hit the ground first?

study (Susskind, 1979) suggesting that teachers often don't have a clear understanding of the way they question students.

Susskind reports that during the study, teachers were asked four questions:

- How many questions do you think you ask in a 30-minute period?
- How many questions would be desirable?
- How many questions do your students ask?
- How many questions would be ideal?

On average, participants responded that the correct number of questions to ask was 15, and they believed that they asked 15 questions during their lessons. Teachers also said they thought the correct number of questions students should ask was 15 and that they thought students in their classes asked 10. The reality was quite a bit different, however. On average, teachers asked 50.6 questions (many more than the predicted number of 15), and students asked 1.8 questions (many fewer than the predicted number of 10; see Figure 6.8).

Improving questioning skills usually begins with the teacher getting a clear picture of current reality. In addition, learning how to improve questioning, like learning many other things, involves finding new perspectives on our reality. Teachers need to have a way to see their questions from new perspectives. When teachers understand the concepts of open and closed, opinion and right or wrong, and knowledge, skill, and big idea questions, they have a way of seeing that will enable them to make significant changes in how they ask questions.

Figure 6.8   Questioning Skills: Teacher Predictions Versus Reality

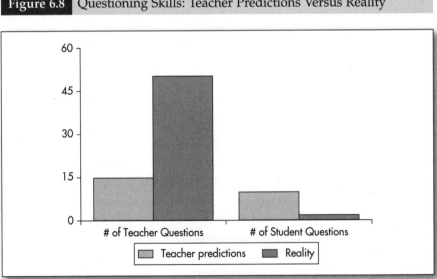

Coaches working with the Kansas Coaching Project use a simple method to get a clear picture of the type, kind, level, and number of questions being asked. As Marti Elford did when she coached Lana Thompson, instructional coaches note every learning-related question spoken by the teacher and then meet with the teacher to code the kind, type, and level, often using the question chart in Figure 6.9.

Figure 6.9	Question Chart

Download this form at www.corwin.com/highimpactinstruction

Question	Type	Kind	Level

Type: Right or Wrong, Opinion

Kind: Closed-ended, Open-ended

Level: Know, Understand, Do

Other Ways of Looking at Questions

At the Kansas Coaching Project, we have found that analyzing the type, kind, and level of questions is an excellent way of improving questions, but there are other approaches coaches use. Other ways of looking at questions are described below.

Bloom's Taxonomy. As I've mentioned at different points in this book and this chapter, Bloom's taxonomy of educational objectives (1956) is frequently referenced when people discuss questions. Indeed, when my colleagues and I at the Kansas Coaching Project first began studying teacher questions, we started by coding questions into the six levels proposed by Bloom: Knowledge, Comprehension, Application, Evaluation, Analysis, and Synthesis.

Bloom's Levels of Questions

- Knowledge
- Comprehension
- Application
- Evaluation
- Analysis
- Synthesis

Quality Questions. In *Quality Questioning: Research-Based Practices to Engage Every Learner* (2005), Walsh and Sattes marshal extensive research to support their assertion that "quality questions and questioning are at the heart of good teaching and learning" (p. v). They describe four criteria for quality questions: quality questions "(1) promote one or more carefully defined instructional purposes, (2) focus on important content, (3) facilitate thinking at a stipulated cognitive level, (4) communicate clearly what is being asked" (p. 23).

Walsh and Sattes' Criteria for Quality Questions

- Promote one or more carefully defined instructional purposes
- Focus on important content
- Facilitate thinking at a stipulated cognitive level
- Communicate clearly what is being asked

Constructivist and Intensive-Explicit Questions. The distinction between constructivist and intensive-explicit instruction should also shape the kind, type, level, and frequency with which teachers ask questions. During intensive-explicit instruction, the teacher uses questions primarily to check for understanding and keep students engaged. For that reason, during intensive-explicit instruction, teachers often ask closed, right or wrong, knowledge questions, and ask a lot of them in a short period of time. Indeed, research on intensive-explicit instruction suggests that teachers should ask at least four questions every minute to maintain student engagement (Council for Exceptional Children, 1987).

During constructivist instruction, the teacher uses questions primarily to push thinking, to prompt deeper thought, and to provide a setting where students can make personal connections with learning and explore learning from multiple perspectives. For that reason, during constructivist instruction, a teacher's line of questioning is the opposite of a teacher's during intensive-explicit learning. During constructivist instruction, teachers ask a small number of open, opinion, big idea questions. Indeed, one or two questions are often sufficient to prompt a powerful classroom conversation. Too many questions will inhibit classroom learning (see Figure 6.10).

One of the most important things teachers can do is determine what kind of learning they are involved in and then make sure they have the kind of questions that are appropriate for that kind of learning.

Using Questions Effectively With Students

Ask Questions of All Students. If questions are to keep all students engaged, then all students must know that they are responsible for answering all questions. When teachers name a student and then ask a question, what often happens is that most, if not all, of the other students in the room stop doing the thinking that is being prompted by the question. However, when a teacher poses a question, pauses for all students to think about the answer, and then calls on a student, many more students do the thinking prompted by the question.

Hands Up, Hands Down. Whether or not students raise their hands to answer a question depends on the purpose of the question and the teacher's pedagogical style. Generally, during intensive-explicit instruction, I suggest that teachers don't ask students to raise their hands so that all students know they may be called on to answer the question (often a closed, right or wrong question). During the free-wheeling discussion and dialogue of constructivist instruction,

Figure 6.10	Intensive-Explicit or Constructivist Questions	

Question	Intensive-explicit	Constructivist
Type	Closed	Open
Kind	Right or wrong	Opinion
Leve	I Knowledge or skill	Big idea
Number of Questions	Many: Up to more than four per minute	Few: As few as one to five per lesson

however, asking students to raise their hands allows a teacher to mediate classroom discussion and provides a procedure that allows more students to engage in the conversation. Having students raise their hands also recognizes that in some cases students may not wish to share their opinions for discussion.

Everyone Answers the Question They Are Asked. During intensive-explicit instruction, to maintain engagement, I recommend that teachers use a simple routine to make sure that everyone answers every question and no one is ever allowed to say those three counterproductive words: "I don't know." The routine is repeat, rephrase, reduce, reach out.

Repeat

The first response to a student who says "I don't know" is to simply repeat the question. For example, if you ask, "What are the subject and the predicate of the sentence?" and a student says those three words, "I don't know," you simply repeat the question, exactly as you first posed it.

Rephrase

It is surprising how effective it is to merely repeat the question. However, if that method leads to a repeat utterance of the three nasty words, the second step of this strategy is to restate the question using different words. Thus, a teacher might rephrase the question about subjects and verbs by asking, "Every sentence has an action and a noun that does the action; what are they in this sentence?"

Reduce

If rephrasing fails to prompt an answer, the next step is to ask a smaller version of the question. A teacher asking about subjects and verbs, then, might ask, "Let's look for one part of my question. What are the verbs or action words in this sentence?"

Reach Out

In a small number of cases, a student may genuinely not know and, therefore, also say, "I don't know." At that point, a teacher might ask the student to "reach out" to get the answer. One teacher mentioned in a workshop that if her students struggle to answer a question, she asks them if they'd like to "phone a friend." If the student says yes, then students who know the answer put their hands up to their ear as if they are talking on the phone, and the student can call on anyone who gives the answer.

After hearing the correct answer, to make sure that the student deepens his or her knowledge, the teacher should ask the student to repeat the answer, for example, in the above scenario, by describing how to find the subject and verb in a sentence.

Teachers rarely get to the reach out phase of this process, especially after students learn that everyone is expected to answer every question. Of course, teachers must scaffold questioning appropriately so that students are not embarrassed by being exposed in class as not knowing content. That issue is addressed by the next strategy.

Celebrate Mistakes. As Einstein is frequently quoted as having said, "Anyone who has never made a mistake has never tried anything new." This is a good adage to be taken to heart in the classroom. Teachers need to acknowledge students for trying whenever they answer a question and repeatedly stress that mistakes are windows of opportunity. Teachers should never ridicule or even tease students who make mistakes but go out of their way to encourage students for every answer, correct or incorrect. Teachers can even acknowledge their own mistakes to make it clear that everyone makes mistakes and that it is through mistakes that we can learn.

If we want students to respond to questions, we need to encourage them to answer them. In Chapter 14, I describe what teachers can do to increase effective, positive feedback. One important strategy for encouraging responses, however, is just to stop doing things that discourage kids from responding. Don't ridicule, make buzzer noises, or ignore students who are answering.

Avoid Giving Away the Answers to Right or Wrong Questions. The purpose of asking right or wrong questions is to assess student understanding by determining if students can correctly answer questions. Giving away the answer renders a right or wrong question useless.

Teachers can give away the answer in many ways, but in particular through nonverbal communication, perhaps smiling a bit too positively when proposing an answer, or through tone of voice, perhaps raising their voice at the end of a statement when sharing a correct answer. The easiest way for teachers to learn whether or not they are giving away answers is to video record them and then have them review their nonverbals and tone of voice.

There are two reasons, I think, why teachers give away the answer. First, they feel pressure to move forward with the lesson, and if they discover that students can't answer the question, they will have to stop and reteach whatever is being learned until it is mastered. More significant, however, might be the simple fact that cuts to the heart of the fear that all teachers face: *What if the students don't know the answer and I don't know what to do?* It is to prevent this feeling of fear that we discussed formative assessment (Chapter 3) and all of the various teaching practices emphasized in this book.

Provide Sufficient Wait Time. When we ask questions, Susan Scott tells us, we need to respect "the sweet purity of silence." This is not easy at first. We live in a noisy world, and waiting in silence almost seems unnatural; it can be uncomfortable for teachers to wait for a few seconds in silence. Being uncomfortable with silence, many teachers feel the need to fill in the gap with their own answers, thereby communicating that not answering is OK and, often, keeping students from giving answers they know.

I learned a simple strategy for wait time watching Susan Leyden and Sarah Weller as they talked about questioning in a video coaching session. This is a paraphrase of the conversation. "I learned about wait time," Sarah told Susan, "during a course at Lewis and Clark College. Our prof said to us, I know that none of you likely smokes cigarettes, but the idea of smoking does give you a good idea of how much time to allow for wait time. What you do is ask your question, then imagine taking a drag on your cigarette. Then inhale the smoke and let the nicotine hit. Then after a pause, exhale. That's how long the wait time should be."

I'm not advocating smoking, but Sarah's story does provide a good way of thinking about wait time.

Turning Ideas Into Action
Students

1. Dan Rothstein and Luz Santana (2011) argue that students should be guided to ask their own questions. The authors suggest the Question Formulation Technique (QFT), which involves teaching students to (a) produce a lot of questions, (b) improve their questions, and (c) prioritize their questions.

2. Teachers can ask students to help them perform a thinking audit by having each student write on a slip of paper, from 1 to 5, how much thinking he or she did during a classroom discussion (with 1 being none and 5 being a lot) and asking them to write down what could be done to encourage them to do better thinking during questioning.

Teachers

1. Teachers can coach themselves on questioning techniques by audio recording their lessons and then listening to questions and coding them.

2. Video recording of students during lessons can show the effectiveness of each question. Teachers can watch students and listen to questions to see what kind, type, or level of question is most effective at increasing energy and engagement in class.

3. Video recording can also be used so that teachers watch their wait time and their nonverbal communication during lessons to see if they are providing sufficient wait time or if they are giving away answers to questions. Both audio and video recordings can reveal a lot of useful data about questions and questioning techniques.

Instructional Coaches

1. The easiest way to coach teachers on questioning is to video record a teacher asking questions and then meet to code the type, kind, and level of each question. One of the benefits of coaching around questions is that, as several coaches have explained to me, it takes the coach out of the process.

2. Coaches can also coach teachers on questioning without using video by using the question chart in Figure 6.9. In this case, the coach writes down every instructional question asked during a class (except questions such as "Does anyone have a pencil for Luke?") and then during the coaching conversation after the lesson collaborates with the teacher to code the questions.

3. When collaborating with teachers around questioning, consider setting student goals related to student engagement (more than 95% time on task), learning (more than 85% highly proficient on exit tickets), or attitude (more than 3.5 out of 5 on the thinking audit). Teachers might also set goals for themselves, such as to use 95% open, opinion questions during classroom discussion.

Principals

1. One of the most important issues teachers need to consider is whether or not they are using the right questions for the right type of learning. Administrators can facilitate group discussion about questioning, constructivist instruction, and intensive-explicit instruction.

(Continued)

(Continued)

When schools develop a shared vocabulary around teaching practices and learning theories, the quality of conversation should be significantly improved.

2. Consider reading Walsh and Sattes, *Leading Through Quality Questioning: Creating Capacity, Commitment, and Community* (2010), to learn strategies for using better questions while leading collaboration in your school.

What It Looks Like

The question chart (Figure 6.9) can be used by anyone who wishes to gather data on questioning. The chart is simple to use. When observing another person's class or when observing their own class on video, observers write down every learning-related question asked by the teacher. Then, the observer codes the type, kind, and level of question.

The form can be used by individual teachers who are interested in improving their own instructional practice, or it can be used by administrators to gather data on questioning in a classroom or across a school.

The form can also be used by instructional coaches, as Marti Elford did in the story above. When coaches gather data with the form, they may wish to save the coding of the questions until they meet with their collaborating teacher so that they can code and discuss each question with the teacher.

To Sum Up

- Asking the right question at the right time improves student thinking, increases engagement, and fosters learning.

- Open questions prompt unlimited responses.

- Closed questions prompt limited responses.

- Right or wrong questions are asked to confirm whether or not someone has the correct understanding of knowledge, skills, or big ideas.

- Opinion questions ask for someone's perspective on a topic, and they are questions that essentially can't be answered incorrectly.

- Knowledge questions explore what students know about a topic.

- Skills questions explore how well students can do something.

- Big idea questions explore concepts, themes, content structures, and broad topics.

- In effective intensive-explicit classrooms, teachers frequently ask a lot (four per minute) of closed, right or wrong, knowledge, and skill questions.

- In effective constructivist classrooms, teachers usually ask a small number of open, opinion, big idea questions.

Going Deeper

Jackie Acree Walsh and Beth Dankert Sattes have done great work promoting the importance of quality questions. Their book *Quality Questioning: Research-Based Practices to Engage Every Learner* (2005) makes the case for effective questions, nicely summarizes some important research findings on questioning, and offers practical strategies teachers can use to improve questioning in any class. *Quality Questioning* would be a good next step for anyone interested in going deeper into effective questioning.

Walsh and Sattes' *Leading Through Quality Questioning: Creating Capacity, Commitment, and Community* (2011) provides excellent strategies that administrators, coaches, and PLC members can adopt to improve questioning during collaborative conversations.

Dan Rothstein and Luz Santana's *Make Just One Change: Teach Students to Ask Their Own Questions* (2011) is a provocative and persuasive book that, as the title would suggest, provides a variety of strategies to help students be more skilled at creating powerful questions to drive their own learning. The book explains how teachers can guide students to create a lot of questions, distinguish between open and closed questions, and then use those questions as the focus for learning. Also, the discussion of questions and divergent and convergent thinking adds to my comments about questioning and constructivist and intensive-explicit approaches to learning. You can learn more about *Make Just One Change* by watching Dan Rothstein's Ted Talk on the topic, at ted.com.

When Marti Elford met to talk about coaching for this book, she told me that her long-range professional goal is to be able to ask questions as effectively as Steve Barkley. Marti has seen Steve lead workshops at our Teaching, Learning, and Coaching Conference in Kansas on a couple of occasions.

Although all of Steve's books address questioning, the book *Questions for Life: Powerful Strategies to Guide Critical Thinking* (2009), which he co-authored with Terri Bianco, focuses on how powerful questions can be catalysts for improved critical thinking. Their book is packed with suggestions that could help anyone asking questions, and I found their discussion of cue words in questions to be especially useful.

Anita Archer is a master presenter with great practical ideas to share. In *Explicit Instruction: Effective and Efficient Teaching* (2011), she and Charlie Hughes dedicate a significant part of their book to discussing how teachers adopting an intensive-explicit stance can use questions and guide student responses to maintain engagement and monitor student learning.

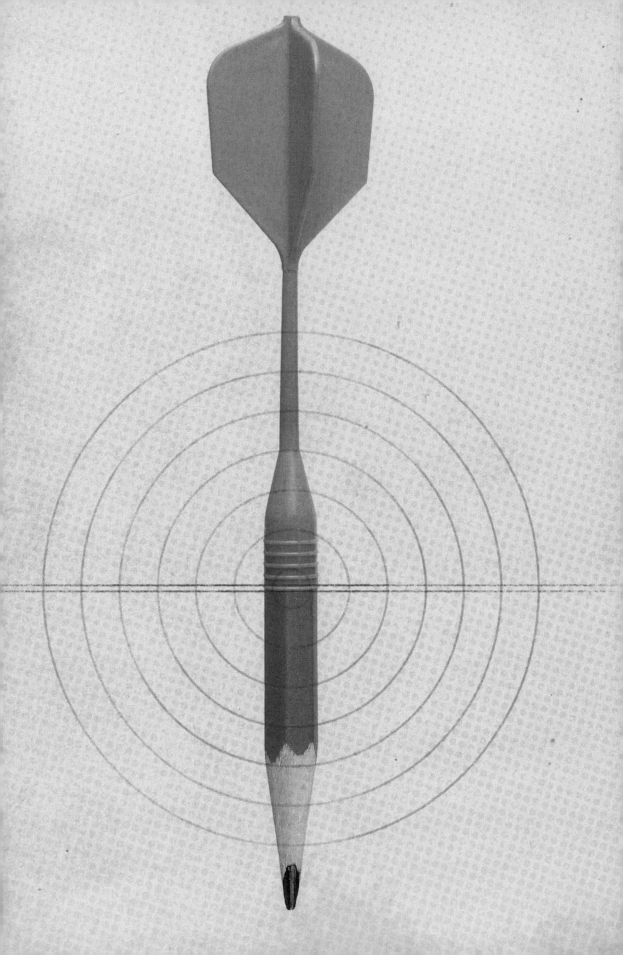

Chapter 7:
Stories

is about

using narratives to enhance learning

by understanding → why
- Engage
- Motivate
- Build community
- Enhance learning

by choosing an → organizing structure →
Escalation
Hero-conflict-resolution
Building and upsetting expectations
Self-revelation
Epiphanies

by knowing the story's → purpose →
Anchor new knowledge
Build prior knowledge
Prompt thinking and dialogue
Generate interest
Inspire hope
Offer new perspectives
Build community

by crafting a → story line →
1. Draw a line from birth to today.
2. List events on the line.
3. List people on the line.
4. Identify associated stories.
5. Flesh out the best stories.

7

STORIES

If stories come to you, care for them. And learn to give them away where they are needed. Sometimes a person needs a story more than food to stay alive. That is why we put these stories in each other's memory. This is how people care for themselves.

—Barry Lopez

"I want to start our class with a story."

Hannah Grant (not her real name) stood in front of her students, 14 children ages 11 to 14, mostly girls, who were taking her art class in a small alternative school.

Miss Grant had taught art long enough to know that by the age of 11 many of her of students had given up on being artists, or they had let other people convince them that they didn't have any talent for drawing or painting. On the first day of class, more than anything else, Hannah wanted her students to know that creating art is a tremendously rewarding experience and that they shouldn't let others' opinions hold them back. So she decided to start with a story.

"There was a little girl who lived on a farm," she said, "and the farm was her favorite place in the world."

All eyes were on Miss Grant. One girl shot up her hand to ask a question: "Were you the little girl?"

"Well, yes, I was," Hannah admitted, "but let me tell you the story. There were many animals on the farm, and one of the things the little girl used to love to do was sit on her porch and watch them. Of all of the animals, without a doubt, her favorite was a beautiful goose."

"One day the little girl was especially happy, and she thought, 'I wish I had a camera to take a picture of this goose.' Then she realized that if she drew a picture that might be as good as a photo."

With every student watching, Hannah continued her story.

"The little girl took out a pencil and paper, and the goose stood still for her so she could do her drawing almost as if the goose knew it was being drawn. When the little girl finished, she was very proud of her drawing. 'Who needs a camera?' she thought. 'I love to draw.'"

"After she grew up, the girl moved to a big city. She really missed her family and her home on the farm, and sometimes when she felt especially lonely, she pulled out the picture of the goose. Looking at it made her feel a little less lonely. Many years after the girl had made the drawing, she still loved her picture of the goose."

"One day she decided to show the picture to a man she knew in the big city. He took a quick look and immediately began to criticize the drawing. 'This really doesn't look like a goose; it looks more like a duck,' he started. 'The neck is way too long. The shading should be darker. And the eyes don't look right.'"

When Miss Grant told her students what the man said about the picture, the children hissed as if seeing the evil villain in a silent film (Sarah took quiet satisfaction from their reaction since the man who made the comments was her ex-husband).

"After that, the girl put away her goose, and for a long time she stopped thinking about being an artist. Then one day, the girl realized that she still wanted to draw and paint, and she decided she wasn't going to let anyone else tell her whether or not she was an artist. She started to draw and paint all the time. And she loved it. She loved the smell of paint. She loved to watch a blank page turn into a drawing. She loved the idea of trying to make something beautiful."

Then Miss Grant showed the students some pictures she had created. When the students saw her paintings and drawings, they realized it would have been a great shame if their teacher had given up art.

"And you can be an artist, too," she said after sharing her paintings and drawings. "Don't think for a second you can't. In our class, you're going to have a lot of time to enjoy being an artist. I did it. You can do it, too."

"Do you have the picture of the goose?" asked the children.

"Well, yes, I do," Miss Grant said, and, with a slight flourish, she held up her drawing (see Figure 7.1). Everyone was hooked. The students dove into their first assignment furiously. Even Hannah's instructional aide came up to her and asked, "Do you really think I could draw?"

"Absolutely," Hannah said, "everyone can be an artist." Her course was launched with a story.

Why Use Stories?

Miss Grant's story accomplished a lot in a few minutes. She immediately engaged her students. She communicated her faith in their abilities. She revealed something about herself, which made her more human and approachable. She motivated the children to dive into their assignments with gusto. She communicated the important lesson that her students shouldn't let others' opinions keep them from exploring their own talent. She built community by telling a story to which the students could relate.

The idea of using stories, as Hannah Grant did, is not one of the most common topics raised when effective teaching practices are discussed. We talk about curriculum, formative assessment, content knowledge, and precise modeling—all of which are important. But stories also deserve a place on the list of effective practices. Stories, after all, have been an effective mode of communication since humans began to communicate. Chances are the teachers you have known who used stories effectively left their mark on you.

Figure 7.1   Hannah Grant's Goose Drawing

I learned about the power of stories in 1997 when I traveled to Winnipeg, Ottawa, Toronto, Hamilton, and Montreal, Canada, to interview adult university students for a qualitative study I was conducting for the Eaton School of Retail at Ryerson University in Toronto. I talked to more than 80 Eaton's of Canada employees, who were also taking university courses. I spent over an hour in each one-to-one conversation with every student, asking him or her all kinds of questions about learning experiences in colleges and universities.

During those conversations, everyone talked about the teachers in their classes. In almost every interview, the students told me that the best teachers were the ones who told stories. Stories helped them learn because they were entertaining and engaging, because they provided a concrete context in which to place abstract ideas, and because they helped them remember what was being learned. Stories helped them connect with their teachers. Stories made ideas real.

Stories in Intensive-Explicit and Constructivist Instruction

As with all of the teaching practices described in this book, stories can be used within intensive-explicit or constructivist instruction. When stories are used for intensive-explicit instruction, a teacher's goal is to ensure students learn whatever is being taught as understood by the teacher. That is, the goal is to ensure that the picture in the students' minds is exactly the same as the picture in the teacher's mind. When stories are used for this kind of learning, students anchor their understanding of ideas in something everyone can relate to—a story. Teachers who use intensive-explicit instruction explicitly show the connections between stories and the content being learned.

The goal for constructivist instruction, on the other hand, is to create a learning experience that provides the freedom for all students to build their own understanding, or to create their own picture of what is being learned. When stories are told for this kind of learning, students are encouraged to build their own understanding of the story from the vantage point of their own prior knowledge. During constructivist learning, the students connect the dots.

Stories for Intensive-Explicit Instruction

One of my favorite stories is told in a scene on the old TV show *WKRP in Cincinnati*. The DJ, Venus Flytrap, has a conversation with Arnold, a young man working at the station. Venus convinces Arnold to stay in school by betting him that he can teach him "the basics of the atom in two minutes." To convey his message, Venus tells a story.

"There are three gangs on the street," Venus starts, drawing a big circle on the wall of the storage room where they happen to be sitting. "Now here is the neighborhood, and right here in the middle of this neighborhood is a gang called the New Boys." Venus then explains that there are two other gangs, the Elected Ones and the Pros. The Elected Ones are "really negative dudes," who are "always circling around the neighborhood. They don't like nothing." The Pros are "very positive cats." "Interesting thing," Venus says, "the Pros and Elected Ones hate each other so much that they keep the same number of members in the gang, just in case."

Venus goes on. "The Pros and the New Boys [the third gang Venus mentions] . . . they call their hangout, the nucleus," which, Venus says, is a "really tough word, it's Latin, but I kind of think of Swahili, and it means center."

"I'll give you another Swahili word," says Venus, "it's *tron*. It means *dude* . . . All these gangs like that name so well that they all decided to use it . . . the Pros start calling themselves the Protons, the New Boys start calling themselves the Neutrons, and the Elected Ones start calling themselves . . ." Venus turns to Arnold, who predicts correctly, " . . . the Electrons."

Venus' simple little story ensures that Arnold remembers all the parts of the atom. Not surprisingly, when Venus gives him a pop quiz, Arnold gets every question right. Venus, whom Arnold calls Professor DJ, smiles and tells Arnold, "You've got it man! You get an A!"

Venus' story is an excellent example of a story used appropriately for intensive-explicit instruction. Stories, like thinking prompts described in Chapter 5, work because they provide a known anchor for learning—they make learning sticky. As Heath and Heath have written in *Made to Stick* (2007),

> A story is powerful because it provides the context missing from abstract prose. It's back to the Velcro theory of memory, the idea that the more hooks we put into our ideas, the better they'll stick. . . . This is the role that stories play—putting knowledge into a framework that is more lifelike, more true to our day-to-day existence. (p. 214)

We remember ideas better when we connect them with something else. For example, for decades marketers have known that we remember their products better if we connect a song with their product, and all of us have probably been unable to shake a catchy tune that we've heard on an advertisement. Teachers have also learned that music can be used to help students remember information, and many students have remembered important information that was sticky because it was learned with the help of a song.

Labarbara Madison explains how music helps her students remember.

Video 7.2
www.corwin.com/ highimpactinstruction

Venus' goal with his story was to ensure that his young student remembered the parts of the atom exactly as he explained them. When you are telling a story within intensive-explicit instruction, it's important to know exactly the critical elements you want your students to remember and exactly how your story will anchor that learning.

One way to develop and plan a story for intensive-explicit instruction is to create a simple t-chart where you list the critical elements of a concept, fact, or historical event in the left-hand column and identify the parts of the story that will represent those elements in the right-hand column. Venus, for example, might have created a t-chart that looks like Figure 7.2.

Stories for Constructivist Instruction

Teaching that enables constructivist instruction provides an opportunity for students to explore and create their own understanding of whatever is being learned. Thus, when stories are used within constructivist instruction, they are powerful precisely because they are evocative rather than explicit. H. B. Danesh's comments (1994) about analogies help us understand how stories work within constructivist instruction:

> Analogies are powerful instruments of education because each person understands the concepts according to his or her own level of growth and maturity. In addition, an analogy can

Figure 7.2 T-Chart for Venus' Story

Atom	Story
Electrons	Elected Ones
Protons	Pros
New Boys	Neutrons
Atom particles	Gang members
Emptiness of an atom	The neighborhood
Nucleus	Hangout

be simplified or elaborated upon according to the age, intellect, and emotional capacities of the individuals involved. (cited in Rowshan, 1997, p. 28)

Ernst Kurtz and Katherine Ketcham (1994) have also described how the indirect communication of stories can be especially powerful. In *The Spirituality of Imperfection: Storytelling and the Journey to Wholeness*, the authors observe that "stories become 'new' to us when something in our own experience makes us ready to hear them. . . . Story . . . cannot be commanded or forced; it must float loosely within its vehicle, the better to lodge in each hearer's individual spirit." In support of their beliefs about stories, the authors include an ancient parable:

> One spiritual leader cautions: "If you respect your listeners enough to tell the story, respect them enough to draw their own conclusions." And another master began one of his books with a story that consoles anyone who must confront the impossibility of "explaining" story:
>   A disciple once complained, "You tell us stories, but you never explain their meaning to us."
>   Said the master, "How would you like it if someone offered you fruit and chewed it up before giving it to you?"
>   No one can find your meaning for you.
>   Not even the master. (p. viii)

Although a story told within constructivist instruction begins with one teller, the teacher, it only truly becomes real when listeners, students, hear it and make it personally meaningful. The teacher creates and tells a story, and students re-create the story in their minds. As Richard Stone (1996) has commented, listening to a story can be as creative an act as telling:

> When you hear my story it is transformed into a tale that feels intimately like your own, even palpably real and personal, especially if you repeat it to another. . . . After a few tellings, it no longer matters from where these anecdotes and tales originated. They take on a life of their own, permeating our experiences. (p. 57)

The notion that stories come alive through a creative partnership between teller and listener is not new. Iser (1978), for example, observed that all texts require a creative act to be understood. According to Iser, reading a story or any other text involves "the mediation of places of indeterminacy." All texts and stories contain ambiguities or gaps, and the reader's task is to make sense of the text by filling those gaps: Reading is an act of bringing meaning to the experience of literature. In this way a reader transforms an ambiguous text into a living work of art. Like a photograph appearing in a developer's tray, meaning appears through the symbiotic interaction of reader and text.

Stories told during constructivist instruction require co-construction; they demand that we "fill in the gaps." Storytellers use literary techniques to convey their messages more richly than explicit language *because* they communicate indirectly. Through analogies, symbols, similes, and myths, stories communicate with power because they evoke rather than tell. The simple symbol of a nation's flag, for example, evokes thousands of responses in us simply because we are free to make up, to some extent, our own minds about what the flag means—even in ways that we may not be able to articulate.

Purposes of Stories

Teachers can use stories to accomplish several goals in the classroom, including (a) anchoring new knowledge, (b) building prior knowledge, (c) prompting thinking and dialogue, (d) generating interest, (e) inspiring hope, (f) offering new perspectives, (g) describing epiphanies, and (h) building community. Each of these is described below.

Anchoring New Knowledge. Teachers can make it easier for students to learn and understand new knowledge if they use stories to make the new knowledge concrete and accessible. In the movie *Big*, there is a delightful example when the lead character, Josh Baskins, played by Tom Hanks, helps a child learn his algebra by telling a story about a football game. Stories that are used as anchors must be simple enough to be easily understood. Venus Flytrap's story is an example of an anchor story. Effective anchor stories are crafted so that the links between the concrete story and the abstract ideas are extremely easy to see. Often, especially during intensive-explicit instruction, the teacher explicitly draws the connections between elements within the story and the ideas being learned.

Building Prior Knowledge. Stories can also enrich student learning by providing additional, contextual information that students need to know in order to appreciate whatever is being learned. The stories of a teacher who walked in the civil rights marches in the sixties, for example, might help students better understand the civil rights movement being discussed in U.S. history class. Similarly, an art teacher who has camped and canoed in Canada's Algonquin Park could help students better identify Tom Thomson's paintings by telling stories about her experiences in the park. Stories that are used to supply prior knowledge should be vivid, filled with details that make it easy for students to picture the topic being introduced.

Prompting Thinking and Dialogue. Teachers can use stories as thinking prompts in the classroom. For example, a teacher might start a conversation about ethical behavior by telling a story about a young boy who steals when he is hungry. Stories that are used as thinking prompts must be simple enough to be easily understood, but at the same time, they must be complex enough so that they can be interpreted in several ways. A simple story that leads to an obvious interpretation rarely engenders meaningful conversation, but a simple story that can been seen from many perspectives can prompt rich dialogue.

Generating Interest. Stories are often used as "hooks" to capture student attention. In fact, presenters have probably used stories to catch audience attention for as long as there have been presenters speaking to audiences. Effective interest generators are often surprising, emotional, humorous, or compelling in some other way. Interest generator stories should be captivating, tightly organized, and brief.

Inspiring Hope. Teachers can use stories to motivate students to action by telling success stories that students can relate to their own circumstances. Stephen Denning (2005) refers to these as "springboard stories." Inspiring stories are most effective when they are brief and include few details. By keeping details to a minimum, teachers make it easier for students to see themselves in the story. Most important, inspiring stories must sound realistic to students while also clearly showing that students can be successful. Stories that sound implausible, no matter how positive the outcome, can decrease hope.

Offering New Perspectives. Teachers can help students see perspectives other than their own by telling stories that communicate the elements of an event through another person's eyes. Many of the stories on storycorp.net, a website where listeners can hear people tell their life stories, are excellent examples of stories providing new perspectives. In one story, for example, a homeless man explains that although alcohol derailed him from a meaningful and successful life, he still had worth. "There's a lot more to me than you might think just looking at me," he said. The intelligent, moving story he tells about redeeming his life with the help of a mentor is further proof that this homeless person has a lot to contribute to all of us.

Stories can also give students new perspectives on themselves. As James Loehr has written (2007), we shape our ideas about our lives by the stories we tell about ourselves:

> The idea of "one's own story" is so powerful, so native, that I hardly consider it a metaphor, as if it's some new lens through which to look at life. Your life *is* your story. Your story *is* your life. . . . If you are human, then you tell yourself stories—positive ones and negative, consciously and, far more than not, subconsciously. . . . Telling ourselves stories helps us navigate our way through life because they provide structure and direction. (p. 4)

New perspective stories are most captivating if they are vivid, emotional, and written so that students feel sympathy for the central protagonist.

Describing Epiphanies. James Joyce popularized using the word *epiphany* to refer to the point in a story when a central character has a profound insight into some aspect of life. In one of Joyce's best-known short stories, "The Dead," for example, the main character, Gabriel, awakens for the first time to the actual nature of his relationship with his wife.

I had an experience like this when I was a teenager, working one summer at a youth hostel in Banff, Alberta, Canada. Every day, it seemed, people would come to the hostel and try to stay for free by lying and telling me they didn't have any money. Over time, I grew tired of being lied to so often, and I became skilled at grilling people until they admitted that they could pay. I didn't care what their story was; if they told me they were broke, I would glare at them until they told the truth, and if they were already telling the truth, too bad.

One day that summer I walked down the main street, Banff Avenue, and saw a policeman directing traffic where a traffic light was out. It was hot, and he was clearly unhappy. He directed the traffic by glaring at each car and angrily gesturing where the car was to go. He didn't want to be there, and he wasn't giving any thought to the people in those cars—he just wanted the cars out of his intersection as quickly as possible.

Watching the policeman, I had a sudden flash of insight. "That's me," I thought. "When I grill people at the hostel, I have forgotten that they are people with real stories and real lives regardless of their situation." At that moment, I resolved to do my best to remember that whenever I talk to anyone in any situation, I am talking to a real person.

Most of us have had these moments, and they mark our character. If we retell our epiphanies as stories, when they are appropriate, they can help our students gain important knowledge, skills, and big ideas. And because epiphanies document a moment of real insight, students often remember the stories long after they leave our classrooms.

Building Community. Stories also shape the kind of learning community that is created in a class in a manner similar to thinking prompts. Stories that authentically elicit warmhearted emotions can foster those same kinds of positive emotions in class. However, stories that belittle others or evoke negative emotions can produce negative emotions. Stories that build learner-friendly cultures are authentically inspirational, positive, and hopeful. Authenticity is especially critical. If teachers use a story that students think is hokey, it can have an effect opposite to what the teacher intended.

When people listen to a story, they often connect the emotions they feel with their own experiences. This creates community. Our petty thoughts and preconceptions separate us, but stories bring us together. Stories serve numerous functions: They enable us to shape or structure the general chaos of personal experience; they convey truths too simple or too complex to be stated out loud; they help us make sense and meaning of memories and experiences; they prompt us to wrestle with problems and create our own meanings; and they connect us with larger ideas and, perhaps most important, to each other. As W. R. S. Ralston has stated (1873), "One touch of storytelling may, in some instances, make the whole world kin."

Finding Stories

Your memories are an encyclopedia of moving, humorous, and profound stories. In fact, whenever people get together anywhere in the world, much of the conversation is simply people sharing stories. The trick is to remember all those stories and then retell them in a way that others recognize as storytelling.

A simple exercise may help you create stories that draw from the raw material of your personal experience. By developing a personal time line that summarizes the events that take place in your life, or a portion of your life, moving from birth to the present, you can begin to open up the rich reservoir of stories buried in your memories.

1. Start by drawing a horizontal line across a page to represent the chronology of your life. Include on the time line the critical incidents you've experienced, memorable people you've worked with,

and so on. Your time line should be a kind of graphic autobiography. Following this, identify the points on the time line where interesting or illustrative events occurred. These people and points will all be prompts to remember your stories.

2. Pick one event from your life that you think would make an excellent story. Once you have chosen a story you want to work on, write down the main elements of the story. You might want to brainstorm ideas by jotting them down on a piece of paper or developing a mind map; the important thing is to tell the whole story. In story writing workshops I've conducted, we've used tape recorders to make it easier for participants to describe the details of a future story.

Once you have recorded the details, work to embellish the story. For example, describe the feelings you felt when you experienced the story. What feelings do you think an audience should feel? Similarly, what sensual details are important? What are the sights, scents, sounds, touches, and tastes you experienced or that your story should evoke?

3. Finally, consider all the characters in the story. Does your story contain heroes or villains, and if so, who are they? Who are other important people in the story whom you might have overlooked? Once you have recorded all the events, details, and characters, you can turn to developing a structure that audiences will easily recognize as a story.

Ryan Berger talks about using stories in the classroom.

Video 7.3
www.corwin.com/
highimpactinstruction

Organizing Stories

By definition, a story is a structure for organizing and retaining events that serves an important function in any culture. As Norma Livo and Sandra Rietz (1986) have observed,

> "Story" is a way of knowing and remembering information—a shape or pattern into which information can be arranged. . . . And it is an ancient, perhaps natural order of the mind—primordial, having grown along with the development of human memory and or language itself. "Story" is a way of organizing language. Even very young children recognize "story" and can shape language and ideas into its forms. (p. 15)

Perhaps the single attribute that separates a story from other forms of communication is its structure (Chatman, 1978; Cohan & Shires, 1988; Livo & Rietz, 1987; Todorov, 1977). In essence, a story consists of events placed in a sequence to delineate a process of change, the transformation of one event into another. This sequence

STORIES 187

of events represents a kind of grammar, a structure that audiences recognize as a story. Frequently, that story grammar moves from a state of order to chaos, and back to order.

Whatever structure you choose for your story is a matter of your own choosing. Nonetheless, the following suggestions provide you with a generic structure for your story: Begin by describing the setting, problem or disruption, and solution. List the events leading to the problem, and then list events leading to the solution. If there is a moral, explain it.

- **Escalation.** A series of story components (for example, events) are structured so that each new component is more intense or powerful than the previous one.
- **Hero-Conflict-Resolution.** A hero we sympathize with encounters an obstacle or conflict and (in some admirable way) overcomes the conflict or obstacle.
- **Building and Upsetting Expectations.** A story appears to be moving in a particular direction, but then a twist in the narrative is included to surprise or entertain the listeners.
- **Self-Revelation.** To enhance your relationship with your students, tell a story about your own life that provides some information about your personality or life.
- **Epiphanies.** Epiphany stories are built around a single event that leads to profound new insight into such things as principles, character, or beliefs.

Integrating Stories Into Teaching

If you want to use stories more frequently in your classroom, you'll need to be intentional about how you use them. The following suggestions are intended to help anyone use more stories during the learning experiences they lead.

Develop Your Personal Library of Stories. You will find stories in your experiences, in the experiences of friends, family, or colleagues, in books or articles, on television, in movies, in the news, overheard in coffee shops, or just about anywhere. When you keep your eyes and ears open, you will find that stories pop up all around you.

I recommend that teachers keep a story journal where they can write down stories whenever they discover them. Your notes don't have to be long, just long enough to record the salient details you'll need to remember the whole. The journal can be written in an actual notebook, on your computer, or in the cloud on your smartphone. Jocelyn Washburn, a professional developer in Virginia, keeps a story journal with her at all times and jots down story ideas whenever they come to her. Then, before she leads a professional development session, she looks through her journal and chooses which stories she will use in her sessions.

Integrate Stories Into Your Lessons at Their Most Effective Points. Once you have your library of stories, you need to find the most appropriate point to integrate them into your lessons. I consider two factors. First, what is an instructional area that I need to enhance because it is (a) complicated, (b) especially important, or (c) foundational for learning that will continue throughout the year? A teacher who plans to refer to the scientific method throughout the year, for example, might illustrate it by telling a particularly memorable story that she can refer to whenever students discuss the scientific method.

Second, is there a story I can tell that will interest students? If I have a story that I know will capture my students' attention, I will work hard to find an appropriate way to weave it into my lesson.

Stories can be used to illustrate complex ideas that are difficult to fully grasp without a narrative. Aspects of the concept of empathy, for example, might be much better illustrated by a story than by a carefully crafted checklist.

Frame Stories With Introductory and Summative Comments. How you introduce and sum up a story will depend on whether or not your story is being used for intensive-explicit or constructivist instruction. When a story is being used within intensive-explicit instruction, you may want to introduce it, explicitly stating that you are sharing the story so that students will remember some specific content. For example, you might say, "I want to tell you a story about a basketball game so that you always remember the order of operations." In addition, when you finish the story, you may want to return to the salient points and make sure students are 100% clear on the connection between the story and whatever they are learning.

When stories are told for constructivist reasons, on the other hand, leave the conclusions to the students so that they can draw their own conclusions about what they have heard.

Stick to the Learning. One of the few criticisms I have heard about teachers who use stories is that some teachers tell stories that are not relevant to the learning. Stories are entertaining, and they can make the classroom enjoyable, but the purpose of the classroom is learning. For that reason, teachers should identify their learning goal before they choose their story. The primary goal of a teacher's story should always be enhanced learning.

Think About Who Should Be the Hero of Your Story. By telling stories about ourselves, by revealing something about ourselves, we may make it easier for students to see similarities between themselves and us. By talking about our personal challenges, struggles, and possible successes, we can share important lessons and encourage students when they run up against their own roadblocks.

However, if students are to appreciate your story, they need to see how the story can be connected to their own experiences. In other words, your story has to become their story. For that reason, you should think carefully about making yourself the focus of your success stories. Talking about glory days might be tempting, but if students think their teacher is bragging, they will likely be turned off rather than be engaged by a story. This is especially true of success stories, where through heroic effort you have succeeded. Teachers may find the success stories they tell are more effective if they begin them by saying "There's a person I know . . ."

Stories achieve a lot when they are used to educate. At its best, a story provides an audience with insight into the tacit dimensions of whatever is being discussed. A story provides a context for understanding. A story conveys emotion, humor, and humanity. In short, to hear an effective story is to be reminded that we are alive, sharing the world with other people who know and have experienced events similar to those that make up our lives. Figure 7.3 lists a few guidelines for developing effective stories.

Figure 7.3	Effective Stories

Effective stories are . . .	✓	Comments
Not Lame. Is the story of interest to students or just the teacher?		
Concise. Cut out every word that you can. Shorter stories are more powerful.		
Vivid. Have you included enough details to pain a rich picture?		
Emotional. Will the story touch students' hearts?		
Surprising. Can you make the story more effective by including a surprise ending?		
Humble. Stories that celebrate a teacher's successes can be off-putting to students.		

Download this form at www.corwin.com/ highimpactinstruction

Telling Stories

There is an art to telling stories, and the great storytellers like Bill Cosby or Garrison Keillor can keep audiences spellbound for hours. But we don't have to be as polished as a world-famous entertainer to use stories effectively. Indeed, each of us tells stories every day, and moving stories from the kitchen table to the classroom is a shorter journey than you might think. Here are a few simple suggestions for the elements of an effective story (see Figure 7.4).

Planned Ahead of Time. Our stories are more effective if we think carefully about the main elements of the story before we tell it. Factors to consider include (a) what the learning goal is that the story will enhance, (b) who the hero is, (c) what the complication or problem is, (d) what the resolution is, (e) what the essential plot elements are, and (f) what the moral or lesson of the story is.

Spontaneous. Too much planning can be a bad strategy, however, if your stories feel too contrived or inauthentic. Stories provide people with a vicarious experience of the events being described; that is, your students should experience feelings that are somewhat similar to your hero's when she or he went through the experiences told in the story. For that reason, strive to tell stories that feel spontaneous.

Conversational. Telling a story in the classroom shouldn't feel any different than telling a story in the kitchen. We don't need to call up

Figure 7.4 How to Tell a Story

Well-told stories are . . .	✓	Comments
Planned ahead of time		
Spontaneous		
Conversational		
Simple		
Short		
Appropriately paced		

our inner Chris Rock to capture everyone's attention. Much more important is to simply let the details reveal the story. Although we might be telling the story to 30 or more students, each listener should feel like we are telling the story to him or her.

Simple. Strive to find the easiest way to explain the events of your story. Some of the most powerful stories, like parables, are shorter than a hundred words. The parable of the prodigal son, for example, beautifully illustrates the power of loving grace in less than 200 words. Authors Chip and Dan Heath (2007) write the following about the importance of simplicity in storytelling:

> It's hard to make ideas stick in a noisy, unpredictable, chaotic environment. If we're to succeed, the first step is this: Be simple. Not simple in terms of "dumbing down" or "sound bites." You don't have to speak in monosyllables to be simple. What we mean by "simple" is *finding the core of the idea* [author's italics]. Finding the core of an idea means stripping down an idea to its most critical essence. (pp. 27–28)

Short. If you can cut something out without changing the meaning of the story, do so. Short stories are more powerful; besides, they allow more time for students to experience other learning in the classroom.

Appropriately Paced. A quick pace is usually more engaging than a slow one (Archer & Hughes, 2011). Storytellers can modulate their use of pace to emphasize different aspects of a story, pausing for dramatic effect, speeding up during exciting moments, slowing down to emphasize important ideas, and changing volume to distinguish characters, maintain attention, or provoke surprise.

Turning Ideas Into Action
Students

1. Consider having your students create their own stories to inform their learning or to help them remember key content.

2. You may want to ask your students to create their own story line and prompt them to make connections between their stories and what they are learning.

(Continued)

(Continued)

Teachers

1. Teachers can learn a lot about their stories by simply audio recording their stories to see how effectively they deliver them. Most smartphones come with an audio record app that records fairly high-quality sound, and with the right hookup, teachers can listen to their stories on the way home over their car audio system.

2. A lot can also be learned by watching how stories are told in books, on the news, and in films and documentaries. Watching the nightly news can become just another way to improve your game as a teacher.

3. Keeping a story journal and reviewing it every week is a great way to make stories a habitual part of your instruction.

Instructional Coaches

1. One of the most powerful things instructional coaches can do is to gather time-on-task data at different points during a lesson to see how engaged students are during storytelling. If the story is effective, engagement should be at or close to 100%.

2. Instructional coaches can also work with teachers individually or in teams to develop a bank of stories that can be used in a school. In a school of 50 teachers, if every teacher contributes 50 stories to a common bank, perhaps a wiki on which teachers upload stories, teachers will have 2,500 stories that they can access for use in their classrooms.

Principals

1. School leaders can promote the use of stories by creating opportunities for teachers to create and share stories. Teachers can attend workshops on storytelling and/or share video of stories they have told in the classroom.

2. Stories remind us of our shared humanity. The opportunity to create and share stories can have a positive effect on student learning, but it can also have a positive effect on the culture within a building. For centuries, cultural heritages have been fostered and shared through a tradition of telling stories. Why not start such a tradition in your school?

What It Looks Like

Teachers can assess how effective their stories are by comparing how well students remember content that they learned with the help of a story with content they learned without a story.

To Sum Up

- When stories are used within constructivist instruction, they should be told in an open-ended way that allows each student to draw his or her own conclusions.

- When stories are told within intensive-explicit instruction, the teacher should explicitly connect the elements of the stories to the content being learned.

- Stories can be used to (a) anchor new knowledge, (b) build prior knowledge, (c) prompt thinking and dialogue, (d) generate interest, (e) inspire hope, (f) offer new perspectives, (g) describe epiphanies, and (h) build community.

- Teachers can use a story line to develop a library of stories to use in their lessons. They should consult the story line when they plan instruction.

- Common story structures include escalation, hero-conflict-resolution, building and upsetting expectations, self-revelation, and epiphanies.

- Effective stories are not lame; in addition, they are concise, vivid, emotional, surprising, and humble.

- Well-told stories are planned ahead of time, spontaneous, conversational, simple, short, and appropriately paced.

Going Deeper

Several excellent books have been written to help us improve our ability to tell stories when teaching. Although most of the books described below are not from the education field, all of them provide information that could be helpful to any educator interested in including stories in his or her lessons.

Stephen Denning's *The Leader's Guide to Storytelling: Mastering the Art and Discipline of Business Narrative* (2005) provides both an excellent explanation of the power of stories and numerous practical, innovative, and useful suggestions. One of Denning's most important comments is as follows:

> The idea that storytelling is a kind of rare skill, possessed by relatively few human beings, is utter nonsense. Human beings master the basics of storytelling as young children and retain

this capability throughout their lives. One has only to watch what goes in an informal social setting—a restaurant, a coffee break, a party—to see that all human beings know how to tell stories. (p. xviii)

Richard Stone's *The Healing Art of Storytelling: A Sacred Journey of Personal Discovery* (1996) offers excellent insight into how the stories we tell ourselves or others can be toxic or healthy. With ample examples from other publications, Stone explains how healing stories can be important for people who are struggling to become healthier or shake off addictions. The book also includes many practical suggestions on how to craft stories.

I found Jim Loehr's *The Power of Story: Rewrite Your Destiny in Business and in Life* (2007) to offer a great clarification of what stories are and how they shape our thinking. For me personally, his book also spoke to how important it is for us to control our lives by thinking about how our own stories can block us or help us flourish.

Two other business books, Jonah Sachs' *Winning the Story Wars: Why Those Who Tell (and Live) the Best Stories Will Rule the Future* (2012) and Ryan Mathews' and Watts Wacker's *What's Your Story: Storytelling to Move Markets, Audiences, People, and Brands* (2008) also do an excellent job of explaining why we should tell more stories and how we can structure stories to be highly effective.

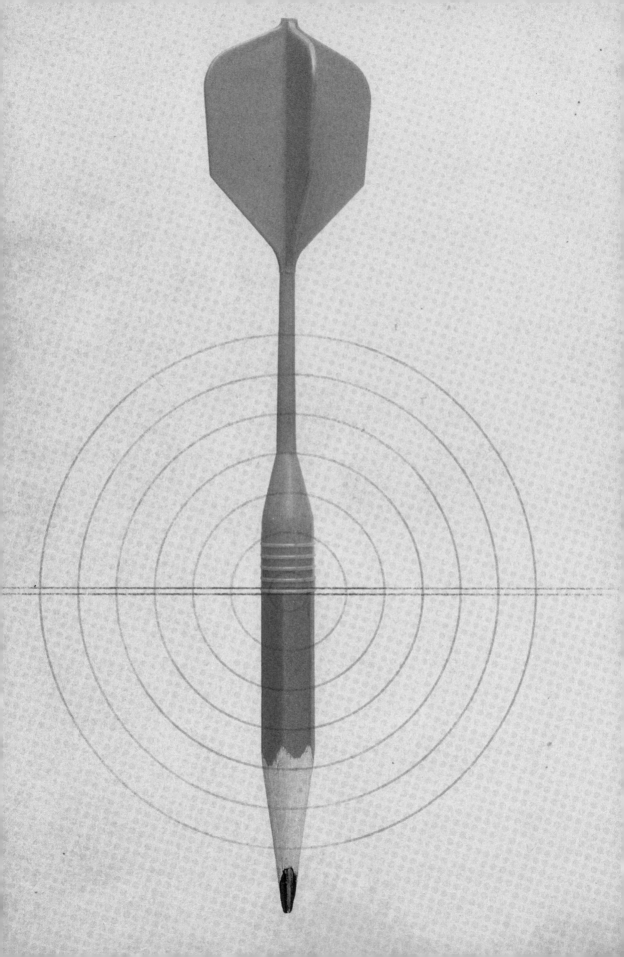

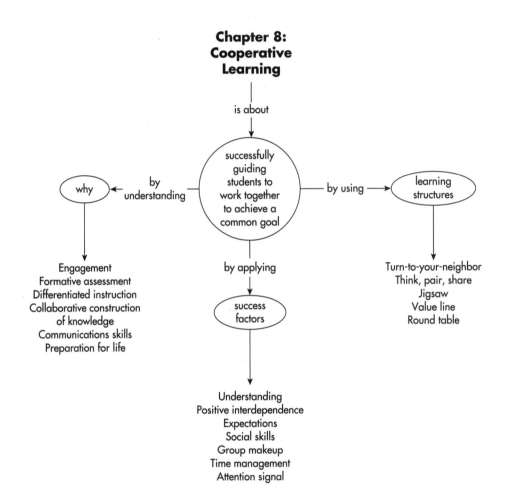

**Chapter 8:
Cooperative
Learning**

is about

successfully
guiding
students to
work together
to achieve a
common goal

by
understanding

why

by using

learning
structures

Engagement
Formative assessment
Differentiated instruction
Collaborative construction
of knowledge
Communications skills
Preparation for life

by applying

success
factors

Turn-to-your-neighbor
Think, pair, share
Jigsaw
Value line
Round table

Understanding
Positive interdependence
Expectations
Social skills
Group makeup
Time management
Attention signal

8

COOPERATIVE LEARNING

Diana Milan (not her real name), a student in Sarah Langton's sixth-grade science class, was not having a good year. Diana had long, thick, beautiful hair when she first came to Sarah's class. However, early in the year her family got head lice. "Diana's dad," Sarah's instructional coach, Michelle Harris, told me, "got so frustrated that they couldn't get rid of the lice that he shaved his daughter's head. After that she would wear her hoodie every single day and never put it down," Michelle said. Always a shy girl, Diana now tried to be invisible in school.

But Diana was fortunate to be in Ms. Langton's class because Sarah was deeply committed to helping each of her students succeed. One way she tried to improve was by collaborating frequently with instructional coach Michelle Harris. In Chapter 3 I described how Sarah and Michelle collaborated to implement formative assessment.

To start the coaching process, Sarah watched a video of her class. "The video," Michelle said, "helped her see that she was only calling on the same few kids in the class." Sarah realized, as she explained to Michelle, "that there was a whole group of students she wasn't really reaching."

Watching the video was "shocking" to Sarah, Michelle said. "I think she was sad, anxious, and ashamed, and felt a sense of urgency. You only have so much time in a year and you think what you are doing works. Then you watch the video and you think, Holy crap, I've spent eight months on this, and it's not working. Now I only have two months left to do something," Michelle said.

"I remember Sarah saying," Michelle told me, "'They are just tuning out. Everyone around them is raising their hand, and they are just sitting there. They just sit. I am calling on the same kids and I'm trying hard not to. I need to know how I can get these kids to participate. Twenty to thirty percent of my students are not participating.'"

The students who didn't raise their hands were the English language learners. After watching the video, it became clear to Sarah that she didn't know whether the students didn't know the subject matter or whether their English skills were not adequate enough for them to speak out in class. Ultimately, she didn't know if they understood the questions.

Sarah was well aware that sixth grade was pivotal for her students. As Michelle explained to me, Sarah knew that "by the time you get to sixth grade, the achievement gap that everybody talks about starts to widen . . . and if students never feel success, they spend the whole day never talking in an academic way. And by the time they get to tenth grade, they just drop out." It was this fact that made Sarah desperate to find a way to get those kids to feel successful.

With Michelle, Sarah set the goal for coaching that at least 70% of her nonparticipating students would talk in every classroom discussion. Eventually, after collaborating with Michelle, Sarah decided to try think, pair, share—a learning structure that prompts students to (a) consider their prior knowledge, (b) discuss and confirm their understanding with another student, and (c) then share their understandings with the rest of the class. Michelle explained why they decided to try this learning structure:

> The idea behind think, pair, share is that students access background knowledge by listening to others talk about a topic. Some kids just need that little trigger, especially kids who are not comfortable with their academic vocabulary. So once students feel like they can participate in a conversation—even if it is just with a partner—they are more confident and are more likely to raise their hand and participate in class. It is kind of like a self-fulfilling prophecy. Once they start to experience academic success, they begin to think, "Okay, I can do this school thing."

In planning for using this learning structure, Sarah carefully chose partners who would be most appropriate for the students who were struggling. For example, Diana, the girl with the hoodie, was paired with an encouraging, positive girl with whom she was already comfortable talking.

Sarah knew that students needed to use the learning structure successfully, so she modeled think, pair, share for the students and put up a poster that described how to do it. She told the students, "Here's what you'll be talking about, and here's what I expect to hear when you are talking." In addition, she walked around the room to monitor students and ensure they used the learning structure effectively.

"When the students finally got to the point that they were doing think, pair, share, Sarah had an epiphany," Michelle told me. She suddenly realized, "these kids do know a lot about what I am teaching them; they just aren't confident enough to call it out in the middle of class." That is, in listening in on the kids who never responded, Sarah realized they knew the material.

Sarah's students beat the goal! Sarah was thrilled. "I remember her being so happy that she had been able to determine that those students understood," Michelle said. The whole dynamic of the class changed because everyone was participating. The students who were English language learners "sat a little taller, smiled a little more," and they showed their peers that they knew the content. That, Michelle said, "had a very positive impact on the community in the classroom. That's so important at the middle level—that kids see each other as smart and 'with it.'"

Diana became a different student. Michelle said "she participated in class . . . started to smile a lot more, she was opening up a lot more, talking a lot more." And, like the other kids in class, she was "visibly more confident." And in the process, Michelle said, "her reading scores improved dramatically. She went from being at least two years behind to grade level. She was getting it—passing her tests and quizzes and doing her work." "Most important," Michelle reported, "she stopped hiding beneath her hoodie. Experiencing success, she learned that she didn't have to hide; she could leave sixth grade open to learning."

What Is Cooperative Learning?

The think, pair, share strategy that Sarah Langton used so successfully is one of many effective cooperative learning structures. Briefly, cooperative learning is learning that is mediated by the learners rather than directed by the teacher. In cooperative learning, students work in groups of various sizes and control their own learning. During cooperative learning,

> students work together to accomplish shared goals. Students are assigned to small groups and instructed to learn the

assigned material and to make sure that the other members of the group also master the assignment. Individual accountability is checked regularly to ensure that all students are learning . . . [and] students perceive that they can reach their learning goals if and only if the other students in the learning group also reach their goals. (Johnson & Johnson, 1986, p. 554)

According to Robert Slavin (1983), cooperative learning is "a set of alternatives to the traditional instructional system" (p. 3). Slavin writes that cooperative learning involves

techniques that use cooperative task structures, in which students spend much of their class time working in 4–6 member heterogeneous groups. They also use cooperative incentive structures, in which students can earn recognition, rewards, or (occasionally) grades based on the academic performance of their groups. (p. 3)

For our purposes, building on Johnson and Johnson (1986) and Slavin (1983), cooperative learning is any structured, systematic learning activity in which groups of learners work together to achieve a common goal.

Why Use Cooperative Learning?

Teachers and researchers alike have found that cooperative learning is a high-impact instructional strategy (or a collection of strategies) because it ensures student engagement, facilitates formative assessment, facilitates differentiated instruction, allows students to collaboratively construct knowledge, develops communication skills, and prepares students for the work world. Each of these areas is discussed below.

Ensures Student Engagement. Research on how the brain takes in information, such as that summarized by John Medina in *Brain Rules: 12 Principles for Surviving and Thriving at Work, Home, and School* (2008), shows what most of us have learned from personal experience: People struggle to stay engaged when they experience the same activity, such as lectures, for long periods of time. Cooperative learning changes the way students learn from teacher-mediated to student-mediated, and simply because this structure changes what students are doing, it can increase student energy and engagement.

Watch Sandi Silbernagel use two cooperative learning structures—mix, pair, share and jot thoughts.

Video 8.1
www.corwin.com/
highimpactinstruction

More important perhaps, well-constructed cooperative learning gives every student a learning task at every minute during an activity. And as a result, students have no other option than to be engaged and learn.

Facilitates Formative Assessment. As mentioned at different points in this book, formative assessment is an important instructional strategy because (a) student engagement and learning increase when students clearly understand how well they are doing, and (b) teachers are able to adapt their instruction based on their knowledge of how well each student is doing.

Cooperative learning provides many opportunities for formative assessment because it asks students to produce some kind of product (e.g., a prepared verbal response, a written commentary, a graphic organizer) that demonstrates their level of understanding. When teachers review what students produce, they can quickly see whether or not students have learned the knowledge, skills, and big ideas they are exposed to in class and then, if necessary, make decisions about how they need to modify instruction to promote better learning.

Facilitates Differentiated Instruction. One of the challenges teachers face today is having to teach a classroom of students who have extremely diverse academic skills, interests, and strengths. Cooperative learning allows teachers to group students in ways that allow for greater differentiation of learning. Thus, a teacher might allow students to choose a topic they wish to work on (using the modified open-space techniques described in Chapter 12) and work with others on a topic that is especially interesting to them. Similarly, a teacher might group students with others who have the same strengths so they can work on a task that will allow them to flourish. Other options include grouping students with other students who have similar academic needs or with students who have different academic strengths so that they can help each other learn the knowledge, skills, and big ideas in the course.

Allows Collaborative Construction of Knowledge. Students deepen and refine their understanding by talking about what they are learning. In part, this occurs because, as Vygotsky explained (1978), each person's learning begins at a different point. Well-structured cooperative learning brings together students who are in different stages of understanding, and the conversation moves students along their own zone of proximal development (Vygotsky).

When I talk to people who are further along in their learning than I am, our conversation moves my understanding closer to their level of understanding. As Vygotsky has written, "what children can do together today, they can do alone tomorrow" (as cited in Bennett, Rolheiser, & Stevahn, 1991, p. 16).

In addition, striving to find words for their ideas compels students to clarify and deepen their learning since they need to know what they are talking about if they are going to talk about it with others. Cooperative learning often prompts students to find new ways to express their ideas—that is, to paraphrase—which also supports student learning.

Develops Communication Skills. School teaches knowledge, skills, and big ideas related to content areas such as math, English, science, social studies, the arts, related studies, and other topics. But school also has a responsibility to teach students knowledge, skills, and big ideas that are outside the main academic content, such as how to communicate effectively and build relationships with others. If students are to learn how to interact successfully with others, in school, in society, at home, and later in life, they need to practice effective communication, and that can be done during cooperative learning.

Much like swimming, which would be difficult to learn if you never got in the water, communication skills are difficult to learn without real-life practice and feedback. Cooperative learning provides opportunities for students to practice listening, speaking clearly, taking turns, making eye contact, paraphrasing, and so on. Also, if available, students can periodically use micro-cameras to review their communication skills and see where they are strong, where they can improve, and what progress they have made as communicators.

Prepares for Life After School. Patrick Lencioni begins *Five Dysfunctions of a Team* (2002) with a bold claim about the work world: "Not finance. Not strategy. Not technology. It is teamwork that remains the ultimate competitive advantage, both because it is so powerful, and so rare" (p. vii). Similarly, Massachusetts Institute of Technology organizational theorist Edgar H. Schein, in his foreword to Amy Edmondson's *Teaming: How Organizations Learn, Innovate, and Compete in the Knowledge Economy* (2012), writes, "Even though our culture tends to accept groups and teams only when pragmatically necessary to win or get a job done, teams and teaming are at the foundation of society and community" (p. xi).

Collaboration is increasingly becoming the way through which business and community work gets done. As part of preparing their students for life beyond school, teachers can use cooperative learning to teach the important life skill of how to work effectively with others. When students are taught how to be successful in teams, and when they are taught those skills by actually working with others, they learn vitally important professional skills.

Critical Factors for Success When Using Cooperative Learning

Clearly Understand the Learning Structure. Implementation of cooperative learning can look deceptively easy—"let's put the kids in groups and let them teach each other." It is important to guard against what Michael Fullan referred to as "false clarity." "False clarity," Fullan writes, "occurs when change is interpreted in an oversimplified way; that is, the proposed change has more to it than people realize" (2001, p. 77). If teachers have false clarity about why students will use cooperative learning, what students are to do and how they are to act, there is a real danger that the activity could fall apart.

To prevent this from happening, teachers can ensure that they have a deep understanding of the cooperative learning structure they plan to use by writing out (a) the learning goal of the activity; in other words, what is the specific proficiency that the cooperative learning structure is being used to help students learn; (b) what students have to do during the activity; and (c) how students have to behave (i.e., as explained in Chapter 13, how students should act, talk, and move during the activity).

In addition, to guard against false clarity, teachers should also apply the other success factors listed here (see Figure 8.1).

Create Positive Interdependence. In *Cooperative Learning: Where Heart Meets Mind* (1991), Bennett and colleagues expand on Johnson and Johnson's findings (1991) that teachers must strengthen positive interdependence for cooperative learning to be successful.

Bennett et al. (1991) give excellent examples of how teachers can foster positive interdependence. For example, the authors suggest that teachers can promote positive interdependence by ensuring students have shared goals, such as creating a product, completing an assignment, or analyzing information or by providing resources in a way that requires cooperation, such as providing a group of students with one textbook, one pencil, and one learning sheet.

Positive interdependence, the authors suggest, can also be promoted by assigning roles to students in groups, such as checker, time keeper, questioner, encourager, reader, or summarizer. In addition,

Figure 8.1 Success Factors Checklist

Success Factors	✓
The teacher clearly understands the learning structure.	
The teacher has created a psychologically safe environment.	
The teacher has written expectations for how students should act, talk, and move while they perform the cooperative learning activity.	
Students have learned the expectations for how to act, talk, and move during the cooperative learning activity.	
Students have learned and use appropriate social skills to interact positively and effectively during the activity.	
The teacher has carefully considered the optimal makeup of each group of students.	
The teacher has given students sufficient time for each activity, without providing so much time that the learning loses intensity.	
Students have additional activities they can do if they finish their tasks before others in the class.	
The teacher has planned additional activities to use during the class if activities take less time than planned.	
The teacher has planned how to adjust the lesson plan if activities take more time than planned.	
The teacher uses an effective attention signal.	

positive interdependence can be created by giving a group a unique identity such as a name or special place to meet in the classroom.

Create a Psychologically Safe Learning Environment. Amy Edmondson, the Novartis Professor of Leadership and Management at Harvard University, has dedicated much of her academic life to studying how people work and learn together. Although her research has focused on adult teams in organizations, her findings have implications for schools. One of Edmondson's primary findings is that people need to feel psychologically safe in order to be productive and learn. Edmondson writes that "in corporations, hospitals, and government agencies . . . interpersonal fear frequently gives rise to poor decisions and incomplete execution" (2012, p. 118). Edmondson continues:

In psychologically safe environments, people believe that if they make a mistake others will not penalize them or think less of them for it. They also believe that others will not resent or humiliate them when they ask for help or information. This belief comes about when people both trust and respect each other, and it produces a sense of confidence that the group won't embarrass, reject, or punish someone for speaking up. (pp. 118–119)

The psychological safety that Edmondson's research has identified as essential for organizational learning is also important for classroom learning. If students are afraid to speak up, take risks, or ask for help, their opportunities to learn will be limited.

Based on her research, Edmondson suggests strategies leaders can use to create psychologically safe teams (see Figure 8.2). With some adaptations, many of her suggestions can be employed by teachers establishing cooperative learning.

Be Accessible and Approachable. Leaders can "encourage team members to learn together by being accessible and personally involved" (Edmondson, 2012, p. 138). Similarly, teachers can take a personal interest in the success of each student in each cooperative learning grouping and make it clear that they are available to answer any questions students may have about what they are learning, how they are learning it, and anything else that might help students learn.

Acknowledge the Limits of Current Knowledge. "Strange as it may seem," Edmondson writes, "many leaders are unwilling to publically express the fact that they don't have the answers to every issue or challenge. . . . Acknowledging uncertainty . . . [however] . . . creates an

Figure 8.2	Edmondson's Leadership Behaviors for Cultivating Psychological Safety

- Be accessible and approachable
- Acknowledge the limits of current knowledge
- Be willing to display fallibility
- Invite participation
- Highlight failures as learning opportunities
- Set boundaries
- Hold people accountable for transgressions

Source: Edmondson (2012).

implied invitation to offer information or expertise" (2012, p. 140). So too in the classroom, when a teacher makes it clear that some knowledge is provisional and that she too is a learner and, therefore, doesn't have all the answers, she invites students to be learners along with her.

Display Fallibility. "To create psychological safety," Edmondson writes, "team leaders must demonstrate a tolerance of failure by acknowledging their own fallibility" (2012, p. 140). Like leaders in organizations, teachers can encourage students to risk failure by admitting that they are not perfect.

Invite Participation. "When people believe leaders and managers want to hear from them and value their input, they're more responsive" (Edmondson, 2012, p. 141). Like Sarah Langton, whose story was included at the beginning of this chapter, teachers are always looking for ways to include all students in learning. What is vitally important is that *all* students are included, and teachers need to be intentional about watching and including all students.

Highlight Failures as Learning Opportunities. Many stories typically are told about organizations, that may or may not be true, but that illustrate the importance of celebrating failures as learning opportunities. Edmondson (2012) includes a story, told by Paul Carroll about Tom Watson, Jr., at IBM and one of his executives who lost $10 million in a mistake. "Watson asked, 'Do you know why I've asked you here?' The man replied, 'I assume I'm here so you can fire me.' Watson looked surprised. 'Fire you?' he asked. 'Of course not. I just spent $10 million educating you.' He then reassured the executive and suggested he keep taking chances" (p. 142).

"By avoiding punishing others for having taken well-intentioned risks that backfired," Edmondson writes, "leaders inspire people to embrace error and failure and deal with them in a productive manner" (2012, p. 141). Teachers should also set out to create a culture where students know it is OK to make mistakes. They can accomplish this by being supportive of all responses, encouraging student effort, and refraining from ridiculing incorrect responses.

Set Boundaries. "Paradoxically," Edmondson writes, "when leaders are as clear as possible about what constitutes blameworthy acts, people feel more psychologically safe than when boundaries of acceptable action are subject to guess work" (2012, p. 143). As explained below and in other sections of this book, teachers need to be very clear about what students are to do and not to do during any activity.

Hold People Accountable for Transgressions. "It's the job of leaders," Edmondson writes, "to help people see that unacceptable behaviors do occur and must be equitably addressed" (2012, p. 144). Again, this finding has application in the classroom. Once teachers establish the boundaries for cooperative learning, they need to ensure that students respect those boundaries.

Ensure Students Have Learned the Expectations. As explained in Part III of this book, to ensure that students act in ways that promote their learning, teachers need to write down and teach the expectations for (a) what students are to do in an activity (i.e., what meaningful, appropriate engagement looks like); (b) how loudly students should talk and what they should and should not talk about; and (c) what kind of movement is acceptable for any activity or transition.

Teachers should not assume that telling students the expectations will lead to students automatically following them. For that reason, teachers need to spend a significant amount of time on ensuring students learn and can follow the expectations. This might involve using the "I do it," "We do it," and "You do it" teaching routine described in Chapter 3.

Teach Social Skills. My colleague Sue Vernon has created a comprehensive, research-validated curriculum on social skills for cooperative learning. According to Vernon (1996),

> Working together in an effective way demands special skills and cannot be left to chance. Learning the prerequisite skills often requires much time and practice. If such skills are taught well, however, students can become exceedingly effective members of a team. (p. 1)

In her book *The Score Skills: Social Skills for Cooperative Groups* (1996), Vernon presents a set of carefully designed, explicit lessons to teach students "five social skills [that] provide the foundation for students to work together in the classroom as coworkers or as teammates in a pleasant, cooperative, and effective manner while building a successful learning community" (p. 4). Vernon's research (reported in her book) suggests that social skills instruction can have a profound impact on how students interact. Vernon proposes students learn five skills built around the acronym SCORE. Specifically, students are taught how to **s**hare ideas, **c**ompliment others, **o**ffer help or encouragement, **r**ecommend changes nicely, and **e**xercise self-control.

In addition to Vernon's SCORE skills, I suggest teaching at least two other social skills. First, since cooperative learning activities will flounder if students all talk at once, I suggest teaching students how to take turns. Second, I suggest teachers take time to teach students how to listen to each other.

Listening is not just a strategy for cooperative learning; it is a skill students can use in all areas of their lives inside and outside of school. To ensure student acquisition, teachers should (a) explain the skills, (b) model the skills, and (c) provide ample opportunity for students to practice their listening skills. By teaching students how to listen, teachers increase their ability to learn (people learn more when they hear what is being taught), decrease behavior problems, and ensure students learn an important life skill.

Determine the Optimal Makeup of Every Group. Before moving students into groups, teachers should consider at least two factors—the size of the group and who will work with whom. At first, before students have learned all of the expectations for the cooperative learning structure they're going to experience, it may work best to start with smaller groups, usually pairs, since smaller groups are easier to manage. Teaming students in pairs is also a good idea in classes where teachers are still helping students to learn how to communicate positively and effectively.

Teachers also need to consider which students should work together. Sometimes teachers may want to group students according to their interests or strengths so that they focus on particular tasks or content. At other times, teachers may want to group students who have different strengths together to ensure that each group includes students who can approach challenges with different perspectives. In yet other cases, teachers may want to avoid putting some students together who might keep each other off task during learning.

Manage Time Effectively. Time management makes or breaks any cooperative learning activity. First, teachers must give the right amount of time for students to complete cooperative learning activities. If students don't have enough time, (a) they won't learn what they need to learn from an activity, (b) they will feel like the effort they put into the task was a waste of time, and (c) they will be less inclined to work hard during the next cooperative learning activity. On the other hand, if students have too much time, the activity may lose intensity, and students may stop being engaged.

One way to help manage time is to give students a second activity they can do once the first activity is completed. This second activity should be a meaningful learning activity that can keep students engaged until all groups are finished. In this way, a teacher can keep students engaged and provide sufficient time for all students to finish.

Teachers also have to manage overall instructional time. Cooperative learning can be unwieldy, and, especially at first, it can be hard to determine how much time a cooperative learning activity might take. For that reason, teachers need to plan to make adjustments if an activity takes longer than planned—the most likely scenario—or too little time—which is also possible.

On those occasions when cooperative learning takes longer than anticipated, teachers must be prepared to cut down on or eliminate other learning experiences they might have planned. Conversely, when cooperative learning takes less time than expected, teachers must be ready with extra learning experiences that students can complete to take maximum advantage of learning time during a class period.

Use an Attention Signal. Cooperative learning engages students in interesting and often very enjoyable learning experiences. As a result, regaining students' attention after they have participated in a cooperative learning activity can be a challenge. Many teachers find it useful to teach students an attention signal to regain their attention. For example, they can teach students that when they raise their hand and say, "May I have your attention, please?" the students are also to raise one hand and stop talking, as soon as possible. Other signals include clapping out a rhythm that students clap back, flicking the lights, or playing a sound, such as chimes or a bell, to get attention.

Learning Structures

Researchers have developed and studied several cooperative learning structures that teachers can use to help students acquire and master what they are learning. For example, teams, games, tournaments (Devries & Edwards, 1974), and student teams—achievement divisions (Slavin, 1978)—are cooperative learning structures in which team goals and team successes are predicated upon all members of a team learning the objectives being taught. Special cooperative learning structures have been used to teach reading and writing, such as cooperative integrated reading and composition (Stevens, Madden, Slavin, & Farnish, 1987), in which "students follow a sequence of teacher instruction, team practice, team preassessments, and quiz" (Slavin, 1990). Further, group investigation (Sharan & Sharan, 1976) is a cooperative learning structure in which groups of students (from two to six students) work together using group inquiry, discussion, and cooperative planning to organize and complete group projects that require each student to complete individual tasks.

Watch Tiffani Poirier use games to teach the concept of place value.

Video 8.2
www.corwin.com/
highimpactinstruction

In my experience, the following five learning structures can be easily implemented in many different classrooms with many different groups of students: turn-to-your-neighbor (Johnson & Johnson, 1991); think, pair, share (Lyman, 1987); jigsaw (Aronson, 1978); value line (Kagan, 1990); and round table (Kagan, 2009). Each structure is described below.

Turn-to-Your-Neighbor (Also Turn-to-Your-Partner, Turn-and-Talk). Turn-to-your-neighbor, one of the simplest cooperative learning structures, is also very effective for increasing engagement, checking student understanding, and preparing students to engage in large-group discussion (see Figure 8.3). While it is easy for students to master, as is the case with all of the other learning structures, teachers must explicitly teach students how to act, talk, and move when they "turn to their neighbor."

During turn-to-your-neighbor, the teacher organizes students into pairs and then, at various points throughout the class, prompts students to turn to their neighbor (the student in the class with whom they have been paired) and have a conversation about what they are learning. For example, students might share their opinion about a provocative topic, paraphrase different components of content being covered during a learning session, or ask each other questions to confirm that they have mastered the material.

Turn-to-your-neighbor breaks up the routine of a class, provides a way for students to prepare for classroom discussion, and enables students to confirm their learning. However tempting it is to use this learning structure, overdoing use of turn-to-your-neighbor is no better than overdoing any teaching practice, and being asked to turn to your neighbor every five minutes can be just as boring as having to listen to lectures all of the time. For that reason, it is important to use a variety of learning structures, such as those included in the rest of this book and in this chapter.

Think, Pair, Share. During think, pair, share activities, students first individually learn or reflect on new content and then record their thoughts in some formal way such as writing on notepaper or in a journal (see Figure 8.4). Students might be prompted to write down their opinion on a topic to be discussed, an answer to a question, or a prediction related to what is being discussed in class.

After students have written down their thoughts, they share with a classmate what they have written. In some cases, students are checking their understanding by confirming that they have the same

Figure 8.3 Turn-to-Your-Neighbor Checklist

Students know . . .	✓
Who their learning partner will be before they start.	
What tasks, if any, they need to do before they turn to their neighbor.	
What tasks they need to do with their partner (for example, confirm their understanding, compare answers, share an opinion).	
The outcome they need to produce for the class (a written product, a comment to share with the class, thumbs up, and so forth) at the end of the conversation.	
How they should communicate with each other (in particular, how they should listen and talk).	

Download this form at www.corwin.com/ highimpactinstruction

understanding as their partner. In other cases, the teacher prompts students to explain or justify their answer to their partner. When students are prompted to give their opinions, the teacher might prompt students to identify ways in which their answers are similar and different.

After students have talked with their partners about their thoughts, the teacher prompts them to share with the larger class what they have learned. In some cases, teachers simply ask students to raise their hands and share what they have discussed; at other times they ask students to take turns replying. At yet other times, teachers have the students organize themselves, by choosing, for example, to be the sun or the moon, hotdogs or pizza, and so forth, and then asking the sun or hotdogs to be the first to share.

It is important that students think and write down their thoughts before they share them, in part, because this allows them to access their prior knowledge. When students don't take time to think before they talk, many are inclined to simply agree with their partner without considering what they already know, which would defeat the purpose of the learning structure.

Jigsaw. During jigsaw activities, students are divided into small groups, and each group is prompted to learn a portion of content being covered during the class, often a few pages of a textbook or some other reading material (see Figure 8.5). Sometimes teachers give students graphic organizers or cloze diagrams to help them note and organize their understanding of what they are learning.

Figure 8.4 Think, Pair, Share Checklist	
Students know . . .	✓
Who their learning partner will be before they start.	
Exactly what the thinking prompt is to which they are responding.	
How much time they will have to write their response.	
That they are to use all the time they are given to think and write about their response.	
The outcome they need to produce for the class (a written product, a comment to share with the class, thumbs up, and so forth) at the end of the conversation.	
How they should communicate with each other (in particular, how they should listen and talk).	

After each group has learned a different portion of content, the teacher puts the students in new groups, with every new group containing at least one member from each original group. For example, if there are five original groups, each new group includes at least one member from the original five groups. In the new groups, students, in sequence, teach what they learned in their first group to the members of the new group. In this way, a lot of information can be learned and shared in ways that should be highly engaging for students.

Jigsaw is more complicated than some of the other learning structures described here, and it is important to set students up for success. Usually, this means that teachers must ensure that students know exactly what they are to do in their original group and in their second group. For example, teachers may want students to check with each other to make sure everyone understands what they are to do before they begin. Also, teachers must ensure that students are clear on exactly what group they have to go to in the second stage of jigsaw. The entire activity can fail if each new group doesn't include a member from each previous group. Having students write down a number for their second group and then double-check to make sure that each new group has the correct members helps ensure students always move to where they need to be.

Students are usually very engaged during jigsaw, so it is important for teachers to move around the room and check that what students have learned is correct before they move to the next group to teach.

Figure 8.5 Jigsaw Checklist	
Students know . . .	✓
What group they will be in for the first activity (perhaps by writing down the number for their group).	
What group they will be in for the second activity (again, perhaps by writing down the number for their group).	
How they are to work together to learn and summarize what they are learning.	
The product they need to create to share with the second group.	
Before moving to the second group, that what they have created has received their teacher's stamp of approval.	
How they should communicate with each other in both groups (in particular, how they should listen and talk).	
How they will record (usually take notes or fill out a learning sheet) what they learn from their fellow students in their second group.	

Download this form at www.corwin.com/ highimpactinstruction

Value Line. Value line (Kagan, 1994, 2009) is a fun and energizing learning structure because it prompts the students to get out of their chairs and move around the room. It can also be a stimulus for rich and meaningful discussion since it leads to a visual depiction of students' opinions or understandings (see Figure 8.6).

During value line, the teacher first presents an issue, topic, or question and then assigns a value scale to each possible student response. For example, the teacher introduces a 1–10 scale where 1 equals strong agreement and 10 equals strong disagreement. The teacher then asks students to form a line based on how they rank their responses on the scale. After students line up, the teacher guides a discussion about the topic. After the discussion, the teacher may ask students to reevaluate where they wish to stand in the line.

For value line to be successful, teachers must ensure that students clearly understand the question they are considering and have sufficient time to consider it. I've found that it is a good idea to have students write down the number that best reflects their opinion before they move to their spot in the number line. Students also need to know how to act, talk, and move during the activity. Specifically, they need to know when and how quickly to move to prevent students running across the room disturbing or distracting the class. In addition, students need to know what to talk about during the activity, how loud to talk, and what to do when they arrive at their spot on the line. Finally, students need to know why they are being asked to participate in the learning structure.

Some classrooms are too small or too crowded for this learning structure, so when teachers believe value line is an important learning structure to support students' mastery of knowledge, skills, or big ideas, they may choose to take students outside to build a number line. In the linked video clip from the Teaching Channel, Alastair Inman, a science teacher from Lexington Junior High, takes students outside to use a value line to deepen their understanding of the history of the earth.

An alternative to value line is to post one of four possible answers to a question in each corner of the classroom and then ask students to go to the corner that best represents their answer or perspective. Again, this works best in larger rooms were students have room to move around, but it is a simple way to get students moving and to start discussion.

Round Table. Round table, another learning structure, prompts students to generate a lot of information quickly. The activity provides an opportunity for every student to share his or her unique knowledge, and students find it to be highly engaging (see Figure 8.7).

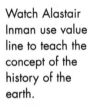

Watch Alastair Inman use value line to teach the concept of the history of the earth.

Video 8.3
www.corwin.com/
highimpactinstruction

Download this form at www.corwin.com/ highimpactinstruction

Figure 8.6	Value Line Checklist	
Students know . . .		✓
What the question is that they are considering.		
How much time they have to consider the question.		
Where the numbers for the value line are located in the room.		
Why they are being asked to line up in a value line.		
When to move and how quickly.		
What to talk about and how loud to talk.		
What to do when they get to their spot on the number line.		

During round table, the teacher divides the class into groups, and students write down ideas on a piece of paper and then pass the paper to the student next to them so that he or she can add ideas to the paper. Every student gets a turn at answering the question before the activity is completed. I have found that students are most engaged when each student has a piece of paper that he or she rotates to a neighbor when given the prompt. When there is only one piece of paper to be circulated, students spend too much time watching and not enough time thinking and writing.

Round table can be used to review what students have learned or to begin a lesson by prompting students to discuss their prior knowledge. For example, in a study of the novel *The Catcher in the Rye*, students could use round table to look at Holden Caulfield's character from many perspectives. Thus, in a group of three, each student would start with a piece of paper with a question about characterization. One student could be prompted to write down how Holden describes himself. Another student could be prompted to write down what Holden's actions reveal about his character. And the third student could write down how others view Holden. After a short time, perhaps three minutes, the teacher could ask the students to pass their notes to the student on their right, and once the papers are passed, students can then write down what they know about the second question.

Once all of the questions have been addressed, the class may be asked to share what they have learned. In this way, students can show what they know, learn from their fellow students, and gain a deeper understanding of the big idea, in the above case, how authors reveal characters in works of fiction.

Figure 8.7	Round Table Checklist

Download this form at www.corwin.com/highimpactinstruction

Students know . . .	✓
Each question they are responding to.	
How much time they have to consider the question.	
Where they are to pass the paper.	
How they will sum up what they have learned or discovered.	
How they will share with the rest of the class what they have learned.	

Turning Ideas Into Action

Students

1. The easiest way to find out how effective a cooperative learning structure has been or whether or not students have acted consistently with the expectations for the activity is to ask the students themselves. For example, following an activity, teachers might give students an anonymous, brief survey to rank, from 1 to 5, how well they acted with respect to specific expectations, such as listening, taking turns, encouraging each other, and so forth.

2. Students can also be asked to assess their level of engagement, noting whether they were (a) authentically engaged, (b) strategically compliant, or (c) off task.

3. Students could be asked to write down suggestions for how a learning structure could be improved to increase their learning and enjoyment. Asking for students' opinions takes only a minute at the end of the class, but by involving students in such a way, teachers may increase students' engagement in learning and also get some great suggestions.

Teachers

1. Teachers who have never used cooperative learning should probably begin with an easy-to-implement learning structure such as turn-to-your-neighbor.

2. Even when introducing a seemingly simple learning structure, teachers should review the learning structure carefully to be certain they understand exactly what students will do during the activity.

3. Teachers should also carefully review the success factors checklist to ensure that the learning structure will be successful.

4. Teachers should consider visiting other teachers who use cooperative learning effectively to pick up tips on how to implement it effectively.

Instructional Coaches

1. In most cases, if an instructional coach is helping a teacher implement cooperative learning, it is not because the teacher hasn't heard of cooperative learning but because the teacher has had some concerns or fears about dramatically changing the way learning occurs in his or her class. For that reason, coaches must be especially attentive to the critical factors for cooperative learning success listed above.

2. Coaches must do everything in their power to ensure that a teacher's first attempt at cooperative learning doesn't fall apart. For that reason, ICs are wise to suggest simple cooperative learning

structures such as think, pair, share before turning to more complicated structures such as jigsaw.

3. Coaches might also suggest that teachers write out the guidelines for the learning structure to ensure that they fully understand all of its aspects. Teachers will be much more likely to continue to use cooperative learning if their first experience is successful, and ICs can do a lot to increase the likelihood that a teacher will be successful.

4. Instructional coaches can be a second set of eyes for teachers, observing students to see that they understand their roles and that they are on task. ICs can also talk with students briefly to see if they know what they are supposed to be doing, if they are doing it, and if they are learning during the activity.

Principals

1. What matters most when using cooperative learning is that students are actually learning. For that reason, administrators conducting walk-through observations may want to pay special attention to the conversations that are taking place within cooperative learning groups. Those conducting observations can observe whether (a) students are on task, (b) all students are engaged in the activity, and (c) the activity is appropriate for meeting the learning goal.

2. Perhaps the two most important issues for administrators to consider are (a) when teachers are not using cooperative learning, should they be? and (b) when teachers are using cooperative learning, would some other form of learning be more efficient? In some cases, it may take students more time to learn through cooperative learning than through some other way. In other situations, administrators may be in classrooms where students stop being engaged because there is too much teacher-directed instruction, and they may propose teachers use cooperative learning (and other high-impact instructional strategies) to increase engagement and learning.

3. Since teachers need to implement cooperative learning effectively if it is going to succeed, and since seeing how others implement cooperative learning can be very helpful, administrators should look for ways to free up teachers to watch others who fluently guide students through learning structures. For example, substitutes could be hired to free up teachers, or administrators could fill in for a lesson so that teachers can observe someone else.

What to Look For

Cooperative learning is most helpful for responding to two basic student needs—engagement and learning. For this reason, teachers may choose time on task (95% of students are on task) or student achievement (all students are proficient; more than 80% are highly proficient) as an improvement goal.

(Continued)

(Continued)

In my experience, measuring time on task during cooperative learning is difficult to do in a standardized way (such as assessing one student every five seconds). A more appropriate way is to simply observe each group and note whether or not students are engaged in the task at hand.

Teachers can use two simple methods to assess whether or not students have learned what they are supposed to have learned during cooperative learning activities. Teachers can give students a short quiz after a cooperative learning activity or give students an exit ticket at the end of class to assess whether they have learned what was intended during the activity.

Some teachers and coaches identify teacher goals along with student goals. For example, instructional coach Michelle Harris sometimes gathers data on teacher talk and student talk. This can be easily done by using the stopwatch function on a smartphone (or an actual stopwatch). Many coaches keep track of student talk on their stopwatch and then consider the rest of instruction as teacher talk. For more precise numbers coaches can use two devices for recording time, one to record teacher talk and another to record student talk, with the remaining time being labeled as transition time.

The checklists in this chapter can also be used as observation tools to assess how fluently a learning structure is being implemented.

To Sum Up

Cooperative learning may be defined as any structured, systematic learning activity in which groups of learners work together to achieve a common goal. As such, cooperative learning is a high-impact instructional strategy because it

- Ensures engagement by providing every student with a task and by varying the way in which students learn
- Facilitates formative assessment
- Facilitates differentiated instruction
- Allows students to collaboratively construct knowledge
- Develops students' communication skills
- Prepares students for life after school

Cooperative learning is most successful when teachers

- Clearly understand the learning structure students will use
- Create positive interdependence

- Teach expectations
- Teach social skills
- Determine the optimum makeup of groups
- Manage time successfully
- Use an attention signal

Five learning structures that are easy for teachers to use with different students in different settings are

- Turn-to-your-neighbor
- Think, pair, share
- Jigsaw
- Value line
- Round table

Going Deeper

In one way or another, most authors and researchers describing cooperative learning owe a debt to David and Roger Johnson. Their book *Learning Together and Alone: Cooperative, Competitive, and Individualistic Learning* (1975) laid the groundwork for many other descriptions of cooperative learning, highlighting the importance of positive interdependence and individual accountability. In addition, their work provides excellent advice on practical matters such as the teacher's role during cooperative learning, choosing the appropriate size for cooperative learning groups, assessment and evaluation within cooperative learning, and the differences between cooperative, competitive, and individualistic learning.

Barrie Bennett, Carol Rolheiser, and Laurie Stevahn's *Cooperative Learning: Where Heart Meets Mind* (1991) is another excellent and useful description of cooperative learning. Their book contains numerous bullet points, checklists, and learning sheets that teachers can use as a resource. Overall, the book is easy to understand and filled with practical advice.

Perhaps no one has done more to disseminate ideas related to cooperative learning than Spencer Kagan. His book *Cooperative Learning* (Kagan & Kagan, 2009) is packed with learning structures (Kagan has created more than 200 "Kagan Structures") that can be used in many different settings with many different students for many different purposes. Thus, the book is ideal for anyone who wants to get a deeper understanding of learning structures that can be used during cooperative learning.

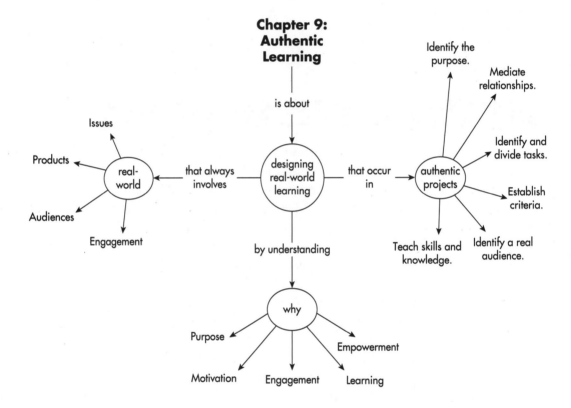

**Chapter 9:
Authentic
Learning**

is about

designing
real-world
learning

that always
involves

real-
world

Issues

Products

Audiences

Engagement

that occur
in

authentic
projects

Identify the
purpose.

Mediate
relationships.

Identify and
divide tasks.

Establish
criteria.

Identify a real
audience.

Teach skills and
knowledge.

by understanding

why

Purpose

Motivation

Engagement

Empowerment

Learning

9

AUTHENTIC LEARNING

If you drop in on Amy Schmer's sixth-grade science class at Preston Middle School in Fort Collins, Colorado, there is a good chance you'll see 10- and 11-year old children passionately exploring topics that ordinarily are discussed by professional biologists. The students might be doing research on how to provide a new clean water source for wildlife, discussing the challenges of nonnative plants and the role livestock plays, or passionately discussing the needs of screech owls, great horned owls, and northern pygmy owls with an expert ornithologist from Estes Park. Whatever the students are doing, likely they are doing it with a level of engagement and excitement that would thrill any educator.

The educators at Preston Middle School have been partnering with David Neils, an educational activist who has spent more than 17 years guiding schools toward ensuring that students do real learning, authentic learning. David is passionate about students and refuses to accept the notion that children can go through school bored and compliant. He told me:

> Something is amiss in our educational system when youth don't have the confidence, the skill, the ability to put forth their own ideas and make something happen. You see a lot of high school students even today who are unprepared for life after high school. Their plans are shallow; they are based on whims or as basic as "I'm going into engineering because I think I can make a lot of money." They are not connected with

professionals in a way that allows them to leverage who they are. I feel that youth can start doing authentic learning soon after they can walk, and authentic work should be the hallmark of their education up through graduate school.

David and I have collaborated for more than a decade, and his deep commitment to students is so forceful that on more than one occasion we have ended up in passionate arguments. (My wife, Jenny, is quick to remind me that my stubbornness contributes significantly to the heated nature of some of my conversations with David.) Sometimes David and I disagree, but mostly he makes me think deeply about what education is for and how we can do a better job. Ultimately, David has the results to show that his passion is well directed.

David's work has been widely recognized. He's been mentioned by acclaimed authors such as Po Bronson and Sir Ken Robinson, and featured in articles in *Fortune* and *US News and World Report*. People celebrate David's pioneering work in creating The International Telementor Center, which exploits the connectivity of the Internet so students can learn from experts and mentors who work around the world in organizations such as Hewlett Packard, MasterCard, Intel, Google, Merck, Wells Fargo, and the George Lucas Educational Foundation.

Telementoring for David, though, is not an end in itself; telementoring is a tool for supporting what really matters to him—authentic learning experiences for students. David once told me, "I would love to be able to manage this program and never have to look at a computer. But telementoring is the only way to efficiently and successfully connect fantastic professionals with students in a way that works with the existing structure."

When he isn't working directly with schools, David loves to photograph and videotape mountain lions and other predators, and he frequently spends time in the Colorado mountains near his home. One area close to his home is Sylvan Dale Guest Ranch (sylvandale .com), a 3,000-acre mountain getaway used for weddings, business meetings, and other outdoor adventures. While photographing next to the ranch, David realized that the land would be a fantastic place for students to do science projects, so he called the owners to see if they'd be interested in students visiting the property. As it turns out, Susan Jessup, the ranch owner, told David that her father always wanted young people to do real science on the ranch. "So," David told me, "we were given access to the 3,000 acres of the ranch holdings to do authentic science work for multiple years, and in addition to the 3,000 acres, we had another 4,000 acres of leased land on a national forest available to us. We had an outdoor 7,000-acre classroom."

After getting the go-ahead from Sylvan Dale Ranch, David met Amy Schmer from Preston Middle School. Amy visited the ranch and quickly recognized that it would be a great place for students to do science, so she asked David to speak to her sixth-grade students. "I shared the opportunity that Sylvan Dale Ranch had given us," David told me. "I let them know what I do, that I run this mentoring program and I'm looking for opportunities for students to do authentic work. They were given the choice to do science outside in the wilderness or do the regular curriculum. Amy wanted the students themselves to agree to the project, and they immediately were on board."

The students were given a number of options. They could focus on plants, water, or wildlife. In early September, the students decided to focus on improving wildlife habitat because that would affect both water and plants. "The decision was made by students. We didn't tell them what to do," David explained, and then described how their project got started:

> The students had to figure out what was happening on the ranch with the species of animals that were there. They learned by conversing with mentors and other wildlife experts about the fact that there are four main areas to focus on if you are going to improve wildlife habitat: forage, water, shelter, or places to rear young. Then they looked at the target species. This is what makes this work authentic—they went after the real issues that professionals in the field care about, issues regarding predators, wild cats, bob cats, mountain lions, coyotes, mule deer, elk, and so on. They had to get an understanding from these biologists of which animals needed the most help and what areas they should focus on.

"What came out on top right away," David said, "was the issue of water." When the students visited the ranch, they discovered that although a big ditch flowed through the property, it could only be reached by bats, birds, and other flying animals. They saw that water was scarce for animals, and they realized that if they put in some kind of water structure it could make a big difference.

David explained to me what happened next:

> Then the students had to work with their mentors to do research: What does that water structure look like? Where have professionals had success putting in water structures? A lot of that work had been done in Utah, so they communicated with their mentors and experts in other states to learn

how to do this. Then they got a guzzler (a 50-gallon tank buried in the ground filled with water) donated by a company. We set up on a Saturday and asked parents and students to come out. We had sixth graders swinging pickaxes—where do you see that? Digging a hole in the ground. Pulling rocks that weighed more than 100 lbs.

We installed this guzzler in early October and set up a trail camera. On October 13, a Friday morning, the students filled it for the first time. Between Friday night and Monday morning, we had 92 bear pictures on the camera. When those pictures were shown to the students the following Tuesday, it changed everything. The level of engagement by these 10- and 11-year-old kids was off the charts. The quality of the conversations was incredible because everything had been real. Nothing had been fabricated. Now they were seeing the results of their work.

"The kids," David said, "were hooked because it was the real deal. When you do something on your own, and you've done collaborative work of excellent quality, and you have a mountain lion show up in three days—that's a big deal." The science didn't end there, however. As it got colder, the guzzler froze, and the students experimented with solutions. They tried putting rubber balls in the water thinking that if the sun shone on the balls, it would heat the water around the balls and the water wouldn't freeze. However, they discovered that as soon as the temperature dropped to about 10 degrees, that didn't work very well.

The students worked with their telementors to discover how other wildlife professionals were keeping their guzzlers from freezing. David explained the next steps:

The students learned about aerators, the voltage requirements, and power inverters. We didn't have any power up there so then they had to figure how big a solar panel do we need, how's it going to work with an aerator, and the right converter to convert ac to dc current. So they decided to get another guzzler tank and set it up outside the classroom so they could test their ideas outside. That took place over a month's time and it was just fabulous work and there were fabulous discussions between students and mentors. They came up with a solution that was bulletproof. They finally got it to where that aerator was running 24/7 and keeping that guzzler from freezing.

The learning continued all year. With the help of their telementors, the students learned a lot about water, aerators, and solar energy. "They are doing work," David said, "that we would never expect from a high school senior." Amy also set up the chance for them to hear guest lecturers. "We had an owl expert from Estes Park come in," David said, "and students had over 50 excellent questions for him. He told me out in the hallway after that session that he had never before had this experience with students, never had even high school students come close to this level of engagement."

When I asked David why he does what he does, supporting projects such as the one completed by Amy Schmer's students at Preston Middle School, he told me he loved the work mostly because students learn that they can make a difference:

> I want youth to know they count for something and they can contribute. And that by contributing, that is where maximum joy is felt while you are here. It is not about amassing anything materially; it's about making a difference for people and other important things on this planet. When you are young it is so easy to go back to that place that you already know as a toddler, and that is where maximum joy is derived. If more youth are in that place, they will have a greater impact and live much more successful lives, the best definition of success, while they are here. Plus, I'm paying my childhood mentor back. That's why I do it.

What Is Authentic Learning?

The *Oxford English Dictionary* contains more than a page of definitions for the word *authentic*, but most commonly we use *authentic* to mean that something is real, or genuine—not a copy or a fake. For example, we might say that we are selling an authentic first edition of John Steinbeck's *East of Eden*, which is to say that since the book is authentic, it is worth a lot more than a later copy of the book. According to the *Oxford English Dictionary*, something that is authentic is "real, actual, genuine."

For our purposes, then, authentic learning is student work that is "real, actual, genuine" in all the aspects experienced by students. Student work is also authentic when it addresses a real issue. Students who are fixing their teacher's computers, for example, are clearly working on an important real-life concern. However, students who are memorizing computer terms simply to pass a test, and who will forget those terms a week after the test, are engaged in learning that is far from real.

Annette Holthaus has the students working on teachers' computers.

Video 9.1
www.corwin.com/
highimpactinstruction

Assignments are also authentic when they produce a real product. For example, the students in Amy Schmer's class created genuine solutions to a real-world problem—how to improve the wildlife habitat at Sylvan Dale Ranch by getting more water to the animals that live there.

Authentic learning is also assessed based on real-world standards. The criteria for judging authentic learning arise naturally from the task—in this case, improving the habitat. Since the real world establishes criteria for excellence, the bar for quality work is often set much higher during authentic learning.

Finally, authentic learning really engages students because they consider it relevant, interesting, and important. Authentic learning is work that students want to do because they see the investment of their time as time well spent. Students completing authentic learning, to use Phil Schlecty's definition (2011), are authentically engaged in the learning. Usually, this is only possible when students have a major voice in defining the project, identifying the driving question at the heart of the work, identifying tasks to be completed, dividing those tasks among students, identifying how to best learn from mentors, and identifying criteria (based on the true demands of the project) for excellence in the work (see Figure 9.1).

Is Authentic Learning Project-Based Learning?

In his review of research on project-based learning (PBL), John W. Thomas writes that "the variety of practices under the banner of PBL makes it difficult to assess what is and is not PBL" (p. 2). William Bender (2012), for example, describes project-based learning as

Download this form at www.corwin.com/highimpactinstruction

Figure 9.1	Authentic Learning Checklist	
Authentic learning always involves . . .		✓
A real-world issue.		
A real-world product.		
Real-world assessment.		
Real student engagement.		

"using authentic, real-world projects, based on a highly motivating and engaging question, task, or problem, to teach students academic content in the context of working cooperatively to solve the problem" (p. 7). In his review of the literature, Thomas identifies five "central" criteria for PBL projects:

- Central, not peripheral to the curriculum
- Focused on questions or problems that "drive" students to encounter (and struggle with) the central concepts and principles of a discipline
- Involves students in a constructive investigation
- Student-driven to some significant degree
- Realistic, not school-like (pp. 3–4)

In many cases, project-based learning and "authentic learning" are one and the same. Project-based learning is authentic so long as the emphasis of the project is on "authenticity" rather than the project itself. To be authentic learning, then, PBL has to meet the criteria mentioned above; that is, it (a) addresses a real-world issue, (b) produces a real-world product that addresses the issue, (c) is assessed using real-world criteria, and (d) really engages students because they find the project interesting, meaningful, and personally relevant.

Students usually collaborate with their peers when they do project-based learning, but this is not always the case with authentic learning. Group work has many advantages, but students can do authentic learning individually or with others. For example, an individual student might conduct a campaign to convince students not to text message while driving or analyze the nutritional quality of a school's cafeteria food and make recommendations for healthier food. What counts here is that the work counts, whether it is done individually or with others.

When students do authentic learning, David Neils told me, "I see it. I see it in their eyes. I see it in the way they talk to each other. I see it in their level of engagement. They know what they are working on is real."

Why Should Students Do Authentic Learning?

This question might sound silly, a bit like asking, "Why should we drink water when we are thirsty?" If students are 100% engaged in what they do, are pushed to meet real-world standards, and do work that makes a contribution to the community, wouldn't it be obvious that they will benefit? Yes. However, reviewing why we might use authentic learning highlights how this kind of learning can help students develop deeper understandings, along with increased motivation, engagement, and empowerment.

Purpose. William Damon, in *The Path to Purpose* (2009), has written persuasively that lack of purpose can interfere with students' ability to lead rich, happy, productive lives. Damon writes:

> The most pervasive problem of the day is a sense of emptiness that has ensnared many young people in long periods of drift during a time in their lives when they should be defining their aspirations and making progress toward their fulfillment. For too many young people today, apathy and anxiety have become the dominant moods, and disengagement or even cynicism has replaced the natural hopefulness of youth. (p. xiv)

Authentic learning isn't a guaranteed way to light a fire in every student whose dominant moods are "apathy and anxiety," but some aspects of this learning should awaken many students to their potential. First, the very act of doing authentic learning helps students see how important it is to set a purpose and act to achieve it since during authentic learning, students should clearly understand why they are doing what they are doing. Furthermore, since authentic learning leads to real-world outcomes that demonstrate the importance of striving to resolve real issues, students see a natural connection between purpose and achievement.

More important, authentic learning at its best kindles a desire in students to learn more about fascinating and meaningful topics that they might otherwise not have known about—a crucial goal for education. By structuring learning experiences so that they are relevant and engaging by demonstrating how important it is to pursue a project with a meaningful mission, authentic learning can lead students to a deeper understanding of the power of purpose.

David Neils saw purpose as an incredibly important part of authentic learning. In conversation, he told me the following:

> Students need to find the intersection between who they are, I'll call it natural ability, and what needs to be done as identified by a leader in the field. But you have to teach the students how to find the need. We don't let them shoot from the hip. The first thing is to have students connect with other people who share their interests. They find out what keeps the leaders

and experts up at night and then discuss what they learned with their mentor. Then they decide where they are going to focus their effort addressing one of the expert's needs. That's a super critical component of authentic learning. Once that happens, all the other dominoes fall.

Meaningful. What makes authentic learning authentic is that students work on real projects that make a significant contribution to their community, their environment, or the world at large. Students at Preston Middle School completed many meaningful projects. One student worked with a telementor from the global health care organization Merck to study malaria, ultimately working with a team of professionals to get mosquito nets to a village in the developing world. Other students developed a public communication program to spread the word on animal health for the Fort Collins Cat Rescue organization and invented a rubber grip to make it easier for students to open lockers.

In each case, during authentic learning, students address an issue or problem that is important and meaningful for the community. By addressing such issues, students gain a sense of pride in what they accomplish.

Personally Relevant. Doing meaningful work is important, but only if it is relevant to the students. If students don't care about a project, they won't give it their best effort. On the other hand, when students tackle a project they care deeply about, their effort often goes far beyond what they realized they could do. By definition, work is only authentic if students truly care about what they are doing. By designing projects that students care about, teachers can lead students to do outstanding work.

The world is full of topics that can deeply engage students, including the environment, animal wildlife, nutrition and health, community development, education, and issues facing the developing world. What matters is that students work on a project that they care about. As Boss and Krauss have written in *Reinventing Project-Based Learning* (2007), a truly outstanding project is one that connects with students' passions and interests:

> John Seely Brown, former chief scientist at Palo Alto Research Center in California, suggests that we should imagine what "passion-based learning" would look like (La Monica, 2006). . . . What would spark your students' curiosity and make them feel that what they are learning is interesting and

important? How would interactions with classmates and others engage them and make them feel a part of something big? What activities, experiences, and tools would excite them? When you tap into students' enthusiasm, you increase the likelihood that they will dive into deep inquiry and come away with essential understanding. Projects with passion help connect with the social and emotional sides of the learning experience. (pp. 52–53)

Motivation. Work that is meaningful, interesting, personally relevant, and chosen by students is likely work that students will be motivated to complete. Researchers such as Edward Deci have broadened our understanding of motivation by helping us see that we are rarely motivated by others' goals. In *Drive: The Surprising Truth About What Motivates Us* (2009), Daniel Pink summarizes that research. He writes: "Goals that people set for themselves and that are devoted to attaining mastery are usually healthy. But goals imposed by others—sales targets, quarterly reports, standardized test scores, and so on—can sometimes have dangerous side effects" (p. 50).

Much of the education students experience in school involves goals that are imposed on them from outside. However, during authentic learning, even though the learning addresses state or common core standards, students have a large say in deciding the specific issue the project will address, how the issue will be addressed, and what will be the criteria for quality work. For many students, having an increased say in learning leads to an increase in motivation.

Engagement. When students are doing work that matters to them, that they choose, and that is important and interesting to them, they are much more likely to be engaged. In a famous *Ed Leadership* article, Strong, Silver, and Robinson (1995) summarized a 10-year research project during which they asked teachers and students to describe the kind of work that is "totally engaging" and the kind of work "you hate to do." They found distinct patterns in the responses:

Engaging work, respondents said, was work that stimulated their curiosity, permitted them to express their creativity, and fostered positive relationships with others. It was also work at which they were good. As for activities they hated, both teachers and students cited work that was repetitive, that required little or no thought, and that was forced on them by others. (p. 8)

Authentic learning addresses all of these issues. Students work on projects that they choose and that excite their curiosity. In addition, authentic learning provides an opportunity for students to express themselves, and, when well facilitated, authentic learning leads students to experience success, doing work that they are proud to have done.

Learning. Earlier in this book, I distinguished between procedural knowledge, which is acquired and learned during performance of tasks, and declarative knowledge—knowledge that is expressed in books, texts, lectures, and most classroom learning. Both forms of learning are important, and in many cases declarative knowledge is a necessary prerequisite for procedural knowledge. But because procedural knowledge is what we do, this type of learning can have a deep impact.

Since authentic learning takes place in the field, so to speak, with students addressing real-world issues, much of what they learn during authentic learning is procedural knowledge. Students learn such skills as how to identify a problem, develop action plans, find expert advisers, communicate with mentors, develop communication plans, conduct research, invent new products, and so forth. Since this learning occurs during real-world experiences, students are much more likely to remember what they have learned. This is especially important since much of what students otherwise learn in school rarely becomes procedural.

Empowerment. When students do authentic learning—working on tasks that matter, applying real-world solutions that are judged by real-world standards—they have the opportunity to learn that their own actions can make a difference. Few things are more empowering than overcoming challenges and accomplishing a task that you care about and that makes a positive impact on your community.

David Neils told me about Cohen, a boy in sixth grade, who especially benefited from doing authentic learning. Cohen worked with a mentor in Beijing who helped him plan, market, and run a summer camp for kids through a partnership that he set up with Colorado State University. Then, after filling his camp in three days, Cohen decided he wanted to do more. David told me his story.

> Cohen found me a week after his camp sold out. He said, "Since my camp is full, I have some extra time between now and the end of the school year, so my mentor and I are working on another project." So I said, "What are you working on now?" Cohen answered, "We've done our homework and we realize that kids with disabilities do so much better in school

Caryl Crowell takes students outside to learn science.

Video 9.2
www.corwin.com/
highimpactinstruction

if they get exercise. We know, based on the research we have done, that these kids here at Preston could be getting a lot more exercise. I am working on a proposal with my mentor that I am going to share with my principal, and I hope that some of my ideas are adopted." Two weeks later, he set up an hour-long meeting with the principal. After the meeting, he ran around the school trying to find me. "Mr. Neils," he stated proudly, "my proposal was basically accepted. They have already made changes for next year so that the kids with disabilities get more exercise." He had tears in his eyes. Now that tells you everything, right?

Designing Authentic Learning

When teachers provide authentic learning for students, they move from being the primary sources of knowledge to being facilitators of the learning process. The goal remains the same—to ensure maximum student learning—and teachers are no less busy. However, during authentic learning, teachers have to attend to aspects of learning that are less important during more traditional forms of learning.

Perhaps the most important facilitation task that teachers perform when students do authentic learning is to make sure students make choices about every significant part of the project. To ensure that authentic learning is successful, teachers guide students through many aspects of the work, including (a) guiding students as they choose a project and identify its purpose, (b) supporting students as they find and mediate relationships with mentors and experts, (c) guiding students as they identify and divide tasks, (d) working with students to establish criteria for quality work, (e) guiding students as they identify a real audience for their work, (f) directly teaching students when they need to learn social or other skills to complete a project. Each of these areas is described in Figure 9.2.

IDENTIFY THE PURPOSE OF THE PROJECT

For authentic learning to begin, the work requires a purpose. That purpose can be expressed as a question, objective, or problem. John Larmer from the Buck Institute suggests that projects begin with a driving question. "A driving question," he writes, "clearly states the purpose of the project. It gives focus to all the tasks students do . . . [and the driving question ensures] . . . students always know, 'Why are we doing this?'" (p. 40).

| Figure 9.2 | Successful Authentic Learning Checklist |

In designing authentic learning . . .	✓
Identify the purpose of the project.	
Mediate relationships with mentors and experts.	
Identify and divide tasks.	
Establish criteria for success.	
Identify a real audience.	
Teach necessary skills and knowledge.	

Download this form at www.corwin.com/highimpactinstruction

The temptation is to simply tell students what the project will be and then push them to complete it. But such an approach dramatically decreases student motivation. If students are to truly embrace authentic learning, they need to make a choice to do the project. It is hard for anyone, adult or child, to feel excited about an experience that they have been told to do. A better strategy is for students to discuss the work and, ultimately, vote, perhaps through a secret ballot, on the topic for authentic learning.

Teachers should help students to understand exactly what they are being offered. In the best situations, this might involve, as it did for Amy Schmer's students, taking a field trip to a ranch in the Colorado Rockies. Unfortunately, that isn't always possible, so teachers can use other strategies, such as sharing compelling videos that present possible issues, inviting guest speakers, having guest conversations with experts via Skype or Facetime, and reading newspaper articles, websites, or other media.

For authentic learning to truly be authentic, this stage is crucial—students must be "all-in" on the project, which means they have to see it as relevant (a project that they care about), interesting (a project that captures their imagination), and meaningful (a project that they believe will make a difference and that they would like to spend time on). Students should not be satisfied until they have chosen a project that meets those criteria (see Figure 9.3).

To ensure that the work that students do is indeed authentic, teachers should constantly be on the lookout for work that will make

Figure 9.3	Project Criteria Checklist

Is the project . . .	✓
Relevant?	
Interesting?	
Meaningful?	

a difference for students. They also need to work to understand their students' interests by talking with students one-on-one, giving students interest surveys, and taking every opportunity to learn about students by interacting with them.

The challenge at this stage of the project is to align the student work with the broader learning goals within a school, such as the Common Core State Standards. As stated in Part I, if teachers are unintentional about standards, their students will miss out on learning foundational, essential knowledge, skills, and big ideas. However, learning that covers all the standards but provokes no real learning—a far too common situation when teachers are expected to follow pacing guides—does not prepare students for success. When proposing possible topics, teachers need to think carefully about how authentic learning experiences can ensure that students learn what they are expected to learn while also ensuring that what students do is real work.

Finally, teachers need to be aware of Mintzberg and Christensen's distinction between deliberate and emergent strategy. Good plans for learning must be deliberate, focusing and guiding student learning experiences so that students learn some of the knowledge, skills, and big ideas that teachers, curriculum guides, and standards identify as essential. But especially during authentic learning, teachers must also be ready to embrace emergent opportunities for learning. Real work is messy and nonlinear, and if students are doing real work, surprising and important opportunities for learning will present themselves almost daily. To miss those opportunities is to miss a major reason for doing authentic learning.

MEDIATE RELATIONSHIPS WITH MENTORS AND EXPERTS

A critical characteristic of authentic learning is that students learn with and from other people, who share important knowledge and help them complete their project. This usually involves directly contacting experts in the field being studied (wildlife biologists in the case of Amy Schmer's class) and mentors, who provide support and guidance as students move through the project. Experts help students understand important aspects of the issue they are tackling and help students see what kind of questions they are studying. While mentors primarily help students find information that they need, they can provide support in any aspect of learning.

Teachers facilitate this kind of learning in many ways. First, they need to find mentors who can work with students. One way is to work with organizations such as David Neils' International Telementor Program (ITP), which brokers mentoring relationships for students. Alternatively, they can reach out to community organizations that are interested in providing mentoring support. To protect the students, all mentoring interactions must occur at school, or if they involve email, all emails must be public. ITP has built-in safeguards to ensure that all interactions are filtered, monitored, and archived. No email is exchanged. All mentoring communications occur through a secure web space at www.telementor.org. As of this date, nearly 46,000 students throughout 11 countries have been mentored through ITP.

Teachers must also guide students to identify experts they can contact and from whom they can learn. Teachers can usually lead students to identify experts, or mentors can help, or sometimes they can be found without any help. Students may need to learn about appropriate and effective written communication at this point as well. However, the teacher should intervene as little as possible. This process needs to be led by the students themselves. As David Neils told me, "All of the conversations—the inviting of experts—everything is driven by the students. And when they get to a fork in the road, the teacher lets the students decide which direction to take. This produces a lot of energy."

IDENTIFY AND DIVIDE TASKS

Once students have committed to a project, they need to identify what tasks have to be completed and who will do them. In many cases, when students are tackling a project that they truly believe in, and they have the freedom to identify tasks and determine who will do them, they are capable of doing this on their own. In other situations, and when tasks are more complex, teachers may need to guide conversations to make sure appropriate tasks are identified and tasks are divided equitably. Teachers might also want to teach students how use organizational tools like a Gantt chart—a planning tool used in project management to sort tasks and responsibilities (see ganttchart .com for more information).

What makes this part of the process authentic is that there should be no meaningless tasks, no work done just to fill time. The work that students do should help them address a real-life problem, or they shouldn't be doing it. There are no time-killing, mind-numbing worksheets in authentic learning.

ESTABLISH CRITERIA FOR SUCCESS

One of the aspects of authentic learning that makes it "real" is that the work is judged by real-world criteria. One way to do this is to simply assess whether or not the students did a satisfactory job of solving a problem they were addressing. For example, the students in Amy Schmer's class judged their work based on whether or not they were able to solve the water problem at Sylvan Dale Ranch, which, as it turns out, they did.

Other standards arise naturally from the project that has been embraced. For example, if students are doing an experiment, they should conduct real science. That is, they should address an issue that is being addressed by scientists in the field, not a simple experiment that has been repeated thousands of times at science fairs across the nation. In addition, students should apply the scientific method—identifying research questions, using random assignment, controlling for error, and applying measures that are considered valid and reliable.

Students can identify the criteria for judging their work by contacting or reading the work of experts in the field or with the help of their mentors who can guide students to find the information that they need. Teachers can also facilitate discussion of quality work by showing products of differing quality and asking students to identify the differences. During truly authentic learning, subpar work simply is not acceptable. Real problems require high-quality solutions.

IDENTIFY A REAL AUDIENCE

Another way to make a project real is to have a real audience for what is being created. A real audience provides focus to a project. As they work at whatever their project is, students can ask themselves, "What will our audience really think of what we are doing?"

Thus, students who are engaged in community improvement projects might invite a local politician to class, and students who want to set up a business might invite a business leader to hear about their plan. Depending on the project, students could invite the school principal, the mayor, customers buying a product, a CEO, or anyone else who would be appropriate to evaluate their work. In addition, inviting someone into the classroom to offer candid feedback can be an exciting and meaningful culminating act for a project.

Teachers need to prepare the external audience somewhat to make sure that they not only provide candid and substantial feedback, but offer it in a constructive way. If an external evaluator offers only positive and superficial comments, students miss a potentially meaningful learning opportunity. However, if an external evaluator is brutally critical and overlooks students' genuine accomplishments, it can end a project poorly and inhibit learning.

TEACH THE SKILLS AND KNOWLEDGE STUDENTS NEED TO COMPLETE A PROJECT

To complete any project, students need to learn important skills. For a science project, for example, students will need to learn about the scientific method and various ways of measuring outcomes. For a communication project, students may need to learn some fundamentals of marketing, the elements of persuasion, or more basic writing or design skills. And to succeed at any collaborative effort, students will need to learn important communication skills.

Teachers can teach important skills and knowledge in real-world contexts that help students remember them by directly teaching the skills and knowledge students need to learn to succeed. When students understand why they are being taught, and they see how the skills and knowledge help them succeed, they are usually much more engaged in the learning.

Experiential Learning: One Alternative

The lessons learned from authentic learning can be applied to other learning experiences for students. In particular, experiential learning can embody many of the components of authentic learning. I define experiential learning as any learning activity that allows students to experience the phenomenon they are exploring, acting out the behaviors, strategies, or other knowledge, skills, or big ideas being learned.

Effective experiential learning provides learners with a simulation of some or all elements of content being covered during a learning session. Thus, learners are provided with an experience that simulates reality. Experiential learning can be manifested in a variety of ways, including students role-playing, listening, or putting on a poetry reading, experiencing firsthand what it feels like to work within different economies.

Students have their own poetry reading in Miss Gray's language arts class.

Video 9.3
www.corwin.com/
highimpactinstruction

Experiential learning helps students see how well they can use new concepts they are learning, reminds learners of the concrete attributes of a particular phenomenon being studied, and allows learners to gain new insights into their thoughts, assumptions, and behaviors. What matters in experiential learning is that learners experience content in a way that simulates the real-life cognitive, emotional, and sensual elements of the content being covered.

In communication classes at Ryerson Polytechnic University, Susan FitzRandolph uses experiential learning to reinforce learning about cross-cultural communication. In her classes, after covering content on cross-cultural communication, Susan divides her class into three teams and explains that each team is now going to learn to embody a unique culture. The teams are directed to different breakout rooms, with their cultural instructions in hand, and they then quickly learn the characteristics of a culture that they will role-play when the three teams are brought together. Of course the cultures are strikingly different: in one group, personal space is 20 centimeters, in a second, personal space is 60; one group has a sacred ritual it performs, another group is atheistic; one group believes in socializing, dining, and drinking, whereas another group believes time is money and forbids some kinds of dining and drinking, and so on.

When Susan reunites the groups, she asks them to work together to make a business deal, but inevitably the teams have great difficulty dealing with their cultural differences. Often, the debriefing of this experience leads to learners gaining startling insights into their attitudes toward people from a variety of cultural backgrounds.

Chris Korinek helps students learn about economic systems by simulating those systems.

Video 9.4
www.corwin.com/
highimpactinstruction

Final Story

When David Neils and I were discussing his work at Preston Middle School, he told me a story that captured what students were experiencing by doing authentic learning. This story seems to crystallize the difference between authentic learning and more traditional forms of learning:

At the end of the school year, Amy's father-in-law passed away, and she was gone for 10 days, so I helped cover her class. They had a substitute in there when I was also working with the class. At the time there were forest fires raging in Colorado. Amy felt it would be great if the students developed a little background knowledge of fire ecology, and because she was dealing with her personal situation, she thought the best place to start was an article in the textbook used in the class. So the substitute said to the students that she wanted them to get out the textbook. One of the students looked at me with this horrified look on his face and said, "What? We are not the textbook group. We do real stuff in here. Somebody needs to tell him. That's not us!"

Turning Ideas Into Action

Students

1. Ensure students are active partners during authentic learning, choosing the topic, the experts to contact, what to learn from mentors, and, with teacher guidance, the criteria for success.

2. Encourage students to provide suggestions for how to improve future authentic learning projects.

3. Encourage students to talk about their interests, passions, concerns, and fears. Authentic learning is only meaningful if students truly care about the project they are addressing.

Teachers

1. Dedicate a lot of time to talking with students to identify the issues and topics that most interest them.

2. Continually be on the lookout for settings for authentic learning.

3. Contact community groups to find agencies that can provide safe and supportive mentoring for students.

Instructional Coaches

1. Begin learning about authentic learning by partnering with one teacher on a small but high-quality project.

2. Be on the lookout for resources teachers can use to design great projects, such as experts, mentors, project sites, technological tools that can help with the work, and so on.

3. Visit websites such as www.telementor.org and www.bie.org to learn about other projects to develop a library of projects that can be shared with teachers.

Principals

1. Perhaps most important, let teachers know they have the freedom to experiment with innovative learning such as authentic learning. This kind of learning cannot be taught using a pacing guide.

(Continued)

(Continued)

2. Engage in dialogue with other administrators in your district about the merits of authentic learning versus a more exclusive reliance on traditional learning.

3. Arrange for your teachers to visit schools where authentic learning is being implemented successfully.

What It Looks Like

The best way to measure the impact of authentic learning is through measures of students' attitudes such as those surfaced by the Tripod Survey (tripodproject.org), the Gallop Student Poll (gallupstudentpoll.com), or surveys created by teachers to study students' attitudes about learning.

To Sum Up

- Authentic learning is learning that involves real-world issues, products, and audiences.

- Students are deeply engaged by authentic learning because it is interesting, relevant, and meaningful.

- Done well, authentic learning helps students discover the importance of purpose and motivates, engages, and empowers them.

- Because it occurs in the real world, authentic learning helps students acquire procedural knowledge.

- Teachers who design authentic learning move from being disseminators of knowledge to being facilitators of learning.

Going Deeper

The Buck Institute for Education is a leader in the dissemination of training and support for project-based learning (PBL). Their website (www.bie.org) is a natural first stop for learning more about project-based learning. Further, their book, *PBL Starter Kit* (Larmer, 2009), is a clear, easy-to-read introduction to the subject.

The International Telementor Center (www.telementor.org), developed by David Neils, who is featured in this chapter, has provided mentoring via the Internet for hundreds of authentic learning projects conducted around the world. The Telementor Center brings together professionals who can mentor students as they conduct their projects.

Suzie Boss and Jane Krauss' *Reinventing Project-Based Learning: Your Field Guide to Real-World Projects in the Digital Age* (2008), published by the International Society for Technology in Education, provides excellent suggestions for how technology can be used as a central resource with PBL.

William Bender's *Project-Based Learning: Differentiating the Instruction for the 21st Century* (2012) provides excellent suggestions on how PBL can be designed to bring out students' unique strengths and respond to their different learning needs.

PART III

COMMUNITY BUILDING

Instructional coach Lea Molczan and reading specialist Jody Johnson had lunch together every day in Lea's classroom. They always planned their lessons together, and lunch was the only time they could find to collaborate. Every day Jody would pull a student desk up beside Lea and together they would plan their lessons and brainstorm ideas. Surrounded by Lea's books, posters, inspirational quotations, and New Orleans Saints souvenirs, the two talked about all the things that might come up whenever two friends eat together. Almost always, though, they found themselves talking about Jody's seventh-grade reading intervention class.

Jody was an accomplished teacher with more than two decades of experience, and she was almost always highly successful with her students. But the eight boys and two girls in this particular class were struggling. Most of them had a limited understanding of English and were probably the least successful students in the school. The students were failing most classes, never passed benchmark tests, and felt like failures among their peers. Reading for pleasure was the last thing on their minds. Many of the students had given up.

What bothered Jody most about the class was that the students had become used to failing. They didn't expect to learn, so they invested most of their effort in avoiding learning. One student, we'll call him Dennis, especially refused to participate. He came to class, sat in the back, put his head on his desk, and didn't do anything. Five months into the school year, he still refused to pick up his folder at the start of the class.

Every day Jody wondered what Dennis and his classmates might do to upset her lesson. During read-aloud time the students were reading the young adult comic novel *Big Nate: In a Class by Himself*,[1] in which the central hero sets a record for the highest number of detentions. Jody asked how many of the students in the class had been in in-school suspension (ISS)—the punishment given to students when all other forms of punishment have failed. All students raised their hands. "They all had vivid experiences of being in different ISS rooms across different schools; in fact, some were somewhat proud of this fact," Lea said.

The students' misbehavior wore Jody down. She was at a low point with them and felt like a novice, not an experienced professional with 20 years of success under her belt. Every day "as lunch was winding down," Lea said, "Jody experienced this overwhelming sense of dread. She felt like she was losing momentum. She felt like she was failing them."

"The thing about Jody was," Lea continued, "that she saw something in her students. They had potential to be successful. She really felt that these were kids other people had given up on, and she didn't want to give up and consequently took their failures very personally." Jody and Lea looked for books that might interest the students. They brainstormed different ways Jody might teach. Jody tried everything she could think of to reach her students. She changed the activities. She tried various rewards and punishments. She offered more or less "Coco Time" (Coco was the pet hamster that all the students loved to visit). Nothing worked.

One day Lea decided to video record the class. Afterward she and Jody watched the video separately, and what they saw was that the start of the class was a mess. So much time was being wasted. Some students would be ready, but others would take forever to pick up their folders. Students would socialize, throw stuff around the room, and do anything but get prepared to learn. Jody's corrections didn't make a dent, even though she corrected the students frequently. What Lea and Jody saw in the video was that more than 10 minutes was wasted at the start of class, and the period was only 45 minutes long. The chaos at the start also spilled over into the rest of the lesson, making the whole period an ordeal for everyone. No wonder Jody dreaded the class.

Lea and Jody decided to teach the students expectations, one of the central community-building practices described in this chapter. Together they identified expectations for all activities and transitions, especially for the first few minutes of class. They wrote down what the goal of each activity was (to be ready to start class in 3 minutes), what kind of talking was acceptable (inside quiet voice), and what kind of movement was expected (go to the back of the room, pick up your folder, return to your desk, be ready to start). They set the goal that class would start within 3 minutes.

To make the expectations stick, they added a component that made a big difference. Jody was a master storyteller, and although the students were usually not engaged in other learning activities, they loved the way she read about Big Nate. Jody told her students that they would get read-aloud time until 11:22 every day (the class started at 11:12). If it took them 8 minutes to get ready, they would get 2 minutes of reading, but if they were ready in 2 minutes, they would get 8 minutes.

The kids beat the 3-minute goal. After Jody taught the expectations and put the new routine in place, class always started in less than 3 minutes. By teaching expectations and reinforcing them as skillfully as she did, Jody added 7 minutes of learning for each student every day. Spread over the 181 days of a school year, that added up to more than a month of additional learning.

In addition, starting so quickly and smoothly affected the rest of the period. Students were engaged and learning more. Jeff Levering, a researcher observing Jody's class, reported that even Dennis became an active learner. "I mean, now he's engaged. It is really quite remarkable . . . it has been a 180-degree shift with him."

Jody's teaching was changing, too. Barb Millikan, another researcher observing Jody's class, saw a dramatic change in the frequency with which Jody praised the students. Before she created expectations with Lea and taught them to the students, Jody, Barb reported, placed a heavy emphasis on correction: "If praise was 1, the number of corrections had to be 5 or 6." After Jody taught expectations, Barb and Jeff's observation data showed that Jody was much more positive. In a typical post-expectations class, for example, Barb recorded 42 praises to 13 corrections. Jody was more positive and was especially excited to see that Dennis was engaged. Jody, Barb said, "is more motivated as the kids are more motivated."

Researchers Barb Millikan and Jeff Levering spent many hours observing Jody's class and saw firsthand the changes in the class. When I asked Barb to describe what she saw in Jody's room, she emailed me the following:

> The last time Jeff and I observed the class we were . . . stunned
> by the dramatic difference in her students. The class was

orderly. Students sat in the first two rows of class, right in front of Jody. [Dennis] sat in the front row, raised his hand, attended to Jody's every move, and treated his classmates with respect. On the board was a note written by a student that said: Just try to keep us from reading a book! When class started, the students asked Jody to leave the room. She agreed to leave saying, "I know you must have a good reason for this. Remember, I stop reading at 11:22 a.m." Jody stood outside the door while the students, chattering, signed notes on a homemade card they had created for her. One student blurted out, "She's not leaving is she?!" "No, dummy, she's not leaving; we're just thanking her for being our favorite teacher." All of them breathed a little easier.

When Jody returned to class, the lesson proceeded as usual. Jody complimented students about how they were really readers and could read a whole book now. At the end of class, one student stayed to give Jody the card. Her eyes welled up as she read the notes. She said, "This was my worst class at the beginning of the year. Because of this work it's now my favorite class." Dennis' note read, "From your favorite student to my favorite teacher." "He's the one who hated me and gave me such a bad time most of the year," Jody said, weeping at the realization that she had really helped him turn around.

After Jody taught and reinforced expectations, not surprisingly, student learning improved. In fact, almost all the students met proficiency on the state test, and all students increased their scores by at least 10 points—the entire class increasing by 170 points. For Lea and Jody, this was "phenomenal." "These were kids," Lea said, "who had never met [proficiency] in four years. And so they just felt this huge sense of accomplishment. Like 'Oh, I really am not dumb.'" By implementing powerful community-building strategies, Lea and Jody dramatically improved how much Jody's students learned. More important, perhaps, they made it possible for the students to see that they could succeed.

The strategies Lea and Jody used—identifying, teaching, and reinforcing expectations—are part of a collection of teaching strategies I group together under the category "community building," often referred to as "classroom management" or "behavior management." Community building is an essential component of good teaching.

In every class, every day, our goal should be maximum learning per second so that our students get the most benefit possible from the learning experiences we create. Community building can help with this goal, but it is not a Band-Aid used to keep students quiet and in their seats or to cover for poor, uninspiring instruction. Effective teachers, like Jody, employ community building as a part of an entire approach to fostering learning, also using the strategies of content planning, effective instruction, and formative assessment to encourage the most learning per second.

In this part of the book, I describe six easy-to-implement, powerful strategies for building positive, productive learning communities. In Chapter 10, I'll discuss how teachers can create learner-friendly cultures that encourage respect, productivity, and learning. In Chapter 11, I'll explain why teachers should build power with students rather than pushing for power over students. In Chapter 12, I'll describe how teachers should structure learning activities that organize student learning while providing a great deal of freedom for students to make important choices about their learning, an approach I call "freedom within form."

In Chapter 13, I'll explain why teachers who wish to create an effective setting for student learning may also choose to create and teach expectations for all activities and transitions students experience. In Chapter 14, I'll describe strategies teachers can use to reinforce those expectations with positive attention, and in Chapter 15, I'll discuss how teachers can redirect behavior with fluent corrections.

Note

1. The *Big Nate* series by Lincoln Peirce tells the hilarious stories of Big Nate as he negotiates the complexities of junior high.

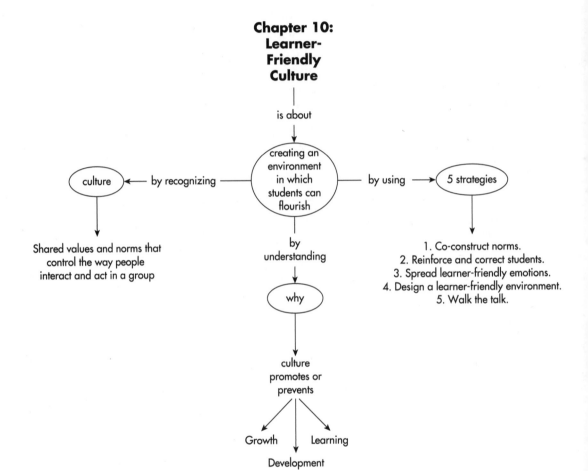

**Chapter 10:
Learner-
Friendly
Culture**

is about

creating an
environment
in which
students can
flourish

culture ← by recognizing

by using → 5 strategies

Shared values and norms that
control the way people
interact and act in a group

by
understanding

why

culture
promotes or
prevents

1. Co-construct norms.
2. Reinforce and correct students.
3. Spread learner-friendly emotions.
4. Design a learner-friendly environment.
5. Walk the talk.

Growth   Learning

Development

10

LEARNER-FRIENDLY CULTURE

The only thing of real importance that leaders do is to create and manage culture. If you do not manage culture, it manages you, and you may not even be aware of the extent to which this is happening.

—Edgar Schein

When I visited Sandi Silbernagel's second-grade classroom in St. Tammany Parish, Louisiana, as part of my work on Talking About Teaching for the Teaching Channel, I saw a great example of the positive impact of culture. During one of my visits, Ms. Silbernagel and her students read Tynia Thomassie's *Feliciana Feydra LeRoux: A Cajun Tall Tale* (2005), and Sandi carefully attended to minute details to create the most learner-friendly culture.

I spent two days watching Sandi teach, and it was very evident that she carefully plans each lesson to create a learner-friendly culture. For her lesson on Tynia Thomassie's Cajun tall tale about a young girl's adventures in the Louisiana swamp, for example, Sandi arranged stuffed alligators and crabs around the room so she could refer to them during the reading of the story. She also scanned the book to display it on her Smart Board so that all students could see it and interact with it on the big screen.

Sandi's plans helped her create a powerful learning experience for her students. She asked the children to gather on a colored carpet for the reading of the book. As Sandi guided her students through the book, she prompted them to demonstrate on the Smart Board how they used their reading strategies (right there clues; search and check; prediction) to deepen their understanding. She also showed students a YouTube video of a swamp so they could get a vivid picture of where the heroine was going. Sandi even shared pictures of her great-grand-mother, who lived in a home very much like the home of their hero. Every student was locked in as Sandi guided them through the story.

When they were done reading, Sandi played Johnette Downing's song "Feliciana LeRoux" about the very story they had just read. Then, as a coup de grace, she gave each child a chance to eat some alligator sausage, just like the alligator in her story. Literally, the children saw, heard, touched, and even tasted what they were learning about.

Much of what Sandi did doesn't get written down in a lesson plan, but the learning experience her students had would not have been possible if Sandi hadn't attended to culture. Yes, the students didn't need to see the stuffed swamp animals. Yes, Sandi could have read from the book and held up the pictures rather than pointing to the larger images on the Smart Board. Yes, she didn't need to play the song in order to teach the reading strategies. And yes, she didn't need to cook up alligator sausage. But years from now, even if students forget the actual words or events of the story, they will remember how they felt in the classroom created by Ms. Silbernagel, and many will remember and apply the reading strategies they learned in her class. Such is the power of a learner-friendly culture!

Why Worry About Culture?

Culture is manifested in everything we see, hear, feel, smell, touch, and taste. Charles Hill and Gareth Jones, the authors of *Strategic Management* (2001), define culture as "the specific collection of values and norms that are shared by people and groups in an organization and that control the way they interact with each other and with stake-holders outside the organization." Culture is the invisible force that shapes behavior in a country, an organization, or a classroom. Effective leaders (in major corporations and kindergarten classes) recognize how much culture accelerates or inhibits success or growth. For that reason, they do everything in their power to create the most successful culture.

School or classroom culture can promote or prevent student growth, development, and learning. When cultural norms promote hard work, kindness, openness, or respect, those norms can help all the members of any group be more productive, supportive, and respectful. But when norms guide group members to lower their standards—selfishness or gossip, for example—they can keep group members from coming close to realizing their potential. A destructive culture may lead us to live, as William James has said, "lives inferior to ourselves" (cited in George Sheehan, *Personal Best*, p. 30).

The trouble with culture is that it works indirectly and invisibly. We cannot see the forces that shape and control behavior, so as Edgar Schein writes, "we may not even be aware of it." But everything counts in the school and the classroom. An irritating school buzzer turned up too loud has a negative effect on attitude. A loud PA system that seems to interrupt every class every day distracts students and also annoys everyone who hears it. A room filled with overflowing boxes of papers and general messiness may subtly undermine the sense of order that students feel inside. And a class in which students frequently make disrespectful comments may make students feel unsafe and unwilling to participate. Little factors, by themselves, may not make an enormous impact, but add them up, and they can make or break students' learning experiences. When it comes to school culture, the little things are the big things.

Culture is difficult to see; yet, it is everywhere. Every interaction, every learning experience exists within a culture, and one aspect of effective instruction is creating a learner-friendly culture. I recommend five ways to shape a culture that positively influences how every student learns every day.

> **Five Ways Teachers Can Create Learner-Friendly Cultures**
>
> 1. Co-construct norms with students.
> 2. Reinforce students when they act consistently with the cultural norms.
> 3. Spread learner-friendly emotions.
> 4. Design a learner-friendly learning environment.
> 5. Walk the talk.

Co-Construct Norms With Students

Norms are the invisible forces that shape behavior within a culture. In a classroom learning community, norms are different than expectations (more on this topic in Chapter 13). Expectations address each individual activity or transition; norms apply equally to every situation. Thus, treating everyone with respect is a norm, but using your whisper voice to talk quietly with a partner is an expectation that would apply only to some particular learning situations.

Teachers can shape a learner-friendly culture by proposing productive or positive norms for their learning community or involving students in creating the norms. Teachers and students can create norms on any number of topics, but common themes include (a) approach to learning, (b) respectful interactions, (c) conversation, and (d) support.

One way to involve students in co-constructing class norms is to ask them to answer the following four questions by writing down their honest answers anonymously.

1. How should we approach learning?
2. What are some ways that we can communicate respect to each other?
3. What should our classroom discussions look like?
4. How should we support each other?

After gathering the students' responses, and prior to the next class, the teacher can review the students' responses, summarize all of the ideas submitted, and lead a discussion about them. In some cases, students can vote (perhaps by secret ballot) until everyone (or at least a majority) agrees on the norms. The nominal group technique described in Chapter 12 is one way to structure this activity. Such a discussion can address many important questions, including What are norms and how do they work? What is a community? Can we create a community? What is respect? Why should we support each other? and What is the purpose of school?

Some teachers prefer to write their classroom norms on their own and hand them out to their students. Others prefer to use the term *rules* rather than *norms*. For me, "norms" better captures the idea of community and partnership, but if "rules" is clearer or better fits your methods, go for it.

Teachers may also wish to turn to a proven curriculum that has been developed to help teach norms. For example, Sue Vernon has created a research-validated curriculum that contains explicit guidelines for creating norms for a learning community. Her book *Talking Together* (2000) presents several lessons to teach students: (a) how to listen to others during classroom discussion, (b) how to work with a partner, (c) how to share ideas in class, (d) how to demonstrate respect, (e) how to respect differences between us, and (f) how to support each other.

What matters is that teachers identify and teach norms to create a positive, productive learning community. Culture can make or break students' learning, and culture, more than anything, is the embodiment of norms.

Reinforce Students When They Act Consistently With the Cultural Norms

Writing an inspirational list of community norms and then never referring to them will not create a learner-friendly culture. Thus, teachers should (a) clarify in their own minds what each norm means, (b) watch students to call attention to situations where students demonstrate respect for norms, and (c) correct students when they act in ways that are not consistent with the norms. The strategies of being a witness to the good and fluently correcting students, described below, should be employed to shape a positive learning culture.

During her lesson on the Cajun tall tale, Sandi was very attentive to her students, both when they acted consistently with classroom norms and when they violated them. I kept track of Sandi's comments and found that in a typical minute she would say eight positive statements. Nevertheless, she also corrected students when they didn't follow norms. Sandi intervened with students to ensure they spoke respectfully or prompted them to apologize to fellow students, if necessary. For Sandi, a critical part of culture is ensuring that students feel safe, and she does everything she can to achieve that.

Spread Learner-Friendly Emotions

Daniel Goleman, the leading expert on emotional intelligence, points to another way in which culture can be shaped. In *Social Intelligence* (2006), he explains that research on the brain shows that emotions are infectious. If you drive across the state with a friend who just caught an infectious fever, you may well be the one with the fever at the end of the trip. In the same way, if someone you interact with is happy or grumpy, you can end up feeling happy or grumpy. What the research suggests is that other people's emotions almost seem to rub off on us, and leaders need to be attentive to what feelings are being spread around in their organization or classroom. Here is how Goleman states it:

> When someone dumps their toxic feelings on us—explodes in anger or threats, shows disgust or contempt—they activate in us circuitry for those very same distressing emotions. Their act has potent neurological consequences: emotions are contagious. We catch strong emotions much as we do a rhinovirus—and so can come down with the emotional equivalent of a cold. . . .
>
> Every interaction has an emotional subtext. Along with whatever else we are doing, we can make each other feel a little better, or even a lot better, or a little worse—or a lot worse . . . we can retain a mood that stays with us long after the direct encounter ends—an emotional afterglow . . . or afterglower. . . .

These tacit transactions drive what amounts to an emotional economy, the net inner gains and losses we experience with a given person, or in a given conversation, or on any given day. By evening the net balance of feeling we have exchanged largely determines what kind of day—"good" or "bad"—we feel we've had. (pp. 13–14)

The fact that we catch each other's emotions has implications for how we should teach. That is, teachers need to be aware of the way they share their emotions with others. A teacher who is quick to be angry or express frustration, and who is not mindful of the impact of negative emotions, will infect students with those emotions, and those students inevitably will infect other children as well. In contrast, leaders who are quick to express warmth, happiness, and love foster positive emotions in others. Each of us shapes the emotions of those we touch. Part of teaching is recognizing that, in a very real sense, we create the emotions around us.

Teachers can do several other things to spread positive emotions. For example, they can prompt students to act in a respectful manner toward each other, such as by saying "thank you" after interacting with each other. Students can also be taught to give effective, authentic praise and encourage each other. Teachers can also use thinking prompts to shape culture. The video clips, vignettes, stories, poems, and songs teachers use all influence the learner-friendliness of a classroom. Each time a teacher chooses to use a thinking prompt, he should ask, "what kind of emotion will this introduce into our community?" If the emotion is one that is counter to productive learning, he should probably reconsider using it.

Design a Learner-Friendly Learning Environment

Bill Strickland, winner of a MacArthur Foundation Genius Grant, and founder of the Manchester Bidwell Educational Center in Pittsburg, Pennsylvania, designs beauty into the core of his school. In his Ted Talk,[1] Bill makes a powerful argument for the importance of believing in our students and points out that one way we communicate our faith in our students is the way we design our students' learning environments.

In *Make the Impossible Possible* (2007), he explains that when you walk into his school, you are "confronted by something beautiful every time you turn around" (p. 13). He writes about describing his center, designed by a student of Frank Lloyd Wright, to students at Harvard:

> The soaring lobby . . . was flooded with light from the banks of tall windows. Accents of natural wood brightened the space, and immediately arched alcoves led to the way to quiet halls. I pointed out the small touches—the rich carpets, the designer tile, the handmade stained-glass inserts in the office doors, the bouquets of fresh flowers. "This place is my idea of a perfect human shelter," I said. It generates order and serenity and stability and optimism, things many of our students do not enjoy in abundance in their private lives. Poor people live in a world where beauty seems impossible. We make it possible. Then the world and eventually the future look very different to them. (pp. 12–13)

For Strickland, the learning environment is a critical part of the learning experience. The environment isn't an add-on; indeed, the setting is as important as the curriculum or the activities—maybe more important.

> The beauty we've designed into our center isn't window dressing; it's an essential part of our success. It nourishes the spirit, and until you reach that part of the spirit that isn't touched by cynicism or despair, no change can begin. You can't show a person how to build a better life if they feel no pleasure in the simple act of being alive. That's why I built this place, and why I fill it with sunlight, and quilts, and flowers. So some black kid who thinks the world is as stale and grey as the ghetto, or some white kid from some hardscrabble blue-collar neighborhood ravaged by layoffs and chronic underemployment, can find out what an orchid smells like. (p. 17)

Bill Strickland created his own school, but what if you are a teacher with just one classroom? What can you do to create a learner-friendly environment? Sandi Silbernagel's actions answer that question. Her classroom, like Bill Strickland's Manchester Bidwell Center, presents students with warmth and beauty everywhere they turn.

Prior to the start of the school year, Sandi decorated her room with posters, paintings, plants, toys, colorful carpets, and comfortable couches and chairs. She also put lamps around the classroom so her students wouldn't have to work under the glare of fluorescent lighting, and finished off her decorating with twinkle lights suspended across the ceiling.

The result is a joyful, beautiful place for children to learn. "I really thought of, as a 7-year old, what would I want my classroom to look like," Sandi told me, "and what came to mind is just 'comfortable.'" Any teacher can create a positive learning environment by asking that simple question: What would I want if I was a student in my class?

Sandi Silbernagel explains how she creates her classroom.

Video 10.1
www.corwin.com/
highimpactinstruction

Not every classroom needs to have twinkle lights, but every classroom should be designed to produce optimal learning. There is much teachers can do to create a learner-friendly environment, and some of them are quite simple. First, teachers can be careful to make sure the classroom is organized and tidy. A room that has boxes piled along a wall or file folders spilling over a desk suggests that a lack of order is acceptable. A lack of order in the way the room is put together might reinforce a lack of order in the way students approach their work.

As Sandi did, teachers can also do their best to make the classroom warm and friendly. Warmer lighting can create a more positive learning environment. Similarly, posters, art, or other beautiful objects can create a classroom that students enjoy being in.

One particularly powerful way to shape culture is to post quotations that promote respect, personal growth, or intellectual curiosity. A teacher I observed in North Carolina posted quotations around her room to inspire her students. When I visited her classroom, I saw sayings such as, "The limits of my language are the limits of my universe" by Ludwig Wittgenstein, philosopher, and "We are more alike, my friends, than we are unalike" by writer and poet Maya Angelou.

These are just a few strategies; what matters with culture is that teachers recognize that everything shapes culture. The norms that are created, the way norms are reinforced, the way emotion is spread, and even the way a room looks all contribute to creating a learner-friendly culture. So too do all the other strategies in this section, including the way teachers use the huge amount of power they are given when they are offered the chance to teach.

Walk the Talk

In 1995, I led an organizational learning project with the Canadian Post Office. As part of the project, I interviewed retail managers about leadership and what kinds of leaders the managers respected (and didn't respect). The one comment I heard more than any other during those interviews was that people respected leaders "who walked the talk"— who did exactly what they expected of the people who reported to them.

Not long after I completed my work with Canada Post, Peter Senge and his colleagues published *The Dance of Change: The Challenges to*

Sustaining Momentum in Learning Organizations (1999), and they reported that their research with organizations led to exactly the same finding—leaders who want to shape culture and lead change must "walk the talk." Here are a few of Senge and his co-authors' observations:

- If managers are not authentic in their convictions and sincere in their behavior, there will be little trust and, consequently, little safety for the reflection that leads to authentic change (p. 194).
- Mismatches between bosses' behavior and espoused values do matter (p. 195).
- People do not expect perfection, but they recognize sincerity and openness—and their absence. When a local boss relapses from a style of open inquiry into authoritarian behavior, the repercussions can be felt for months (p. 195).

Walking the talk isn't just important for leaders in businesses, however. Leaders in classrooms need to walk the talk just as much as leaders in business, and if, for example, teachers expect students to treat each other with respect or be prepared, they must treat their students with respect and be prepared themselves. Indeed, because students frequently look to their teachers as models for their behavior, teachers must consciously and intentionally model the cultural norms they expect from their students.

This is simple to do, but it requires discipline on the part of the teacher. If teachers expect students to hand in papers on time, they must return papers on time. If teachers expect students to listen to them and each other, they must be experts at listening and always listen to their students.

Senge and his colleagues write that "the challenge of 'walking the talk' is more complex than it often appears" (1999, p. 195). This is especially true in the classroom, where the challenge and pressure of moving through the day with 32 students can inhibit a teacher's ability to really see how she or he is acting. For that reason, we suggest teachers use strategies that help them determine how well they are "walking the talk." Teachers, as I've mentioned throughout this book, can learn a great deal by video recording their classroom and watching to see how well their actions embody the norms for the class. An even easier tactic teachers can use is to audio record a lesson on a smartphone or other recorder and then listen to the recording through their car stereo on their drive home. Asking students for feedback, perhaps by having students complete a short survey, can also be enlightening.

All of us have blind spots when it comes to our own behavior. For that reason, if we truly want to shape a learner-friendly culture, we should do what we can to understand clearly how well we do, or do not, walk the talk. When it comes to shaping culture, President Kennedy's paraphrase of Emerson is perfectly apt: "What we are speaks louder than what we say" (Senator Kennedy at the Mormon Tabernacle, Salt Lake City, Utah, September 23, 1960). We need to learn what we do, and then walk the talk.

Turning Ideas Into Action

Students

1. Involve students in designing the classroom. Ask them to bring in toys, quotations, works of art, music, or other artifacts that might shape a learner-friendly culture.

2. Talk about the learning environment with students and encourage them to be active creators of their classroom. Ask them what helps them learn and what interferes with their learning.

Teachers

1. Do what Sandi Silbernagel did—ask yourself what kind of classroom your students would learn best in and do your best to create it. This might involve finding comfortable furniture, lighting, carpet, music, books, art, quotations, or other artifacts that can have a positive impact on culture.

2. Develop an orderly environment. Creativity often involves some degree of messiness, but a lack of order in the classroom may be reflected in a lack of order in student work. A warm, humane, but orderly environment is best.

3. Expand your awareness of the environment by being on the lookout for good ideas. Every trip to a retail store, library, shopping mall, office space, or home can be a chance to deepen your appreciation of environment.

Instructional Coaches

1. Use the learning environment tool (see the book's companion website at www.corwin.com/highimpactinstruction) as a method of assessing the learner-friendliness of a classroom environment.

2. Use your smartphone or digital camera to create a library of examples of effective ways in which designers (in school and outside) create positive environments. Make every trip to the mall or art gallery an opportunity to learn how lighting, color, order, layout, and other factors affect environment.

Download a learner-friendly environment survey at www.corwin.com/highimpactinstruction

3. Suggest to teachers that they redesign their classrooms at the same time that they introduce new behavioral strategies, such as new expectations for activities and transitions. If the classroom looks different, the teacher sends a message that the class is entering a new phase of learning.

Principals

1. Bring the staff together to discuss the entire school's learning environment. Consider showing excerpts from Bill Strickland's Ted Talk or Sandi Silbernagel's Talking About Teaching episode[2] and engage staff in discussions about how the school's learning environment can be improved.

2. Use the learning environment tool (see the book's companion website at www.corwin.com/highimpactinstruction) as a method of assessing the learner-friendliness of a classroom environment. Ask every employee in the school to conduct the learner-friendly analysis so you can get feedback on how to improve the school's environment.

3. Use a professional development day to raise "learning environment awareness." Ask all staff to visit interesting environments (such as beautiful or interesting stores like Anthropology, The Apple Store, a local café, or public buildings such as an art gallery, city hall, or the library). Ask staff to act like anthropologists noting down everything they see. Then reconvene with staff to discuss what they saw and what the school might do to improve its learning environment.

4. Use the learning environment tool (see www.corwin.com/highimpactinstruction) for conducting walk-through observations.

5. "Walk the talk" by using the learning environment tool to design your own office and the school office.

6. Make sure that the school is designed for students and not the convenience of adults. Involve all staff in discussions around environment so that everyone recognizes the important role environment plays and is committed to creating a learner-friendly environment.

What It Looks Like

Use the learning environment tool (see www.corwin.com/highimpactinstruction) to assess the overall environment of the school and assess the following: (a) overall order, (b) ease of access to all parts of the room and all students, (c) cleanliness, (d) aroma, (e) color and quality of paint, and (f) signs of life, including plants, art, light, quotations, and other factors.

To Sum Up

- Culture is in large part invisible, but it has a huge impact on student learning.

- Every classroom will have a culture; the question is, will the culture be shaped by students or by the teacher?

- To create a learner-friendly culture, teachers can

  Co-construct norms with students

  Reinforce students when they act consistently with the norms

  Spread learner-friendly emotions by recognizing that emotions are shared like a virus

  Design a learner-friendly environment by attending to the organization, color, art, quotations, lighting, and other aspects of the room

  Walk the talk by acting in a manner that is consistent with the norms and expectations created for students

Going Deeper

My colleague Sue Vernon has created a number of useful, inexpensive practices teachers can use to create learner-friendly cultures. Sue's community-building series helps students learn skills that are important for their full participation in a learning community. *Talking Together* teaches students how to listen, encourage others, respect diversity, and basically treat each other with kindness. *Organizing Together* teaches students the organizational skills they need to be productive learners. Other very helpful practices in the series include *Following Instructions Together* and *Taking Notes Together*. More information on the series may be found at http://www.edgeenterpris esinc.com.

Daniel Goleman's work has greatly enhanced our understanding of the role emotional intelligence plays in life. His book *Emotional Intelligence* (2006) popularized the extremely influential concept of emotional intelligence. His book *Social Intelligence: The New Science of Human Relationships* (2007) describes what occurs when people interact, and in particular, explains how emotions spread among groups. Goleman's *Primal Leadership: Learning to Lead With Emotional Intelligence* (2004) is a great overview of Goleman's ideas as they apply to leaders, including teachers.

Bill Strickland's *Make the Impossible Possible: One Man's Crusade to Dream Bigger and Achieve the Extraordinary* (2007) is Bill Strickland's story of how he grew from humble beginnings to create the impressive Manchester Bidwell Educational Center in Pittsburg, Pennsylvania.

Notes

1. You can see Bill Strickland's Ted Talk here: http://www.ted.com/talks/lang/en/bill_strickland_makes_change_with_a_slide_show.html.

2. You can see Sandi teaching and my interview with her at http://www.teachingchannel.org/videos/wraparound-learning-experience.

Chapter 11:
Power
With, Not
Power
Over

is about

treating students with respect

by understanding

by building

power

power over

power with

When teachers use power to dominate, it can be detrimental for everyone.

When teachers choose power with, authentic power is developed with children.

power with

Empathizing

Connecting through one-to-one interactions

Listening

Defusing confict

Communicating respect

11

POWER WITH, NOT POWER OVER

Nearly all [people] can stand adversity, but if you want to test [their] character, give [them] power.

—Abraham Lincoln

It takes two to have a power struggle.

—Jim Fay

In a rural school some time back, a seventh-grade student was marshaled into the eighth-grade classroom for a boys' health class. The youngster sat in a girl's desk since all the eighth-grade boys were sitting in their desks and the girls had gone across the hall for girls' health.

At the end of the lesson, before the seventh-grade boys headed back to their room, the girls came back to their seats. The girl who returned to the desk where the boy had been sitting shouted out to her teacher that her pencil, which she'd left behind, was now gone. "Where's the pencil?" the teacher asked the boy.

The seventh grader had no idea, and that's what he told his teacher. "But you must have taken the pencil," the teacher said. "Where is it?" Again, the boy knew nothing about the pencil and told his teacher so. The teacher pushed him harder and harder, and the boy kept denying having taken the pencil, telling the truth. Eventually, the teacher grabbed the boy by his shirt, pushed him against the wall, and yelled at him to hand over the pencil. The boy, frightened and humiliated, had nothing to say.

Watching the whole incident, perhaps taking pity on the boy, another student spoke: "I don't think the pencil was there before class." The teacher had to let the boy go, and the incident, for the moment, was over. Except it wasn't over. That night, at a sporting event, intent on continuing the humiliation, a high school student grabbed the seventh-grade boy and repeated the process, jokingly pretending to be the teacher and roughing up the boy in front of other older students. The experience from the morning was repeated at night except this time the humiliation was much more intense.

I know this story is true. I was the boy. The teacher became my eighth-grade teacher when I moved up from seventh grade. And although he may have wanted to teach me many important concepts, skills, or big ideas, what I remember about him is the way he treated me during that incident in health class the previous year. When teachers abuse power, they do a terrible disservice to students.

How teachers use power in the classroom can have an enormous impact on the community they create and how much their students learn. Every classroom gives teachers a great deal of structural power. Teachers plan the lesson, ask the questions, evaluate students' work, and assign grades. Teachers pass or fail students and often have the power to remove children from their classroom. Teachers are older, more educated, and more skilled in the ways of human interaction than their students.

Teachers can use their inherent power to leave their mark on the lives of their students. The mark can be profoundly positive or it can wound students for life.

When a teacher uses power for good, wonderful learning can happen. For example, teachers can design challenging assignments that unlock students' interests or help students discover who they can be. George Lucas sums up most students' experiences when he writes, "apart from my parents, my teachers have done the most to shape my life."

Unfortunately, power is not always used for good. Just like every other human being on the planet, teachers can be tempted to exert power in ways that are destructive. When teachers use power to dominate, often simply because the feeling of domination is intoxicating, that exertion of power over students can be detrimental to everyone in the classroom, including the teacher. I refer to this as "power over."

The Dangers of Power Over

Power over shows up in psychological bullying, asserting that there is only one truth (the teacher's), and the constant reminder to students that they have inferior status. In the worst-case scenarios, students feel impotent when confronted by a dominating teacher. Feeling powerless or hopeless, everybody loses the desire to learn.

Power over students, however, is not always as obvious as psychological bullying. It can surface when teachers subtly ridicule a student in front of her peers, when they lecture students to show who is boss, when they glare at a student who is out of line, and when they use their much greater knowledge and experience to show up a student in an in-class debate.

Power is especially seductive because it corrupts minute-by-minute, day-by-day. Each time we exert power over a student, we move a little closer to becoming the dictator we always vowed we would never become. Robert Sutton (2010) draws on a wide body of research to describe how "power over," which he calls "power poisoning," can keep leaders from understanding their subordinates' concerns and needs. Sutton references Dacher Keltner's research (2003) on power dynamics. One especially fascinating study of Keltner's cited by Sutton is the "cookie experiment":

> Three-person student teams were instructed to produce a short policy paper. Two members were randomly assigned to write it; the third member evaluated it and determined how much to pay the two "workers." After about thirty minutes, the experimenter brought in a plate of five cookies. It turned out that a little taste of power turned people into pigs: not only did the "bosses" tend to take a second cookie, they also displayed other symptoms of "disinhibited eating," chewing with their mouths open and scattering crumbs. (p. 33)

The "cookie experiment" is just one of many studies from Keltner's 15 years of clinically analyzing power. Keltner (quoted in Sutton's book, 2010) summarizes in graphic and dramatic terms what he has learned about the potential hazards of power:

> People with power tend to behave like patients who have damaged their brain's front orbitofrontal lobes . . . a condition that seems to cause overly impulsive and insensitive behavior. Thus, the experience of power might be thought of as having someone open up your skull and take out that part of your brain so critical to empathy and socially appropriate behavior. (p. 221)

Power, Sutton explains, doesn't affect everyone the same way because "there are empathetic and civilized bosses." But power can poison our ability to see the world through others' eyes if we are not careful. "There is ample evidence," Sutton writes, "that power turns people into insensitive jerks" (pp. 220–221).

I understand the attractions of power and recognize how pleasant power feels. I feel the pleasures of power in a little way every day I am home with our Labrador retriever Dodger. Thanks to my wife Jenny's dog whisperer skills, Dodger minds me when I tell him to do various things. If I snap my fingers and say, "Sit down," he sits down. Every time. I enjoy how it feels when I snap my fingers and watch him sit down. Indeed, I feel a little bit of pleasure every time Dodger does my bidding.

Controlling my dog is one thing; controlling people is another. As Patricia Evans has written in *Controlling People: How to Recognize, Understand, and Deal With People Who Try to Control You* (2002), people's need for control may lead them to act in destructive ways that they fail to recognize. Evans writes:

> Most people who act in oppressive ways, consciously or unconsciously, attempting to control others, are trying to meet a particular need that overrides their good intentions. Misdirected, they have sought to meet this need in extraordinarily destructive ways, *even while unaware of the need itself.* Ultimately, destructive behaviors never succeed in fulfilling the need. As a result, we are witnesses to cycles of destruction. (p. 22)

Whenever my need for control runs up against someone else's need for autonomy, problems arise. "Each of us," negotiation experts Roger Fisher and Daniel Shapiro (2005) have written, "wants an appropriate degree of autonomy" (p. 73). When we use power over to control students, our coercive attempts may actually make things worse, more out of control.

As the diagram in Figure 11.1 suggests, power over can increase misbehavior. When a teacher tries to force students to act a certain way, that force limits students' autonomy. Often power over pushes students to act more autonomously. When this occurs, teachers may try more coercive methods of control, which in turn produces more resistance, more conflict, ending in a vicious cycle, and, of course, less learning for all.

Few people have more direct power over others than teachers. Like a boss with plenty of reports, teachers observe, direct, evaluate, reward, and punish students. And like good bosses, teachers must be vigilant that they don't let power poison their perceptions and end up creating the control-autonomy vicious cycle.

| Figure 11.1 | Control-Autonomy Vicious Cycle |

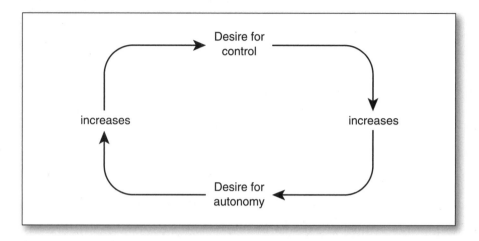

Power With

"Power with" is an alternative to power over; it involves authentic power we develop *with* students, as opposed to power over, which is coercive power we hold *over* students to keep them in place. Teachers taking the power with approach practice empathizing with, connecting with, and respecting students. Each of these is described below.

EMPATHIZING WITH STUDENTS

> *Empathy is the very means by which we create social life and advance civilization.*
>
> —Jeremy Rifkin (2009, p. 10)

Power with our students begins with the simple desire to empathize with them, to deeply understand how they are experiencing our class and school, and how they think and feel about what is important in their lives. As Jeremy Rifkin has written in *The Empathic Civilization: The Race to Global Consciousness in a World in Crisis* (2009), we use the term *empathy* "to describe the mental process by which one person enters into another's being and comes to know how they feel and think. . . . Unlike sympathy, which is more passive, empathy conjures up active engagement—the willingness of an observer to become part of another's experience, to share the feeling of the experience" (p. 12). Empathy, Rifkin writes, "is sparked by a deep emotional sharing of that other person's state, accompanied by a cognitive assessment of the other's present condition and followed by an affective and engaged response to attend to the needs and help ameliorate their suffering" (p. 13).

If we empathize with students, we are more likely to connect with them and less likely to need or want to resort to power over. There is much we can do to understand our students better. Empathy begins with a simple commitment to understand our students, the desire to truly see the world through their eyes. I know that this sounds frightfully close to a vacuous platitude, but the simple desire to see our students as real people with real thoughts and feelings is the starting point for empathy.

When we commit to understanding our students, we ask more questions of them and of ourselves. When we ask our students questions, we ask anything that might help us better understand them without any expectation of an answer. But the simplest technique might be to ask ourselves questions, taking a moment each day to focus on one student in every class and ask, "What is this student experiencing right now?"

In essence, empathy is about being intentional about understanding. My colleague Keith Lenz suggests that teachers can understand their students better by using the HALO effect, considering how High-, Average-, Low-, and Other-achieving students will experience any kind of learning we are planning. He suggests literally imagining the faces of students as we plan our lessons. I know one group of teachers who put photographs of their students on the center of the conference table in their collaborative planning room just so they would never forget what the focus should be for all their conversations.

Individual teachers can use the same strategy, looking at photos of their students as they plan their content. In addition, teachers can do a mental roll call by imagining their classroom and thinking about the students and where they sit in class, pausing to consider each student as he or she pops into their mind. When teachers can't remember which student sits where, that is a good prompt for them to make an effort to better understand their students.

Teachers can also learn a lot about their students by using more formal methods to gather information. For example, they might give students a short survey about their interests, asking students to describe their favorite music, books, websites, sports teams, or hobbies and their long-range goals. My colleague Mike Hock's *Possible Selves* (2003), for example, guides students through a series of activities that prompt them to identify their goals, strengths, and weaknesses and develop an action plan for achieving their goals.

Writing prompts help teachers gain a better understanding of their students by asking them to write on such topics as a person they respect, a challenge they have overcome, something that makes them feel proud, and so forth. Martin Seligman's Three Good Things Exercise (2011) has been proven to increase people's positive emotions, but it also is a way by which we can learn more about our students:

> We instruct the students to write down daily three good things that happened each day for a week. The three things can be small in importance ("I answered a really hard question right in language arts today") or big ("The guy I've liked for months asked me out!!!"). Next to each positive event, they write about one of the following: "Why did the good thing happen?" "What does this mean to you?" "How can you have more of this good thing in the future?" (p. 84).

We can also learn a lot by asking students for anonymous feedback. For example, we can give students a simple question to respond to on an exit ticket they complete before ending class. The ticket could ask students to describe on a scale of 1 to 10 a topic such as How engaged were you today? How safe do you feel in my classroom? How interested were you in today's topic? Teachers could also simply ask students to write one word that describes how they feel "right now."

When she was an instructional coach in Cecil County, Maryland, Sherry Eichinger helped teachers get anonymous feedback by interviewing students one-on-one or in small groups about how they were experiencing class. One of the teachers she collaborated with, Sharon Thomas, reported that she found Sherry's interview information to be a "tremendous help." Sherry's interview data gave Sharon insight into the students' interests and concerns and also opened the door to closer relationships with her students. In an email to me, Sharon described the impact of the interviews as follows:

> They also reported liking the class activities and reading selections, which I thought (based on behavior) they universally despised. Interestingly, the answers on these issues did not vary widely for behaviorally challenging kids versus kids who were more cooperative. All of the kids said that they very much appreciated being asked for their thoughts. They also asked for more choice in reading selections, and we instituted more of that as a result. Something else that was very important to me was that, because of that personal contact, they viewed Sherry as part of the classroom after interviews, not as

a "visitor." That led to them interacting more naturally with her every time she came in. . . . The toughest kid in the class was particularly enamored of her after the interview, and she became a key aid in enlisting his cooperation.

Empathizing With Students

- Commit to striving to see the world through your students' eyes.
- Ask: What is each student experiencing right now every day in every class?
- Consider how high-, average-, low-, and other-learning students are doing in your class or how they will experience a planned learning opportunity.
- Keep photos of your students on your desk to remind you of them when you are planning lessons.
- Give surveys to uncover students' interests.
- Consider having your students try a program like *Possible Selves* to uncover their goals, strengths, and weaknesses and to make an action plan for growth.
- Give students writing prompts that provide more insight into their lives, such as asking them to describe a person they respect, a challenge they have overcome, or something that makes them feel proud.
- Prompt students to do Martin Seligman's Three Good Things Exercise.
- Ask students for anonymous feedback.
- Consider asking your instructional coach or other school staff to interview your students.
- Take challenging classes, such as foreign language courses, that help you better understand the experiences of students who are struggling in our class.

Another way teachers can deepen their understanding of their students is by enrolling themselves in challenging classes. (I gained a deeper insight into learning while having a significantly frustrating time understanding instruction in a class on how to use my digital camera!) Teachers can also learn a lot about students by sitting in other teachers' classes to watch how students experience school.

Few things are more damaging to learning than the power tripping that occurs when teachers let power poison their perceptions and limit their empathy. Conversely, few things are more nourishing to learning than teachers who clearly understand how students feel. Empathy can be like Miracle-Gro® for kids.

We can embrace power with by walking a mile in our kids' shoes. When we do, my guess is we will find that our better understanding of our students often empowers them to be more open to learning. We can do something as simple as asking ourselves: "How would I feel if I was a student in this class, at this moment?" If we have genuine empathy for our students and see our classrooms through their eyes, we can avoid dominating destructive power over our students and move closer to power that is used to unleash potential rather than pin students down.

CONNECTING THROUGH ONE-TO-ONE CONVERSATIONS

I learned about the power of connecting through one-to-one conversations when I was in ninth grade. At that time, I saw many school rules as only in place to keep me in place, and I did my best to fight those rules frequently. And I did worse things than fighting the rules. One of the worst was treating teachers cruelly, especially when I was part of a group. (Cruelty is easier when you do it with others.)

One teacher I treated very poorly was Miss Stumpf, a newly minted English teacher. In Miss Stumpf's class I took every opportunity to communicate that I didn't care. I went into her class, an alienated teenager, looking for ways to sabotage whatever learning experience she had planned.

One day as I was walking home tired after a tough football practice (we always had tough practices after we lost, and we always lost!), Miss Stumpf drove by, stopped, and asked me if I wanted a ride. (This was back in the early 1970s when teachers still felt safe making such simple offers.) I was very happy to not have to walk and accepted the ride.

Something amazing happened when we talked. I found myself speaking with her in the same way I would talk to my friends or family. In a matter of seconds, literally, my understanding of her was transformed. In the midst of our friendly interaction, I realized that she really cared about my success. I realized too that the teacher that I had treated so terribly was just as real a person as I was, and a lot nicer. From that day forward, I had a different relationship with Miss Stumpf. The reason for the change was simple: I now saw her as a real person.

My experience with Miss Stumpf exemplifies something Martin Buber talks about in *I and Thou* (1958). When we see others as objects, we can do terrible things to them simply because we don't recognize that they are real. Of course, we know that they are just as human as we are, but we don't see them having the same feelings as we do. However, when we see people as real, as subjects rather than objects, we see them as fellow human beings. Seeing through empathetic eyes rather than cold dehumanizing eyes transforms our relationships with others.

One of the simplest ways to move from being an object to a subject is to do what Miss Stumpf did; have one-to-one conversations. I've written about one-to-one exchanges as an important part of instructional coaching, but I see them as important relationship builders in all settings, and especially in the classroom. We can (and I think should) make one-to-one conversations a ritual of our classrooms. They can be scheduled throughout the school year. They might take place informally outside of class, or formally in class while all other students are engaged in an activity that doesn't require teacher direction.

One-to-one conversations could focus on student progress, but they can also focus on our own progress. We can ask children for feedback on what is and isn't working for their learning. What matters in these simple exchanges is that we try to connect with our students and reveal ourselves as real.

Sandi Silbernagel explains how she reveals information about herself to build relationships.

Video 11.1
www.corwin.com/highimpactinstruction

> **Connecting Through One-to-One Conversations**
>
> - Schedule them throughout the year.
> - Discuss student progress.
> - Ask for feedback on what is and isn't working.
> - Use effective communication strategies to build connections with students, especially listening.

Organizational theorist Peter Senge is credited with a statement that I love: "The way forward is about becoming more human, not just more clever." Senge's words are just as meaningful in the classroom as they are in the boardroom. And one way we can become more human is through more one-to-one conversations.

Of course, one-to-one conversations won't be effective if we fail to connect with students when we talk with them. For that reason, one of the most important skills any teacher needs to master is effective listening.

LISTENING

The more deeply you understand other people, the more you will appreciate them, the more reverent you will feel toward them.

—Stephen Covey

You can clarify how important listening is in all aspects of life by doing something simple. Imagine a person you know, a real person, who is not a good listener. Think about what it is like when you talk to her, and what she does. Chances are, she cuts you off in midsentence. She might look bored while you talk. She might look like she can't wait to share her thoughts and words, whenever you start to talk. Her actions make you feel she doesn't think what you have to say really means anything. She might even look as if she thinks she's much smarter than you.

Now imagine a real person that you consider a great listener. Chances are when you talk to her, she lets you have the floor. She appears to be curious and interested in what you have to say. Her actions make you feel like your words and ideas are important; she makes you feel like you count, that you are valuable.

Leaving aside every other characteristic of these two people (their intelligence, leadership skills, gender, race, ethics, etc.), chances are you have a better opinion of the person who listens than you do of the one who cuts you off—just because she listens to you.

Much has been written about listening. If you pick up a book about leadership or relationship building, chances are there will be a chapter on listening. We are given lots of advice. Good listeners make eye contact; they empathize; they paraphrase; their body language reflects back the stance of the speaker. Good listeners get inside the paradigm of the speaker. This is all good advice, but I believe the heart of listening is nothing more than making the commitment to do it.

If we really want to hear what another person has to say and allow him or her to speak, and we process what is being said, I believe the rest of the listening strategies will take care of themselves. When we reduce listening to its essence, it primarily means just to stop talking and focus on the speaker. If we really want to hear what the other person wants to say, he or she will know. It's as simple as that.

Listening is important for leaders, for all of us in any relationship, and I believe it is especially important in the classroom. When we listen to students, we show respect for them, and we reduce behavior problems by encouraging a positive and respectful classroom culture. Listening communicates our belief that students have something worthwhile to say and that they are smart, valuable people. Listening also models respectful behaviors that all people would be wise to demonstrate.

Truly listening is a humble act. If we listen to our students, we communicate that everyone in the classroom has something worthwhile to say. We also get the opportunity to learn more by really hearing what our children are saying. And when we really listen to our students, they often reward us with real insights.

COMMUNICATING RESPECT

In her book *Respect* (2000), Sarah Lawrence-Lightfoot tells a story from her childhood that captures what can happen when we respect others. Dr. Lawrence-Lightfoot describes how she felt and what she learned when a family friend sketched a picture of her as a young girl. The story, which I first included in *Instructional Coaching: A Partnership Approach to Improving Instruction* (2007), paints a vivid picture of why teachers should communicate respect for their students and how to do so:

> The summer of my eighth birthday, my family was visited by a seventy-year-old black woman, a professor of sociology, an old and dear friend. A woman of warmth and dignity, she always seemed to have secret treasures hidden under her smooth exterior. On this visit, she brought charcoals and a sketch pad. Mid-afternoon, with the sun high in the sky, she asked me to sit for her. . . .
>
> What I remember most clearly was the wonderful, glowing sensation I got from being attended to so fully. There were no

Listening

- Commit to listening to every student.
- Make sure that the student is the focus of the conversation, not you.
- Talk in a way that opens up rather than shuts down a conversation.

distractions. I was the only one in her gaze. My image filled her eyes, and the sound of the chalk stroking the paper was palpable. The audible senses translated into tactile ones. After the warmth of this human encounter, the artistic product was almost forgettable. I do not recall whether I liked the portrait or not. . . . This fast-working artist whipped the page out of her sketch pad after less than an hour and gave it to me with one admonition: "Always remember you're beautiful," she said firmly. To which I responded—beaming with pleasure and momentary embarrassment—"Now I know I'm somebody!"

In the process of recording the image, the artist had made me feel "seen" in a way that I had never felt seen before, fully attended to, wrapped up in an empathic gaze. (p. 211)

Respecting students, seeing them, communicating that they are "somebody" begins with a deep desire to acknowledge that we see our students as valuable, as people, no matter how old or young, with important ideas and feelings to share. If teachers carefully listen to students, acknowledge their ideas, validate what they say, and stop actions that communicate a lack of respect (sarcasm, singling out students, ridiculing students, cutting students off in midsentence), we can have a profound impact on students.

I saw a great example of a teacher respecting students when I watched my friend Jean Clark teaching a seventh-grade English class in Cecil County, Maryland. During class discussion, Jean hung on to each word each student spoke. She did this by totally focusing on each student when he or she was talking and by then communicating her joy and interest in what each student said. Stopping after one comment, for example, Jean said to the other students, "Did you all hear what this young man said?" Then she turned to the boy who was speaking and said, "That was so wise. Please say that again." The boy lit up and gladly repeated his insight, and every student in the room saw that their words counted. In addition, the students also saw that Ms. Clark saw them as real people who counted.

Wendy Hopf explains how she builds trust with students.

Video 11.2
www.corwin.com/
highimpactinstruction

Communicating Respect

- Commit to seeing students as people with important ideas to share.
- Validate what students say.
- Avoid sarcasm, singling out students, cutting students off in midsentence, or other actions that communicate a lack of respect.

DEFUSING CONFLICT

As I noted above, power over can lead to a vicious, destructive cycle when a teacher tries to force students to act a certain way (by forcefully telling them that they have to do something). That force increases a student's desire to meet his or her need for autonomy (refuse to comply with a forceful command), the student's resistance increases a teacher's desire for autonomy, so he becomes more forceful (threatening the student with punishment), and on and on.

One way to defuse this vicious cycle is to ensure that the student-teacher conversation never becomes personal. Once things become personal, as Roger Fisher and William Ury explain in *Getting to Yes* (1991), conflict resolution becomes very difficult. According to Fisher and Ury, effective negotiators keep negotiations from becoming personal by addressing interests rather than positions. If I focus on my position in a negotiation, my goal is to win and make sure you lose. If I focus on interests, my goal is to find a negotiated solution that best meets both of our interests.

In negotiations, Fisher and Ury explain, there are always shared and compatible interests as well as conflicting ones. For example, in the classroom, a teacher might want students to improve as readers by doing a great deal of reading, and students might be willing to read a great deal if they get to choose a topic that is of high interest to them. Thus, by acknowledging students' interests by giving them a chance to choose reading material on a high-interest topic, a teacher can meet her goal of increasing the amount of reading done by students. (More on this is included in Chapter 12, Freedom Within Form.) If a teacher insists on choosing the reading and pushing for her position, power over, and most likely much less reading will take place. As is often the case, power over actually decreases teachers' ability to meet their goals.

Turning Ideas Into Action

Students

1. Give the students the student survey available on the book's companion website at www.corwin.com/highimpactinstruction.

2. Teach students listening skills and explain that it is your intention to model the practices in every class, every day.

3. Give students numerous opportunities to explain how they feel in class and how they would like the classroom to be adjusted to support their learning needs.

Teachers

1. Record your conversations (inside or outside of school) to see how effectively you listen.

2. Video record your classes to observe how well you use the power with strategies.

(Continued)

Download student surveys at www.corwin.com/highimpactinstruction

(Continued)

3. After you have been the victim of power over (for example, from a TSA official, immigration officer, or Department of Motor Vehicle clerk), write down as much as you can about your experience and consider how your students might feel if they are victims of power over.

Instructional Coaches

1. Share this chapter with teachers in a book study setting and discuss such questions as these: "How would you define power over and power with? What does power with look like to you? How can we know for sure if we are doing power with?"

2. Conduct schoolwide surveys of students, assessing their perceptions of how often they experience power over, how psychologically safe they feel, and how much they think teachers care about them.

Principals

1. Commit to modeling power with during all of your interactions with people (children and adults) in the school.

2. Lead schoolwide conversations with staff to define power with and power over. Consider using the *Unmistakable Impact* process to identify power with strategies to be embraced and power over strategies to be eliminated.

3. Once everyone can describe power with and power over and has committed to eliminating power over practices, be vigilant in naming power over when you see it and encouraging teachers to change their practices. Adults should never be allowed to bully children.

What It Looks Like

Embracing power with, not power over, is as much about not doing certain things as it is about what not to do. If people embrace power with, they shouldn't yell, belittle, interrupt, or bully others. If students feel they are respected, that should be reflected in surveys of student attitudes.

To Sum Up

• "Power over" occurs when people use power in destructive ways, to dominate and control, often because it feels pleasant to be in control.

• When one person's need for control butts up with another person's need for autonomy, it can become a vicious cycle.

- Power with involves authentic power people develop *with* students.

- Teachers can increase power with by

  Empathizing with students

  Connecting with students

  Respecting students

  Listening

  Effectively defusing conflict

Going Deeper

Robert Sutton's *Good Boss, Bad Boss: How to Be the Best and Learn From the Worst* (2010) is, as the title indicates, a book about management and leadership, but Sutton's insights also have a lot of application for teachers. Sutton discusses such topics as "power poisoning," mentioned above, balancing love and accountability, Lasorda's Law of control mentioned in Chapter 12, assuming the best, creating psychological safety, and encouraging "small wins." Almost every idea in Sutton's book has application to the task of leading a group of students in a classroom.

Patricia Evans has written several important and educational books about verbal abuse and controlling people. Verbal abuse can be even more destructive than physical abuse, and everyone should know how to recognize and avoid it. Two books worth reviewing are *The Verbally Abusive Relationship: How to Recognize It and How to Respond to It* (2010) and *Controlling People: How to Recognize, Understand, and Deal With People Who Try to Control You* (2002).

Martin Seligman has come to be called the father of positive psychology, and his book *Learned Optimism: How to Change Your Mind and Your Life* (2006), like Carol Dweck's *Mindset* (2006), clearly explains how our ways of thinking can significantly inhibit our ability to learn. Seligman's *Flourish: A Visionary New Understanding of Happiness and Well-Being* (2011) is a comprehensive overview of positive psychology and includes many activities teachers can share with students, such as the Three Good Things activity mentioned in this chapter.

Jeremy Rifkin's *The Empathic Civilization: The Race to Global Consciousness in a World in Crisis* (2009) eloquently makes the case that people are inherently empathic beings and that the movement forward of our global communities hinges on our moving into a more empathic way of interacting.

Chapter 12:
Freedom
Within Form

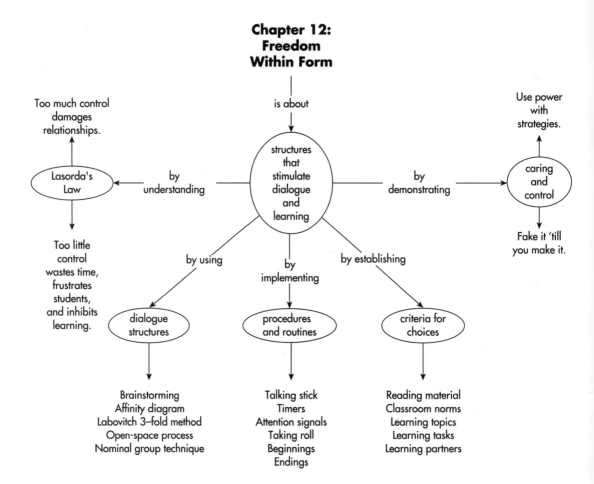

Too much control
damages
relationships.

Lasorda's
Law

is about

by
understanding

structures
that
stimulate
dialogue
and
learning

Use power
with
strategies.

by
demonstrating

caring
and
control

Too little
control
wastes time,
frustrates
students,
and inhibits
learning.

Fake it 'till
you make it.

by using

by
implementing

by establishing

dialogue
structures

procedures
and routines

criteria for
choices

Brainstorming
Affinity diagram
Labovitch 3–fold method
Open-space process
Nominal group technique

Talking stick
Timers
Attention signals
Taking roll
Beginnings
Endings

Reading material
Classroom norms
Learning topics
Learning tasks
Learning partners

12

FREEDOM WITHIN FORM

Anyone can improvise with no restrictions, but that's not jazz. Jazz always has some restrictions. Otherwise, it might sound like noise. The ability to improvise . . . comes from fundamental knowledge and this knowledge limits the choices you can make and will make.

—Wynton Marsalis (in Iyengar, 2010, p. 214)

If the structure does not permit dialogue, the structure must be changed.

—Paulo Freire

Former LA Dodgers manager Tommy Lasorda was one of the most successful (and colorful) managers in the history of Major League baseball. A member of the Baseball Hall of Fame, he won two World Series championships, four National League pennants, and eight division titles in his 20 years of managing the Dodgers. Asked to describe the secret of his success, Lasorda used a simple analogy: "I believe that managing is like holding a dove in your hands. If you hold it too tightly, you kill it, but if you hold it too loosely you lose it" (quoted in Sutton, 2010).

In *Good Boss, Bad Boss* (2010), Robert Sutton writes that this analogy, which he refers to as "Lasorda's Law," captures the delicate balance that every good boss seeks between managing too much and too little. According to Sutton, "Managers who are too assertive will damage relationships with superiors, peers, and followers; but managers who are not assertive enough won't press followers to achieve sufficiently tough goals."

Lasorda's Law also applies in the classroom. An effective teacher maintains control while ensuring that there is sufficient freedom. Too much control damages relationships. Too little control leads to frustrated students, wasted time, and too little learning. Skillful teachers create learning situations in which students are authentically free to make decisions, set goals, and construct their own learning, while at the same time creating structures that ensure learning is productive, positive, and meaningful. I refer to this balancing act between choice and control as freedom within form.[1]

The Paradox of Freedom

Most people recognize that we learn best when we have some freedom or autonomy. As numerous research studies have shown, students are most motivated by learning when they set their own goals, and rarely motivated by goals that are set for them (see selfdetermi nationtheory.org for many articles on this topic). Unless a goal matters to an individual student, chances are that student will not be very interested in learning (Pink, 2011).

In addition, telling students what to do without providing some degree of freedom often leads to resentment. People, adults and children, want to control their actions, and when leaders control others without acknowledging their needs for autonomy, that creates resistance. As the saying goes, "When you insist, I will resist." Ironically, a teacher's attempt to control students can lead to more disruptions if she doesn't recognize the universal need we all have for some control over what we do.

When a teacher's desire for control collides with a student's need for self-direction, the results can be messy, and the conflict often significantly inhibits learning. Students must experience some form of autonomy if they are to get the most out of their learning experiences. Being autonomous means that people are free to make their own decisions; that they have choices. Indeed, "choice," as Barry Schwartz wrote in *The Paradox of Choice* (2004), "is essential to autonomy . . . [and autonomy] . . . is absolutely fundamental to well-being" (p. 3).

Paulo Freire, in *Pedagogy of the Oppressed* (1970), describes autonomy as "the indispensable condition for the quest for human completion" (p. 31) and sees education without autonomy as dehumanizing. This is in part what Freire was referring to in his famous criticism of "banking education," a form of schooling, he writes, "in which the scope of action allowed to the students extends only as far as receiving, filing, and storing the deposits" (p. 58). During banking education

> the teacher . . . leads the students to memorize mechanically the narrated content. Worse yet, it turns them into "containers" into "receptacles" to be "filled" by the teacher. The more completely he fills the receptacles, the better a teacher he is. The more meekly the receptacles permit themselves to be filled, the better students they are. (p. 58)

Banking education dehumanizes because it leaves no room for choice—and if students cannot choose, they cannot reflect. Reflection is impossible without choice since it involves making up our own minds about learning. When we remove freedom, we remove reflection, and removing reflection makes learning a dehumanizing experience.

While freedom is essential for learning, simply opening up the classroom to an infinite number of choices is not the solution. As Barry Schwartz (2004) has explained, too much choice is little better than no choice:

> When people have no choice, life is almost unbearable. . . . But as the number of choices keeps growing, negative aspects of having a multitude of options begin to appear. As the number of choices grows further, the negatives escalate until we become overloaded. At this point, choice no longer liberates, but debilitates. It might even be said to tyrannize. (p. 2)

If too many choices tyrannize, and too few choices dehumanize, what can a teacher do? Too much freedom leads to anarchy; too little freedom leads to student resentment, resistance, and apathy. Should teachers focus on freedom and just accept that freedom is messy and students will inevitably feel frustrated and waste learning opportunities? Or should teachers focus on control and just accept that resistance is inevitable and many students will never be motivated? The solution is both: Honoring students' freedom by providing meaningful choices throughout the fabric of the entire day, *and* providing sufficient form for learning by designing experiences that enable students to take advantage of the freedom they are granted in the classroom—freedom within form.

This chapter describes approaches and strategies that teachers can employ to make freedom

Freedom Within Form

- Dialogue structures
- Procedures and rituals
- Choices guided by criteria
- Caring and control

within form a central part of their learning community. Strategies and approaches include (a) employing dialogue structures that organize collaboration while respecting the autonomy of each individual, (b) using procedures and rituals to liberate and organize learning, (c) offering choices that are guided by clear criteria, and (d) being caring and controlling in the classroom.

Dialogue Structures

When students work together, they often run up against the paradox of freedom. On one hand, they will be alienated from group activities when they don't have choices about the tasks at hand. On the other hand, if groups are loosely structured with unclear goals and no direction and every student has input whenever and however he or she wishes, some voices will likely be drowned out, and some children may end up leaving the process more frustrated than empowered. Keith Sawyer (2007), writing about creative teams, describes how the paradox of freedom lies at the heart of much of the collaborative work of any team:

> The key to improvised innovation is managing a paradox: establishing a goal that provides a focus for the team—just enough of one so that team members can tell when they move closer to a solution—but one that's open-ended enough for problem-finding creativity to emerge. (p. 45)

Sawyer's comments are about adult teams, but they are equally applicable to students. In *Unmistakable Impact*, I identify dialogue structures as one way to balance the need for freedom and form. Too much freedom leads to chaos; too much control leads to alienation. This is where dialogue structures come in. Dialogue structures are activities that are propelled by students' free choices but organized so that outcomes are reached effectively.

To understand what a dialogue structure is, let's start by analyzing the concept of dialogue. As David Bohm (1996) has written, dialogue is "thinking together." In *On Dialogue* (1996), Bohm explains that the etymology of *dialogue* reveals that the word describes a form of communication where meaning moves back and forth between and through people. The original Greek meaning of "logos" is "meaning" and the original Greek meaning of "dia" is "through." Bohm explains:

> The picture or image that this derivation suggests is of a *stream of meaning* flowing among and through us and between us . . .

out of which will emerge some new understanding. It's something new, which may not have been in the starting point at all. It's something creative. And this *shared meaning* is the "glue" or "cement" that holds people and societies together. (p. 1)

Dialogue structures unleash the free-flowing sharing of ideas by organizing student collaboration. The following are examples of structures teachers can use with students.

Brainstorming, Affinity Diagrams, and the Labovitch Method. Brainstorming is a dialogue structure familiar to most. First described by Alex Faickney Osborn in *Applied Imagination* (1953), brainstorming is a simple process whereby a group of people lists ideas or thoughts about a particular topic. A family might sit around the kitchen table brainstorming possible names for a new puppy, and a group of students might brainstorm ways their class could do something important for children in the developing world.

While brainstorming is a free activity, it works best when it is organized by guidelines. Two rules are basic to effective brainstorming.

Focus on Quantity

During brainstorming, a group should try to come up with as many ideas as possible; the more ideas the better. The assumption here is that sometimes the best ideas come at the end of a brainstorming session.

Withhold Criticism

Criticism should be put on hold during brainstorming so that people feel free to generate more, and more innovative, ideas. If participants aren't worried about how good or bad an idea is, they are more likely to make suggestions. Evaluation of the ideas can occur after every idea has been listed.

The idea of brainstorming was adapted by Japanese anthropologist Jiro Kawakita, who created affinity diagrams. The affinity diagram process involves three steps. First, students pick a topic to be discussed and write down their ideas on sticky notes. Second, they affix all their sticky notes to the white board or a wall in the classroom. Then, usually without talking, they sort the notes into groups that are related. Affinity diagrams allow a large amount of information to be generated and organized very quickly.

My friend and former colleague Ben Labovitch, a master teacher at Humber College in Toronto, Canada, uses a method of analysis with his students that incorporates aspects of brainstorming and affinity diagrams. Ben uses what he refers to as the Three-Fold Method of Analysis to model interpretation of literary works, but the Three-Fold Method may be used in any subject area that involves analysis, which is probably most subjects (see Figure 12.1).

For the first step of the threefold analysis, Ben asks students to come to class ready to identify sections that stand out as important or memorable in a novel or other work they have just completed. During the class, following the methods of brainstorming, Ben writes down every important scene students suggest without judgment.

Once the white board is filled with scenes the students have identified as important, Ben follows the methods of affinity diagrams, asking students to group the scenes into different categories. For example, if his students were reading *Huckleberry Finn*, they might identify groupings of scenes that show Huck's growing awareness of racism, the symbolic meaning of the river, or Mark Twain's use of irony.

After brainstorming and grouping, Ben asks students to identify the big ideas or messages that they see. Ultimately, the big ideas become the thesis statements for essays, the groupings of scenes become the source for the main ideas, and individual scenes become the supporting details for each student's essay.

Open Space. Harrison Owen's *Open Space Technology* (1997) describes a group conversation process that is driven entirely by the interests and choices of participants. Although open space is frequently used by groups of adults interested in exploring topics from multiple perspectives (e.g., multinational corporations looking to identify breakthrough innovations or small not-for-profit organizations looking to identify effective fundraising), open space can be used in all sorts of ways in the classroom (see Figure 12.2).

During open space, participants list topics they would like to discuss and then organize themselves by joining with others who are interested in the same topics. Whoever proposes a topic to be

| Figure 12.1 | Labovitch's Threefold Method of Analysis |

1. Ask students to identify their favorite scenes in a work they have read and list all the scenes on the board.

2. Ask students to group the scenes in ways that seem to make sense to them.

3. Identify big ideas, which can become thesis statements for an analysis of the work.

| Figure 12.2 | The Open Space Process in School |

1. Students create a list of topics they want to discuss.

2. The student suggesting a topic agrees to host the discussion.

3. Students choose which topic they want to discuss.

4. According to the Law of Two Feet, students can move to another group if they're not learning in the group they initially chose.

5. Students may be asked to create a product (such as a brainstormed list or graphic organizer) and share it with the rest of the class at the end of a lesson.

discussed is expected to serve as a host for the conversation and generally keep the conversation moving once students move into groups. After all topics have been proposed, and perhaps posted on paper in different parts of the room, students join the group that most interests them. If students don't feel they are contributing to or learning from a given group, they are free to move to another group. Owen calls this the Law of Two Feet, suggesting that if a conversation isn't working for someone, they are free to use their two feet to find another one.

Teachers can adapt aspects of open space for use in the classroom in a variety of ways. For example, a secondary science teacher might use open space to prompt deeper understanding of climate change by asking students to identify what they want to explore in a major project. Students might then identify a list of topics, such as scientific explanations of the causes of climate change, climate change's impact on glaciers, a public relations campaign to educate the general public about the topic, a call to action describing what individuals can do about climate change, interviews with public figures to identify their views on the topic, and so forth.

The host for each topic of discussion is the student who proposed the topic, and students choose which topic they want to explore. If students don't like the topic, they are free to propose a new one. If a topic is proposed that no one wants to do except the host, the host has the option of joining another group or working individually.

Aspects of open space may be used in any subject area. Students reading *To Kill a Mockingbird*, for example, might self-organize into discussion groups to discuss such topics as whether or not the book is still relevant today, personal applications of the book's main theme, the writer's craft, and so forth. Open space may also be used for content review, with students hosting discussions of content they know well, and other students joining groups to deepen their understanding. When using open space in this way, teachers may want to give all students a chance to be an expert and a learner, so that everyone gets to both share their knowledge and receive assistance.

Teachers can also choose to use only one or two strategies from open space. For example, a teacher might list the topics students will discuss, but let the students choose what they want to discuss. Or a teacher might assign "hosts" for a classroom discussion, let the group choose their own host, or arrange for "hosting" to be a responsibility that every student experiences. Teachers may also decide not to introduce the Law of Two Feet. The amount of freedom teachers provide depends on how well students have learned to use their freedom (through the teaching and reinforcing of expectations, procedures, and rituals, as described below), which in turn determines how much scaffolding is necessary. The challenge is recognizing that too little choice leads to alienation from the task, but that too little structure leads to inefficient learning and frustration. So the sooner students can experience more freedom in an orderly manner, the sooner they will be more engaged in learning.

To increase the likelihood that open space will be effective, teachers should teach the skills students need to be successful. This includes the strategies in this part of the book (expectations for activities, procedures, learning rituals, etc.) as well as skills specifically needed for open space. Thus, teachers might teach students how to host discussions, how to listen and encourage other students to speak up during discussion, criteria for the work produced during group work, and so forth. The open space process is a rich opportunity for students to work on content that they are personally interested in while also learning about collaboration. Finally, by providing a structure for free choices, open space is also a great example of freedom within form.

Structured Choices. When teachers provide students with the opportunity to have meaningful input into their learning, students sometimes have to make decisions before everyone can move forward. For example, when a group of students are working together on a project, they may need to make decisions about the direction of their project. Other decisions might address how students will work together, how students will contribute to their community, what content will be covered in a particular topic (in settings where such freedom is possible), or simply how students will celebrate a group or individual success.

One way to address these decision points is by simply opening up discussion—much can be learned from a freewheeling conversation. However, a lot of time can be burned up discussing what treats will be served at the end-of-year party and similar topics, and often teachers would rather have their students use that time to learn something more important.

To move the discussion forward while also providing students with meaningful choices, teachers can provide structured choices. A *structured choice* is one that is controlled by the teacher but that also gives students some meaningful choices. For example, if a class needs to decide on how it will do some form of public service, a teacher can offer a structured choice by asking all students to write down their ideas and hand them in. She can then sort through the suggestions, identify the most popular ones, and have the students vote on the choice they prefer. By offering a structured choice, the teacher can still give each student a voice in the process but ensure that a minimal amount of time is taken for the decision.

One well-known method for structuring choices is the nominal group technique, a simple four-step dialogue structure that can be used to lead a group to a decision. Students can work in groups or work together as one large group when using this approach. The steps are as follows:

Nominal Group Technique

1. Generate ideas
2. Record
3. Discuss
4. Vote

Step 1: Generate Ideas

The process begins with the teacher presenting a question or problem and asking students to write down their ideas on slips of paper or index cards. Each student writes down his or her ideas without consulting other students.

Step 2: Record

During the next stage, all the students' ideas are recorded. To do so, the teacher might gather all the notes and write down everything she finds or ask students to read their ideas out loud as she records them. If students are working in groups, the host of the group discussion can record comments on chart paper or some other form of poster paper.

Step 3: Discuss

The teacher or host of the discussion (if students are meeting in small groups) then directs the students' attention to each of the ideas and asks for comments. Anyone who wants to say something about a topic should feel free to speak up.

Step 4: Vote

Once the discussion is complete, students vote privately. Sometimes students generate a list of criteria for the vote, at other times the teacher gives students criteria, and at yet other times students do not need criteria. All the votes are tallied and shared with the group.

Structured choices and nominal group technique can be used to make decisions about actions that might or might not take place in a classroom, or the process can be directed at content in the class. For example, in a contemporary history class, students could explore ways to address social problems related to the environment, poverty, the developing world, teenage pregnancy, or whatever is most important for learning. Students could also explore solutions to historical problems. For example, a teacher might lay out the interests of all countries sitting at the table to draft the Treaty of Versailles, without giving the details of the treaty, and ask students to suggest possible solutions. Students could even be prompted to use nominal group technique to solve scientific or mathematical problems.

Other Dialogue Structures. There are many other dialogue structures that can be used in the classroom. Formative assessments, such as exit tickets (see Chapter 3), can be used to ask students, "What was the most important thing you learned today?" "What important questions do you still have?" or "What was the muddiest point in _____?" (Angelo & Cross, 1993, pp. 154–158).

Pro and con grids, in which students are asked to come up with a minimum number of pros and cons on a topic, can be used to enable students to see an issue from more than one perspective. Or students can be asked to use the FOG method of analysis to identify whether ideas in a piece of writing are Facts, Opinions, or Guesses (Straker, 1997, pp. 27–34). What counts with all of these structures is that students have a real voice and choice in learning and that that freedom is organized so that everyone truly can contribute in meaningful ways.

Procedures and Rituals

If students are to experience the kind of freedom inherent in dialogue structures, rituals and procedures must be in place to ensure that that learning doesn't go awry. One way to do that is to teach students certain procedures and rituals that organize experiences and keep learning productive.

Procedures. In *Teach Like a Champion* (2010), Doug Lemov describes a video of a teacher, Doug McCurry, teaching his students to hand out papers. In the clip, McCurry explains that students are to "pass across rows; start on his command; that only the person passing gets out of his or her seat if required and so on." Then McCurry has the students practice the procedure until they can do it fluently. He even times the students until they can pass out papers in less than 10 seconds.

Lemov reports that when he shows this clip in workshops, some teachers inevitably find fault with what they see as poor instruction. Then Lemov explains why he thinks McCurry is actually using highly effective instruction:

> Assume that the average class of students passes out or back papers and materials twenty times a day and that it takes a typical class a minute and twenty seconds to do this. If McCurry's students can accomplish this task in just twenty seconds, they will save twenty minutes a day. . . . Now multiply that twenty minutes per day by 190 school days, and find that McCurry has just taught his students a routine that will net him thirty-eight hundred minutes of additional instruction over the course of a school year. (p. 7)

Although some may question whether or not students would or should hand out papers 20 times a day, Lemov's point is a good one. Teaching student procedures saves time and, perhaps more important, creates the kind of order necessary for student freedom to exist. When students have learned the procedures for small-group discussion, for example, it is much easier for them to participate in open-space kinds of activities. But if students haven't learned how to listen to each other, discuss ideas constructively, and take turns, the kind of freedom offered in open space will end up being chaotic and unproductive.

In *Classroom Management for Secondary Teachers*, Emmer, Evertson, and Worsham (2003) explain how important it is for teachers to explain procedures:

> It is just not possible for a teacher to conduct instruction or for students to work productively if they have no guidelines for how to behave or when to move about the room, or if they frequently interrupt the teacher and one another. Furthermore, inefficient procedures and the absence of routines for common aspects of classroom life, such as taking and reporting attendance, participating in discussions, turning in materials, or checking work, can waste large amounts of time and cause students' attention to wane. (p. 17)

Teaching students exactly how to do the procedures Emmer and colleagues list may seem to inhibit student freedom, but the reality is that freedom is not possible unless procedures are explained, modeled, and practiced. Only when students know exactly how to do tasks such as hand out papers, pass out supplies, or move desks into different groupings are they able to experience freer dialogue structures and other learning experiences.

Teachers adopting the freedom-within-form approach set out to teach routines and procedures that increase freedom. One way to accomplish this seeming paradox is through the use of learning rituals that structure students' experiences while making it easier for them to participate as they see fit. I use the term *ritual* here to refer to an action or set of actions that are used in a routine, consistent way. A number of learning rituals that foster freedom within form are described below.

Talking Stick. The talking stick ritual originated with indigenous North Americans and was likely first used during tribal council circles. The talking stick, often a carved wooden staff, was passed around the circle to whomever chose to speak. Since only the person holding the stick was allowed to talk, the ritual ensured that everyone had a chance to speak and everyone listened to the speaker. When the speaker was finished, he or she passed the stick to somebody else, and if that person wished to speak, he or she would hold the stick while speaking. In this way, every speaker had an opportunity to speak, and no single voice was allowed to dominate and silence others. The ritual increased each speaker's freedom since every speaker had an equal chance to speak.

When I observed Sandi Silbernagel teach in Slidell, Louisiana, I saw how she used a variation on the talking stick ritual. When Sandi brought her second-grade students together for a discussion circle, she gave them a stuffed animal (a talking crab) to pass around to see who wanted to add comments to the discussion. Whoever held the talking crab had the chance to speak, and everyone else was expected to listen. What worked for aboriginal tribal council circles worked just as well in Sandi's classroom, for each of her students had an opportunity to speak up and everyone listened to each speaker. Freedom was increased by form.

Timers. Teachers can also increase freedom through the use of timers. Teachers can use timers—such as those that are built into Promethean Boards or Smart Boards, or simple kitchen timers—to let students know how much time they have for an activity. Explaining precisely how long students can work on a cooperative learning activity helps maintain student focus and often increases how much students learn.

Attention Signals. There are many ways that teachers can get students' attention. These include counting to five, ringing a bell, raising one's hand, and saying "may I have your attention please." By ensuring that every student understands and responds to an attention signal, teachers can maintain control and significantly increase the amount of time students are actually learning.

Taking Roll. To ensure that the least amount of time is consumed by taking roll, teachers should create a simple ritual and use it each day. There are many ways to do this, but what matters is that the students have something meaningful to work on while the teacher takes roll. By doing it the same way every day, the teacher ensures that students always know what to do while she takes roll.

Beginnings. To get the day off to a good start, many teachers start each class with a warm-up activity such as silent reading, journal writing, or a review assignment. Some teachers begin by asking students to review the learning map, if one is being used. Others begin class with an advance organizer in which they explain what will be learned, why it is important, how the new knowledge fits with what has been learned, and what students need to do.

Endings. Rituals can be used just as effectively at the end of a class as at the beginning. Teachers can end class by prompting students to add newly learned content to their learning map (see Chapter 4) or by asking students to complete an exit ticket (see Chapter 3). Teachers can also simply ensure that every class ends with a post organizer in which the teacher guides students, through questions, to discuss such topics as (a) what was learned today, (b) how does what was learned fit with the bigger ideas being learned in the unit, and (c) what will be learned tomorrow.

Learning rituals create an orderly learning environment, and as such they make it easier for teachers to provide freer experiences for students. In a classroom where simple rituals are in place and acted upon every day, there are many ways for the free spirit of a child to find its natural place. In a classroom where there is a lack of order, the free spirit of a child must fight to find expression and often never is given a voice at all.

Choices Guided by Criteria

Freedom is primarily about making choices, so teachers who want to create freedom in their classrooms make student choice a central part of what happens in every class, every day. Students can make meaningful choices about many important and foundational aspects of their learning, including (a) the norms and expectations of their learning community, (b) the material they will read, (c) the learning activities they will complete, (d) how they will do their work, and (e) who they will work with.

Simply providing choices without some structure to guide those choices may not lead to productive learning. Giving students complete freedom to choose everything about their learning, for example, without establishing guidelines or criteria for work could lead to poor-quality student products and limited student learning. If students' free choices are truly to lead to optimal learning, that freedom must be contained and set free with some kind of structure. Here are a few suggestions for how to balance choice with criteria.

Reading Material. In *The Book Whisperer: Awakening the Inner Reader in Every Child* (2009), Donalyn Miller provides a great example of how the freedom of choice can be set free by form. Based on her experience teaching reading, Miller asserts that "providing students with the opportunity to choose their own books to read empowers and encourages them . . . Readers without power to make their own choices are unmotivated."

Miller believes that allowing students to have free choice is an essential part of engaging them in reading. However, she is also very clear that simply letting students pick books is not sufficient to inspire and develop readers. First, Miller says that in her class it is simply not acceptable for students to choose not to read. Second, all students are told that she expects them to read 40 books in a year. In addition, Miller references the work of Australian researcher Brian Clairbourne to suggest several guidelines for learning:

- **Immersion.** Students need to be surrounded with books of all kinds and given the opportunity to read them every day.
- **Demonstrations.** Students require abundant demonstrations on the structure and features of texts, how to use texts for different learning goals, and how to access information in them.
- **Expectations.** Students will rise to the level of the teachers' expectations.
- **Responsibility.** Students need to make at least some of their own choices when pursuing learning goals.
- **Employment.** Students need time to practice what they are learning in the context of realistic situations.

- **Approximations.** Students need to receive encouragement for the skills and knowledge they do have and be allowed to make mistakes as they work toward mastery.
- **Response.** Students need nonthreatening, immediate feedback on their progress.
- **Engagement.** Reading must be an endeavor that . . . has personal value to students, students see themselves as capable of doing, is free from anxiety, [and] is modeled by someone they like, respect, trust, and want to emulate. (p. 36)

For Miller, choice is a critical part of student learning, but that choice must be balanced by criteria and guidelines for action. Criteria can also shape many other aspects of what takes place in a classroom.

Classroom Norms. Clearly describing rules and procedures can be an important part of creating an effective learning community, but once again, rules and norms are best created through a combination of freedom and form. Marzano et al., in *Classroom Management That Works*, explain that "research . . . indicates that rules and procedures should not be simply imposed on students. Rather, the proper design of rules and procedures involves explanation and group input" (p. 16).

One way to create norms is to use some version of structured choices or nominal group technique. In that way, all students can have input, and even vote on the norms, and once they are created, norms can provide the structure for many free learning experiences.

Learning Topics. When students choose their own topics, they often bring prior knowledge to the learning task, and that prior knowledge enables them to experience deeper learning. However, not all learning experiences fit all topics, and not all topics are sufficiently challenging. Teachers may need to articulate what types of topics are acceptable and what types are off-limits.

Learning Tasks. Students can also make choices about how they learn. Indeed, when students choose how they want to learn, they frequently choose activities that especially speak to their strengths. A student who is interested in video, for example, might learn an enormous amount more from creating a video than from writing a paragraph, so providing choice can greatly enhance his or her learning. To ensure high-quality work, teachers might establish specific criteria for what quality work involves (research, organization, editing, creativity, thoroughness) and confirm the criteria with students before they start the assignment. In this way, students have the freedom to choose their work, and teachers can rest assured they will do quality work.

Learning Partners. Students often want to choose their learning partners. The risks are that students working with friends might distract each other from the learning at hand or that some students might be skipped over in the selection process. For that reason, a teacher can ask students for suggested partners, and after reviewing students' choices, make the ultimate decisions about student pairings. Also, if a teacher has carefully taught expectations for all activities and transitions, she can use those as ground rules for all activities. When clear expectations have been laid out for all activities, much more freedom can be offered in choice of partners.

Caring and Control

The Measures of Effective Teaching Project, best known as the MET project, has mounted a comprehensive study to "test new approaches to measuring effective teaching" (see metproject.org). Their work brings together partners from multiple organizations, including Harvard University, Teachscape, the New Teacher Center, Stanford University, and Educational Testing Service, all focused on the shared goal of building "fair and reliable systems for measuring teacher effectiveness that can be used for a variety of purposes."

The MET project has worked with more than 3,000 teacher volunteers in six school districts and employed a comprehensive range of assessments, including student achievement, classroom observations and teachers' reflections, measures of teachers' pedagogical knowledge, student perceptions of the classroom instructional environment, and teachers' perceptions of working conditions and instructional support at their schools.

A central part of the MET project is the Tripod survey instrument developed over 10 years by Harvard researcher Ron Ferguson, which "assesses the extent to which students experience the classroom environment as engaging, demanding, and supportive of their intellectual growth." The survey asks students if they agree or disagree with a variety of statements. After giving the survey to thousands of students in elementary and secondary classrooms,[2] the authors found the following:

> Student perceptions of a given teacher's strengths and weaknesses are consistent across the different groups of students

they teach. Moreover, students seem to know effective teaching when they experience it: student perceptions in one class are related to the achievement gains in other classes taught by the same teacher. (p. 9)

After reviewing an enormous amount of data, the researchers identified two variables that most consistently identified effective instruction: caring and control.[3] These results are similar to what we have observed in schools. If a teacher is in control but lacks caring, his controlling approach may lead to resentment, as students feel their autonomy limited by someone who doesn't seem to understand their situation. If a teacher is caring but not in control, however, students might ignore classroom expectations and boundaries and waste a considerable amount of time.

A conversation I had with instructional coach LaVonne Holmgren, a highly experienced educator whom I featured in my book *Instructional Coaching: A Partnership Approach to Improving Instruction* (2007), reinforces these findings. "What the students tell me," LaVonne said, "is that there are two kinds of teachers, mean ones and easy ones. The students resent the mean ones, and they walk all over the nice ones. Effective teachers need to learn how to be nice and in control, not one or the other."

In Chapter 11, Power With, Not Power Over, I explained several ways by which teachers can be caring toward their students. They can empathize, listen authentically, demonstrate respect, be a witness to the good, and model caring behavior for all students to see. More than anything else, caring is about seeing children as people who deserve the same respect as we give to adults.

But what about control? One way teachers maintain control is by demonstrating a respectful level of confidence. This means teachers carry themselves in a way that nonverbally communicates that they are in control. For example, they make eye contact, turn their bodies toward students, speak clearly and confidently, and so forth.

This is easier said than done. Thus, telling novice teachers that they need to be confident is a bit like telling batters that they shouldn't strike out. They know what they are supposed to do, but they're not sure how to do it. Robert Sutton (2010), in his discussion of effective leaders, offers some sage advice. He asserts that good bosses (and I extend his ideas to good teachers) exude confidence even when they don't feel confidence. Sutton writes:

Faking it until you make it can trigger a self-fulfilling prophecy: by acting as if you know what you are doing and in control, even if it isn't true at first, such confidence can inspire you and others to achieve great performance. (p. 52)

For teachers, this means that they must remain calm, no matter what craziness descends on the classroom. Books on conflict resolution and relationship building, such as *Difficult Conversations* (2009) by Douglas Stone, Bruce Patton, and Sheila Heen or *Fierce Conversations* (2002) by Susan Scott, although designed for the corporate world, can teach us a lot about how to remain calm and in control under pressure; besides, teachers can apply the Name It, Reframe It, and Tame It strategies described in my book *Unmistakable Impact: A Partnership Approach for Dramatically Improving Instruction* (2011).

Acting in control is a start, but it does not make up for poor planning and boring assignments. The easiest way for teachers to increase their confidence and control is to use effective teaching practices such as those described throughout this book. When teachers develop and share learning maps that describe appropriately challenging unit plans, use formative assessments, engage students through the use of stories, thinking prompts, cooperative learning, or other practices, and provide students with relevant, challenging assignments and activities, they will find it much easier to project confidence.

The community-building strategies described in this part of the book also help teachers lead the classroom with confidence. Teachers who develop and teach expectations for all activities and transitions, and reinforce those expectations with frequent praise and calm consistent corrections, will find themselves more and more at ease. In addition, teachers who build relationships with students and create learner-friendly environments will find it easier to be in control every day in every class. Finally, when students' needs for autonomy are respected, students are much more likely to work within structures. Giving students real choices makes it easier to control students when there really is no choice.

Control is important, but it does not mean that teachers need to control every student's every action. Kids need to play; they need to have fun; and fun is just as important in the classroom as it is on the playground. Indeed, when teachers create a setting where students know that their teacher has things under control, they are much more likely to genuinely enjoy and get the most out of their learning—the ultimate goal of effective teachers everywhere.

Lori Sinclair explains how she organizes her class for freedom within form.

Video 12.1
www.corwin.com/
highimpactinstruction

Turning Ideas Into Action

Students

1. Give students the Tripod survey to see how they feel about their experiences in the classroom. The survey identifies care, control, clarify, challenge, captivate, confer, and consolidate as critical variables that correlate with effective teaching.[4]

2. Prompt students to complete exit tickets or other informal surveys that ask about their interest in learning. If student interest is low, it may be because students don't feel they have real control over their learning.

Teachers

1. Video record yourself to observe how your physical actions communicate that you care about your students and that you are in control.

2. Observe other teachers to see how they communicate care and control.

3. Watch videos of presenters on websites such as www.Ted.com to identify communication skills presenters use to convey care and control.

4. Experiment with different ways in which you can give your student more choice and monitor students to see if choice changes their interest in learning experiences.

Instructional Coaches

1. Use the various engagement assessment tools described below and available at the book's companion website at www.corwin .com/highimpactinstruction to monitor the impact of the freedom within form strategies described here.

2. Develop a video library of teachers implementing the strategies described in this book so that they can see many examples of the freedom within form practices.

3. Offer to interview students to see if they truly do feel autonomous in their classroom.

Principals

Lead a book study with teachers around this chapter. Consider discussing such questions as these:

- How important is choice for student motivation?
- Will students be motivated to learn if they don't have choices about what they learn?
- What choices are possible? What are nonnegotiables in the classroom?

(Continued)

Sandi Silbernagel explains how she assesses engagement.

Video 12.2
www.corwin.com/
highimpactinstruction

Download information on assessing time on task at www.corwin.com/highimpactinstruction

(Continued)

What It Looks Like

One way to assess the impact of freedom within form is by assessing student engagement. Students will most likely be engaged in learning when they are free to make choices that lead them to see learning as meaningful *and* when sufficient structure is provided for them to act on that freedom. If there is a lack of engagement, probably one of those two factors needs to be adjusted—more freedom, or more form.

Engagement can be assessed in a number of ways. Many educators assess time on task, that is, how many students look like they are engaged. Time on task can be measured by counting the number of students in a class, counting the number who are on task, and then calculating a percentage. In a class of 25 students, for example, if 20 are on task, then the on-task percentage is 80%. A good goal for time on task is 90 or 95%. For more information on time on task, see the book's companion website, www.corwin.com/highimpactinstruction.

Another way to gather data on engagement is to simply ask the students to tell you if they are engaged. Teachers can accomplish this by explaining to students each of the levels of engagement and then asking for feedback. In her second-grade classroom, Sandi Silbernagel from Slidell, Louisiana, gives her students Popsicle sticks and has them put them in cans marked for the three levels of engagement, so she can assess their level of engagement.

Teachers can also get feedback on students' level of engagement by surveying them at different times during a class. I call this experience sampling. This is accomplished by giving students a simple form such as the one included in Figure 12.3, with numbers arranged across the page under the headings *engaged, compliant,* and *noncompliant.* Discussion of the form can be a springboard for a healthy dialogue about the importance of engagement in learning. Teachers might ask students what engages them or how they can find personal connections in learning to make learning more relevant and thus engaging, or what could be changed in class to increase their learning.

Once everyone understands the three levels of engagement, the teacher can explain that she will be setting a timer to ring every 10 minutes (the timer may be a simple kitchen timer or the timer on a cell phone) and that when the bell on the timer rings, students are to circle the number that best reflects their level of involvement.

Teachers can learn a lot by keeping track of what students are doing at each ring. They should review their data the day they do the engagement sampling and look for trends. They can also calculate a mean and then repeat the sampling a few weeks later to see if student engagement has changed. If you try out a new practice, you can also use the form to see how effectively it engages students.

| Figure 12.3 | Engagement Form |

DATE:

INSTRUCTIONS:

Each time you hear the bell, please rate how engaging the learning activity is in which you are involved. You are only to rate whether or not the learning activity is engaging for you.

noncompliant			compliant			engaged
1	2	3	4	5	6	7
1	2	3	4	5	6	7
1	2	3	4	5	6	7
1	2	3	4	5	6	7
1	2	3	4	5	6	7
1	2	3	4	5	6	7
1	2	3	4	5	6	7
1	2	3	4	5	6	7
1	2	3	4	5	6	7
1	2	3	4	5	6	7
1	2	3	4	5	6	7
1	2	3	4	5	6	7
1	2	3	4	5	6	7

Download this form at www.corwin.com/highimpactinstruction

To Sum Up

- Form without freedom is oppressive and decreases interest and motivation.

- Freedom without form is chaotic and wasteful.

- Teachers can create freedom within form by

    Using dialogue structures such as brainstorming, affinity diagrams, and the Labovitch three-fold method

    Teaching students clear expectations for procedures, such as handing in papers and gathering materials, and rituals for such events as the start and end of class

    Providing choices based on criteria

    Adopting a caring attitude toward students while also maintaining control of the learning

Going Deeper

Several publications lay the theoretical groundwork for this chapter, and all of the them deserve further study. Daniel Pink's *Drive: The Surprising Truth About What Motivates Us* (2011) is a great summary of much of the research on motivation. Pink's statements about goals as motivation are important for any educator to review. Two books, Barry Schwartz's *The Paradox of Choice: Why More Is Less* (2005) and Sheena Iyengar's *The Art of Choosing: The Decisions We Make Every Day* (2011), convincingly make the case that while choice is an essential part of a free, authentic life, too much choice can be just as limiting as too little choice.

David Bohm's *On Dialogue* (1996) is a concise, wise book about the importance of dialogue as a part of life. Paulo Freire's *Pedagogy of the Oppressed* (1970) is a profound, important, and challenging work about the role freedom and dialogue play in humanizing education, in conversation, and in life.

Harrison Owen's *Open Space Technology: A User's Guide* (2008) offers excellent suggestions on how any facilitator (e.g., a teacher or an organizational consultant) can lead open space sessions. Donalyn Miller's *The Book Whisperer: Awakening the Inner Reader in Every Child* (2009) is the best example of freedom within form that I have read.

Notes

1. My wife, Jenny, introduced me to the concept of freedom within form, an idea that extends back to classical times. Jenny learned it from her friend and mentor Charlotte Ostermann.

2. A total of 963 elementary classrooms with more than five students responded, and 2,986 secondary classrooms with more than five students responded.

3. For more information on the MET project methodology see www.met project.org.

4. You can learn more about the Tripod project at www.tripodproject .org.

Chapter 13:
Expectations

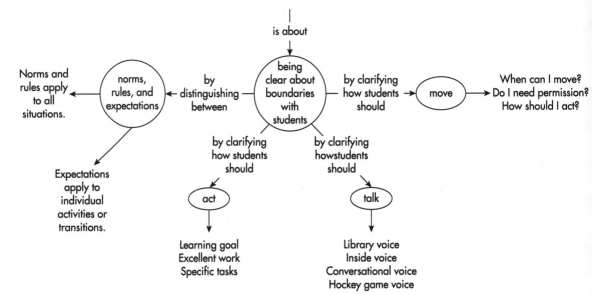

is about

being clear about boundaries with students

by distinguishing between → norms, rules, and expectations

Norms and rules apply to all situations.

Expectations apply to individual activities or transitions.

by clarifying how students should → move → When can I move? Do I need permission? How should I act?

by clarifying how students should → act → Learning goal Excellent work Specific tasks

by clarifying howstudents should → talk → Library voice Inside voice Conversational voice Hockey game voice

13

EXPECTATIONS

W hen Lea discussed expectations with Jody, the story included at the start of this section, she shared her copy of Randy Sprick's book *CHAMPs: A Positive and Proactive Approach to Classroom Management* (2009). Randy is one of the founders of the positive behavior movement and the author of numerous helpful books about community building or classroom management in systems, schools, and classrooms. He is also a colleague with whom I have worked for most of the past decade and whom I greatly respect. Together with Wendy Reinke, Tricia Skyles, and Lynn Barnes, we wrote *Coaching Classroom Management*.

I first learned about Randy while visiting Jody King, Director of Special Education in Cecil County, Maryland, a mostly rural school district on the north tip of the Chesapeake Bay.

Jody invited me to Cecil County to talk with her teachers about instruction and coaching, and she and I visited many classrooms in schools across the district. She is a modest, warmhearted, self-effacing person, who interacted with everyone in a kind, gentle, soft-spoken way. However, when we talked about Randy Sprick, she couldn't help sounding very proud, as she described how her district's implementation of Randy's ideas had had a significant, positive impact on student behavior and teacher morale.

As we drove from school to school, Jody and I had many conversations about what was working in Cecil County. At that time, I was looking for practical tools for classroom management for a project in Kansas. She was convinced that Randy's work would meet my needs, and before I left Maryland, Jody gave me her personal copy of Randy's *CHAMPs*. "You need to read this book," she said. I promised her I would.

The next day, as luck or fate would have it, I woke up in Baltimore to see thick, wet snowflakes falling outside my hotel window, the first snow of the year. This was perfect snow for making a snowman, but not for flying. Although my flight was scheduled to be the first one out, the snow kept my plane on the ground. I spent a few hours on the runway, and even more in the airport. With time on my hands, I read *CHAMPs*. When I landed in Kansas City more than 10 hours late, I had read most of the book, and like Jody, I was a believer.

Two weeks later, I was sitting in a conference room at the Heathman Hotel in Portland, Oregon, listening to Randy talk about classroom management. He is a wonderful presenter, similar to a collegial teacher who bails you out by sharing numerous practical tips, but also a lot like a stand-up comedian who keeps you on the edge of your seat with highly engaging stories. Randy had me laughing so hard that I had to brush tears out of my eyes as I frantically tried to write down all the ideas he shared.

Randy has written many books about community building, on topics ranging from districtwide behavior programs to skills for bus drivers or creating safe playgrounds. However, when teachers talk to me about his work, they keep coming back to teaching expectations. This isn't surprising, as I've often heard Randy say, "If you look at the past 90 years of research on behavior management, the one finding that rises above all the rest is the importance of writing, teaching, and reinforcing expectations. If we want students to act a certain way, we need to know what that way is, and then teach it to the students."

Sandi Silbernagel explains why and how she teaches expectations.

Video 13.1
www.corwin.com/
highimpactinstruction

"Expectations" Versus "Rules" and "Norms"

Randy believes that effective expectations must be specific and designed for the majority of learning activities and transitions occurring in the classroom. He suggests teachers create expectations around five variables, summarized in the simple acronym CHAMPs, which stands for Conversation, Help, Activity, Movement, Participation.

Randy isn't the only person to write about the importance of expectations; in fact, he is not particularly tied to his CHAMPs framework. In *Discipline in the Secondary Classroom* (2006), he suggests a different framework, which might be more appropriate for older students: Activity, Conversation, Help, Integrity, Effort, Value, Efficiency, which produces the acronym ACHIEVE. Many

Sprick's Framework for Expectations

- Conversation
- Help
- Activity
- Movement
- Participation

others also write about the importance of teaching expectations. In *Classroom Management That Works: Research-Based Strategies for Every Teacher* (2001), Marzano, Pickering, and Pollock write that "probably the most obvious aspect of effective classroom management involves the design and implementation of classroom rules and procedures." Fred Jones, in his frequently used *Tools for Teaching* (2007), writes about the importance of general rules and specific procedures and routines. There is a great deal of research that teaching and reinforcing expectations has a significantly positive impact on student behavior.

One thing I have learned from Randy is that using the terms *rules*, *expectations*, and *norms* interchangeably muddies the waters. For me, and as used in this book, *rules* or *norms* describe suggested behavior that should occur in all situations. The term *expectations*, on the other hand, describes suggested behavior that occurs in unique, individual activities or transitions. Thus, a norm that "we treat each other with respect" can be acted on when students walk into the classroom, during direct instruction, when students take tests, or when they work in small groups. However, the kind of conversation students can have during each activity or transition will vary greatly and, as a result, an expectation cannot be applied to all situations. The way students should talk with each other, or even if they should talk with each other at all, will likely be completely different when students are walking into the classroom, listening to direct instruction from the teacher, writing tests, or working in small groups. In short, so that students know exactly what they are supposed to do at all times, teachers should write expectations for all activities and transitions.

Expectations may be written about any behaviors, but three areas seem especially important:

1. **Act.** Explaining the activity and what students have to do

2. **Talk.** Explaining what kind of talking, if any, can take place

3. **Move.** Explaining what kind of movement can and cannot take place in a classroom

I summarize these variables as ATMs—action, talk, movement. Students can make deposits or withdrawals in a community based on how they respond to expectations. The three variables are described below.

High-Impact Expectations

- Act
- Talk
- Move

Act. In this part of expectations, the teacher describes what kind of work the student needs to be doing. Specifically, the act part of expectations describes at least three things: (a) what learning goal the student should be working toward, (b) what excellent work looks like, and (c) what specific tasks the student has to do. By answering the simple questions in Figure 13.1, teachers can write useful "act" expectations.

Talk. In this part of expectations, teachers explain what kind of talking, if any, students may engage in. Essentially, these expectations put boundaries around what and how students should talk, or if they should talk at all. Thus, when writing expectations around talking, teachers describe whether or not talking with fellow students is part of an activity, and, if so, what topics are and are not appropriate. In addition, teachers should clarify what level of talk is acceptable for each activity. I like to use four levels: (a) library voice, as quiet as you can be but still be heard; (b) inside voice, a little louder than library voice, but quieter than our usual conversational level; (c) conversational voice, in which talking occurs at the level of an ordinary conversation, but raised voices and shouting are to be avoided; and (d) hockey game voice (any sport would do), in which loud shouting is allowed (see Figure 13.2).

Figure 13.1	Questions for Developing "Act" Expectations for Students

What learning goal should I be working toward?

What does excellent work look like?

What specific tasks do I need to do (e.g., take notes, organize notes, clean up, brainstorm, listen, contribute ideas, paraphrase others' ideas, problem solve, write or speak in complete sentences)?

Figure 13.2	Questions for Developing "Talk" Expectations for Students

Can we talk during this activity?

What topics are appropriate?

What topics are not appropriate?

How loud can we talk (library voice, inside voice, conversational voice, hockey game voice)?

In most classrooms, level four is rarely, if ever, suggested, but describing level four gives the teacher a standard for clarifying the other levels of communication with students, as in "Remember, we're not using our hockey voices for this activity."

Move. When and how students may move out of their chairs and around the room is a final important variable for expectations. This often involves student requests to sharpen a pencil, get supplies or resources such as a dictionary, or to go to the restroom. As every teacher knows, some students go out of their way to get their teacher's and fellow students' attention by taking a long time to walk across class to the pencil sharpener, stopping to chat with other students en route, spending several minutes at the sharpener, and then repeating the long, slow walk back to their desk. The simple task of sharpening a pencil can distract an entire class for a few minutes (2 minutes × 30 students = 60 wasted learning minutes), so it is important to explain expectations.

Expectations should state when, if at all, students may leave their seats; whether or not students need permission to leave their seats; and how students should act when they leave their seats (How quickly should I move? May I talk with anyone else? How many times can I repeat the process?). These ideas are captured in the questions in Figure 13.3.

Randy Sprick recommends developing expectations for each activity or transition students will experience. He identifies independent seat work, small-group reading instruction, teacher-directed instruction, group activity, oral written tests (such as spelling), individual written tests, peer tutoring, and individual seat work as common activities. Similarly, he identifies getting a book out and opening to a particular page, moving to and from small reading groups, getting out supplies, movement of small groups, handing out paper and supplies, handing in papers (tests, etc.), before bell, class travel, and cleanup at the end of the day as common transition activities. He provides excellent examples of expectations for all of these activities

Figure 13.3   Questions for Developing "Move" Expectations for Students

For what reason, if any, may I leave my seat?

Do I need permission to leave my seat during those times?

How should I act when I leave my seat? (How quickly should I move? May I talk with anyone else? How many times can I repeat the process?)

and transitions in *CHAMPs: A Proactive and Positive Approach to Classroom Management* (2009). Still more may be found by searching online for CHAMPs images.

Writing expectations is a great start, but students need to learn the expectations if they are to have an impact on their learning behavior. Therefore, teachers must take sufficient time at the start of the year to ensure that all students understand all expectations. Some teachers give students graphic organizers, such as the one in Figure 13.4, so students can record notes on expectations for each activity.

Teaching Expectations

Teachers usually introduce and teach expectations in one of two ways. Some prefer to teach all of the expectations at once, ensuring that students record all expectations on the first day of class. In this way, they can lay a solid foundation for the various learning activities and transitions that will occur in class.

Other teachers prefer to teach expectations for learning activities and transitions at the point when they are first introduced during the class. Thus, teachers would teach expectations for teacher-directed instruction right before teacher-directed instruction and teach expectations for

Download this form at www.corwin.com/ highimpactinstruction

Figure 13.4	Act, Talk, Move

ATM for _____

Act: _____

_____

_____

Talk: _____

_____

_____

Move: _____

_____

_____

getting materials out of their desks right before asking students to bring out their notebook and pencils.

What is important is that teachers approach teaching expectations just as seriously as they approach teaching content. Thus, many of the teaching practices described in this book could be used to ensure students learn the expectations. For example, learning maps in Chapter 4 could be used for students to record expectations; experiential learning such as role-playing in Chapter 9 could be used by students to practice acting consistently with expectations; and exit tickets and other informal assessments from Chapter 3 could be used to determine whether or not students know the expectations. What counts is that students understand all expectations for every activity.

Involving Students in Writing Expectations

One way to increase student commitment to expectations is to ask students to help you write them (Marzano, Pickering, & Pollock, 2001). For many of us, this makes intuitive sense. When we have a voice in something, we are more likely to agree with whatever is created. Thus, when teachers introduce students to a new activity or transition, they can ask students for their suggestions on how a transition can be done more efficiently or which talking level should be allowed. I have found that it is a good idea to write out your expectations in advance so that you have thought through the various reasons why you might want to address the specifics of movement, talk, or action in particular ways.

When teachers ask students to help write expectations, they can also use that time to engage students in conversations about other aspects of learning and community. For example, teachers and students might talk about what respect is and why it is important, or what settings and situations enhance or interfere with learning. Such conversations can also serve another important function by providing an opportunity for teachers to explain and students to explore why each expectation is important. As I explained in Chapter 11, Power With, Not Power Over, explaining why communicates respect, motivates students to act, and decreases resistance. Saying "because I said so" to some students is almost guaranteed to produce an "I don't think so" response.

How Expectations Help Teachers

Teachers who have not developed expectations for all activities and transitions are forced to make a multitude of decisions every day.

Every few minutes of every day, they must decide whether students are talking too loudly, distracting others, moving for a good reason, or moving to get attention. Having to make so many decisions is mentally taxing and wears some teachers out. Writing down and disseminating expectations makes it easier to reinforce or correct the behaviors teachers want from their students. Clear expectations provide a solid foundation for teacher interactions with students around behaviors.

Also, if teachers are unclear in their own minds about expectations, they will be inconsistent when correcting or reinforcing behavior. If on some days teachers correct students for talking during independent seat work and not on others, it can confuse and frustrate students and increase students' resistance to any corrections. When students say, "it's not fair," the truth is that if expectations change every other day, the students are right. Wavering expectations can increase negative interactions between students and teachers when students feel they are being unfairly corrected for something that was acceptable the day before, or if they are being corrected for something that was acceptable for another student. When everyone knows the rules of the game, everyone walks on much more solid ground.

Perhaps the most important advantage for teachers is the impact that expectations can have on student behavior. Ensuring that everyone knows what is expected, in every activity and every transition, is an important first step in creating a positive learning community. Reinforcing those expectations is step two.

Turning Ideas Into Action

Students

1. Ask students for their suggestions for expectations.

2. Use informal assessments like checks for understanding to gauge whether or not students have learned the expectations.

3. Give students brief surveys throughout the year to get their opinions on how well classroom expectations help them learn from and enjoy all activities.

4. During activities, ask students to tell you what the expectations are to check for their understanding.

5. Ask students to assess how well they did with respect to acting consistently with expectations.

Teachers

1. List all learning activities and transitions.

2. Identify your expectations by answering the ATM questions (Act, Talk, Move).

3. Teach the expectations using other Big Four teaching practices, such as role-playing and exit tickets.

4. Continually assess how students are doing with respect to acting consistently with expectations.

Instructional Coaches

1. Deepen your knowledge of expectations by reading other books on the topic, especially Randy Sprick's *CHAMPs: A Proactive and Positive Approach to Classroom Management.*

2. Collaborate with teachers to develop and refine precise expectations for most activities and transitions.

3. Collaborate with teachers to use effective instruction and assessment strategies to ensure students learn content.

4. Periodically offer to ask students brief questions to see if they understand expectations during class time observations and collaborate with teachers to use other good teaching strategies.

Principals

1. Lead study groups to discuss expectations for common areas in the school such as the cafeteria and halls.

2. Where appropriate, guide the school to make developing and teaching expectations a part of the instructional improvement target.

3. Ask teachers to share their expectations with you and each other, and look for expectations when you enter a classroom. If there is no evidence of expectations, have a serious conversation with the teacher about expectations and learning and propose several strategies a teacher can use to develop them (such as reading *CHAMPs: A Proactive and Positive Approach to Classroom Management,* enrolling in an online course, or working with an instructional coach).

4. Resist the temptation to have a small committee create CHAMPs for the entire school. Those who write the expectations might

(Continued)

(Continued)

implement them, but for the rest of the staff, expectations that they haven't created are just one more thing coming down the pike. If teachers are to understand and implement expectations, they must create their own and have follow-up experiences that lead to implementation.

What It Looks Like

1. Are expectations posted? When conducting a classroom observation, a simple bit of data principals can look for is evidence that expectations are being used in a classroom. Expectations may be posted on the wall, or shared via the Smart Board, data projector, overhead, blackboard, or some other way. If they are being used in a classroom, they should be posted.

2. Are students acting consistently with the expectations? If expectations are posted, an equally important question is whether or not students are acting consistently with the expectations.

3. How much time is spent on transitions? A third way to observe the effectiveness of expectations is to assess how much time is dedicated to transitions. If transition time is quite high, the teacher likely has to revisit or refine expectations. Teachers, coaches, and principles can assess transition time by making a video recording of the class (an audio recording might also serve as useful data). Coaches and principals can also observe for transition time by using their smartphone to keep track of how time is spent during a lesson.

To Sum Up

- Writing up and teaching expectations is one of the most important strategies teachers can employ if they want to build positive learning communities.

- Norms or rules describe suggested behavior that should occur in all situations.

- Expectations describe suggested behavior that occurs in unique, individual activities or transitions.

- High-impact expectations teach students how to act, talk, and move during all activities and transitions.

- Expectations can be taught all at once or for one activity or transition at a time.

- Students may be more committed to expectations if they are involved in creating them.

Going Deeper

Most of what I know about expectations (indeed community building, in general), I learned from Randy Sprick, whose *CHAMPS: A Proactive and Positive Approach to Behavior Management* (2009) is a valuable tool describing how to create expectations for all activities and transitions and offering excellent examples of expectations for most activities and transitions students might encounter in elementary school. *CHAMPs* also contains very practical information about most other aspects of classroom management. While the information in *CHAMPs* is most appropriate for elementary teachers, Sprick's book *Discipline in the Secondary Classroom: A Positive Approach to Behavior Management* (2008) offers similar practical information for secondary teachers. *CHAMPs* would be most appropriate for teachers teaching classes up to Grade 8, and *Discipline in the Secondary Classroom* would be most appropriate for teaching in Grades 9 and up. In my opinion, if you can only buy one book on classroom management, *CHAMPS* or *Discipline in the Secondary Classroom* are excellent choices.

Two other popular books filled with practical strategies are Robert Marzano et al.'s *Classroom Management That Works: Research-Based Strategies for Every Teacher* (2001), which discusses the practical implications of a large number of studies for classroom and behavior management, and Harry and Rosemary Wong's *The First Days of School: How to Be an Effective Teacher* (1998), which does not draw on the same research base as Marzano, but nonetheless contains many useful strategies that can help any teacher.

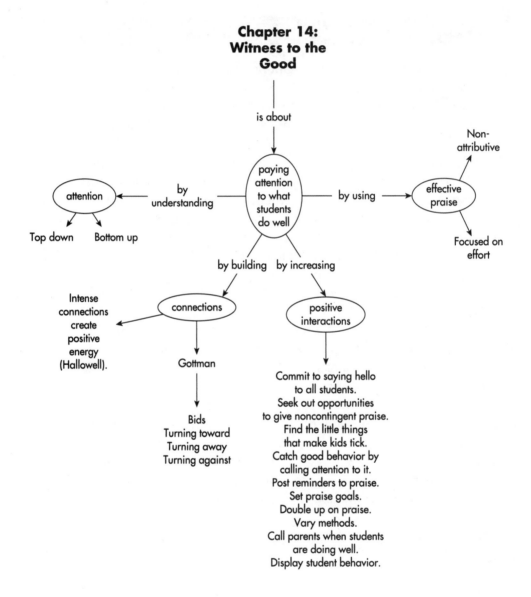

**Chapter 14:
Witness to the
Good**

is about

paying
attention
to what
students
do well

by
understanding

attention

Top down   Bottom up

by using

effective
praise

Non-
attributive

Focused on
effort

by building   by increasing

connections

Intense
connections
create
positive
energy
(Hallowell).

Gottman

Bids
Turning toward
Turning away
Turning against

positive
interactions

Commit to saying hello
to all students.
Seek out opportunities
to give noncontingent praise.
Find the little things
that make kids tick.
Catch good behavior by
calling attention to it.
Post reminders to praise.
Set praise goals.
Double up on praise.
Vary methods.
Call parents when students
are doing well.
Display student behavior.

14

WITNESS TO THE GOOD

We do not believe in ourselves until someone reveals that deep inside us something is valuable, worth listening to, worthy of our trust, sacred to our touch. Once we believe in ourselves we can risk curiosity, wonder, spontaneous delight or any experience that reveals the human spirit.

—E. E. Cummings

The simple act of paying positive attention to people has a great deal to do with productivity.

—Tom Peters

Creating and teaching expectations is only the first part of the process of building a positive, productive learning community. Expectations that don't have an impact on students don't serve any useful purpose. We need to encourage and reinforce students to act within the boundaries laid out by what we have created and taught. One way to do this is by paying attention to students when they act consistently with expectations. If we let them know that we see them acting appropriately, we increase the amount of appropriate behavior. A teacher's attention is an extremely powerful reinforcer for student behavior. How and where a teacher directs her attention has a great impact on what happens in her classroom.

A simple metaphor might help illustrate how important a teacher's attention can be. My colleague and friend Devona Dunekack has a

Christmas cactus that sits prominently in a window in her living room. The plant thrives in the sunlight coming in through the window. Over time, all the plant's leaves turn toward the sun to soak up the life-giving energy, and Devona has to rotate it since every leaf is pointed toward the window and almost none of the plant's beauty is visible inside.

In the classroom, a teacher's attention affects children the way the sunshine affects Devona's cactus. Children adjust their behavior to get the warm sunshine of their teacher's attention. Thus, if a teacher only attends to students who misbehave, correcting students when they don't act consistently with expectations but failing to comment when they act consistently with expectations, the teacher may unintentionally encourage misbehavior. Students who want to be noticed by their teacher may misbehave just to get their teacher's attention (Reinke, Lewis-Palmer, & Merrell, 2008). If a teacher mindfully watches to see when students are actively engaged in meaningful work or when they treat each other respectfully, and comments on what she sees, more and more students will engage in meaningful work and treat each other respectfully.

I refer to the act of watching for the positive things students do as "being a witness to the good." We are being a witness to the good when we are attentive and intentional about noticing everything our students do—not just the misbehavior. We are being a witness to the good when we are especially attentive to the times when students are making the best of learning opportunities. We are being a witness to the good whenever we recognize and encourage students for acting in ways that are consistent with expectations.

But being a witness to the good is not always easy. For most of us, noticing the students who are *not* following the expectations is much easier than noticing the students who are following them. If we have a better understanding of how our attention works, we get a better understanding of why being a witness to the good can be difficult.

Top-Down and Bottom-Up Attention

Winifred Gallagher, in *Rapt: Attention and the Focused Life* (2009), helped me understand why it is difficult—almost unnatural—to be a witness to the good. Gallagher describes two types of attention that we may bring to any experience such as those we see in the classroom. *Bottom-up attention* is the attention we use when we notice something we can't help noticing. For example, if I catch the scent of fresh-baked chocolate chip cookies, that scent will get my attention.

I can't help but notice that sweet aroma. Bottom-up attention can notice pleasant things like cookies, or unpleasant events like a crying baby. What defines bottom-up attention is that it is something we can't avoid noticing.

Top-down attention, on the other hand, occurs only when we prompt ourselves to look for something. For example, we might be driving down the road watching for a sign that marks where we need to turn off the highway. If we are not vigilant, we might miss our turn and get lost. With top-down attention, we must be intentional to notice what we notice. If we don't tell ourselves to see whatever we are looking for, we miss it.

In the classroom, students who are off task or misbehaving catch our bottom-up attention. If you are looking at 32 students and one is out of line, which student will you notice? We can't help but notice the student who blows off the learning. To truly be witnesses to the good, we need to teach ourselves to see all that is going well and not just the aberrations; in other words, we need to use top-down attention.

To use the earlier metaphor of the cactus plant, if our attention is like sunshine, then we need to make sure that bottom-up attention to misbehavior doesn't dominate the way we interact with students. Indeed, we need to make sure we give a lot more attention to the good than the not-so-good. Some authors say the proportion of positive to negative attention should be nine-to-one times; others say three-to-one. Some studies outside of the classroom are telling. John Gottman, for example, reports that at least a five-to-one positive to negative ratio exists in healthy and successful marriages (1994). Gottman writes, "Unstable marriages are likely to be those that, over time . . . fall into a pattern that does not maintain the balance of positivity to negativity at a high level" (p. 380). Similarly, Marcial Losada and Barbara Fredrickson (Losada, 1999; Fredrickson & Losada, 2004) studied 60 different companies and observed their work teams, coding their meeting conversations, and they found that the most productive teams had a 2.9-to-one positive to negative ratio. Whatever numbers we like, a majority of our attention needs to reinforce positive and productive behavior.

Positive Attention and Learning

There are many reasons why it is important to be a witness to the good. One of the most important is reinforcing behavior. Another important reason is that being a witness to the good encourages connection. A major learning inhibitor is lack of connection. When students feel connected to their learning, to their peers, and to their teacher, they are much more likely to get the most out of their learning opportunities. Edward Hallowell, a psychiatrist and author of several books on leadership, focus, and productivity, identifies connection as one of the most important variables distinguishing excellent performers. Although Hallowell is describing employees in the workplace, his comments about the importance of connection in *Shine: Using Brain Science to Get the Best From Your People* (2011) could easily apply to students:

> *Connection* refers to the bond an individual feels with another person, group, task, place, idea, mission, piece of art, pet, or anything else that stirs feelings of attachment, loyalty, excitement, inspiration, comfort, or a willingness to make sacrifices for the sake of connection. The more intense the connection, the more effective the employee will be. Intense connection creates positive energy, and the more positive energy a person brings to work, the better work he will do.
>
> By contrast, disconnection refers to disengagement and distance from a person, group, task, idea, or mission. . . . Disconnection is one of the chief causes of substandard work in the modern workplace. But it is also one of the most easily corrected. (p. 75)

One of the leading scholars studying the science of human connection is John Gottman at the University of Washington, mentioned above. Gottman (2001) conducted research by creating an on-campus apartment where couples would stay for a weekend at a time so that researchers could study how they interacted. To record a couple's interactions, researchers placed cameras in the living and dining rooms of the apartment and video recorded all interactions between 9:00 a.m and 9:00 p.m. Then they reviewed the video, breaking down the recordings, in some cases, into segments that are less than a second long. Based on their analysis, Gottman and his colleagues determined that emotional connection is the critical variable in healthy relationships and that there are specific acts, both conscious and unconscious, that foster or inhibit healthy connections. Gottman summarizes his findings as follows:

> A very fundamental and simple idea has emerged from our research: We have discovered the elementary constituents of closeness between people, and we have learned the basic principle that regulates how relationships work and also determines a great deal about how conflict between people can be

regulated. That basic idea has to do with the way people, in mundane moments in everyday life, make attempts at emotional communication, and how others around them respond, or fail to respond, to these attempts. (p. xi)

According to Gottman, the crucial move in relationships is what he calls a bid, a message we send, verbally or nonverbally, that says to somebody that we want to be connected to them:

> Even our best efforts to connect can be jeopardized as a result of one basic problem: failure to master what I call the "bid"—the fundamental unit of emotional communication. . . . A bid can be a question, a gesture, a look, a touch—any single expression that says, "I want to feel connected to you." A response to a bid is just that—a positive or negative answer to somebody's request for emotional connection. (p. 4)

What Gottman found after studying thousands of hours of video recordings of couples interacting is that emotional connection is fostered or squelched by the way in which we make and respond to bids for connection. When someone makes a bid to us, we can increase emotional connection by responding positively toward it, what Gottman refers to as "turning toward the bid." When people turn toward bids, Gottman writes, those positive responses "typically lead to continued interaction, often with both parties extending more bids to one another. Listening to this kind of exchange is kind of like watching a Ping-Pong game in which both players are doing very well" (p. 7).

In unhealthy relationships, people miss the chance to turn toward the bid, and either turn against the bid by responding in a belligerent or argumentative way or turn away from the bid by ignoring the bid or not responding at all. Gottman found that when parents turn away from or turn against their children, for example, it can have long-term, negative consequences:

> Our studies indicate that children whose parents consistently thwart their bids for connection often suffer long-term consequences as a result of constantly experiencing more negative emotions and fewer positive emotions. They have trouble developing the social skills to get along with friends, for example. They don't do as well academically, and they have more problems with physical health. (p. 18)

Gottman's research provides another reason why teachers should be a witness to the good. When teachers catch their students doing something right, they foster emotional connection between themselves and their students. And, as we've seen, connection is critical for student success. Not every student will feel a connection with the teacher, and not every student needs to. But we do a disservice to students if we don't foster relationships in which students feel that some kind of connection is possible.

Lori Sinclair talks about being a witness to the good.

Video 14.1
www.corwin.com/
highimpactinstruction

How to Be a Witness to the Good

At its most fundamental level, being a witness to the good is simply about taking the time to see and comment on the actions our students do that foster personal or group learning. Over the years, many of my colleagues (including Randy Sprick, Wendy Reinke, the coaches working with the Kansas Coaching Project, and the coaches from Beaverton, Oregon) have given me excellent suggestions on how to increase positive attention, many of which are included in *Coaching Classroom Management.*

One strategy for increasing attention to the positive is to make a list of behaviors teachers especially want to watch for each day. Such behaviors might be simple actions, such as getting ready for class at the bell, staying focused on a learning activity, listening when other students are talking, or using the correct talking level during an activity.

Being a witness to the good, however, does not mean we have to focus only on particular student behaviors. This strategy is primarily about building connections with students. Hallowell (2011), mentioned above, suggests that we "start simply by intending to connect":

> Make it a priority. Instead of relying on metaphorically beating people up, build relationships. Become curious and interested in others. . . . Using the tool you know best—yourself—to connect with others and help others connect, you can bring out the best in the people you lead. (p. 98)

In a short clip on England's Teacher TV, the UK website, no longer available, that was packed with videos of great teaching, a teacher describes what she does to build connections with her students. Each Friday she sits down and lists the names of all of her students. Then she looks over the list to see whom she has forgotten and who is at the bottom of her list and thinks about the particular strengths of the students she missed or thought of last. The following Monday and the rest of the week, she seeks out these students and calls attention to their strengths. Then at the end of the week, she repeats the process, always focusing on students' strengths, and always focusing on building connections. There are many other strategies teachers can employ; some of them are included in the list in Figure 14.1 (many of these ideas were first described in Sprick, Knight, Reienke, McKale, & Barnes, 2010).

Keeping Track of Positive Interactions With Students

In the classroom management and positive behavior literature, when we attend to how often we interact positively with students, we often refer to ratios of interaction (Reinke, Lewis-Palmer, & Merrell, 2008). As mentioned above, there is no set rule for the number of positive versus negative interactions, but the lowest number I've seen is

Figure 14.1	Increasing Positive Interactions

Download this form at www.corwin.com/highimpactinstruction

- Commit to saying hello to every student as he or she enters the classroom (put special emphasis on kids with whom you may have had a recent negative interaction).
- Seek out positive (appropriate) interactions that are not contingent on behavior.
- Find the little things that make kids tick (activity, team, interest, etc.) and talk about them with them.
- Catch the good behavior by drawing attention to it (thanking students, commenting, etc.).
- Focus praise or attention on effort rather than attributes (talk about a student's hard work rather than a student's intelligence).
- Pay attention to academic and behavioral opportunities for praise.
- Post reminders to praise (sticky note to yourself on the Elmo; poster in the class, on your lesson plans).
- Set specific praise goals (today every student who gets the book out will be praised).
- Set goals based on irrelevant prompts (every time a teacher enters my room, I'll praise three kids).
- Double up on praise by naming all students who are doing something appropriate (Michelle, Lea, Susan, and Jenny, thanks for getting your book out so quickly).
- Vary methods of praise.
- Call (or email) the parents of children who are doing well.
- Send home postcards to parents to praise kids.
- Prominently display student work in the classroom.
- Ignore minor misbehavior if the behavior is attention seeking.

giving at least three times as much positive attention to students as negative attention. In our many informal studies of teachers in action, I rarely see teachers who have a positive ratio; indeed, often the ratio is one-to-six or even more weighted toward the negative.

Positive attention is not the same as a talking positively. I find it helpful to keep in mind the idea of attention being like sunlight. Positive attention is based on what students are doing when we attend to them, not the tone of our voice. Telling a student, "Alexa, I know you're such a great student that you'll get back to work right now" sounds positive, but it still brings attention to the negative. In that moment, we are giving Alexa our attention because she is off task, and that is how we need to record it. This is not to say we shouldn't correct students—we absolutely must—and in the next section, I'll describe effective corrections. However, if we want to encourage behaviors with our attention, we need to ensure that our attention to the positive happens much more often than our attention to the negative.

We can learn a lot about how we spend our attention by video or audio recording a class and counting how many times we attend to the positive versus how many times we correct students. We can also keep track of how often we give group or individual attention to students. Or we can see how we interact with students depending on their gender, race, or other distinguishing characteristics.

If you decide to video record a class, start by setting up a micro-camera behind you as you teach. Once the class begins, push record, and although the video won't capture your face, it will show you how your students respond to you.

After the class, when you watch the video, if you have a seating chart, you can put a plus underneath each student's name when you are a witness to the good and a minus sign when you correct a student. If you give the entire class positive or negative attention, you can write a plus or minus on the side of the chart.

Of course, you could simply keep track of pluses and minuses or you could record how often you praise boys or girls, or review whatever other data you think it might be fruitful to notice.

In one school district the coaches I was working with visited more than one hundred classes. We found that, on average, the ratio of interaction was that for each positive statement there were six negatives. What would be the impact on learning and classroom culture if that ratio was reversed? What if you have a one-to-six ratio in your class?

Most teachers who gather data on their classes are surprised, sometimes shocked, by what they see. The video, however, doesn't lie. By getting a clear picture of what is really happening in the classroom, teachers can begin some truly powerful professional learning—and that could have a powerful impact on student learning.

Can Being a Witness to the Good Be Bad?

Positive attention fails whenever it is not perceived as being positive. At the most fundamental level, positive attention will fail if it is inauthentic. Children are just as adept as adults at spotting fake comments, and they react just as adults do. Hallowell puts it this way:

> You have to be genuine in your efforts to connect. . . . A manager who reads [about positive interactions] and says, "I get it, I should wear a smiley button at work," will get the opposite result of what he works for. Fake smiles and forced connections backfire. But if you try to put your most positive self forward, if you notice and appreciate others in simple and honest ways . . . you will go a long way toward creating the all-important positively connected atmosphere. (p. 86)

Harvard researchers Robert Kegan and Lisa Lahey (2001) offer a second suggestion on how to share positive information, which they refer to as "a language of ongoing regard." A "language of ongoing regard" has specific characteristics. Kegan and Lahey stress that authentic, appreciative, or admiring feedback must be (a) direct, (b) specific, and (c) non-attributive. By "non-attributive," Kegan and Lahey explain that our positive comments about others are more effective when we describe our experience of others rather than the attributes of others. They describe the problem with non-attributive praise as follows:

> It may seem odd to you that we're urging you not to make statements of this sort: "Carlos, I just want you to know how much I appreciate how generous you are" (or "what a good sense of humor you have" or "that you always know the right thing to say"), or "Alice, you are so patient" (or "so prompt," "so never-say-die," "always there when you are needed"), and so on. . . . These seem like such nice things to say to someone. What could possibly be the problem with saying them?
>
> The problem we see is this: the person, inevitably and quite properly, relates what you say to how she knows herself to be. You can tell Carlos he is generous, but he knows how generous he actually is. You can tell Alice she is very patient, but she knows her side of how patient she is being with you. (p. 99)

Non-attributive praise focuses on the evidence you see that points toward a general attribute, rather than a general attribute. Thus, rather than telling a student, "you're a kind person," we say, "the way you complimented Jordan really encouraged him." Similarly, rather than saying "you're a hard worker," we say, "I bet you put a lot of effort into this paper because it is very well written."

Carol Dweck's research on praise, which she summarizes in her frequently cited book *Mindset: The New Psychology of Success* (2006), further enriches our understanding of how to be a witness to the good. In an interview published on www.highlightsparents.com, she summarized her findings:

> Parents must stop praising their children's intelligence. My research has shown that, far from boosting children's self-esteem, it makes them more fragile and can undermine their motivation and learning. Praising children's intelligence puts them in a fixed mindset, makes them afraid of making mistakes, and makes them lose their confidence when something is hard for them. Instead, parents should praise the process—their children's effort, strategy, perseverance, or improvement. Then the children will be willing to take on challenges and will know how to stick with things—even the hard ones.

To be a witness to the good, then, sounds like a fairly complex task. Our "language of ongoing regard" must be authentic, direct, specific, and non-attributive, and focus on effort rather than intelligence. This does not mean that we should worry about the nuances of every comment we make before we say anything. What matters is this. First, we must communicate to our students that we see them acting appropriately. Our comments must be real, for otherwise they may backfire. But if our ratio of interaction is six corrections for each positive statement, job one is to turn around that ratio. Second, after we have developed the habit of noticing and communicating what we see going well, we can work at refining our language—striving to focus on effort, rather than smarts, using specific, direct, non-attributive comments.

Once again a micro-camera may be used to record our comments and give us a record of the way we share positive attention. If we practice focusing on effort, and frequently record our lessons or work with an instructional coach, we can develop habits that truly help our students learn and grow.

Turning Ideas Into Action

Students

1. Consider giving students a student survey so you can learn about the things that most interest them, similar to the example available at the book's companion website at www.corwin.com/highimpactinstruction. The survey could ask students about their favorite sports teams, music, books, TV shows, or other interests. It could also ask students about the activities they do, whether or not they have pets, or anything else that might tell you something about what they enjoy or what they are passionate about.

2. After you receive the completed surveys, review them carefully to learn as much as you can about students and then take time for one-to-one conversations in which you talk with students about their unique interests and passions.

3. Give students direct instruction, experiential learning, or challenging assignments that empower them to be a witness to the good. If students develop their ability to see and comment on the good things they see their fellow students doing, everyone wins.

4. Consider giving your students an assignment to try out a positive intervention in their school or at home and report on what they find. Imagine what might happen if a whole school (students, teachers, and other adults) was focused on trying to be a witness to the good.

Teachers

1. Find a way to get a clear picture of your ratios of interaction; that is, how often you comment on the positive versus the negative. Getting a clear picture of this might involve recording your lessons with a video or audio recorder such as a smartphone or having an instructional coach visit your classroom and gather data, as described below.

2. Once you know your current reality, set a goal to increase your ratio to at least three-to-one, though I recommend higher, at least five-to-one.

3. Consult the list of strategies for increasing positive attention or work with a coach to implement strategies that markedly increase your attention to the positive.

4. Keep recording your class to monitor your progress. You might accomplish this by video or audio recording or by having an instructional coach record data.

5. Consider gathering data on your attention to the positive and the number of disruptions in your class. A disruption is anything a student might do that interrupts the teacher teaching or students learning. Research suggests that as your attention to the positive goes up, disruptions go down (Reinke, Lewis-Palmer, & Merrell, 2008).

(Continued)

(Continued)

Instructional Coaches

1. Practice observing teachers until you are extremely consistent with your observations. It is a good idea to practice along with another coach (either in a class or watching a video) until you both consistently score your observations in the same way.

2. Study the list of ways to increase positive interactions and practice implementing them with teachers until you have a rich collection of ideas about how to increase positive interactions with students.

3. Add to your list of ways to increase positive interactions with students by interviewing teachers, observing classrooms, and reviewing relevant books, such as *Coaching Classroom Management*.

4. Coach teachers by gathering data, setting goals, video recording the class, modeling practices, and collaborating to identify ways to increase the positive half of ratios of interaction.

Principals

1. Guide schoolwide discussion about ratios of interaction and consider establishing with staff a goal ratio, such as five-to-one.

2. Conduct walk-throughs that focus on ratios of interaction.

3. Consider leading book studies on books such as Martin Seligman's *Flourish* or Carolyn Dweck's *Mindset* to foster dialogue around the importance of a positive learning environment.

4. Monitor your own interactions to make sure you are walking the talk by being a witness to the good done by the people you encounter.

What It Looks Like

1. "Attention" refers to anything a teacher says or does that indicates she is attentive to a student's behavior.

2. When attention is focused on student behavior that promotes individual or group learning, we refer to it as positive attention.

3. When attention is focused on student behavior that distracts or diminishes individual or group learning, we refer to it as negative attention.

4. Ratios of interaction can be recorded by using forms similar to the one in Figure 14.2. More information on how to score ratio of interaction is available at www.corwin.com/highimpactinstruction.

5. Pluses and minuses can also be marked on a seating chart (see Figure 14.3). You can note a plus under the names of students each time they receive positive attention and a minus under the names of students each time they receive negative attention. Positive or negative comments directed to the entire class may be noted on the margins of the seating chart with pluses and minuses.

| Figure 14.2 | Ratio of Interaction |

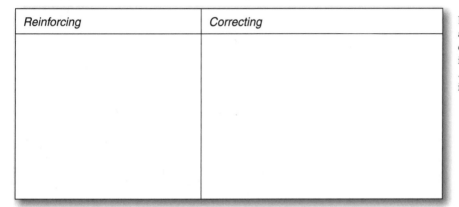

Reinforcing	Correcting

Download this form and more information on scoring ratio of interaction at www .corwin.com/high impactinstruction

| Figure 14.3 | Seating Chart |

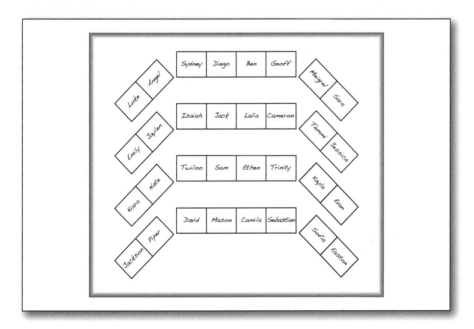

To Sum Up

- Paying attention to what students do well reinforces learner-friendly behavior.

- Being a witness to the good isn't always easy because we are more likely to notice inappropriate behavior than we are to notice learner-friendly behavior.

- Being a witness to the good builds connections, and connections create positive energy (Hallowell, 2011).

- There are many things teachers can do to increase positive attention.

- Teachers can keep track of the frequency of their positive comments by using video or audio recording or by using other methods.

- Effective positive comments are non-attributive (Kegan & Lahey, 2002), and they focus on effort rather than fixed traits such as intelligence (Dweck, 2007).

Going Deeper

Coaching Classroom Management: Strategies and Tools for Administrators and Coaches (2010) by Randy Sprick, Wendy Reinke, Tricia Skyles, Lynn Barnes, and myself contains many tools educators can use to gather data in the classroom, including tools for gathering data on such aspects of classroom management as ratio of interactions.

Several other books lay the theoretical foundation for being a witness to the good. Winifred Gallagher's *Rapt: Attention and the Focused Life* is an interesting discussion of how our use of attention shapes our life experiences. Among other things, Gallagher spells out the distinction between top-down and bottom-up attention. John Gottman's many books provide insight into how emotional connection can make or break a relationship. *The Relationship Cure: A 5-Step Guide to Strengthening Your Marriage, Family, and Friendships* (2002) is an accessible overview of his research and strategies that can help any relationship.

Two books, in particular, have deepened my understanding of how to share positive information. Kegan and Lahey's *How the Way We Talk Can Change the Way We Work* (2001) leads readers through an enlightening process to unpack personal barriers to change and explains the importance of direct, non-attributive praise. In *Mindset: The New Psychology of Success* (2006), Carol Dweck explains her research on how growth and fixed mindsets can affect or impede personal growth and how the way we praise our students or children can reinforce productive or counterproductive patterns of thought.

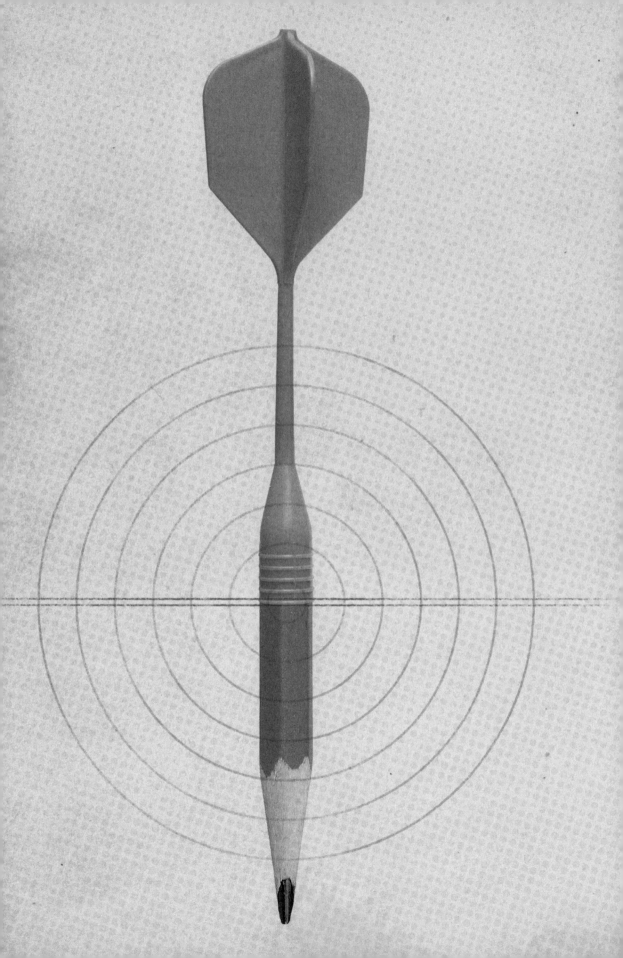

**Chapter 15:
Fluent
Corrections**

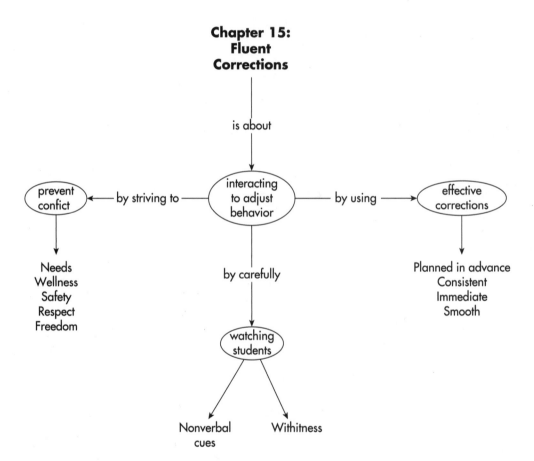

is about

interacting
to adjust
behavior

prevent
confict

← by striving to ―

by using →

effective
corrections

Needs
Wellness
Safety
Respect
Freedom

by carefully

Planned in advance
Consistent
Immediate
Smooth

watching
students

Nonverbal
cues

Withitness

15

FLUENT CORRECTIONS

The fact is that people are good. Give people affection and security, and they will give affection and be secure in their feelings and their behavior.

—Abraham Maslow

The enemy of art is the absence of limitations.

—Orson Welles

Two weeks after starting as an instructional coach at a middle school in a large city in the midwestern United States, Tom Jurado ran into Kristin Wilson, a new teacher in the school. Somewhat exasperated, Kristin said to Tom, "I've been looking for you. You've got to help me reach my students." Tom offered to observe Kristin's class, and two days later he dropped by to see what was happening. Tom was unprepared, however, for what he saw in Miss Wilson's classroom.

To say that Kristin's class was out of control would be a strong understatement. It appeared to Tom that every student was off task at some point during the class. Kristin was respectful and kind toward the students, but they totally ignored her requests, arrived late, engaged in loud side conversations, and shouted to students in the hall. Two girls had turned their backs to their teacher, with one braiding the other's hair. Another two students were playing cards, and three students were text-messaging friends.

"Wow," thought Tom, "this looks like a class where I can make a difference." When he sat down to talk with Kristin, however, he had a hard time getting words into the conversation. Kristin told him about the students' lives, the challenges they faced, the abuses they had experienced. "I don't know if anyone has ever been kind to these students," she said. "If nothing else, I'm going to treat them with respect." Kristin then talked about giving the kids a safe, free space to be themselves. It seemed as if she didn't see any problems with her class. But when Tom asked if she was happy with the lesson, she was overcome with emotion and just shook her head no. At that point, the bell rang, and Kristin had to go back to her class, leaving Tom to wonder what to do next.

Tom Jurado and Kristin Wilson aren't real people. They are characters I created for a case I share with educators during workshops. But the situation is definitely real because when I discuss this case, teachers, coaches, and principals all offer their own versions of this scenario. Some people talk about working with teachers like Kristin, but more frequently they confess that they were a lot like her when they started out as teachers. "That girl in the case, Kristin," more than one workshop participant has said, "that was me."

What comes out during our workshop conversations is that most people believe that respecting students involves more than being nice. As many participants have said in various ways, "If we want to respect students, we need to make sure they learn a lot. We need to hold them to high expectations. And we need to create a setting where they can flourish. To do that, we need to make sure that they are on task, respectful, and getting the most out of their learning experiences."

Without question, writing and teaching expectations and being a witness to the good by maintaining a positive ratio of interaction (at least five-to-one) are both very important strategies. But teachers also must correct students when students step outside the boundaries established through expectations. To praise students without ever correcting them is a bit like planting and fertilizing a garden but never weeding it. Pretty quickly, weeds will overtake the garden, and your flowers won't grow. In the classroom, misbehaviors are the weeds, and unchecked, they can take over and make it difficult for any meaningful learning to occur.

Some teachers are uneasy correcting students because they don't want to have to deal with the negative or angry reaction they might get. In some cases, teachers are afraid that students will refuse to do what they are asked to do, which could lead to a nasty power struggle and erosion of the teacher's authority in the classroom. Rather than dealing with the emotional complexity of correcting a student, some teachers choose to ignore the behavior.

Other teachers believe or hope that by being kind to students, they will be able to maintain a productive learning environment. Sadly, love without structure and discipline is often not enough, just as structure and discipline without love is insufficient. In his popular handbook, *Tools for Teaching* (2007), Fred Jones puts it this way:

> It is the undying hope of green teachers that if they just love their students and are nice to them, everything will turn out fine. This is the sweet dream of the uninitiated. It will get a smile from anyone more experienced in raising children.
>
> You cannot afford to walk into a classroom of thirty young people and "wing it" with your favorite home remedies contained in a bag of tricks. You will be backed into a corner and, when you sense that you are losing the group, you will do what you have to do to get it back.
>
> To succeed, you will need both love and skill. Love without expertise is powerless. Unless you manage effectively, you will become tired and frustrated and, ultimately, lose your capacity to nurture. (pp. 160–161)

Preventing Conflict

The most effective way to keep students on track is to prevent conflict from arising in the first place. Harvard researcher and negotiation expert William Ury has written extensively about resolving conflicts in all settings—the world, the workplace, the home, and the school. In *Getting to Peace: Transforming Conflict at Home, at Work, and in the World* (1999), Ury explains that prevention is the best way to control conflict. His motto is, "Contain if necessary, resolve if possible, best of all prevent" (p. 113). For Ury, "our challenge is to learn to embed prevention in the fabric of normal life" (p. 116). The same challenge exists for a teacher who wants to create a safe and productive learning environment.

Building on the work of Maslow (1954), Ury suggests that frustrated needs stand at the heart of most conflicts and negotiations, whether they occur at a United Nations roundtable or a kindergarten student's desk. "Whatever the surface issues in dispute, the underlying cause of conflict usually lies in the deprivation of basic human needs like love and respect. Frustration leads people to bully others, to use violence, and to grab someone else's things" (p. 118).

Ury's comments have direct implications for teachers. One way to prevent conflict from arising in the classroom is to consider whether a student is misbehaving because a fundamental need is being unmet.

In particular, Ury identifies wellness, safety, respect, and freedom as needs that everyone shares. By considering whether or not their students have these needs and thinking about how they can ensure their students "feel well, safe, respected, and free" (p. 118), teachers can often prevent problem behaviors from ever arising.

Needs	
• Wellness	• Respect
• Safety	• Freedom

Wellness. This need can have a huge impact on student behavior, but unfortunately, it is often the most beyond a teacher's control. Whether or not students are eating well, sleeping enough, avoiding drugs, and staying healthy can significantly affect how they behave in the classroom. School systems help by offering free and reduced-price lunch for many students, and teachers can help by encouraging students to get sufficient sleep and by communicating with parents about how important sleep is for learning. Some schools offer after-school workshops for parents on nutrition, healthy living, and other wellness-related topics, and many programs exist to teach students about the dangers of some drugs.

Teachers can also make it easier for students to get sufficient sleep by monitoring how much homework they assign. Practice is an important part of learning, but assigning so much homework that students have to stay up late to complete it may ultimately interfere with learning by not allowing students to get enough sleep. You can learn a lot by occasionally asking students how much time they spent doing homework the previous night.

Safety. For Maslow, being safe means you are removed from danger. In school as in life, danger can be both physical and psychological. If a student is afraid that another student is going to beat him after school, for example, it is hard for that student to concentrate on learning how to multiply fractions. To increase student safety, many schools institute antibullying programs and teach students nonviolent communication and problem-solving skills so that they can learn how to resolve issues without violence.

In the classroom, teachers should strive to create environments that are psychologically safe. If students are to learn, they need to feel they can express themselves without fear of being insulted or verbally attacked by anyone in the room. Clearly articulating norms and expectations that reinforce psychological safety is of utmost importance. To create a safe learning community, teachers must ensure that expectations are learned, reinforce those expectations by being a witness to the good, and correct students when they are not acting consistently with them.

Respect. A fundamental need for all people—children as well as adults—is the need to feel respected. Ury (1999) describes our need for respect as follows:

> Human beings have a host of emotional needs—for love and recognition, for belonging and identity, for purpose and meaning to live their lives. If all these needs had to be subsumed in one word, it might be "respect." People want to be recognized and respected for who they are. (p. 121)

Respect is both given and received. We can be respectful, and we can be respected. To be respected, usually, we must be respectful of others, even when they don't appear to respect us. This can be especially true in the classroom. Students can upset classroom balance in a thousand different ways, and a teacher may be tempted to express anger or frustration. However, when we lose composure and lash out at a student, it almost always causes more trouble in the long run.

A great deal of conflict can be avoided if students feel respected. Teachers can show their students respect through simple actions such as authentically listening to all students, empathizing, acknowledging students' effort and ideas, and being a witness to the good. But in many ways, we show respect by what we don't do. We shouldn't interrupt students who are talking, ridicule their ideas, use the power of position to talk over students, yell, or resort to sarcasm. Simply put, when we treat children with respect, we treat them as we would treat any adult we respect; we treat them as we would want to be treated. (Much more on this topic is included in Chapter 11.)

Freedom. According to Ury (1999), "the need for autonomy, for exercising a measure of control over one's life, runs deep. Even small children want to be able to do things themselves without help from adults" (p. 123). Most schools significantly limit students' freedom, and this can be another source of conflict in the classroom.

One way teachers can meet their children's need for autonomy is by offering them choices. Even simple choices can go a long way toward decreasing tension in the classroom. I watched a masterful young teacher in a seventh-grade Spanish class in North Carolina use

questions to deal with a student who was testing her to see how far
he could push the boundaries. Here is what I heard:

> "I don't want to do the group activity," he said.
>
> "That's fine," she said. "You can have a choice. If you
> don't do the group activity, you can read the chapter and
> write answers to all the questions at the back of the chapter.
> What would you like to do?"
>
> "All of them?" he said.
>
> "Yup. It's your choice."
>
> "I think I'll work with the group then."
>
> "Good choice," she said, and the student was back on track.

Teachers can give students autonomy and weave choice into the
general proceedings of every day. Students can choose which topics they
want to work on, the format they'd like to use, the books they'd like to
read, and how much time they'd like to spend on each activity. Students
can also have a voice in creating classroom expectations and norms and
be active participants in creating a learning community. The goal should
be to create a community of learners where everyone collaborates
around at least some decisions, a community that embodies at least some
of the principles of democracy. Ury (1999) writes the following:

> Democracy is about much more than voting. . . . It is about
> participating in decisions and negotiating agreements within
> a context of shared power. Voting can easily become divisive,
> ending in an outcome with winners and losers. In collabora-
> tive democracy, by contrast, people make every effort to reach
> a consensus that includes the full group. (p. 157)

To meet students' need for automony, then, teachers should build
choices into the structure of all student activities. More ideas about
how to do this are described in Chapter 12.

Watching Students

"Conflict does not just break out," William Ury (1999) writes, "but
escalates through different stages. . . . [For this reason perhaps] the
single most important action we can take is paying attention to danger signals" (p. 171).

Ury's comments apply to the classroom, where most big problems
start as little ones. Many chaotic learning environments or major
conflicts between teachers and students can be avoided if problematic
behavior is nipped in the bud before it ever has a chance to grow into

an event that sidetracks everyone's learning. By watching students and addressing little misbehaviors, teachers can often keep larger conflicts from erupting.

Teachers need to watch vigilantly so they can encourage students when they act consistently with expectations, and so they can bring students back on track when they act inconsistently with expectations.

Jacob Kounin's research, conducted more than 40 years ago, identified the importance of teachers staying attentive to all students (1970). After reviewing 49 videotapes of first- and second-year teachers, Kounin identified what was being done by the teachers with the best classroom management techniques. The most effective teachers, he found, demonstrated "withitness"; that is, they watched their students and interacted immediately when their students behaved inappropriately.

To be "withit," teachers must be goal-oriented observers, and they must look carefully at students frequently throughout the day to assess their engagement, joy, and comfort level. Teachers need to recognize nonverbal cues suggesting that students are confused and check in with students frequently to see how they are progressing. Teachers also need to move around the classroom frequently and listen to students in groups. Anita Archer and Charles Hughes (2011) suggest that teachers take notes while listening to groups working and report back what they heard students say—another way of being a witness to the good.

Watching students is important, but what you do when you see students violate expectations is critical. Done effectively, corrections maintain a focus on both student learning and mutual respect. To be effective, corrections must be calm, planned, consistent, immediate, and smooth. Each of these attributes is described below.

Effective Corrections

Calm. Any attempt to correct students will likely be unsuccessful if the teacher loses her cool. If she gets angry, her anger can significantly distract students from learning.

Children who feel they have been singled out by a teacher are often distracted for the rest of the school day. And communicating anger or frustration affects more than the student who receives the comments. As noted above, emotions are infectious, and when a teacher communicates anger or frustration toward a student, that negative emotion can interfere with the learning experienced by all students.

When teachers lose their cool, their actions communicate that anger is an acceptable response in civilized groups. But in most cases, it should not be. If a teacher wants students to remain calm during

class and, ultimately, in the rest of their lives—an essential life skill—
he absolutely must do all he can to remain calm in the classroom.

In *Unmistakable Impact: A Partnership Approach for Dramatically
Improving Instruction* (2011), I discuss three simple strategies people
can employ to remain calm: "name it," "reframe it," and "tame it."
When we "name it," we recognize the behaviors that are most likely
to trigger negative emotions in us. We can call these behaviors "hot
buttons." Different teachers may have different hot buttons. For some
teachers, a hot button might be students who talk back; for others it
might be students who refuse to do the work or students who insult
their fellow students. For some of us, all of these might be hot buttons. Whatever your hot buttons are, the first step in controlling your
emotions is to recognize the behaviors that may set you off. You may
not know what your hot buttons are, but chances are your students
know, and some of them may enjoy pushing those
buttons. For that reason alone, teachers need to be
aware of their own emotional triggers.

Calm Corrections

- Name it.

- Reframe it.

- Tame it.

Sometimes just being aware of your hot buttons is enough to keep you from losing control.
However, a second strategy, reframe it, is also
important. When we reframe an interaction, we
see it from a perspective that reduces our negative
emotions. Sometimes, learning more about stu-
dents can help us reframe a situation. If we know what a child is
going through in her personal life, we are often better able to maintain our cool.

Many children come to school with a multiplicity of needs manifested as fears, worries, anxieties, and pressures. Most students are
smaller than us, but the worries they experience are just as large as
ours. For many children, growing up is difficult, and the anger or
resistance we see in them often has nothing to do with our class but
instead with what they are feeling intensely as they negotiate the
complexities of their own lives. We can reframe an interaction by
reminding ourselves that in many cases, the behavior we see has
nothing to do with us but everything to do with students' needs.

An additional way to reframe an interaction is to mentally separate ourselves from the interaction. If we can keep ourselves from
taking student behavior personally, we have a chance. William Ury
suggests a technique he refers to as going to the balcony. In *Getting
Past No* (1993), he writes that

> going to the balcony means distancing yourself from your
> natural impulses and emotions. . . . The balcony is a metaphor

for a mental attitude of detachment. From the balcony you can calmly evaluate the conflict almost as if you were a third party. You can think constructively for both sides and look for a mutually satisfactory way to resolve the problem. (p. 38)

"Naming" the hot buttons that might stir up our anger or frustration and "reframing" the behavior can help us control emotions, but we may also need to use strategies to "tame" our negative emotions. The most powerful way to tame our emotions is to pause before we respond. Many a teacher has used the tried-and-true method of counting to 10 before responding to students. Another way to maintain control is to paraphrase what you have just heard. In some cases, if you really feel anger stirring up inside, just say, "I need to help . . . Ethan, but I will come back and discuss this with you soon."

My friend Norbert Cyr, a former public affairs officer in the Canadian Army, has given me a way of understanding how and why a teacher should remain calm in the classroom. Once while Norbert and I were watching a learning simulation that was part of the Canadian Army Public Affairs training, we saw a junior officer running to do some task. Norbert, watching the officer, turned to me and said, "An officer should never run; it panics the troops."

Norbert wasn't suggesting that there would never be a situation when an officer should run, but his point was that an officer must exude a calm attitude, no matter how tense the situation is. Part of leadership, he suggested, is to remain calm in situations that might be highly stressful for others. When the leader remains calm, her or his attitude decreases everyone else's stress.

Much the same thing can be said for teachers. During the day-to-day events in the classroom, moments will likely arise when students push your buttons. If at all possible, the teacher should remain calm in the face of tension. The way a teacher moves through difficult moments in a class can have an impact on every student in the room.

Planned. When my children were playing youth hockey, I sometimes found myself thrown into the role of referee during games. Even though the boys and girls I was overseeing were usually quite young, I realized quickly that a lot is going on when 12 squirming bodies are skating on the ice (and their parents are watching in the stands). A hockey game contains a lot of data to be processed, and it can be hard to know what to call and what to ignore.

In order to be consistent and not waste all my attention trying to decide what I should do in every incident, I made a set of guidelines so I would know when I would or would not call a penalty. For example, when a player puts his stick on another player, the referee might or might not call hooking. However, if you call hooking every time a player's stick touches another player's body, you'll send a lot of players to the penalty box, and the game's action will slow to a crawl. So that I could be consistent, I decided that I would call penalties only when a player was pulled down to the ice by another player's stick. This made it easy for me to decide when I would call a penalty, and it also freed up my attention for watching for other things going on in the game.

By planning in advance when I would call penalties, I was able to consistently address player infractions, and I didn't wear myself out trying to determine what to do each time something came up in a game. In the same way, teachers will better serve their students and be able to focus more on the art of teaching by planning their corrections in advance. If a teacher is unsure of what to do every time a student acts in a potentially disruptive manner, the teacher loses some credibility with students, runs the risk of being inconsistent, and is sure to be worn out.

Planning corrections in advance also helps teachers make better decisions in other aspects of instruction. We can only think about so much at one time, and because we have a limited processing ability, the more we have to think about, the more difficult it is to make good decisions. When our brains are overwhelmed with too much information, what cognitive psychologists refer to as cognitive load , we may struggle to make good decisions, or make decisions too quickly. By planning our corrections in advance, on the other hand, we can lighten our cognitive load and free our minds to make decisions in other aspects of teaching.

When I once asked Randy Sprick for advice on correcting students, he had a great suggestion. Teachers, he said, should list all of the most common misbehaviors they encounter in their classroom and then write beside them the correction that they will give students the first, second, and third time they see them. For example, a common behavior might be students having inappropriate side conversations; indeed, Fred Jones, in *Tools for Teachers* (2007), estimates that 80% of the behavior corrected in schools is side conversations. A teacher might decide that the first time a student engages in a side conversation she will look in the student's direction and nonverbally communicate that he must stop talking. The second time, she might say, "I need you to stop talking and get back to work, or you'll need to make up the time after school." The third time, she might say, "I need you to stay after class to make up the time you missed while talking today."

By planning corrections in advance, a teacher ensures that she won't have to reflect and decide how each behavior will be addressed in each situation because she knows what she will correct and how she will correct it. And knowing what to correct and how to correct it makes it much easier to be consistent and respond immediately, two more techniques described later in this section.

No doubt there will be occasions when students will surprise you with the way they sidetrack learning—one of my students in a community college once climbed up on the roof beside my second-story classroom and looked in through the window after I had asked him to leave my class for disrupting students—but in most cases, student misbehavior involves many of the same behaviors: refusing to do the work, talking back, moving around the classroom inappropriately, touching or interrupting other students, and ignoring expectations. The fact that so many behaviors can be predicted is a great help. Since you know what students might do, you can plan how you will respond, and planning makes it much easier to be consistent.

Consistent. When students are upset about corrections, it is often because they feel they have not been treated fairly. Certainly, some students will play the "it's not fair" card to deflect focus from themselves, but sometimes students are correct. If we are not consistent, our corrections may not be fair. When a behavior is acceptable one day and not acceptable the next, or when some students are corrected for a behavior and others are not, children are right to feel that it's not fair. Also, if the rules change every day, it can trigger more disruptive behavior as students retaliate for unfair treatment. At the very least, if students are unclear about what is appropriate and not appropriate, they are less inclined to act consistently with a teacher's expectations.

For all these reasons, if a teacher is going to correct a student (and corrections must inevitably happen in any classroom), she must be consistent. What was unacceptable yesterday must be unacceptable today and tomorrow. The problem is that for many of us, being consistent is difficult. As Aldous Huxley is credited with saying, "consistency is contrary to nature, contrary to life. The only completely consistent people are dead." Indeed, many teachers—as creative, spontaneous people—are more inclined to live in the moment. What is needed is a professional learning method they can employ to become consistent with their corrections.

In my experience with teachers who are working on being more consistent, I have found that they tend to struggle to be consistent at everything all at once and, therefore, feel pretty helpless. Instead, I suggest teachers pick no more than one or two behaviors to focus on. Once teachers have become consistent with their corrections around side conversations, for example, they can move on to becoming consistent with corrections around students moving around the class-room. This doesn't mean that teachers ignore other behaviors, but only that teachers are very deliberate about being extremely consistent with their focus behaviors.

I also recommend that, when possible, teachers work with an instructional coach to develop the habit of consistent corrections. A coach can observe, or even more powerfully, video record a teacher while he is teaching and give immediate feedback on consistency. A camera with a fisheye lens, such as a Go-Pro, can be very helpful for gathering such data. If teachers don't have coaches to partner with, they can video record their class and watch to see how consistent they are being.

When a teacher is consistent with corrections, she will have more authority and be calmer, and students will be more likely to listen to her because they are crystal clear about the boundaries for all activities. Consistency also creates a more learner-friendly environment. And, if students know that behavior is treated consistently, there will be fewer arguments, less anger, and less frustration. The cumulative effect of being consistent with expectations is that it will decrease disruptions and increase learning.

Immediate. When making corrections, teachers should make them as soon as possible after the behavior occurs. There should be no ambiguity about why a student is being corrected. A teacher makes it clear to students why they are being corrected when she corrects students immediately. Of course, if expectations are clear, and if corrections are planned in advance, this is much easier.

By correcting students immediately, teachers also communicate that they are in control of the class and won't tolerate behaviors that violate the expectations that, in many cases, everyone crafted and agreed to together. Immediate corrections help maintain a safe and productive learning environment, and they keep students from violating the expectations.

Smooth. Effective corrections should be as quick as possible, but, to rewrite Einstein's famous quotation, no quicker. Teachers need to clearly communicate the correction and then smoothly move students back to learning. Some students try to deflect corrections by dragging out conversations for as long as possible by arguing that "she was the one talking," "I am working," "you're being unfair," and so forth. Don't go there! Way too much instructional time can be wasted in arguing with students, so simply identify the behavior to be corrected, explain what the student should be doing, calmly and quickly, and then move back to instruction.

But keeping corrections smooth does not mean that teachers should rush through them. It is important that teachers clearly communicate what has to change. This means that teachers should stop what they are doing, turn their body toward the student, make eye contact, and calmly and in a nonconfrontational manner explain what needs to change. As Fred Jones has written, if we correct students too quickly, they will assume they can ignore our correction and go back to their disruptive behavior. Jones writes:

> When we look up and see a disruption, the fight-flight reflex speeds us up. . . . Everything is driving us through the transition from instruction to discipline *too fast*. The students see this speed of movement and conclude that we will deal with the disruption quickly and return to Robert. . . . Slow down so that the disruptive students have no doubt that instruction has been interrupted, and that they are the sole focus of your attention. Only when you commit your time and attention to the problem will the students begin to take you seriously. (p. 182)

Further, smooth corrections should not interrupt the flow of instruction. The teacher should pause an appropriate length of time, give the planned form of correction, and then return to teaching smoothly. Thus, a teacher might ask, "Who thinks they know one theme in this story—John, you need to get your book out—Sarena, what do you think the theme is?" In the best-case scenario, instruction continues, the correction is given, and the teacher and students return to the lesson without missing a beat.

Turning Ideas Into Action

Students

1. Consider involving students in identifying appropriate consequences. If everyone agrees that there should be no side conversations during teacher-led instruction, then ask students what they think should happen if those expectations are ignored. Such a conversation can lead to broader, important conversations about why you will be monitoring to ensure everyone follows guidelines.

2. Have the students complete their own assessment of how they did on acting consistently with the expectations. You might have students complete an exit ticket at the end of class to write down on a scale of 1 to 5 how well they think they did in acting consistently with expectations.

(Continued)

(Continued)

Teachers

1. Craft corrections for the most common misbehaviors you see your students do. For each common misbehavior, identify your first, second, and third actions.

2. Become masterful at corrections by practicing one common behavior at a time. Gather data (by video or audio recording, or by having a coach visit your classroom). Keep practicing until you make it a habit to be consistent for each of the common behaviors.

3. Consider adjusting your consequences if they are too tight or too loose for your students.

4. Make sure your consequences are enforceable. If you can't enforce them, change either your approach or your consequences.

Instructional Coaches

1. Collaborate with teachers to develop consequences for common misbehaviors.

2. Consider partnering with your collaborating teacher to gather data, perhaps video data, until the teacher is consistent with corrections.

3. Create a video library of teachers who masterfully correct students.

Principals

1. Discuss with teachers the importance of corrections being calm, planned, consistent, immediate, and smooth.

2. During walk-throughs, be especially mindful of whether or not behaviors are being corrected consistently.

What It Looks Like

1. Identify a target behavior that a teacher wants to correct, such as side conversations. Each time you see the behavior, note it and note whether or not the correction was calm, planned, consistent, immediate, and smooth.

2. Keep track of the number of disruptions in a class. Disruptions refer to anything a student does that interrupts the learning of a student or the teaching of a teacher. As the ratio of interactions shifts to more positive comments and as corrections become more fluent, disruptions should decrease.

3. Ask students whether or not their teacher consistently corrects their behavior.

To Sum Up

- Teachers must correct students when they step out of bounds. If student misbehavior goes unchecked, it can take over a class, making it difficult for meaningful learning to occur.

- The most effective way to keep students on track is to prevent conflict.

- William Ury writes that we can prevent conflict by understanding underlying needs that have not been addressed, attending to students' wellness and safety issues, communicating respect, and recognizing people's need for autonomy.

- Teachers need to demonstrate "withitness" (Kounin, 1971) by watching students vigilantly so they can encourage them and, when necessary, bring them back on track.

- Effective corrections are calm, planned in advance, consistent, immediate, and smooth.

Going Deeper

All of the books from the Harvard Negotiation Project are packed with helpful strategies for moving through the complexities of interpersonal relations. William Ury's *Getting to Peace: Transforming Conflict at Home, at Work, and in the World* (1999) contains excellent advice on working through conflict in any setting. Ury's and Roger Fisher's book, *Getting to Yes: Negotiating Agreement Without Giving In* (2011), is likely the most influential book about the topic of negotiation, and certainly a lot of community building in the classroom involves negotiation. Stone, Patton, and Heen's *Difficult Conversations: How to Discuss What Matters Most* (2000) contains very useful strategies for spotting conflict and using effective communication strategies such as authentic listening to work through such conflicts. Other useful books from the Harvard Negotiation Project include William Ury's *Getting Past No: Negotiating in Difficult Situations* (1993), Roger Fisher and Scott Brown's *Getting Together: Building Relationships as We Negotiate* (1989), and Fisher and Daniel Shapiro's *Beyond Reason: Using Emotions as You Negotiate* (2005). Anyone with an interest in healthy relationships (shouldn't that be all of us?) will benefit from reading their work.

Fred Jones' popular *Tools for Teaching* (2007) contains helpful strategies that address student discipline, instruction, and motivation. Jones' description of the nonverbal aspects of correcting students is especially useful.

CONCLUSION

Teaching is personal, and when students are not learning with us, we feel frustrated, and sometimes angry, but mostly we feel like we are letting our students down. When teachers struggle with classroom management, the frustration they experience can run into the rest of their lives, coloring everything the way a bright red T-shirt can color all the other clothes in a washing machine. Many teachers have driven home after a difficult day in school, unable to leave behind the unpleasant emotions they felt at school, and found that their toxic emotions disturb their night at home.

When I started out as a teacher at Humber College in Toronto, working with students who were at risk for failure, I had very little preparation for the students I was asked to teach. Not knowing what to do about management, I tried to win their attention with energy and passion for literature and writing, and sometimes it worked. One student in my college special education class looked at me after I gave my motivational speech about the importance of writing and said, "Man, you should have a late-night TV commercial with a 1-800 number!" But the trouble was that he wasn't buying what I was selling.

On many of my early days of teaching, energy, humor, and passion weren't enough. Too often I was talking and teaching, but my students weren't listening, and especially they weren't learning. And my struggles with control seemed to be popping up in all other aspects of my life. I was a hockey coach at the time, and it seemed I could never get my teenagers to listen to me. Even at home, it seemed like my children went out of their way to avoid listening to me. I became increasingly frustrated when I couldn't get my children to agree to simple things like going to bed on time, doing their homework, or cleaning up after themselves around the house. It wasn't until I learned to have more control in the classroom that I began to feel more control in other aspects of my life and learned that teaching children and adults is what I am meant to do.

It is not surprising that a majority of teachers (some studies suggest more than 50%) quit the profession in the first five years on the job. But the good news is that there is much we can do to help teachers create learning communities that foster creativity, encourage joy and fun, and prompt orderly, efficient learning. The high-impact teaching strategies in this book should help any teacher reach more students.

If teachers develop and teach expectations, they will create a fairer, more orderly environment for students and make it easier for themselves to move through the day. When teachers are witnesses to the good, and when they correct students fluently and consistently, they will see their expectations translated into positive and productive learning.

Teachers can also increase the impact they have on students by recognizing the importance of freedom and form, caring and control. And learning will have a better chance of flourishing in environments where teachers build relationships with students rather than trying to overpower them, and where the teacher carefully shapes a learner-friendly culture.

However, the community-building strategies alone are not enough to create learning that has a profound, positive impact on students. We need to carefully plan our units and lessons and utilize assessment so that we know how well each student is doing and so each student knows how well he or she is doing. Finally, we can increase engagement, learning, and joy by using teaching strategies such as thinking prompts, cooperative learning, stories, effective questions, and authentic learning.

No one can implement all of these practices at once, of course. Each strategy takes time, practice, and usually feedback from a coach. I didn't write this book to suggest that the perfect teacher would hop to it and do all of these practices in one swoop. I wrote this book to make sure that teachers know there is hope, that there are practices that can make a difference, and that if teachers commit to learning, experimenting, and mastering these practices, if they strive for personal bests, they will feel the joy of learning, and so will their students.

The most important factor in the classroom is not techniques, strategies, and principles. It is the committed teacher, whose mind and heart are dedicated to doing what it takes to make a difference, to reach more children, to teach in a way that has an unmistakable positive impact on the lives of the children. This book is meant to honor teachers. I hope these strategies help you keep doing your incredibly important work.

REFERENCES AND FURTHER READINGS

Ainsworth, L. (2003). *Unwrapping the standards: A simple process to make standards manageable.* Englewood, CO: Lead + Learn Press.

Amabile, T., & Kramer, S. (2011). *The progress principle: Using small wins to ignite joy, engagement, and creativity at work.* Boston, MA: Harvard Business School Publishing.

Angelo, T. A., & Cross, K. P. (1993). *Classroom assessment techniques* (2nd ed.). San Francisco: Jossey-Bass.

Archer, A. L., & Hughes, C. (2011). *Explicit instruction: Effective and efficient teaching.* New York: The Guilford Press.

Aronson, E., Blaney, N., Stephin, C., Sikes, J., & Snapp, M. (1978). *The jigsaw classroom.* Beverly Hills, CA: Sage.

Arter, J., & McTighe, J. (2001). *Scoring rubrics in the classroom: Using performance criteria for assessing and improving student performance.* Thousand Oaks, CA: Corwin.

Atkinson, R., & Shiffrin, R. (1968). Human memory: A proposed system and its control processes. *Psychology of Learning and Motivation, 11,* 249.

Ausubel, D. (1980). Schemata, cognitive structure, and advance organizers: A reply to Anderson, Spiro, and Anderson. *American Educational Research Journal, 17,* 400–404.

Barkley, S., & Bianco, T. (2009). *Questions for life: Powerful strategies to guide critical thinking.* Cadiz, KY: Performance Learning Systems.

Barkley, S., & Bianco, T. (2011). *Instructional coaching with the end in mind.* Cadiz, KY: Performance Learning Systems.

Bender, W. (2012). *Project based learning: Differentiating instruction for the 21st century.* Thousand Oaks, CA: Corwin.

Bennett, B., & Rolheiser, C. (2008). *Beyond Monet: The artful science of instructional integration.* Toronto, Ontario: Bookation.

Bennett, B., Rolheiser-Bennett, C., & Stevahn, L. (1991). *Cooperative learning: Where heart meets mind.* Bothell, WA: Professional Development Associates.

Bloom, B. (1956). *Taxonomy of educational objectives: Handbook 1. Cognitive domain.* Longman, NY: Longman.

Bohm, D. (1996). *On dialogue.* New York: Routledge.

Boss, S., Krauss, J., & Conery, L. (2008). *Reinventing project-based learning: Your field guide to real-world projects in the digital age.* Washington, DC: International Society for Technology in Education.

Brooks, J., & Brooks, M. (1999). *In search of understanding: The case for constructivist classroom.* Alexandria, VA: Association for Supervision and Curriculum Development.

Buber, M. (1958). *I and thou.* New York: Charles Scribner's Sons.

Bulgren, J., Schumaker, J. B., & Deshler, D. (1994). *The concept anchoring routine.* Lawrence, KS: Edge Enterprises.

Buzan, T. (1993). *The mind map book: How to use radiant thinking to maximize your brain's untapped potential.* London: BBC Books.

Chappuis, J. (2009). *Seven strategies of assessment for learning.* Boston, MA: Pearson Education.

Chatman, S. (1978). *Story and discourse: Narrative structure in fiction and film.* Ithaca, NY: Cornell University Press.

Christensen, C., Allworth, K., & Killon, K. (2012). *How will you measure your life?* New York: HarperCollins.

Cohan, S., & Shires, L. (1998). *Telling stories: A theoretical analysis of narrative fiction.* New York: Routledge.

Connell, R. (2006). *The most dangerous game.* Minneapolis, MN: Filquarian Publishing, LLC.

Coyne, S. (2012). Foreword. In S. Pressfield, *Turning pro: Tap your inner power and create your life's work.* New York: Black Irish Entertainment.

Costa, A. (2009). *Habits of minds across the curriculum: Practical and creative strategies for teachers.* Alexandria, VA: Association for Supervision and Curriculum Development.

Costa, A., & Garmston, R. (2002). *Cognitive coaching: A foundation for renaissance schools.* Norwood, MA: Christopher-Gordon Publishers

Council for Exceptional Children. (1987). *Academy for effective instruction: Working with mildly handicapped students.* Reston, VA: Author.

Cskiszentmihalyi, M. (1990). *Flow: The psychology of optimal experience.* New York: Harper & Row.

Cummings, E. E. (1923). *100 Selected Poems.* New York: Grove Press.

Damon, W. (2009). *The path to purpose: How young people find their calling in life.* New York: Simon & Schuster.

Danesh, H. B. (1994). *The psychology of spirituality.* Victoria, BC: Paradigm Publishing.

Danielson, C. (2007). *Enhancing professional practice: A framework for teaching.* Alexandria, VA: Association for Supervision and Curriculum Development.

Davenport, T. (2005). *Thinking for a living: How to get better performance and results from knowledge workers.* Boston, MA: Harvard Business School Press.

Dean, C. B., Hubbell, F., Pitler, H., & Stone, B. B. (2012). *Classroom instruction that works: Research-based strategies for increasing student achievement.* Alexandria, VA: Association for Supervision and Curriculum Development.

Deci, E., & Ryan, R. (1985). *Intrinsic motivation and self-determination in human behavior.* New York: Plenum.

Denning, S. (2005). *The leader's guide to storytelling: Mastering the art and discipline of business narrative.* San Francisco: Jossey-Bass.

Devries, D. L., & Edwards, K. J. (1974). Student teams and learning games: Their effects on cross-race and cross-sex interaction. *Journal of Educational Psychology, 66*(5), 741–749.

Dochy, F., Segers, M., & Buehl, M. (1999). The relationship between assessment practices and outcomes of studies: The case of research on prior knowledge. *Review of Educational Research, 69*(2), 147–188.

Draper, S. (2007). *November's Blues.* New York: Simon & Schuster.

Dweck, C. S. (2006). *Mindset: The new psychology of success.* New York: Random House.

Ebbinghaus, H. (1913). *On memory: A contribution to experimental psychology.* New York: Teachers College.

Edmondson, A. (2012). *Teaming: How organizations learn, innovate, and compete in the knowledge economy.* San Francisco: Jossey-Bass.

Ellis, E., Deshler, D. D., Lenz, B. K., Schumaker, J. B., & Clark, F. (1991). An instructional model for teaching learning strategies. *Focus on exceptional children, 23*(6), 1–24.

Emmer, E. T., & Evertson, C. M., & Worsham, M. E. (2003). *Classroom management for secondary teachers* (6th ed.). Boston, MA: Allyn & Bacon.

Erickson, H. L. (2007). *Concept-based instruction for the thinking classroom.* Thousand Oaks, CA: Corwin.

Evans, P. (2002). *Controlling people: How to recognize, understand, and deal with people who try to control you.* Avon, MA: Adams Media Corporation.

Evans, P. (2010). *The verbally abusive relationship: How to recognize it and how to respond to it.* Avon, MD: Adams Media.

Feedback for learning. (2012). *Educational Leadership, 70*(1).

Fisher, F., & Frey, N. (2007). *Checking for understanding: Formative assessment techniques for your classroom.* Alexandria, VA: Association for Supervision and Curriculum Development.

Fisher, R., & Brown, S. (1989). *Getting together: Building relationships as we negotiate.* New York: Penguin.

Fisher, R., & Shapiro, D. (2005). *Beyond reason: Using emotions as you negotiate.* New York: Penguin Group.

Fisher, R., Ury, W., & Patton, B. (2011). *Getting to yes: Negotiating agreement without giving in.* New York: Viking.

Fredrickson, B., & Losada, M. (2004, May). The impact of positive leadership. *Gallup Business Journal.*

Freire, P. (1970). *Pedagogy of the oppressed.* New York: Continuum.

Fritz, R. (1989). *The path of least resistance: Learning to become the creative force in your own life.* New York: Ballantine Books.

Fullan, M. (2001). *The meaning of educational change* (3rd ed.). New York: Teacher's College Press.

Fullan, M. (2009). *Motion leadership: The skinny on becoming change savvy.* Thousand Oaks, CA: Corwin.

Gallagher, W. (2009). *Rapt: Attention and the focused life.* New York: Penguin Group.

Gawande, A. (2009). *The checklist manifesto: How to get things right.* New York: Metropolitan Books.

Gladwell, M. (2000). *The tipping point: How little things can make a big difference.* Boston, MA: Little, Brown and Company.

Glanzer, M., & Cunitz, A. R. (1966). Two storage mechanisms in free recall. *Journal of Verbal Learning and Verbal Behaviour, 5,* 351–360.

Glaserfield, E. V. (1995). *Radical constructivism.* Washington, DC: Falmer Press.

Goleman, D. (1995). *Emotional intelligence: Why it matters more than IQ.* New York: Bantam Dell.

Goleman, D. (2004). *Primal leadership: Learning to lead with emotional intelligence.* Boston, MA: Harvard Business School Press.

Goleman, D. (2007). *Social intelligence: The new science of human relationships.* New York: Bantam Books.

Golich, V., Boyer, M., Franko, P., & Lamy, S. (2000). *The ABC's of case teaching.* Pew Case Studies in International Affairs, Washington, DC: Georgetown University, Institute in the Study of Diplomacy.

Gottman, J. (2001). *The relationship cure: A 5-step guide to strengthening your marriage, family, and friendships.* New York: Three Rivers Press.

Gottman, J. (2002). *The relationship cure: A 5-step guide to strengthening your marriage, family and friendships.* New York: Three Rivers Press.

Gottman, J. M. (1994). *What predicts divorce: The relationship between marital processes and marital outcomes.* New York: Lawrence Erlbaum.

Hallowell, E. (2011). *Shine: Using brain science to get the best from your people.* Boston, MA: Harvard Business School Publishing.

Hargrove, R. (2008). *Masterful coaching.* San Francisco, CA: Jossey-Bass.

Harris, K. (1995). *Collected quotes from Albert Einstein.* Retrieved from rescomp.stanford.edu/~cheshire/EinsteinQuotes.html

Hattie, H. (2008). *Visible learning: A synthesis of over 800 meta-analyses relating to achievement.* New York: Routledge.

Hattie, J. (2009). *Visible learning: A synthesis of over 800 meta-analyses relating to achievement.* New York: Routledge.

Hattie, J. (2011). *Visible learning for teachers: Maximizing impact on learning.* New York: Routledge.

Heath, C., & Heath, D. (2007). *Made to stick: Why some ideas survive and others die.* New York: Random House.

Heath, C., & Heath, D. (2010). *Switch: How to change things when change is hard.* New York: Broadway Books.

Hill, C., & Jones, G. (2001). *Strategic management: An integrated approach.* Boston, MA: Houghton Mifflin.

Hock, M. F., Schumaker, J. B., & Deshler, D. D. (2003). *Possible selves: Nurturing student motivation.* Lawrence, KS: Edge Enterprises.

Hollingsworth, J., & Ybarra, S. (2009). *Explicit direct instruction: The power of the well-crafted, well-taught lesson.* Thousand Oaks, CA: Corwin.

Hyerle, D. (1995). *Thinking maps: Tools for learning.* Cary, NC: Thinking Maps.

Hyerle, D. (2009). *Visual tools for transforming information into knowledge.* Thousand Oaks, CA: Corwin.

Hyerle, D., & Alper, L. (2011). *Student successes with thinking maps: School-based research, results, and models for achievement using visual tools.* Thousand Oaks, CA: Corwin.

Iser, W. (1978). *The implied reader: Patterns of communication in prose fiction from Bunyan to Beckett.* Baltimore, MD: The Johns Hopkins University Press.

Issacs, W. (1999). *Dialogue: The art of thinking together.* New York: Doubleday.

Iyengar, S. (2010). *The art of choosing: The decisions we make every day*. New York: Hachette Book Group.

Jensen, B. (2000). *Simplicity: The new competitive advantage in a world of more, better, faster*. Cambridge, MA: Basic Books.

Johnson, D. E., & Johnson, R. T. (1991). *Learning together and alone: Cooperation in the classroom* (3rd ed.). Edina, MN: Interaction Books.

Johnson, D. W., Johnson, R. T., & Holubec, E. J. (1986). *Circles of learning: Cooperation in the classroom*. Edina, MN: Interaction Book Company.

Johnson, D., & Johnson, R. (1975). *Learning together and alone: Cooperative, competitive, and individualistic learning*. Needham Heights, MA: Allyn and Bacon.

Johnson, D., & Johnson, R. (1986). *Learning together and alone: Cooperative, competitive, and individualistic learning*. Englewood cliffs, NJ: Prentice Hall.

Jones, C., & Vreeman, M. (2008). *Instructional coaches and classroom teachers: Sharing the road to success*. Huntington Beach, CA: Shell Education.

Jones, F. (2007). *Tools for teaching* (2nd ed.). Santa Cruz, CA: Fredric H. Jones & Associates.

Jukes, I., McCain, T., & Crockett, L. (2010). *Understanding the digital generation: Teaching and learning in the new digital landscape* (The 21st Century Fluency Series). Thousand Oaks, CA: Co-published with Corwin.

Kagan, S. (1990). *Cooperative learning: Resources for teachers*. San Juan Capistrano, CA: Resources for Teachers.

Kagan, S. (1994). *Cooperative learning*. San Clemente, CA: Resources for Teachers.

Kagan, S., & Kagan, M. (2009). *Kagan cooperative learning*. San Clemente, CA: Kagan Publishing.

Keene, E., & Zimmerman, S. (1997). *Mosaic of thought: Teaching comprehension in a reader's workshop*. Portsmouth, NH: Heinemann.

Kegan, T, & Lahey, L., (2001). *How the way we talk can change the way we work: Seven languages of transformation*. San Francisco: Jossey-Bass

Keltner, D., Gruenfeld, D., & Anderson, C. (2003). Power, approach, and inhibition. *Psychological Review, 110*(2), 265–284.

Ketcham, E., & Kurtz, K. (1994). *The spirituality of imperfection: Storytelling and the journey to wholeness*. New York: Bantam.

Killion, J., & Harrison, C. (2006). *Taking the lead: New roles for teachers and school-based coaches*. Oxford, OH: National Staff Development Council.

Kline, F. M., Schumaker, J. B., & Deshler, D. D. (1991). The development and validation of feedback routines for instructing students with learning disabilities. *LD Forum, 14*, 191–207.

Knight, J. (2005). Crossing boundaries: What constructivists can teach intensive-explicit instructors and vice versa. In T. M. Skrtic, K. R. Harris, & J. G. Shriner (Eds.), *Special education policy and practice: Accountability, instruction, and social challenges* (pp. 242–266). Denver, CO: Love Publishing.

Knight, J. (2007). *Instructional coaching: A partnership approach to improving instruction*. Thousand Oaks, CA: Corwin.

Knight, J. (2011). *Unmistakable impact: A partnership approach for dramatically improving instruction*. Thousand Oaks, CA: Corwin.

Knight, J., Bradley, B., Hock, M., Skirtic, T., Knight, D., Brasseur-Hock., I., & Hatton, C. (2012). Record, reply and reflect: Videotaped lessons accelerate learning for teachers and coaches. *JSD: The Learning Forward Journal, 11*(2).

Kounin, J. (1970). *Discipline and group management in classrooms*. New York: Holt, Rinehart and Winston.

Larmer, J., Ross, D., & Mergandollar, J. R. (2009). *PBL starter kit: To-the-point advice, tools and tips for your first project*. Buck Institute of Education.

Lawrence-Lightfoot, S. (2000). *Respect: An exploration*. Cambridge, MA: Perseus Books.

Lemov, D. (2010). *Teach like a champion: 49 techniques that put students on the path to college*. San Francisco: Jossey-Bass.

Lencioni, P. (2002). *The five dysfunctions of a team: An illustrated leadership fable*. Singapore: Jossey-Bass.

Lenz, B. K., & Deshler, D. D., with Kissam, B. R. (2004). *Teaching content to all: Evidence-based inclusive practices in middle and secondary schools*. Boston, MA: Pearson Education.

Lenz, B. K., Alley, G. R. Schumaker, J. B. (1987). Activating the inactive learner: Advance organizers in the secondary content classroom. *Learning Disability Quarterly, 10*(1), 53–67.

Lenz, B. K., Bulgren, J., Schumaker, J., Deshler, D. D., & Boudah, D. (1994). *The unit organizer routine*. Lawrence, KS: Edge Enterprises.

Lenz, B. K., Marrs, R. W., Schumaker, J., & Deshler, D. D. (1993). *Lesson organizer routine*. Lawrence, KS: Edge Enterprises.

Lenz, B. K., Schumaker, J., Deshler, D. D., & Bulgren, J. (1998). *Course organizer routine*. Lawrence, KS: Edge Enterprises.

Liu, E. (2004). *Guiding lights: How to mentor—and find life's purpose*. New York: Ballantine Books.

Livo, N., & Rietz, S. (1986). *Storytelling: Process and practice*. Littleton, CO: Libraries Unlimited.

Loehr, J. (2007). *The power of story*. New York: Free Press.

Loehr, J., & Schwartz, T. (2003). *The full power of full engagement*. New York: Free Press.

Looney, J. (Ed.). (2005). *Formative assessment: Improving learning in secondary classrooms*. Paris: Organisation for Economic Co-operation and Development.

Losada, M. (1999). The complex dynamics of high performance teams. *Mathematical and Computer Modelling, 30*(9–10), 179–192.

Losada, M., & Heaphy, E. (2004). The role of positivity and connectivity in the performance of business teams: A nonlinear dynamics model. *American Behavioral Scientist, 47*(6), 740–765.

Love, N. (2009). *Using data to improve learning for all: A collaborative inquiry approach*. Thousand Oaks, CA: Corwin.

Luntz, F. (2007). *Words that work: It's not what you say, it's what people hear*. New York: Hyperion.

Lyman, F. (1987). Think-Pair-Share: An expanding technique. *MAA-CIE Cooperative News, 1*, 1–2.

Maslow, A. (1954). *Motivation and personality*. New York: Harper & Row.

Margulies, N. (1991). *Mapping inner space*. Tucson, AZ: Zephyr Press.

Mariage, T. V. (2000). Constructing educational possibilities: A sociolinguistic examination of meaning-making in "sharing chair." *Learning Disability Quarterly, 23*(Spring 2000), 79–103.

Marzano, R. (2004). *Building background knowledge for academic research on what works in schools*. Alexandria, VA: Association for Supervision and Curriculum Development.

Marzano, R. (2007). *The art and science of teaching: A comprehensive framework for effective instruction*. Alexandria, VA: Association for Supervision and Curriculum Development.

Marzano, R. (2010). *Formative assessment and standards-based grading*. Bloomington, IN: Marzano Research Laboratory.

Marzano, R., & Kendall, J. S. (2007). *The new taxonomy of educational objectives*. Thousand Oaks, CA: Corwin.

Marzano, R., Pickering, D., & Pollock, J. (2001). *Classroom management that works: Research-based strategies for every teacher*. Alexandria, VA: Association for Supervision and Curriculum Development.

Mathews, R., & Wacher, W. (2008). *What's your story? Storytelling to move markets, audiences, people, and brands*. Upper Saddle River, NJ: Pearson Education.

Medina, J. (2008). *Brain rules: 12 principles for surviving and thriving at work, home, and school*. Seattle, WA: Pear Press.

Miller, D. (2009). *The book whisperer: Awakening the inner reader in every child*. San Francisco: Jossey-Bass.

Mintzberg, H. (2009). *Managing*. San Francisco: Berrett-Koehler.

Monroe, H., & Henderson, A. C. (Eds.). (1917). *The new poetry: An anthology*. New York: Macmillan.

Morgan, G. (1993). *Imaginization: New mindsets for seeing, organizing, and managing*. Thousand Oaks, CA: Sage.

Moss, C., & Brookhart, S. (2012). *Learning targets: Helping students aim for understanding today's lesson*. Alexandria, VA: Association for Supervision and Curriculum Development.

Murdock, B. B., Jr. (1962). The serial position effect of recall. *Journal of Experimental Psychology, 64*, 482–488.

Nagel, D. R., Schumaker, J., & Deshler, D. D. (1986). *The FIRST letter mnemonic strategy*. Lawrence, KS: Edge Enterprises.

Naisbitt, J. (2006). *Mind set: Eleven ways to change the way you see—and create—the future*. New York: HarperCollins.

Novak, J. (1998). *Learning, creating, and using knowledge: Concept maps as facilitative tools in schools and corporations*. New York: Lawrence Erlbaum Associates.

Osborn, A. F. (1953). *Applied imagination: Principles and procedures of creative-problem solving*. New York: C. Scribner's Sons.

Owen, H. (2008). *Open space technology: A user's guide*. San Francisco: Berrett-Koehler Publishers.

Palmer, P. J. (2009). *A hidden wholeness: The journey toward an undivided life*. San Francisco: Jossey-Bass.

Patterson, K., Grenny, J., Maxfield, D., McMillan, R., & Switzler, A. (2008). *Influencer: The power to change anything.* New York: McGraw-Hill.

Piaget, J. (1954). *The construction of reality in the child.* New York: Ballantine Books.

Peirce, L. (2010). *Big Nate: In a class by himself.* New York: HarperCollins Childrens' Books.

Pink, D. H. (2009). *Drive: The surprising truth about what motivates us.* New York: Penguin.

Popham, J. W. (2008). *Transformative assessment.* Alexandria, VA: Association for Supervision and Curriculum Development.

Pressfield, S. (2002). *The war of art: Breakthrough the blocks and win your inner creative battles.* New York: Warner Books.

Pressfield, S. (2012a). *Turning pro: Tap your inner power and create your life's work.* New York: Black Irish Entertainment.

Pressfield, S. (2012b). *The war of art: Break through the blocks and win your inner creative battles.* New York: Black Irish Entertainment.

Ralston, W. R. S. (1873). *Russian folk tales.* Whitefish, MT: Kessinger Publishing.

Reeves, A. (2011). *Where great teaching begins: Planning for student thinking and learning.* Alexandria, VA: Association for Supervision and Curriculum Development.

Reinke, W. M., Lewis-Palmer, T., & Merrell, K. (2008). The classroom check-up: A classwide teacher consultation model for increasing praise and decreasing disruptive behavior. *School Psychology Review, 37*(3), 315–332.

Reynolds, G. (2008). *Presentation Zen: Simple ideas on presentation design and delivery.* Berkeley, CA: New Riders.

Rico, G. (2000). *Writing the natural way: Using right-brain techniques to release your expressive powers.* New York: St. Martin's Press.

Rifkin, J. (2009). *The empathic civilization: The race to global consciousness in a world crisis.* New York: Penguin Group.

Roam, D. (2008). *The back of the napkin: Solving problems and selling ideas with pictures.* New York: Penguin Group.

Roehler, L. R., & Duffy, G. G. (1984). Direct explanation of comprehension processes. In G. G. Duffy, L. R. Roehler, & J. Mason (Eds.), *Comprehension instruction: Perspectives and suggestions* (pp. 265–280). New York: Longman.

Rothstein, D., & Santana, L. (2011). *Make just one change: Teach students to ask their own questions.* Cambridge, MA: Harvard Education Press.

Rowshan, A. (1997). *Telling tales: How to use stories to help your children overcome their problems.* Oxford, England; Rockport, MA: Oneworld.

Rubenstein, S. (2005). *Raymond Carver in the classroom: A small good thing.* Urbana, IL: National Council of Teachers of English.

Ryan, R., & Deci, E. L. (2000). Self-determination theory and the facilitation of intrinsic motivation, social development, and well-being. *American Psychologist, 55*(1), 68–78.

Sachs, J. (2012). *Winning the story wars: Why those who tell (and live) the best stories will rule the future.* Boston, MA: Harvard Business School Publishing.

Sailor, W., Dunlap, G., Sugai, G., & Horner, R. (2010). *Handbook of positive behavior supports.* New York: Springer Science + Business Media, LLC.

Saphier, J., Haley-Speca, M., & Gower, R. (2008). *The skillful teacher: Building your teaching skill.* Acton, MA: Research for Better Teaching.

Sawyer, K. (2007). *Group genius: The creative power of collaboration.* New York: Basic Books.

Scanlon, D., Schumaker, J., & Deshler, D. (2004). *The order routine.* Lawrence, KS: Edge Enterprises.

Schein, E. (2009). *Helping: How to offer, give, and receive help.* San Francisco: Berrett-Koehler Publishers.

Schlechty, P. (2011). *Engaging students: The next level of working on work.* San Francisco: Jossey-Bass.

Schomoker, M. (2011). *Focus: Elevating the essentials to radically improve student learning.* Alexandria, VA: Association for Supervision and Curriculum Development.

Schumaker, J., Denton, P. H., & Deshler, D. D. (1984). *The paraphrasing strategy.* Lawrence, KS: Edge Enterprises.

Schumaker, J., with Sheldon, J. (1985). *Proficiency in the sentence writing strategy: Instructor's manual.* Lawrence, University of Kansas Center for Research on Learning.

Schwartz, B. (2004). *The paradox of choice: Why more is less.* New York: HarperCollins.

Scott, S. (2002). *Fierce conversations: Achieving success at work and in life one conversation at a time.* New York: Berkley Publishing Group.

Seligman, M. (2006). *Learned optimism: How to change your mind and your life.* New York: Simon & Schuster.

Seligman, M. (2011). *Flourish: A visionary new understanding of happiness and well-being.* New York: Free Press.

Senge, P. (1990). *The fifth discipline: The art and practice of the learning organization.* London: Random House.

Sharan, S., & Sharan, Y. (1976). *Small-group teaching.* Englewood Cliffs, NJ: Educational Technology Publications.

Sheehan, G. (1989). *Personal best: The foremost philosopher of fitness shares techniques and tactics for success and self-liberation.* Emmaus, PA: Rodale Press.

Sheldon, J., Schumaker, J., Sheldon-Sherman, J., Schumaker, J., Sheldon-Sherman, B., & Schumaker, S. (1985). *Fundamentals in the sentence writing strategy.* Lawrence, KS: Edge Enterprises.

Sims, P. (2011). *Little bets: How breakthrough ideas emerge from small discoveries.* New York: Free Press.

Slavin, R. E. (1978). Student teams and achievement divisions. *Journal of Research and Development in Education, 12*(1), 39–49.

Slavin, R. E. (1983). When does cooperative learning increase student achievement? *Psychological Bulletin, 94,* 429–445.

Slavin, R. E. (1990). *Cooperative learning: Theory, research, and practice.* Englewood Cliffs, NJ: Prentice Hall.

Sparks, D. (1999). Assessment without victims: An interview with Rick Stiggins. *Journal of Staff Development, 20*(2).

Sprick, R. S. (2006). *Discipline in the secondary classroom: A positive approach to behavior management* (2nd ed.). San Francisco: Jossey-Bass.

Sprick, R. S. (2009). *CHAMPs: A proactive and positive approach to classroom management* (2nd ed.). Eugene, OR: Pacific Northwest Press.

Sprick, R. S. (2010). *Teacher planner for the secondary classroom: A companion to discipline in the secondary classroom.* San Francisco: Jossey-Bass.

Sprick, R. S., Booher, M., & Garrison, M. (2009). *Behavioral response to intervention: Creating a continuum of problem-solving and support.* Eugene, OR: Pacific Northwest Publishing.

Sprick, R. S., & Howard, L. M. (1995). *The teacher's encyclopedia of behavior management: 100 problems, 500 plans.* Eugene, OR: Pacific Northwest Publishing.

Sprick, R. S., & Howard, L. (2009). *Stepping in: A substitute's guide to behavior and instruction.* Eugene, OR: Pacific Northwest Publishing.

Sprick, R. S., Knight, J., Reinke, W., Skyles, T., & Barnes, I. (2010). *Coaching classroom management: Strategies and tools for administrators and coaches (2nd ed.) with DVD.* Eugene, OR: Pacific Northwest Press.

Sprick, R. S., Knight, J., Reinke, W., Skyles, T., & Barnes, L. (2010). *Coaching classroom management: Strategies and tools for administrators and coaches.* Eugene, OR: Pacific Northwest Publishing.

Sprick, R. S., Sprick, M. S., & Garrison, M. (1992). *Foundations: Developing positive school discipline policies.* Longmont, CO: Sopris West.

Stevens, R. J., Madden, N. A., Slavin, R. E., & Farnish, A. M. (1987). Cooperative integrated reading and composition. *Reading Research Quarterly, 22*(4), 433–454.

Stiggins, R. (2001). *Student-involved classroom assessment* (3rd ed.). Upper Saddle River, NJ: Prentice Hall.

Stiggins, R. J. (2005). *Student-involved assessment for learning* (4th ed.). Upper Saddle River, NJ: Pearson.

Stiggins, R. J., Arter, J. A., Chappuis, J., & Chappuis, S. (2004). *Classroom assessment for student learning: Doing it right—using it well.* Portland, OR: Assessment Training Institute.

Stiggins, R. J., & Chappuis, J. (2011). *An introduction to student-involved assessment for learning* (6th ed.). Upper Saddle River, NJ: Assessment Training Institute.

Stone, D., Patton, B., Heen, S., & Fisher, R. (2000). *Difficult conversations: How to discuss what matters most.* New York: Penguin.

Stone, R. (1996). *The healing art of storytelling: A sacred journey of personal discovery.* Lincoln, NE: iUniverse.

Straker, D. (1997). *Rapid problem solving with Post-it notes.* Great Britain: Gower Publishing.

Strickland, B. (2007). *Make the impossible possible: One man's crusade to inspire others to dream bigger and achieve the extraordinary.* New York: Random House.

Strong, R., Silver, H. R., & Robinson, A. (1995). What do students want? *Educational Leadership, 53(1),* 8–12.

Sutton, R. I. (2010). *Good boss, bad boss: How to be the best and learn from the worst.* New York: Hachettt Book Group.

Swanson, J., Elliott, K., & Harmon, J. (2011). *Teacher leader stories: The power of case methods.* Thousand Oaks, CA: Corwin.

Syed, M. (2010). *Bounce: Mozart, Federer, Picasso, Beckham, and the science of success.* New York: HarperCollins.

Terry, S. (2005). Serial position effects in recall of television commercials. *Journal of General Psychology, 132(2),* 151–164.

Tharp, T. (2005). *The creative habit.* New York: Simon & Schuster.

Thomas, J. W. (2000). *A review of research on project-based learning.* Retrieved from http://www.bobpearlman.org/BestPractices/PBL_Research.pdf.

Todorov, T. (1977). *The poetics of prose.* Ithaca, NY: Cornell University Press.

Tomlinson, C. (1999). *A differentiated classroom: Responding to the needs of all learners.* Alexandria, VA: Association for Supervision and Curriculum Development.

Tomlinson, C. A., & McTighe, J. (2006). *Integrating differentiated instruction and understanding by design: Connecting content and kids.* Alexandria, VA: Association for Supervision and Curriculum Development.

Tovani, C. (2000). *I read it, but I don't get it: Comprehension strategies for adolescent readers.* Portland, ME: Stenhouse Publishers.

Ury, W. (1993). *Getting past no: Negotiating in difficult situations.* New York: Bantam Books.

Ury, W. (1999). *Getting to peace: Transforming conflict at home, at work, and in the world.* New York: Viking.

Vernon, S. (2000). *Talking together.* Lawrence, KS: Edge Enterprises.

Vernon, S. D., Schumaker, J. B., & Deshler, D. D. (2001). *Following instruction together.* Lawrence, KS: Edge Enterprises.

Vernon, S. D., Schumaker, J.B., & Deshler, D. D. (2002). *Taking notes together.* Lawrence, KS: Edge Enterprises.

Vernon, S., Schumaker, J. B., & Deshler, D. D. (1996). *The score skills: Social skills for cooperative groups.* Lawrence, KS: Edge Enterprises.

Vygotsky, L. (1978). *Mind in society: The development of higher psychological processes.* Cambridge, MA: Harvard University Press.

Walsh, J., & Sattes, E. (2005). *Quality questioning: Research-based practice to engage every learner.* Thousand Oaks, CA: Corwin.

West, L., & Staub, F. (2003). *Content-focused coaching: A foundation for renaissance schools.* Norwood, MA: Christopher-Gordon Publishers.

Wiggins, G., & McTighe, J. (2005). *Understanding by design.* Alexandria, VA: Association for Supervision and Curriculum Development.

Wiliam, D. (2011). *Embedded formative assessment.* Bloomington, IN: Solution Tree Press.

Williams, W. C. (2004). *Poetry for young people.* New York: Sterling Publishing.

Wong, H. K., & Wong, R. T. (1998). *The first days of school: How to be an effective teacher.* Mountain View, CA: Harry K. Wong Publications.

Wood, D., Bruner, J., & Ross, G. (1976). The role of tutoring in problem solving. *Journal of Child Psychology and Psychiatry, 17,* 89–100.

INDEX

360
HIGH-IMPACT INSTRUCTION

Dialogue:
affinity diagrams, 283–284
and thinking prompts, 138–140, 147, 148
brainstorming, 283–284
conversational stories, 183
Facts, Opinions, Guesses (FOG)
method, 288
formative assessment, 288
freedom-within-form approach, 282–288
Law of Two Feet, 285, 286
nominal group technique, 287–288
open space, 284–286
partnership approach, 5
pro and con grids, 288
stream of meaning, 139, 282–283
structured choices, 286–288
Three-Fold Method of Analysis, 283–284
See also Communication skills
Dialogue (Isaac), 150
Differentiated instruction:
cooperative learning impact, 201
with guiding questions, 33
Difficult Conversations (Stone, Patton and Heen), 296, 345
Direct instruction, 13
Discipline in the Secondary Classroom (Sprick), 304–305, 313
Double-bubble map, 97, 98f
Draper, Sharon M., 134
"Dreams" (Hughes), 32
Drive (Pink), 21, 230, 300
Dunekack, Devona, 315–316
Dunlap, Glen, 22
Dweck, Carol, 277, 324, 326, 328
Dyer, Wayne, 27

East of Eden (Steinbeck), 225
Edge Enterprises (Lawrence, Kansas), 49, 260
Edmondson, Amy, 202, 204–205
Educational Leadership, 77, 230
Educational objectives:
cognitive taxonomies, 59–60, 164
effective questions, 164
formative assessment, 59–60
Edwards, Ethel, 29–30
Effective questions:
action ideas, 168–170
big idea questions, 161
Bloom's taxonomy, 164
closed questions, 156–158
constructivist instruction, 164–166
formative assessment, 71, 74, 78
improvement strategies, 161–163
instructional coaching activity, 169
intensive-explicit instruction, 164–165, 166
knowledge questions, 160
observation activity, 170
open questions, 155–156

opinion questions, 159–160
quality criteria, 164
Question Chart, 163f
Question Formulation Technique (QFT), 168
Quick Response (QR) code, 160
reading resources, 171–172
reflective approach, 155
research summary, 170–171
right or wrong questions, 158–159, 167–168
sample questions, 156f, 157f, 159f, 160f, 161f
skill questions, 160, 161f
student activity, 168
student engagement strategies, 165–168
student mistakes, 167
study guide, 168–172
teacher activity, 169
teacher predictions versus reality, 162f
teaching experience, 153–155
Eichinger, Sherry, 269
Elford, Marti, 153–155, 163, 171
Elliot Elementary School (Lincoln, Nebraska), 7
Ellis, Ed, 75
Embedded Formative Assessment (Wiliam), 84–85
Emmer, E., 289
Emotional Intelligence (Goleman), 260
Empathic Civilization, The (Rifkin), 267–268, 277
Empathy, 267–270
Ending maps:
learning maps, 89, 101–102, 116–118
sample illustration, 90f
Engagement:
and thinking prompts, 141–142
authentic learning, 226, 230–231
characteristics of, 129
compliance level, 129–130, 299f
cooperative learning impact, 200–201
effective questions, 165–168
engagement form activity, 299f
formative assessment, 55–57, 58
full engagement, 127–128
happiness research, 56–57, 128
high-impact instructional strategies, 129–130
intimate relationships, 128–129
noncompliance level, 130, 299f
Quick Response (QR) code, 129
rebellion level, 130
retreatism level, 130
rewarding employment, 127
Engaging Students (Schlechty), 129
Epiphanies, 184–185, 187
Equality, 5
Erickson, Lynn, 49, 60
Evans, Patricia, 266, 277

CORWIN
A SAGE Company

The Corwin logo—a raven striding across an open book—represents the union of courage and learning. Corwin is committed to improving education for all learners by publishing books and other professional development resources for those serving the field of PreK–12 education. By providing practical, hands-on materials, Corwin continues to carry out the promise of its motto: **"Helping Educators Do Their Work Better."**

Advancing professional learning for student success

Learning Forward (formerly National Staff Development Council) is an international association of learning educators committed to one purpose in K–12 education: Every educator engages in effective professional learning every day so every student achieves.